Prima! Recipes of Choice

The Best Recipes for the Foods You Love to Eat

from

Laurina Filippini Holte

6505 Stonedale Lane

Clifton, VA 20124

Copyright © 2002
Laurina Filippini Holte

Copyright © 2002
Morris Press Cookbooks

All rights reserved. Reproduction in whole or in part without written permission is prohibited.

Printed in the U.S.A. by
Morris Press Cookbooks
P.O. Box 2110 • Kearney, NE 68848
800-445-6621 • www.morriscookbooks.com

ISBN 978-0-9724123-0-8

Library of Congress Control Number 2002094440

Dedication

I would like to dedicate this book to my Husband, Roger, my Children, Lee Anne and Amy Jo, my Mother and Father, Philomena and Natalino, and to Nonno and Nonna, Amato and Zaira.

My interest in cooking began during visits to Nonno's and Nonna's house for Sunday dinner. Their house always smelled the same - irresistible! First, there was the chicken soup - clear, with the tiny pastina, served with a bowl of freshly grated Parmigiano-Reggiano cheese on the side, or perhaps a dish of Verdura (a tasty vegetable soup). Then, that wonderful dish of Tagliatelle with fresh Tomato Sauce was served (the tomatoes having been grown in Nonno's and Nonna's garden). Their garden was perfect. It had all the vegetables you would expect in order to prepare Italian-style dinners. I loved to pick a basil leaf and carry it around with me so I could smell it now and then. I found the perfume to be fascinating. I also loved the Fall when the Concord grapes were ripe and I could pick them and slip the skins off in my mouth. They tasted so good. The strawberries were plump and juicy and tasted somewhat like the wild ones I picked in our own back yard, but they were much larger as they were fertilized with a mixture of manure and water, which made everything grow so big and perfectly. The next course of the meal was usually a Veal Roast, stuck with garlic and flavored with seasonings, served with Roasted Potatoes, stuffed, baked Zucchini Flowers, Whole Wheat Bread, and accompanied by Nonno's homemade wine. (Each Fall, big boxes of grapes were delivered to him.) My favorite desserts were the Strawberries with Lemon squeezed on top and sprinkled with sugar, or the Fresh Pears with Cheese. I loved to go to the cellar and look at those Oak barrels and smell the wine fermenting. My grandparents did not make their own olive oil, but when I visited my great uncles in Tuscany, they would take me to their lower level and show me the huge glass vats of olive oil made from olives picked from their own olive grove, and, of course, their marvelous wine.

My Mother is also a great cook, cooking in both the Tuscan and Abruzzese styles. I never saw her using a cookbook. Everything was in her head, just like my grandparents. She, like they, instinctively knew how cook and flavor food, and make everything delicious. One of the memorable dishes she made for us was the Abruzzese-style Lamb Sauce with Tagliatelle (Fettuccine). Her Christmas Eve dinners were spectacular. They consisted of, among other dishes, a wide array of fish and seafood, such as snails, shrimp, eel, stuffed, baked calamari, fried smelts and fried dough stuffed with anchovies. On Christmas Day, she made hundreds of ravioli (we were a family of nine), all by hand, starting early in the morning. I have carried on the tradition of cooking in this style for my own family and friends. During the Christmas holidays, though, I also include some wonderful Norwegian dishes which my husband loved during his childhood. Needless to say, we end up with far more food than we can eat. I freeze what is left over so that we may enjoy the food for future meals. For people on the go, it's timesaving to cook more than you need of many of these recipes and freeze some for evenings when you just don't have enough time to cook. I have written down the recipes to pass on to my children and to you, my readers, so you can enjoy the same good eating. Also included are recipes I have used for our own dinner and cocktail parties. In this book are the most requested recipes from my Husband, my Children and the people we have entertained over the years. They are the best recipes for the foods you love to eat.

If you have any questions about these recipes, menu planning or substitution of ingredients, please write to me at 6505 Stonedale Lane, Clifton, VA 20124 or please call me at 703.266.0860. My e-mail address is laurina1@juno.com.

My Father loved fly fishing for trout, tying his own flies. This is a 4-pound, 25"-long trout he lured in Trenton Falls, New York.

To Julie,
Please enjoy cooking with Rinia!
Lavinia Filippini Halee 8-30-14

Me with my Husband Roger

Table of Contents

Appetizers/Soups/
    Salads/Sandwiches 1-64
Pasta/Rice/Casseroles/
    Main Dishes/Eggs/Sauces/
    Marinades/Stuffings/
    Vegetables 65-130
Meats And Poultry 131-174
Fish/Seafood 175-190
Breads/Rolls/Pancakes/Muffins/
    Cakes/Frostings/Candy/
    Cookies/Bars 191-266
Pies/Pastry/Desserts 267-294
Beverages 295-304
Sample Meals/Entertaining
Index
Pantry Basics
Herbs & Spices
Baking Breads
Baking Desserts
Vegetables & Fruits
Napkin Folding
Measurements & Substitutions
Equivalency Chart
Food Quantities
Quick Fixes
Counting Calories
Cooking Terms

Appetizers
Soups
Salads
Sandwiches

*Nonna and Nonno with
Aunt Valentine, my Mom and their firstborn*

Helpful Hints

- If the soup is not intended as the main course, count on 1 quart to serve 6. As the main dish, plan on 1 quart to serve 2.
- After cooking vegetables, pour any water and leftover vegetable pieces into a freezer container. When full, add tomato juice and seasoning to create a money-saving "free soup."
- Instant potatoes help to thicken soups and stews.
- A leaf of lettuce dropped in a pot of soup absorbs grease from the top. Remove the lettuce and serve. Or make the soup the day before, chill, and scrape off the hardened fat that rises to the top.
- To cut down on odors when cooking cabbage or cauliflower, add a little vinegar to the water and don't overcook.
- Three large stalks of celery, chopped and added to about two cups of beans (navy, brown, pinto, etc.) makes the dish easier to digest.
- Fresh is best, but to reduce time in the kitchen, use canned or frozen broths or bouillon bases. Canned or frozen vegetables will work well, such as peas, green beans, and corn.
- Ideally, serve cold soups in chilled dishes.
- Perk up soggy lettuce by spritzing it with a mixture of lemon juice and cold water.
- You can easily remove egg shells from hard-boiled eggs if you quickly rinse the eggs in cold water after they are boiled. Also, add a drop of food coloring to help indicate cooked eggs and raw ones.
- Your fruit salads will look better when you use an egg slicer to make perfect slices of strawberries, kiwis, or bananas.
- The ratio for a vinaigrette is typically 3 parts oil to 1 part vinegar.
- Cook pasta for salads al dente (slightly chewy to the bite). This allows the pasta to absorb some of the dressing and not become mushy.
- Fresh vegetables require little seasoning or cooking. If the vegetable is old, dress it up with sauces or seasoning.
- Chill the serving plates to keep the salad crisp.
- Fruit juices, such as pineapple and orange, can be used as salad dressing by adding a little olive oil, nutmeg, and honey.

Copyright © Morris Press Cookbooks

Appetizers/Soups/Salads/Sandwiches

ANTIPASTO

- 6 slices each of salami or soppressata, mortadella, ham, cappicola
- 6 slices each of provolone, Swiss cheese
- ½ c. black olives
- ½ c. green stuffed olives
- two tomatoes cut into wedges
- 3 stalks of celery cut into thin 4" slices
- 1 c. of red roasted peppers
- 1 8-oz. pkg. frozen artichokes, cooked and drained
- ½ c. marinated mushrooms
- ½ c. canned chick peas, drained
- ½ c. hot pickled cherry peppers
- ¼ c. extra virgin olive oil
- 1 tsp. sea salt

Prepare mushrooms using recipe for Marinated Mushrooms in this book. Roll up the the meats and cheeses and arrange around platter. Alternate the olives, tomato wedges and celery inside the circle. Arrange the artichoke hearts and mushrooms next. Then arrange the roasted red peppers. Put the chick peas in the middle and surround with the hot pickled cherry peppers. Drizzle the extra virgin olive over all. Sprinkle lightly with salt.

ARTICHOKE CRAB DIP

- 1 8-oz. pkg. frozen artichoke hearts, cooked, drained and chopped
- 1 lb. cooked crabmeat, drained and chopped
- 1 8-oz. pkg. cream cheese, softened
- 1 c. sour cream
- 1 c. Hellmann's mayonnaise
- 1 clove garlic, pressed
- 1 T. dried onion flakes
- ¼ tsp. salt
- ¾ c. grated Parmesan cheese
- 1 baguette, sliced ½" thick

Blend the softened cream cheese with sour cream and mayonnaise. Add garlic, dried onion flakes, salt and Parmesan cheese. Stir. Fold in artichokes and crab meat. Serve with baguette slices.

BEEF BOURGUIGNON

2 c. peanut oil
1 c. butter

⅓ to ½ lb. beef tenderloin per person
Tomato-Curry Sauce

Put oil and butter into a fondue pot with fire underneath which will keep the beef sizzling. Cut beef into 1" cubes. Pile on platter near pot. Provide long-handled wooden picks or 2-pronged wooden-handled forks so that guests may spear meat and put it into the hot fat, where it is left until done. Serve with bowls of sauce.

Tomato-Curry Sauce:

1 stalk celery, chopped finely
1 onion, minced
1 T. chopped Italian parsley
1 clove garlic, mashed
3 T. olive oil
1 T. curry powder

1 28-oz. can tomatoes, mashed
3 T. tomato paste
1 tsp. salt
½ tsp. pepper
1 tsp. sugar

Sauté celery, onion, parsley and garlic in heated oil. Add curry powder. Stir to blend, cooking gently for 3 minutes. Add tomatoes, sugar and tomato paste. Simmer gently 35 minutes. Add salt and pepper. Cool sauce. Whirl in blender. Re-heat. Serve hot. Makes 3 cups.

BRIE EN CROUTE

2 sheets puff pastry
¼ c. melted butter
1 lb. Brie cheese

¼ c. Italian parsley, minced
¼ c. sliced, toasted almonds
1 egg yolk mixed with 1 tsp. water

Thaw pastry for 20 minutes. Preheat oven to 375°. On a floured surface, roll one sheet of pastry into a 15-inch circle. Brush with melted butter. Roll second sheet of pastry into a 15-inch circle and place over first sheet. Slice Brie in half horizontally into two layers. Sprinkle almonds and parsley on half. Place second layer on top and place in center of pastry. Brush pastry edges with egg mixture and pull up sides of pastry to enclose Brie. Place seam side down on ungreased baking sheet. Brush top with egg mixture. Bake for 20 minutes. Let cool for 10 minutes before serving.

BUTTERY BOURSIN CHEESE SPREAD

1 clove garlic, minced
2 8-oz. packages cream cheese, softened
1 c. butter, softened
1 tsp. oregano
¼ tsp. basil
¼ tsp. dill weed
¼ tsp. thyme
¼ tsp. pepper
¼ tsp. salt

Mix all ingredients together until smooth. Serve with crackers.

CANAPÉS DE NAPOLI

1 c. shredded mozzarella cheese
¼ c. finely chopped Italian parsley
1 c. prosciutto ham, finely chopped
¼ tsp. ground black pepper
½ tsp. nutmeg
¼ tsp. oregano
softened butter
3 dozen miniature rolls

Combine cheese, parsley, ham, pepper, nutmeg and oregano. Cut tops off rolls. Scoop out center. Lightly butter each roll. Spoon 1 tablespoon filling into each roll and replace tops. Wrap in foil and heat until cheese melts.

CAPONATA

2 large eggplants, diced
½ c. olive oil
1 large onion diced into small pieces
3 large stalks celery, diced
1 large green pepper, seeded and diced
1 large red pepper, seeded and diced
1 28-oz. can peeled tomatoes, drained and chopped
2 zucchini, diced
½ c. pitted black olives, sliced
½ c. pitted green olives, sliced
3 T. capers, drained
3 medium cloves garlic, minced
2 T. red wine vinegar
2 tsp. sugar
1 tsp. oregano
1 tsp. salt
1 tsp. pepper
1 tsp. basil
2 T. fresh Italian parsley, minced
1 tsp. thyme
crackers, toasted pita chips or sliced baguettes

Heat saucepan. Add oil and heat oil. Sauté onion, celery and peppers over low heat until tender. Add eggplant, tomatoes and zucchini. Stir. Add olives, capers, garlic, vinegar, sugar, oregano, salt, pepper, basil,

(continued)

parsley and thyme. Stir. Cover pan, reduce heat to low. Simmer 20 minutes, stirring every five minutes. Uncover pan and simmer 10 minutes. Let it sit in the refrigerator five hours to develop flavor if there is time. Serve at room temperature with crackers, toasted pita chips or baguettes.

CELERY AND CARROTS TOSCANO (PINZIMONIO)

5 celery ribs cut into 4" long thin strips
5 carrots cut into 3" thin strips
½ c. extra virgin olive oil
½ tsp. salt (preferably sea salt)
½ tsp. freshly grated black pepper

Whisk oil, salt and pepper together. Put into a small glass. Surround oil mixture with vegetables on a platter. Dip vegetables into oil mixture. Stir mixture if necessary.

CHEDDAR/OLIVE BALLS

¼ lb. grated sharp cheddar cheese
½ c. flour
¼ c. soft butter
½ tsp. paprika
1 8-oz. jar small pimento-stuffed olives, drained

Blend flour and butter. Add cheese and paprika. Mix. Form into a dough. If it's too dry, add a few drops water. Use a teaspoon of dough and wrap it around an olive. Repeat until dough is used up. Seal each one. Chill for about an hour. Set oven at 400°. Bake for 10-15 minutes. Serve warm out of the oven.

CHEESE BALL

1 8-oz. pkg. cream cheese, softened
3 oz. blue cheese, crumbled
⅓ c. drained, crushed pineapple
½ tsp. ground ginger
1 c. chopped pecans

Blend cream cheese and blue cheese. Stir in pineapple and ginger. Mix well. Shape into a ball and chill in the refrigerator. Before serving,

(continued)

sprinkle the chopped pecans on wax paper and roll the ball in the pecans. Serve with crackers.

CHEESE DIP

2 4-oz. cans chopped green chilies
1 15-oz. can chili without beans
1 lb. Velveeta cheese

Set oven at 350°. Mix all ingredients into a 2½-quart baking dish and bake for 45 minutes, stirring every 15 minutes. Pour into a ceramic fondue pot or chafing dish. Keep dip warm over a candle or on a hot plate. Serve with plain Doritos.

CHEESE FONDUE

12 oz. natural Swiss cheese, shredded
4 oz. natural or process Gruyère cheese, shredded
1½ tsp. cornstarch
1 clove garlic
1 c. sauterne wine
1 T. lemon juice
⅛ tsp. nutmeg
¼ tsp. white pepper
1 loaf French or Italian bread, cut into cubes

Combine the cheeses with cornstarch. Set aside. Rub inside of heavy saucepan with garlic clove which has been cut in half (rub the cut side against pan). Discard garlic. Pour the sauterne and lemon juice into pan. Warm over low to medium heat until air bubbles rise and cover surface (Do not cover pan or allow liquid to boil). Remember to stir constantly from now on. Add a handful of cheeses, keeping heat on medium, but do not boil. Add more cheese as it melts. After cheese is blended and bubbling and while still stirring, add ground nutmeg and white pepper. Quickly transfer to fondue pot. Keep warm. If it becomes thick, add warmed sauterne. Spear bread cubes with fondue fork, piercing crust last. Dip and swirl.

CHEESY CHILI DIP

8-oz. pkg. cream cheese, softened
2 T. milk
2 small seeded, chopped tomatoes
1 4½-oz. can chopped green chilis
¼ tsp. salt
¼ tsp. cumin

(continued)

Whip cheese with milk in mixer until fluffy. Stir in tomatoes, chilis, salt and cumin. Serve with plain corn tortilla chips.

CHICKEN DRUMSTICKS

3 lbs. miniature chicken drumsticks (large joint of chicken wing)
¾ c. flour
¾ c. Parmesan cheese
2 tsp. salt
2 tsp. paprika
2 tsp. oregano
tiny pinch of cayenne pepper (if you like the flavor of hot)
1 c. buttermilk
¼ c. extra virgin olive oil

Heat oven to 375°. Mix together flour, Parmesan cheese, salt, paprika and oregano and cayenne pepper. Set aside. Dip chicken drumsticks in buttermilk. Shake off excess. Roll in dry mixture. Place on baking sheet which has been sprayed with Pam. Drizzle with olive oil. Bake for 30 minutes. Serve warm.

CHILES RELLENOS SQUARES

2 4-oz. cans green chiles, drained and chopped
12 oz. grated Monterey Jack cheese
4 large eggs, beaten

Heat oven to 300°. Spray 8" baking pan with Pam. Sprinkle chiles and cheese on bottom of pan. Pour eggs over and bake 60 minutes until firm. Cool 5 minutes. Cut into squares.

CHINESE EGG ROLLS

18 egg roll wrappers
1 c. chopped bean sprouts
3 c. finely chopped cooked shrimp
½ c. finely chopped celery
½ c. finely chopped water chestnuts
¼ c. finely chopped green onions
3 T. peanut oil
1 T. soy sauce
2 tsp. cornstarch
½ tsp. sugar
¼ tsp. salt
¼ tsp. black pepper
½ clove medium garlic, pressed
1 egg yolk mixed with 1 tsp. water
Peanut oil for frying

(continued)

Sauté celery and onion in 3 tablespoons peanut oil for 2 minutes. Add soy sauce, cornstarch, sugar, salt, pepper and garlic. Cook one minute longer, stirring. Add to bean sprouts, shrimp, and water chestnuts. Mix together. Spoon ¼ cup mixture in center of each egg roll wrapper. Fold top of wrapper over filling, tucking under filling; fold left and right edges over filling. Lightly brush remaining edge with egg mixture. Tightly roll filled end toward the remaining edge and gently press to seal. Pour peanut oil to depth of 2 inches into a 8" saucepan or electric frying pan or deep fat fryer. Heat to 375°. Fry, a few at a time, until golden brown, turning once, making sure that oil is reheated to 375° before adding another batch. Drain on paper towels. Serve with hot mustard sauce and sweet and sour sauce. (Recipes in this book.)

COCKTAIL FRANKFURTERS

1½ lbs. frankfurters cut diagonally into ½" pieces
¼ c. finely chopped onion
¼ c. finely chopped green pepper
2 T. butter
1 16-oz. can tomato soup or 2 8-oz. cans tomato sauce

2 T. brown sugar
4 tsp. Worcestershire sauce
1 T. prepared mustard
1 T. vinegar

Heat oven to 350°. In saucepan, cook pepper and onion in butter until tender. Stir in tomato soup or tomato sauce, brown sugar, Worcestershire sauce, mustard and vinegar. Stir until heated. Place frankfurters in casserole. Pour sauce over. Bake for 20 minutes. Put in chafing dish. Keep warm.

COCONUT CURRIED CHICKEN BALLS

4 cooked chicken breast halves minced in food processor
⅔ c. raisins
2 T. rum
1 8-oz. pkg. cream cheese softened
½ c. crushed pineapple, drained
3 T. Hellmann's mayonnaise

1 T. teriyaki sauce
2 tsp. curry powder
½ tsp. ground ginger
½ tsp. salt
½ tsp. pepper
1 c. sliced almonds, toasted
1½ c. flaked coconut

Heat oven to 350°. Put almonds in pan and toast for 5-8 minutes. Watch carefully to be sure they do not burn. Soak raisins in rum. Com-

(continued)

bine cream cheese, pineapple, mayonnaise, teriyaki sauce, curry powder, ginger, salt and pepper. Add raisins, chicken and almonds to cream cheese mixture. Blend. Shape into 1" balls. Roll in coconut. Chill before serving.

COCONUT SHRIMP

4 c. grated coconut
1 c. all-purpose flour
¾ c. golden beer
¾ tsp. baking soda
½ tsp. salt

⅛ tsp. cayenne
1 large egg
6 c. vegetable oil
48 medium shrimp (1½ lb.) peeled, deveined, leaving tail on

Transfer half of the coconut to a shallow pan or pie plate. Beat egg until frothy. Whisk flour, beer, baking soda, salt and cayenne into egg until smooth. Pour oil to 4" deep in a 4-6 quart heavy pot. Heat to 375°. While oil is heating coat shrimp: hold shrimp by tail and dip into batter, letting excess drip off. Then dredge shrimp in coconut, coating completely. Press gently to help coconut stick to shrimp. Transfer to a plate as they are done. Add more coconut to pie plate if needed. Fry shrimp, but do not crowd them. Turn once. Fry until golden. Transfer with a slotted spoon to paper towels to drain. Season lightly with salt. Skim any coconut from oil. Be sure oil is heated to 375° between batches. Serve warm.

CRAB SPREAD

1 lb. cooked, finely chopped crab meat
2 T. Italian parsley, minced
1 tsp. salt
½ tsp. black pepper
1 T. lemon juice
1 T. extra virgin olive oil

1 hard-cooked egg, finely chopped
½ tsp. paprika
⅛ tsp. cayenne
½ c. celery, minced
2 T. Hellmann's mayonnaise

Mix all ingredients together. Chill. Serve with plain crackers.

CRISP SHRIMP WITH SWEET/SOUR SAUCE

1 c. all-purpose flour
½ tsp. paprika
1 tsp. onion salt
12 oz. golden beer
2 lbs. raw shrimp, shelled, deveined, with tails left on

1 c. lemon juice
½ tsp. salt
oil for cooking

Place flour in medium-size bowl. Mix in paprika and onion salt. Gradually add beer, stirring. Let stand a half hour. Add 1-2 tablespoons more beer if batter is too thick. Place shrimp in a container. Sprinkle with salt and lemon juice. Heat oil to 2" in a deep skillet or electric frying pan to 375°. Shake liquid off shrimp. Flour shrimp by shaking a few pieces at a time in a paper bag containing ½ cup flour, then dip shrimp in batter. Shake off excess batter. Fry crisp, turning once. Drain on paper towels.

Sweet/Sour Sauce:

1½ c. orange marmalade
juice of 1 lemon
⅛ tsp. ground ginger

2 tsp. horseradish
2 tsp. salt

Mix all ingredients together.

DEVILED EGGS

6 hard-cooked eggs
½ tsp. salt
½ tsp. French's creamy yellow mustard

¼ tsp. white pepper
3 T. Hellmann's mayonnaise
paprika

Cut peeled eggs lengthwise into halves. Remove yolks and put into a bowl. Mash with fork. Mix in salt, mustard, pepper and mayonnaise. Fill whites with egg yolk mixture, distributing equally among the 12 halves. Sprinkle lightly with paprika. Arrange on plate. Refrigerate up to 24 hours until ready to serve.

DIP FOR RAW VEGETABLES

1 c. sour cream
1 c. Hellmann's mayonnaise
3 T. dehydrated onions
1 T. grated Parmesan cheese
¼ tsp. dill weed
1 tsp. dried oregano
1 tsp. dried basil
1 tsp. dried Italian parsley

Mix all ingredients. Let set in refrigerator for a couple of hours for flavor to develop.

DOLMADES (STUFFED GRAPE LEAVES)

16 grape leaves (packed in jars)
1 lb. lean ground beef or lamb
½ c. cooked rice
¼ c. finely chopped onion
2 T. seedless raisins
2 T. pine nuts
2 tsp. salt
2 T. olive oil
1 c. hot water

Scald grape leaves 2 or 3 minutes in boiling water. Drain. Mix beef or lamb and rice. Set aside. Fry onion, raisins and nuts in olive oil until onion is lightly browned. Mix with salt, beef and rice. Spread the grape leaves carefully on a board. On each, place a tablespoon of the meat mixture. Fold leaf over from top, then bottom, then each side. In the bottom of a large pot place a piece of foil. Put stuffed leaves carefully on this and add hot water. Place a plate on top to keep leaves from moving about. Cover the pan and simmer 30-40 minutes until the water has evaporated. Lift out the leaves carefully and drain if any water remains. Cool in refrigerator and serve cold with Cucumber Yogurt Sauce.

Cucumber Yogurt Sauce:

8 oz. plain yogurt
¼ c. finely shredded cucumber
1 small clove garlic, pressed
1 tsp. dill weed
¼ tsp. finely minced lemon zest

Stir together the yogurt, cucumber, garlic, dill weed and lemon zest in a small mixing bowl. (Lemon zest is just the yellow part of the lemon. Use a lemon zester or potato peeler to cut away the zest.) Makes 1 cup.

EMPANADAS

1 lb. lean ground beef
1 medium onion, finely chopped
3 chili peppers, crushed (omit if you don't like hot foods)
1 green pepper, finely diced
2 cloves garlic, pressed
1 tsp. oregano
½ tsp. thyme
3 T. olive oil
1 large tomato, peeled, chopped, and seeds removed
¼ c. ripe olives, chopped
¼ c. seedless raisins
1 hard-cooked egg, minced
1 tsp. sugar
2 tsp. salt
½ tsp. black pepper

Dip tomato in boiling water for 30 or more seconds for easy removal of skin. Fry beef, onion, garlic, chili peppers and green pepper in oil until meat loses is red color, stirring constantly. Add tomato. Stir well and simmer five minutes. Add oregano, thyme, olives, raisins, egg, sugar, salt and pepper. Mix all ingredients well. Set oven to 400°. Roll dough out on floured surface ⅛" thick and cut into rounds with 3" cutter. Place about 1 tablespoon filling of mixture on each round. Moisten edge of round with water. Fold over. Press edges down to seal. Place on lightly greased cookie sheet and refrigerate until 15 minutes before serving. Brush with beaten egg yolk mixture, sprinkle with a dash of salt and bake for 15 minutes or until browned. Makes about 2 dozen.

Dough:

¾ c. Crisco shortening
1 t. salt
2 c. flour
⅓ c. ice water
1 egg yolk beaten with 2 teaspoons water
salt for sprinkling

Combine flour and salt in a bowl. Cut in shortening with a fork until small particles are formed. Sprinkle water over this mixture, a little at a time, tossing lightly with fork. Add more water if necessary, 1 teaspoon at a time. Work dough into a firm ball (when it clings together, you have added enough water).

ESCARGOTS (SNAILS IN GARLIC BUTTER)

1 can snails with shells (7½ oz. can, 1½ doz. shells)
½ c. melted butter
2 med. cloves garlic, pressed
2 T. finely chopped Italian parsley
1 T. lemon juice
1 tsp. salt
⅛ tsp. nutmeg
1 shallot, finely minced (you may substitute onion)

(continued)

Prepare several hours before serving. Wash snail shells. Drain well upside down on paper towels. Drain snails thoroughly. Set aside. In medium bowl, combine butter with garlic, parsley, lemon juice, minced shallot, salt and nutmeg. Mix well. Place a little butter mixture (about $1/4$ teaspoon) in each shell. Push a drained snail into each shell. Cover with more butter mixture. Arrange filled shells carefully, open ends, up, in a flat baking dish or special escargot dishes. Cover and refrigerate. To serve: preheat oven to 400°. Bake snails in shells, uncovered, 8-10 minutes, or until butter mixture is very bubbly. Serve immediately. Makes 4 first-course or 6 to 8 hors-d'oeuvre servings.

FRIED DOUGH WITH ANCHOVIES

1 recipe Bread Dough in this book
(or purchased dough)

1 can of flat anchovies
olive oil for frying

Divide anchovies into thirds. Wrap a piece of dough about the size of a walnut around a piece of anchovy. Be sure to seal the dough around the anchovy piece by pinching it tightly. As you make them, place them on a piece of floured wax paper. Let them rise until puffy. Heat 2" of oil to 375° in pan or electric skillet. Fry until brown on both sides, turning once. Serve hot.

FRIED DOUGH WITH MOZZARELLA CHEESE

1 recipe Bread Dough in this book
(or purchased dough)

Block of mozzarella cheese
olive oil for frying

Cut cheese into $1/2$" cubes. Wrap a piece of dough about the size of a walnut around a cube of cheese. Be sure to seal the dough around the cheese by pinching it tightly. As you make them, place them on a piece of floured wax paper. Let them rise until puffy. Heat 2" of oil to 375° in pan or electric skillet. Fry until brown on both sides, turning once. Serve hot.

FRUIT KABOBS WITH DIP

18 strawberries cut in half
36 cubes of pear (about 1 pear)
36 pineapple chunks
36 seedless green grapes
48 cubes of Colby or Monterey Jack cheese

1 c. plain yogurt
2 T. honey
grated zest of 2 limes
toothpicks

Alternate three pieces of fruit and one piece of cheese on a toothpick. Repeat until all the fruit and cheese is used up. Mix 1 cup plain yogurt, 2 tablespoons honey and zest of two limes together. Place dip alongside kabobs. Makes 48 appetizers.

GUACAMOLE DIP

2 large Haas avocados peeled, seeded and mashed
3 T. fresh lime juice
½ tsp. salt

½ tsp. pepper
1 T. minced fresh cilantro
2 T. finely minced red onions
3 T. extra virgin olive oil

Mix all ingredients together with a fork. Serve with plain tortilla chips.

HAM AND CHEESE APPETIZERS

8 oz. pepperoni
8 oz. sharp cheddar cheese
8 oz. muenster cheese
8 oz. ham
10 eggs

2½ c. flour
1½ t. baking powder
1 tsp. salt
paprika
nonstick coating for spraying

Set oven to 325°. Cube into ½" pieces the pepperoni, cheeses and ham. In a medium bowl beat the eggs until fluffy with a whisk. Add the flour, baking powder and salt. Whisk. Add the pepperoni, cheeses and ham. Pour into a 12" x 9" x 3" baking dish which has been sprayed with nonstick coating. Sprinkle with paprika. Bake for 50 minutes. When cool slice into 1" squares. Makes approximately 35 squares.

HAM AND CHEESE LOGS

1 c. shredded cheddar cheese
1 8-oz. pkg. softened cream cheese
1 4½-oz. can deviled ham or chopped ham
½ c. pitted chopped ripe olives
1 c. finely chopped pecans

    Mash the deviled ham. Add cream cheese and mix. Add the cheddar cheese and olives. Mix. Shape into two 8" long rolls. Roll each roll into chopped pecans.

HOT CRAB FONDUE

1 8-oz. pkg. cream cheese
1 8-oz. pkg. shredded sharp cheddar cheese
½ c. light cream
½ tsp. Worcestershire sauce
1 medium clove garlic, pressed
¼ tsp. salt
⅛ tsp. cayenne
1 c. Alaskan King Crab, cooked and diced finely
l loaf sourdough or French bread, cubed

    Blend cheeses and cream in top of double boiler over hot water until melted. Add worcestershire sauce, garlic, salt and cayenne. Cook until heated, but do not boil. Add crab. Blend. Put into chafing dish. Serve with cubes of sourdough or French bread.

HUMMUS WITH TAHINI (HOMOS BI TIHINEH) LEE ANNE

1 19-oz. can chick peas, rinsed and drained
1 tsp. salt
1 clove garlic, pressed
¼ c. olive oil
2 T. lemon juice
2 T. minced Italian parsley
¼ c. tahini or 4 T. toasted ground sesame seeds (whirl them in the blender)
1 T. soy sauce
1 tsp. cumin
1 green onion minced
paprika

    Mash the chick peas in the food processor. Put into a bowl and add salt, garlic, olive oil, lemon juice, parsley, tahini or sesame seeds, soy sauce, cumin and onion. Put into serving dish and add a dash of paprika on top. Serve with pita chips or sesame crackers.

INDIAN CURRY BALLS

¼ lb. cream cheese, softened
2 T. Hellmann's mayonnaise
1 c. finely chopped, cooked chicken
½ c. chopped, toasted almonds
1 T. chopped chutney
½ tsp. salt
1 T. curry powder
½ c. chopped, grated coconut

Beat together the cream cheese and mayonnaise. Add the chicken, almonds, chutney, salt and curry powder. Shape into walnut-sized balls and roll in the chopped coconut. Chill for at least 2 hours before serving.

JAPANESE CHICKEN

1 whole, boned chicken breast cut into bite-sized pieces
4 T. soy sauce
2 T. dry sweet sherry
½ tsp. powdered ginger
2 T. sesame seeds
3 T. oil for cooking
toothpicks for serving

Mix together the soy sauce, sherry, ginger and sesame seeds. Marinate chicken pieces in the mix for 2 hours. Heat frying pan. Add the oil. When oil is heated, add the chicken along with the marinade. Sauté in oil until chicken is browned and marinade has evaporated. Serve with toothpicks.

LAYERED BEAN DIP

2 16-oz. cans refried beans
1 medium clove garlic, pressed
2 4-oz. cans chopped green chiles, drained
1 tsp. cumin powder
1 tsp. salt
½ tsp. black pepper
¼ c. chopped green onion
2 ripe Haas avocados, peeled, seeded and mashed
2 T. lemon juice
2 finely chopped tomatoes, seeded and drained
1 small can chopped black olives, drained
1½ c. sour cream
3 c. shredded lettuce
1½ c. shredded cheddar cheese
plain tortilla chips

Mix beans with garlic. Spread beans on bottom of 10" x 10" x 2" serving dish. Sprinkle with chiles, cumin, salt, pepper and chopped onion. Mix mashed avocado with lemon juice. Spread over mixture. Mix tomatoes with olives and spread over. Then spread sour cream over.

(continued)

Mix together the shredded lettuce and shredded cheddar. Sprinkle on top. Serve with tortilla chips.

LIVERWURST PÂTÉ

2 T. Hellmann's mayonnaise
2 T. lemon juice
½ lb. liver sausage, mashed
2 green onions, minced
4 oz. cream cheese, softened
2 T. milk

Blend mayonnaise, lemon juice, liver sausage and onions. Roll into a ball and flatten one side so it looks like a dome. Chill for two hours. Put on serving plate. Blend softened cream cheese and milk together. Spread over pâté and chill until serving time. Serve with crackers.

LORENZO ALLA FILIPPINI

2 T. butter
1 T. minced onion
2 T. flour
½ c. chicken stock
1 c. crab meat
dash cayenne
¼ tsp. salt
¼ tsp. black pepper
1 T. milk
2½ T. grated Parmesan
2½ T. grated Swiss cheese
6 slices toast, crust removed

Heat oven to 450°. Melt one tablespoon butter and cook onion in it without browning. Mix in one tablespoon flour. Add chicken stock, stirring constantly, until smooth. Add crab meat, and simmer gently a few minutes. Season to taste with cayenne, salt and pepper. In another pan, melt remaining butter. Stir in smoothly remaining flour. Add milk and cheeses and cook, stirring constantly, until cheeses are melted and blended. Cool. Form into six little balls. Spread crab mixture on toast, and top each slice with a cheese ball. Place in oven for five minutes. Serve on plates with forks. Makes 6 appetizers.

MARINATED MUSHROOMS

¾ c. extra virgin olive oil
⅓ c. white wine vinegar
1½ tsp. salt
¾ tsp. sugar
½ tsp. basil
6 peppercorns
1 bay leaf
1 medium garlic clove, pressed
1½ lb. fresh, medium-size mushrooms

(continued)

Heat all ingredients except mushrooms. Simmer ten minutes. Stir in mushrooms. Cook 3 to 5 minutes until fork tender. Refrigerate, covered, overnight. Drain mushrooms to serve.

MARINATED SHRIMP

1 lb. shrimp, shelled, deveined
1 qt. water
6 T. extra virgin olive oil
6 T. lemon juice
2 T. vinegar
1 medium clove garlic, pressed
1 tsp. salt
1 bay leaf, crumbled
2 T. minced Italian parsley
¼ tsp. black pepper

Bring water to a boil. Drop shrimp in. Cook until tender (4 minutes). Drain on paper towels and then put into a bowl. In small saucepan, combine oil, lemon juice, vinegar, garlic, salt and bay leaf. Heat to boiling. Pour over shrimp. Add parsley and pepper. Toss. Cover and marinate 4 hours in refrigerator. Drain and serve. Serves 4 for an appetizer.

MEATBALLS WITH SOUR CREAM SAUCE

1 lb. lean ground beef
¼ lb. bacon, diced finely
5 slices whole-wheat bread whirled in blender to make crumbs
1 beaten egg
1 tsp. sugar
¾ tsp. allspice
¾ tsp. nutmeg
1 tsp. salt
1 tsp. pepper
3 T. olive oil
1 16-oz. can beef broth
¾ c. sour cream
toothpicks for serving

Heat oven to 325°. Mix beef, bacon and egg together. Add sugar, allspice, nutmeg salt and pepper. Blend in bread crumbs. Shape into 1" balls. Heat a large frying pan. Add olive oil. Heat oil over medium heat. Brown meatballs, turning as they brown. Add beef broth. Heat through. Transfer meatballs and broth to a baking pan so that they fit in one layer. Cover. Bake for one hour. Stir in sour cream. Heat through without a cover until sour cream is warm. Transfer to a chafing dish. Place toothpicks nearby.

MOZZARELLA PUFFS

2 c. flour
½ tsp. salt
½ tsp. paprika

1 c. softened butter
1 lb. shredded mozzarella cheese

Heat oven to 350°. Sift flour, salt and paprika together. Cream butter. Mix in mozzarella. Add the flour mixture and mix well. Shape into 1" balls. Place on ungreased cookie sheet. Bake for 15 to 20 minutes until they are puffed and golden. Serve hot.

OYSTER CRACKER SNACKS

5 c. oyster crackers
1 (1-oz.) pkg. Hidden Valley Original Ranch salad dressing mix

1 tsp. dill weed
¾ c. corn oil
½ tsp. garlic powder
½ tsp. pepper

Heat oven to 250°. Mix salad dressing mix, dill weed, oil, garlic powder and pepper together in a large bowl. Stir in oyster crackers. Bake in a 9" x 13" pan for 20-30 minutes, stirring gently a couple of times during baking.

PIGS IN BLANKET

2¼ c. sifted flour
1 tsp. salt
¾ c. Crisco shortening

ice water
25 cocktail wieners

Heat oven to 400°. Mix flour and salt together. Cut in shortening until tiny particles are formed. Add just enough ice water to hold ingredients together (about ¼) cup. Divide dough into 25 pieces. Roll each piece into a ball and roll out each ball into a circle large enough to wrap around each wiener. Overlap edges and press together. Bake until pastry is golden, about 20-25 minutes. (Serve with mustard.)

POT STICKERS

1 lb. ground, cooked pork
¼ c. finely grated carrot
1 green onion, minced
1 c. finely chopped water chestnuts
1 T. soy sauce
1 T. rice wine vinegar or dry sherry

1 T. sesame oil
1 tsp. sugar
1 tsp. salt
½ tsp. pepper
2 tsp. grated fresh gingerroot
2 T. cornstarch
48 wonton wrappers

Bring a large pot of water to a boil. In a medium bowl, mix the cooked pork, grated carrot, minced onion, water chestnuts, soy sauce, vinegar or sherry, sesame oil, sugar, salt, pepper, gingerroot and cornstarch together. Place the wonton skins on a work surface and cover them with a damp towel so that they will not dry out. Remove one at a time and place 1 teaspoon filling in the center. Moisten the edges of the wonton with water. Bring two opposite corners to the center, pinching the points to seal, then bring remaining two corners to center, pinching the points to seal. Be sure to seal good. Repeat with remaining wonton skins and filling. Add the pot stickers in batches to the boiling water. Stir gently with a wooden spoon and bring back to a boil. Boil five minutes. With a slotted spoon, transfer the pot stickers to a platter. Serve with dipping sauce.

Dipping Sauce:

3 T. red wine vinegar
½ c. soy sauce
1 tsp. sugar
1 T. sesame oil

1 scallion, thinly sliced
1 medium garlic pressed
2 tsp. grated peeled gingerroot

Combine all ingredients in a bowl.

QUICHES WITH SHRIMP

½ c. soft butter
4 oz. cream cheese, softened
2 T. heavy cream
1¼ c. flour
½ tsp. salt
2 c. minced, cooked, shelled and deveined shrimp

1½ c. heavy cream
3 beaten eggs
¼ c. Swiss cheese, shredded
1 tsp. salt
½ tsp. black pepper
1 tsp. dill weed
⅓ c. grated Parmesan cheese

(continued)

Heat oven to 400°. Cream butter and cream cheese. Beat in two tablespoons cream and work in flour and salt to make a dough. Roll out pastry to ⅛" thickness. Cut into rounds to fit 2" x 1" muffin tins. Dough makes about 2-3 dozen quiches. It's best to have three tins accommodating 1 dozen each. Fit rounds into tins. Distribute shrimp into each round. Combine cream, eggs, Swiss cheese, salt, pepper and dill weed. Spoon mixture over shrimp. Sprinkle tops of tarts with Parmesan cheese and bake 5 minutes. Reduce temperature to 350° and bake 15 minutes longer, or until quiches are set and lightly browned on top. Serve immediately.

QUICHE SQUARES

Crust:

2 c. flour
1 tsp. salt
2 T. Crisco shortening

8 T. butter, softened
5 T. water

Filling:

1½ c. grated Swiss cheese
1 c. finely chopped onion, lightly sautéed in 1 T. butter and cooled
2 c. finely chopped ham
1 c. milk

1 c. light cream
3 eggs
1 tsp. salt
¼ tsp. nutmeg
1 tsp. paprika

Heat oven to 375°. Make crust by working shortening and butter into flour and salt. Add water until dough forms a ball. If you need to add more water, add it a tablespoon at a time. Roll out dough on a floured surface. Line 15½" x 10½" x 1" jelly roll pan with dough. Sprinkle ham over bottom. Spread cheese and onion over ham. Scald milk and cream by heating until tiny bubbles appear. Do not boil. Cool slightly. Beat eggs in large bowl. Add cooled milk and cream, salt, nutmeg and paprika. Pour over mixture and bake 35 minutes. Cut into small squares.

RED PEPPER DIP

½ lb. roasted red peppers, well drained
½ c. sour cream
½ c. mayonnaise
1 medium clove garlic, pressed

1 tsp. freshly grated lemon zest
1 T. lemon juice
pita wedges, plain crackers and/or raw vegetables for dipping

(continued)

Prepare roasted red peppers using recipe in this book. Process roasted peppers in food processor until smooth. Put into serving bowl and stir in sour cream, mayonnaise, garlic, lemon zest and lemon juice. Chill a couple of hours. Serve with pita wedges, plain crackers and/or raw vegetables

RUMAKI

8 slices of chicken livers, 3" long and 1" wide
4 water chestnuts, cut in half
4 slices of bacon, cut in half
onion powder

½ c. soy sauce
¼ c. mirin (sweet sake) or sherry
1 garlic clove, pressed
a slice fresh ginger, minced
½ tsp. turmeric

Sprinkle each piece of chicken liver with onion powder. Fold it around a piece of water chestnut. Wrap a piece of bacon around it. Slip it onto a toothpick, being sure the toothpick goes through center of water chestnut and catches the liver and bacon. Mix soy sauce, mirin or sherry, garlic, ginger and turmeric. Put the bundles in mixture to marinate at least one hour, turning once. Broil until bacon is crisp, turning to brown all sides. Makes 8.

SALMON BALL

1 16-oz. can red salmon, drained
8 oz. cream cheese, softened
2 T. lemon juice
2 tsp. grated onion

½ tsp. salt
½ c. minced parsley
½ c. finely chopped pecans

Remove any bones from salmon. Mash salmon. Mix salmon with cream cheese, lemon juice, onion and salt. Form into a ball. Mix parsley and pecans together. Roll salmon ball in mixture. Chill until ready to serve. Serve with crackers.

SALSA WITH CHIPS AMY JO

1 14½-oz. can diced tomatoes with juice
2 T. cilantro, minced finely
1 jalapeño pepper, diced finely
2 T. diced green pepper
2 T. diced red pepper
freshly ground black pepper
1 T. fresh lemon juice
⅛ tsp. salt
tostados
4 oz. sour cream
1 Haas avocado, mashed and mixed with 1 T. lemon juice

Mash tomatoes with a fork. Add cilantro, peppers, black pepper, lemon juice and salt. Mix together. Serve with tostados, a small bowl of sour cream and a small bowl of mashed avocado with lemon juice on the side.

SAUSAGE BALLS

¼ lb. shredded cheddar cheese
½ c. sifted flour
¼ c. soft butter
½ tsp. paprika
cooked sausage, cut into 25 pieces, each the size of a small olive

Heat oven to 400°. Cut flour and butter together until tiny particles are formed. Mix in cheese and paprika. Form into a dough. (Add drops of water if it doesn't hold together.) Use a teaspoon of dough to flatten around each piece of sausage. Seal each one. Bake for 10-15 minutes, until golden. Serve warm out of the oven.

SCALLOPS WITH REMOULADE DIP

1 lb. scallops, boiled until cooked, drained and chilled
2 c. Hellmann's mayonnaise
1 medium garlic, pressed
1 tsp. French's yellow prepared mustard
1 T. capers, drained
1 T. Italian parsley, finely minced
2 tsp. chives, minced
2 tsp. pickle relish
1 hard-boiled egg, finely minced

Mix mayonnaise, garlic, mustard, capers, parsley, chives, pickle relish and egg together. Serve in a bowl on a large plate surrounded by the boiled scallops, each stuck with a toothpick. Makes about 2 cups dip.

SHRIMP DIP

1 8-oz. pkg. cream cheese, softened
1 10-oz. can frozen condensed cream of shrimp soup, thawed
½ c. sour cream
1 tsp. horseradish
¼ tsp. Worcestershire
¼ lb. tiny shrimp, boiled until cooked

Heat cheese. Blend in soup, sour cream, horseradish and worcestershire. Garnish with tiny peeled cooked shrimp. Put in ceramic pot with candle underneath to keep warm. Serve with crackers, cauliflower, carrots, radishes, pepper strips.

SHRIMP MOUSSE

2 T. unflavored gelatin
½ c. cold water
1 can undiluted tomato soup
1 8-oz. pkg. cream cheese, softened
1 c. Hellmann's mayonnaise
⅓ c. green pepper, chopped finely
1 c. celery, sliced paper thin
1½ c. cooked shrimp, chopped
1 T. grated onion

Soak gelatin in cold water. Heat soup and cheese. Stir until smooth. Add gelatin. Cool. Add mayonnaise, green pepper, celery, shrimp and onion. Put into 6-cup mold or glass bowl which has been very lightly oiled. Refrigerate overnight. Unmold onto serving plate. Serve with crackers.

SHRIMP SPREAD

1 lb. cooked, finely chopped shrimp
1 medium tomato, seeded, drained and chopped
¼ c. finely chopped celery
1 medium clove garlic, pressed
½ tsp. salt
½ tsp. black pepper
2 hard-cooked eggs, chopped finely
1 T. lemon juice
1 T. extra virgin olive oil
½ tsp. crushed oregano
¼ c. mayonnaise

Mix shrimp, tomato, celery, garlic, salt, pepper, eggs, lemon juice, olive oil, oregano and mayonnaise together. Chill. Serve with crackers.

SPANAKOPITA APPETIZERS

4 pkg. (10-oz. size) frozen chopped spinach
1 8-oz. pkg. cream cheese, softened
1 lb. feta cheese, crumbled
½ c. grated Romano cheese
4 eggs, beaten
1 small onion, chopped finely
3 T. olive oil
1 T. dill weed
1 tsp. salt
½ tsp. black pepper
½ lb. butter, melted
15 sheets filo dough

Heat oven to 350°. Defrost spinach, squeeze water out. In large bowl combine spinach with cream cheese, feta cheese, Romano cheese, eggs, onion, olive oil, dill weed, salt and pepper. Arrange 9 sheets of filo dough in buttered 15½" x 10½" baking pan, brushing each sheet with butter. Spread with spinach filling. Cover with 6 sheets of filo dough, brushing each one with butter. Seal edges by tucking under. Brush top with butter. Chill one hour. Gently cut through top layers to mark pieces, first by drawing horizontal lines, and then crossing between the lines with diagonal lines. Bake 45 minutes. When baked, cut all the way through drawn lines.

SPINACH DIP WITH FRESH VEGETABLES

1 10-oz. pkg. frozen chopped spinach, thawed and drained
1 8-oz. can water chestnuts, chopped
1 c. sour cream
1 c. Hellmann's mayonnaise
1 pkg. Knorr (1.4 oz.) vegetable soup mix
½ small onion, finely chopped
3 T. Parmesan cheese, grated
Assortment of fresh vegetables

Combine spinach, water chestnuts, sour cream, mayonnaise, soup mix, onion and cheese together. Serve with an assortment of fresh vegetables such as cauliflower, green and red peppers, carrots, cucumbers, celery.

SPRING ROLLS

20 Spring Roll Skins (purchased)
4 c. vegetable oil for cooking Spring Rolls
3 T. peanut oil
1 can bean sprouts, drained and chopped
6 green onions, thinly shredded
1 c. julienned carrots
1 c. tofu, chopped or 1 c. shrimp (boiled and chopped)
2 c. thinly sliced button mushrooms
1 garlic clove, pressed
¼ tsp. Chinese five-spice powder
1 T. soy sauce
1 tsp. sea salt

For the filling, in a wok or frying pan, heat 3 tablespoons peanut oil and stir-fry bean sprouts, onions, carrots, tofu or shrimp, mushrooms and garlic about 1 minute. Add five-spice powder, soy sauce and salt and continue stir-frying 2 minutes. Cool. Cover skins with a damp cloth so they don't dry out. To fill the skins, lay one out flat on a work surface. Place about 2 tablespoons filling shaped into a roll on a skin. Fold the sides of the skin neatly over the filling. Moisten the edges with water. Then roll up to enclose the filling completely, creating an envelope. Brush around the edges with a beaten egg to seal. Set aside and repeat until all skins are filled. In a sauce pan, an electric frying pan or deep fryer, heat vegetable oil to 375°. Add 4 spring rolls and fry 4 minutes, until crisp and golden, turning once. Drain on paper towels. Keep warm. Reheat oil to 375° and cook 4 more spring rolls. Repeat with remaining rolls. Serve immediately. (If you wish to make your own Spring Roll Skins, recipe follows.)

Spring Roll Skins:

¾ c. all-purpose flour
½ c. cornstarch
3 T. vegetable oil
about 1¾ c. water

In a bowl, stir together flour, cornstarch, oil and enough water to make a thin batter. Heat a lightly oiled, 6-inch, non-stick skillet. Spoon 2 tablespoons batter into center of pan and swirl it quickly around to cover bottom of pan. Cook until the crêpe is dry but not colored and the edges shrink from the sides of the pan. Transfer to a plate. Cover with a damp cloth. Repeat until all the batter has been used. Makes 20 spring roll skins.

STUFFED CELERY

1 c. chopped walnuts
5 oz. Gorgonzola cheese
8 oz. cream cheese, softened
celery stalks cut into 4" lengths

Mix the walnuts and cheeses in a bowl. Stuff the celery stalks with the cheese mixture and arrange on a plate. Keep in refrigerator until ready to serve.

STUFFED MUSHROOMS

2 lb. medium-size button mushrooms, washed, drained and dried
2½ c. bread crumbs
¾ c. grated Parmesan cheese
¼ c. chopped Italian parsley
⅓ c. olive oil
½ tsp. pepper
⅛ tsp. salt
2 medium cloves garlic, pressed

Heat oven to 350°. Remove stems from mushrooms. Finely chop 3 tablespoons of the stems. (Refrigerate the remaining stems and use in tomato sauce or soup.) You may use commercial bread crumbs or make your own as follows: Grate 3 slices of bread in your blender. Toast crumbs in oven at 375° until lightly brown (about 10 minutes). In a bowl, mix together chopped mushroom stems, bread crumbs, cheese, parsley, oil, salt, pepper and garlic. Put about ¼ cup water mixed with one tablespoon oil in the bottom of a large baking dish. Stuff the mushrooms with as much stuffing as will fit, gently patting the stuffing into the mushrooms. Lay the stuffed mushrooms next to each other in the prepared baking dish. Do not get any water on the stuffing. Bake for about 30 minutes. Serve warm.

STUFFED ZUCCHINI BLOSSOMS

21 zucchini blossoms (use only the male blossoms, which sit on a long stem)
7 flat anchovies, cut into thirds
21 ½" cubes of mozzarella cheese
Batter (recipe follows)
3 c. corn or canola oil for frying

Clean zucchini blossoms, leaving about 1 inch of stem on. Lay on paper towels. Blot. Dry. Remove the pistils from the inside very carefully. Discard pistils. Prepare batter. Heat oil to 375°. Stuff the blossoms with a cube of cheese and a piece of anchovy. Twist the ends of the blossoms to close. Dip the blossoms into the batter. Shake off excess and cook

(continued)

a few at a time in the hot oil until golden, turning. Transfer to serving platter lined with paper towels as they are cooked. Repeat until all are cooked. Be sure oil is heated to 375° before adding more blossoms. Serve hot.

Batter:

1¼ c. all-purpose flour
½ tsp. salt
½ tsp. ground black pepper
⅛ tsp. grated nutmeg
¼ c. extra virgin olive oil
3 eggs, separated
1 c. cold water
½ tsp. baking soda

Mix the flour with the salt, baking soda, pepper and nutmeg. Add the olive oil, water and egg yolks. Batter should be smooth. If it too thick, add a couple of tablespoons water, one at a time. Beat egg whites until stiff. Fold into batter with a rubber spatula.

SWEET/SOUR SPARERIBS

3 lb. spareribs, cut into 1½" pieces
2 T. cornstarch
1 T. brown sugar
1 T. salt
2 T. soy sauce
1 clove garlic, pressed
1 slice fresh gingerroot, grated
½ c. salad oil
1 c. vinegar
2 T. brown sugar
½ c. water

Heat oven to 350°. Combine spareribs, cornstarch, the 1 tablespoon brown sugar, salt and soy sauce. Let stand 15 minutes or more. Sauté garlic and gingerroot in hot oil for ½ minute. Add spareribs and cook until browned on all sides. Pour off excess oil. Add vinegar, remaining brown sugar and water. Cook on medium heat until steaming. Place into baking dish. Pour pan drippings over ribs. Cover and bake for one hour or until tender. Remove cover. Baste with pan drippings. Bake 10-15 minutes longer. Put into chafing dish with candle underneath.

TEQUILA DIP

2 medium Haas avocados, peeled, seeded and mashed
2 T. lime juice
8 oz. cream cheese, softened
3 T. tequila
½ tsp. hot sauce
½ tsp. salt
¼ tsp. pepper
nacho chips

(continued)

Mix softened cream cheese with tequila, hot sauce, salt and pepper. Stir in avocado and lime juice. Mix well. Put into serving bowl. Surround with nacho chips for dipping.

VIETNAMESE EGG ROLLS

2 oz. of cellophane noodles soaked in hot water to cover for 10 minutes or until soft, and drained
½ lb. lean boneless pork, minced
1 lb. shrimp, peeled and deveined, and chopped
2 cloves garlic, pressed
2 T. sesame oil
1 egg yolk
6 green onions, chopped
2 T. minced cilantro
2 T. grated fresh gingerroot
½ tsp. salt
20 egg roll wrappers
Vegetable oil for cooking
Hot Mustard Sauce recipe in this book
Sweet and Sour Sauce recipe in this book

Cut noodles into 2-inch pieces; set aside. Cook pork until browned in 2 tablespoons sesame oil. Add shrimp and garlic and cook until shrimp is pink. Add noodles, green onions, cilantro, gingerroot and salt. Cook 2 to 3 minutes. Cool. Spoon ¼ cup mixture in center of each egg roll wrapper. Fold top of wrapper over filling, tucking under filling; fold left and right sides over filling. Brush remaining edge of wrapper with egg yolk; tightly roll filled end toward remaining edge, and gently press to seal. Pour oil to a depth of 2 inches into a wok or saucepan; heat to 375°. Fry, a few at a time, until golden brown, turning once. Drain on paper towels. Be sure oil reheats to 375° before adding more batches. Serve with Hot Mustard Sauce or Sweet and Sour Sauce. (Recipes in this book.)

WONTON FILLED WITH PORK

½ head Chinese cabbage (or use Savoy cabbage)
½ lb. ground cooked pork
1 tsp. rice wine or sherry
½ tsp. pepper
1 tsp. salt
1 T. sesame oil
1 T. cornstarch
2 T. soy sauce
1 can water chestnuts, finely chopped
1 c. finely chopped green onions
1 tsp. finely chopped gingerroot
50 wonton wrappers
3-4 c. peanut or vegetable oil for frying

(continued)

Cook cabbage leaves in boiling water until limp. Drain and cool. Squeeze out water. Chop finely. Mix with cooked pork, rice wine or sherry, pepper, salt, sesame oil, cornstarch, soy sauce, chopped green onions, gingerroot and water chestnuts. Use 1 tablespoon mixture to fill wrappers. Keep wrappers covered with a damp towel so they won't dry out. Moisten edges of wrappers with water. Fold wrappers once to make a triangle. Press edges together to seal. Heat 2" of oil in a sauce pan or electric frying pan or deep fat fryer to 375°. Deep fry until crisp, turning once. Fry in batches, being sure to return oil to 375° before adding another batch. Makes 50.

ZUCCHINI SQUARES

3 c. thinly sliced unpared zucchini
1 c. all-purpose flour
1 tsp. baking soda
½ c. finely chopped onion
½ c. grated Parmesan cheese
2 T. minced Italian parsley
½ tsp. salt

½ tsp. dried marjoram or oregano
¼ tsp. thyme
½ tsp. pepper
1 clove garlic, pressed
½ c. vegetable oil
4 eggs, slightly beaten
paprika

Heat oven to 350°. Grease 13" x 9" x 2" baking pan. Mix all ingredients thoroughly. Pour into pan. Sprinkle lightly with paprika. Bake 25-30 minutes until golden brown. Cut into pieces, about 2" x 1". Serve warm. makes 4 dozen.

ASPARAGUS SOUP

4 T. butter
2 T. flour
6 c. chicken broth
1 lb. asparagus tips, washed and trimmed

½ c. whipping cream or light cream
2 egg yolks
1 tsp. salt
½ tsp. fresh black pepper

Melt the butter in a large saucepan over medium heat, adding flour and stirring. Cook until golden. Slowly stir in 2 cups of the broth and then add the asparagus. Cook over a low heat, simmering, for 30 minutes. Stir occasionally. Cool. Pour the mixture into the blender and mix until it is smooth. Return the mixture to the saucepan and bring to boil. Whisk egg yolks and cream together. Add one cup of the unheated broth to egg yolks and cream. Whisk again. Slowly add to saucepan, stirring. Add remaining 3 cups of broth. Stir. Add salt and pepper. Taste. Add

(continued)

more salt and pepper if you like. Heat over low heat until slightly thickened. Do not boil or the soup will curdle. Serve at once. Serves 6.

BAKED POTATO SOUP

4 large russet potatoes
⅔ c. butter
⅔ c. all-purpose flour
6 c. milk
1 tsp. salt
1 tsp. white pepper

5 green onions, chopped
12 slices bacon, cooked and crumbled
1½ c. shredded sharp cheddar cheese
8 oz. sour cream

Heat oven to 400°. Bake potatoes for 45 minutes or until done. Cool. Cut in half lengthwise and scoop out pulp and mash into small chunks. Set aside. Discard skins. Melt butter in a heavy saucepan over low heat. Add flour, stirring until smooth. Cook 1 minute, until golden. Gradually add milk, stirring. Cook over medium heat, stirring constantly until mixture is thickened and bubbly. Add potato pulp, salt, pepper, 2 tablespoons green onions, ½ cup bacon and 1 cup cheese. Cook until thoroughly heated. Stir in sour cream. Serve with remaining onion, bacon and cheese to sprinkle over.

BEEF BARLEY SOUP

2 lb. beef shank or lean chuck, cut into ½" cubes
¼ c. olive oil
3 carrots, sliced
1 large onion, diced
2 stalks celery, with leaves, sliced
1 tsp. thyme

1 bay leaf
¼ c. Italian parsley
1 14½-oz. can diced tomatoes
2 tsp. salt
1 tsp. black pepper
1 c. barley
5 c. water

Heat oil in large pot. Add beef and brown. Add onions. Brown. Add carrots, celery, thyme, bay leaf, parsley, tomatoes, salt and pepper and water. Simmer for one hour, covered, with cover ajar. Add barley and simmer covered, with cover ajar, for 50 minutes. When barley is cooked, soup is done. Check seasoning. If needed, add more salt.

BLACK BEAN SOUP

1 lb. dried black beans
3 qt. chicken broth
2 medium onions, diced
1 c. chopped celery
1 c. chopped carrots
1 c. ham, diced
1½ T. lemon juice

2 cloves garlic, pressed
4 bay leaves
1½ tsp. salt
1 tsp. black pepper
⅛ tsp. cayenne pepper
½ c. finely chopped red onion
sour cream

    Rinse beans, cover with water and soak overnight. Drain. Place chicken broth in a pot and add beans, ham, bay leaves and salt and pepper. Bring to a boil. Lower heat and simmer, covered, with cover ajar, over a low heat until beans are soft (about 1½ hours). Add onions, celery, carrots, lemon juice, garlic and cayenne pepper. Simmer, covered, with cover ajar, one hour longer. Discard bay leaves. Serve with a teaspoon of red onion and a dollop of sour cream on top.

BROCCOLI SOUP

1 small onion, chopped
1 leek, thinly sliced (white part only)
1 stalk celery, sliced (without leaves)
2 T. butter
1 c. water

2 10-oz. pkg. frozen chopped broccoli
2 tsp. salt
1 dash cayenne
2 T. uncooked rice
2 c. chicken broth
½ c. cream

    Put onion, leek, celery and butter in 2-quart saucepan. Sauté for 2 minutes over medium heat. Add salt, cayenne, rice and one cup chicken broth to onion mixture in saucepan. Simmer 20 minutes. Do not boil. Cool soup. In separate saucepan, cook broccoli in 1 cup water until tender and drain (reserving liquid). Pour chicken broth and onion mixture into blender container. Cover and run on high until liquefied. Pour back into saucepan. Put broccoli and remaining chicken broth in blender container. Cover and liquify. If mixture becomes too thick to flow, add some of the reserved broccoli cooking liquid to thin. Add broccoli to onion mixture in saucepan. Re-heat soup. Add cream. Heat. Do not boil. Serve.

BUTTERNUT SQUASH SOUP

3 T. unsalted butter
2 celery ribs, finely chopped
1 large onion, thinly sliced
1 medium butternut squash (1½ lb.) peeled, and cut into ½" dice
1 small baking potato, peeled and thinly sliced

2 tsp. salt
4 c. boiling water
⅛ tsp. ground mace
¼ c. minced Italian parsley
1 tsp. white pepper

Melt 3 tablespoons butter in a large saucepan. Add celery and onion. Cover and cook over low heat until softened, about 7 minutes. Add the squash, potato, mace and boiling water. Cover and cook, stirring occasionally, until the vegetables are just tender, about 30 minutes. Cool the soup. Purée the soup in blender in batches. and return each batch to the saucepan. Re-heat. Add parsley. Season with salt and white pepper.

CEVICHE

1 lb. fish fillets, cut into ½" cubes (flounder, red snapper, bass, halibut or sole)
½ c. chopped onion
1 jalapeño pepper, finely chopped
½ tsp. Tabasco sauce
½ c. fresh lime juice
1 medium tomato, seeded and chopped

⅓ c. extra virgin olive oil
½ tsp. salt
½ tsp. black pepper
1 clove garlic, pressed
2 T. fresh chopped cilantro
½ tsp. thyme

Combine all ingredients in a bowl. Cover with plastic wrap. Let stand in refrigerator overnight. (The lime juice cooks the fish.) Turn once. When ready to serve, spoon into soup bowls. Serves 4-6.

CHICK PEAS WITH DITALINI SOUP

2 c. dried chickpeas or 1 16-oz. can chickpeas, rinsed and drained
¼ c. olive oil
2 slices bacon, diced
2 cloves garlic, pressed
2 stalks celery, diced finely
¼ c. diced onion

2 T. Italian parsley, minced
1 14½-oz. can diced tomatoes
3 16-oz. cans chicken broth
½ tsp. oregano
2 bay leaves
1 tsp. salt
½ tsp. pepper
½ lb. ditalini

If you use the dried chick peas, soak them overnight. Cover them with water and bring to a boil. Lower heat and simmer for 1 hour. If you use the canned chickpeas, rinse and drain them. Heat the olive oil in a large soup pot. Sauté the onion and celery for 5 minutes. Add the garlic and parsley cook one minute longer. Add the chickpeas, tomatoes, chicken broth, oregano, bay leaves, salt and pepper. Simmer gently for 30 minutes. While the soup is simmering, in a small skillet, fry the bacon until crisp and add the bacon and drippings to the soup. In a large pot, bring 6 cups water to a boil, add the ditalini and cook until al dente. Drain. Add to the simmering soup just before you are ready to serve.

CHICKEN SOUP

1 4-lb. chicken
6 qt. cold water
1 T. salt
3 stalks celery with leaves, cut into 1" pieces
2 carrots, cut into 1" pieces

1 medium onion, chopped
3 whole cloves
2 bay leaves
1 tsp. thyme
6 peppercorns
2 T. tomato paste

Wash the chicken. Put into a large stock pot. Cover with the water. Bring to a boil over high heat. Lower heat and simmer, skimming off the scum periodically. This will take about an hour. When the water is clear, add the salt, celery, carrots, onion, cloves, bay leaves, thyme, peppercorns and tomato paste. Simmer, covered, for 2 more hours. Strain broth and refrigerate. Discard the rest. When ready to use, you may add ¼ cup cooked rice for each 2 cups of soup. You may use ¼ cup cooked egg noodles or pastina for chicken noodle soup. Or, you may use the broth for other purposes.

CHICKEN SOUP WITH MATZO BALLS

See recipe for chicken soup
For the Matzo balls:
1 c. unsalted matzo meal
¼ c. plain seltzer water
1 T. vegetable oil
2 tsp. salt

3 T. fresh dill
¼ c. finely chopped Italian parsley
¼ c. finely chopped fresh chives
4 large eggs, beaten

In large bowl, with fork, stir ingredients until evenly mixed. Cover bowl with plastic wrap and refrigerate for 45 minutes. In large saucepan, heat 2 quarts water to boiling over high heat. Shape matzo-meal mixture into 4 dozen 1" inch balls and place in 15½" by 10½" jelly roll pan. Moisten hands while doing the shaping of the balls. If the mixture is still hard to work with, sprinkle with flour. When water is boiling, drop balls, one by one, into boiling water. Heat to boiling. Reduce heat to low. Cover and simmer 45 to 55 minutes until balls are tender. With slotted spoon, remove balls to paper towels to drain, then transfer to clean jelly roll pan. Heat two cups soup for each person and add 6 balls to each two cups of soup. Enough balls for eight servings.

CORN CHOWDER

1 medium onion, chopped finely
½ c. diced celery
¼ c. diced green pepper
3 T. extra virgin olive oil
1 c. chicken broth
1 16-oz. can whole kernel corn, drained
1 16-oz. can cream style corn

3 small potatoes, peeled and diced small
1 c. milk
1 c. cream
2 T. butter
1½ tsp. salt
1 tsp. white pepper

In 6-quart saucepan, sauté celery, onion and green pepper in oil. Add whole kernel corn, potatoes and 1 cup chicken broth. Cook until potatoes are tender. Add the cream style corn, milk and cream. Simmer gently for 15 minutes. Do not boil. Add butter, salt and pepper and serve.

DUTCH SPLIT PEA SOUP

1 lb. dried green split peas
3 qt. cold water
2 smoked ham hocks
4 slices bacon, diced
1 c. chopped leeks
1 c. chopped onions
2 T. butter
2 c. celery leaves and stalks, chopped
1 medium clove garlic, pressed
1 c. Dutch or Polish sausage, sliced ½" thick
1 bay leaf
½ tsp. thyme
¼ c. chopped Italian parsley
½ c. dry white wine (optional)
½ c. light cream
2 tsp. salt
1 tsp. pepper

Wash peas and bring water to boil. Add peas. Cook for ½ hour, skimming foam off. Add ham hocks, bacon, bay leaf, thyme and parsley. Simmer, covered, with cover ajar, one hour longer. Sauté leeks and onions in butter. Add garlic and sauté. Add these, plus celery, salt, pepper and sausage to peas and simmer, covered, with cover ajar, one hour. Remove ham hocks and cut ham into bite-size pieces. Discard bones. Add ham to soup. Let stand overnight in the refrigerator. Reheat, adding wine and cream. Simmer. Do not boil after cream is added.

ESCAROLE SOUP

6 c. chicken soup
1 head escarole, washed and shredded
¼ c. minced Italian parsley
1 carrot, shredded
1 can cannellini beans, rinsed and drained
salt to taste
pepper to taste
freshly grated Parmesan cheese

Heat chicken soup. Add shredded escarole, shredded carrot and parsley. Simmer for 15 minutes. Add the rinsed and drained beans and heat to boiling. Remove from heat. Season with salt and pepper. Serve with Parmesan cheese.

LOBSTER BISQUE

¼ c. olive oil
1 large carrot, chopped
½ medium onion, diced
2 stalks celery, finely minced
6 c. chicken broth
¾ c. rice
½ tsp. thyme
1 bay leaf

2 T. tomato paste
2 lb. raw lobster meat, cut into small pieces
½ c. dry white wine
½ c. heavy cream
1 tsp. salt
1 tsp. white pepper
dash tabasco sauce

Heat oil in large pan. Add carrots, onions and celery. Sauté for 3-4 minutes. Add the wine. Simmer 5 minutes. Add chicken broth, rice, thyme, bay leaf, tomato paste, salt and pepper. Simmer for 45 minutes. Remove bay leaf. Cool soup. Whirl in blender in batches. Return to heat. Add lobster meat. Cook until lobster turns red. Add cream and stir. Add dash tabasco and more salt, if necessary.

MARYLAND CRAB CHOWDER

1 medium onion, chopped
4 medium garlic cloves, pressed
2 celery stalks, chopped
2 carrots, diced
1 c. frozen green beans, chopped
¼ c. extra virgin olive oil
1 c. water
1 c. dry white wine

1 8-oz. bottle clam juice
5 medium potatoes, peeled and diced
3 14½-oz. cans diced tomatoes
1 6-oz. can tomato paste
1 T. Old Bay seasoning
1 lb. fresh crabmeat, picked over to remove any bits of shell

Heat oil in a 6-quart pot. Sauté onion, celery and carrots in oil for 3 minutes. Add garlic. Cook one minute longer. Add green beans, water, wine, clam juice and potatoes. Bring to a boil, then lower heat and simmer, covered, for 30 minutes. Add tomatoes, tomato paste and seasoning. Return to a boil. Reduce heat and simmer for 30 minutes more. Add crabmeat and simmer for 15 minutes. Add salt if necessary.

MINESTRONE

8 c. chicken broth (If you prefer this to be vegetarian, use water instead. It's still very tasty.)
1 c. onions, diced
3 stalks celery, with leaves, diced
3 carrots, sliced
3 cloves garlic, pressed
¼ c. extra virgin olive oil
1 c. sliced zucchini
3 large potatoes, peeled and diced
1 16-oz. can cannellini beans, rinsed and drained
1 c. green beans, cut into ½" pieces
1 c. peas
1 c. shredded savoy cabbage
1 c. shredded kale
3 stalks swiss chard, diced
1 c. shredded fresh spinach
¼ c. minced fresh Italian parsley
1 T. basil
2 bay leaves
¼ tsp. thyme
3 14½-oz. cans diced tomatoes
2 tsp. salt
1 tsp. black pepper
½ lb. ditalini (this is to be cooked separately and added to soup dishes when served)

Boil chicken broth or water (whichever you choose to use). In a frying pan, sauté onions, celery, carrots and garlic in olive oil. Add to boiling water by scraping pan with spatula. Then add zucchini, potatoes, cannellini beans, green beans, peas, shredded savoy cabbage, kale, swiss chard, spinach, parsley, basil, bay leaves, thyme, tomatoes, salt and pepper. Bring to boil again. Turn heat down and simmer for about 30 minutes. Fifteen minutes before soup is done, bring a pot of water to a boil and add 1 tablespoon salt and ½ pound ditalini. Cook ditalini to al dente. Drain. Put about ½ cup cooked ditalini in each soup dish and ladle soup over ditalini.

PASTA CON FAGIOLI (PASTA AND BEANS)

½ lb. lean ground beef
3 slices bacon, diced, or ¼ lb. pancetta, diced
3 T. extra virgin olive oil
2 carrots, thinly sliced
2 ribs celery, thinly sliced
2 cloves garlic, pressed
3 14½-oz. cans chicken broth (or 6 c. homemade broth)
1 16-oz. can cannellini beans, rinsed and drained
1 bay leaf
1 14½-oz. can diced tomatoes
1 tsp. salt
1 tsp. black pepper
8 oz. ditalini

Heat a skillet. Add 1 tablespoon oil and heat. Sauté beef until brown, breaking up into chunks. Set aside. Sauté bacon or pancetta in 2 tablespoons oil in 10-cup or larger saucepan. Add carrots, celery and garlic.

(continued)

Sauté for 7 minutes stirring. Add bay leaf, chicken broth, tomatoes, beef, salt and pepper. Bring to boil. Lower heat and simmer for about 45 minutes. Fifteen minutes before done, bring a pot of water to a boil. Add 1 tablespoon salt. Add ditalini and cook to al dente. Drain. Add beans and ditalini to mixture and cook 5 minutes longer to heat through.

RIBOLLITA

Heated day-old minestrone
day-old Italian bread
extra virgin olive oil
Parmesan cheese

Place a slice of day-old Italian bread in bottom of soup dish. Pour heated minestrone over the bread. Drizzle oil over and sprinkle with Parmesan cheese.

SOUTHWESTERN CHICKEN SOUP

6 15-oz. cans chicken broth
1 lb. boneless chicken breasts, cubed
½ lb. chorizo sausage, sliced ½" thick
1 large onion, chopped
3 cloves garlic, pressed
¼ c. extra virgin olive oil
1 10-oz. pkg. frozen Italian green beans
1 15-oz. can corn, drained
½ lb. cleaned, sliced fresh mushrooms
2 15-oz. cans diced tomatoes
1 T. cumin
2 tsp. chili powder
2 bay leaves
2 tsp. salt
1 tsp. black pepper
¼ tsp. cayenne pepper

Brown chicken pieces and sausage in olive oil in a large soup pan. Remove from pan. Brown onions for 4 minutes in soup pan. Add garlic. Brown 1 minute. Return chicken and sausage to soup pan. Add chicken broth, cumin, chili powder, bay leaves, salt, black pepper and cayenne pepper. Bring to boil. Lower heat. Simmer, covered, with the cover ajar, for one hour. Add green beans, corn, mushrooms and tomatoes. Return to boil. Lower heat. Simmer for 30 minutes.

STRACCIATELLA

4 c. chicken broth
1 large egg
½ c. cooked pastina

3 T. freshly grated Parmesan cheese

Put the chicken broth in a saucepan and heat. In another pan, cook the pastina al dente. Drain. (Or you may use any very small pasta.) Add the pastina to the broth. Beat the egg with a fork. Drizzle it into the broth. Remove broth from heat. Serve immediately with Parmesan cheese on the side.

TOMATO BISQUE

½ medium onion, minced
¼ c. butter
2 T. fresh Italian parsley, minced
4 c. chicken broth
1 28-oz. can peeled tomatoes
1 bay leaf

1 c. heavy cream
1 tsp. salt
½ tsp. white pepper
1 tsp. sugar
¼ tsp. thyme

Heat the butter in a 10-cup saucepan. Sauté onion for 5 minutes. Add parsley, thyme and bay leaf. Sauté one minute longer. Add broth, tomatoes, sugar, salt and pepper. Simmer for 30 minutes. Remove bay leaf and discard. Cool soup. Purée the soup in a blender in batches. Return to saucepan and re-heat. Add cream and stir. Serve immediately.

WONTON SOUP

See recipe for wontons in this book
18 wontons
7 c. water for boiling
½ c. finely chopped green onions
½ head finely chopped Chinese cabbage

1 T. oil
2 tsp. salt
1 T. soy sauce
⅛ tsp. pepper

Prepare wontons using recipe for Wontons in this book. Bring water to boil. Add onions, cabbage, oil, salt, soy sauce and pepper. Cook for 5 minutes. Add wontons. Cook 5 minutes more. Serves 6.

BARLEY SALAD

4 c. chicken broth
1 c. barley
1 c. shredded carrots
¼ c. minced fresh Italian parsley
¼ c. sliced fresh mushrooms
4 T. extra virgin olive oil
1 T. lemon juice

2 tsp. minced fresh basil or ½ tsp. dried
1 tsp. salt
½ tsp. black pepper
¾ c. chopped peanuts or cashews or toasted almonds

In saucepan, combine chicken broth and barley. Bring to a boil. Reduce heat. Cover and simmer for 50 minutes until cooked. The barley should have absorbed the broth, but if the barley is cooked and there is more broth in the pan, drain. Mix cooked barley, carrots, parsley and mushrooms in a bowl. In another bowl, mix oil, lemon juice, basil, salt and pepper. Pour dressing over barley mixture. Toss. Chill for 3 or 4 hours. Stir in nuts before serving.

CALIFORNIA SHRIMP BOAT

2 Haas avocados
1 c. cooked shrimp
1 c. sliced black olives
1 c. fresh mushrooms, thinly sliced
⅓ c. celery, minced
2 T. green onion, finely chopped
1 T. lemon juice

½ c. Hellmann's mayonnaise
2 T. tarragon vinegar
1 T. fresh Italian parsley, minced
¼ tsp. dill weed
½ tsp. salt
¼ tsp. white pepper
2 c. shredded lettuce

Combine shrimp, olives, mushrooms, celery, onion and lemon juice. Toss lightly. Cover and refrigerate. Make dressing as follows: Mix mayonnaise, tarragon vinegar, parsley, dill weed, salt and white pepper. Pour over salad. Toss. Chill. Before serving, prepare avocados by peeling, cutting in half and removing pits. Top each half with an equal portion of salad mixture. Serve on bed of shredded lettuce. Serves 4.

CAPRESE SALAD

3 vine-ripened tomatoes, cut into ¼" slices
1 lb. mozzarella, cut into ¼" slices

24 leaves fresh basil
salt and freshly ground black pepper
extra virgin olive oil

(continued)

On a beautiful shallow serving platter, alternate the tomato, mozzarella and basil leaves. Drizzle the oil over and sprinkle with salt. Grate fresh black pepper over all.

CHICKEN SALAD

3 c. cubed cooked chicken breast
1/4 c. water chestnuts, sliced
1/2 c. chopped celery
1/2 c. toasted, slivered almonds
1 c. green seedless grapes, cut into halves
1 8-oz. can pineapple chunks, drained
3/4 c. Hellmann's mayonnaise
1 tsp. curry powder
2 tsp. soy sauce
2 tsp. lemon juice
1/4 tsp. salt
1/4 tsp. white pepper
2 c. shredded lettuce

Combine chicken with water chestnuts, celery, almonds and grapes in a large bowl. In another bowl, mix mayonnaise, curry powder, soy sauce, lemon juice, salt and pepper. Pour over chicken mixture. Toss. Chill. Spoon onto nests of lettuce, Garnish with pineapple chunks. Serves 4-6.

CHINESE CHICKEN SALAD

For the salad:

3 c. shredded, cooked chicken breast
2 c. capellini cooked al dente and broken in half and drained
3 T. scallions, thinly sliced
1 red bell pepper, cut into thin strips
1/3 c. cashew nuts
1 T. cilantro, minced
1/2 c. fresh bean sprouts
Dressing

In a large bowl, mix together the cooked, shredded chicken, cooked and broken capellini, scallions, red bell pepper, cashew nuts, cilantro and bean sprouts. Pour dressing over chicken mixture and toss. Serve chilled.

(continued)

Dressing:

2 T. soy sauce
2 T. sesame oil
1 small clove garlic, pressed
¼ c. peanut oil
1 tsp. sugar

3 T. rice vinegar
¼ c. peanut butter
2 T. sesame seeds
¼ tsp. salt
¼ tsp. black pepper

In a small bowl, mix together the soy sauce, sesame oil, garlic, peanut oil, sugar, rice vinegar and peanut butter. Stir in sesame seeds, salt and pepper.

CHINESE VEGETABLE SALAD

1 6-oz. pkg. frozen Chinese pea pods, thawed
2 medium cucumbers, peeled, halved, seeded and sliced ¼" thick

1 medium carrot, shredded
1 c. thinly sliced Chinese or Savoy cabbage
½ red bell pepper, thinly sliced
Dressing

Cook the pea pods in boiling water for 1 minute. Drain and blot with a paper towel. Mix the pea pods, cucumbers, carrot, cabbage and red bell pepper together in a bowl. Pour dressing over vegetables and toss.

Dressing:

1 T. peanut or corn oil
1 tsp. chili powder
1 clove garlic, pressed
¼ c. soy sauce
2 T. rice vinegar

3 T. sesame oil
2 T. brown sugar
1 tsp. finely minced fresh gingerroot

In a small bowl, mix together the peanut or corn oil, chili powder, garlic, soy sauce, rice vinegar, sesame oil, brown sugar and gingerroot.

COBB SALAD

2 c. diced, cooked chicken breasts
2 Haas avocados, peeled, pit removed and sliced crosswise
½ head romaine lettuce, shredded
1 bunch watercress, leaves only
6 slices bacon, cooked crisp and crumbled
2 medium tomatoes, seeded, drained and chopped
2 ounces blue cheese, crumbled
2 hard-cooked eggs, chopped
3 T. green onions, finely sliced
Dressing

Gently toss the chicken, avocados, lettuce, watercress, bacon, tomatoes, blue cheese, eggs and onions in a bowl. Pour the dressing over salad and toss.

Dressing:

1 tsp. sugar
1 tsp. Dijon mustard
1 small clove garlic, pressed
½ tsp. salt
½ tsp. black pepper
1 T. red-wine vinegar
2 tsp. balsamic vinegar
½ c. extra virgin olive oil

In a small bowl, mix together the sugar, mustard, garlic, salt, pepper, red-wine vinegar and balsamic vinegar. Whisk in the oil until well blended.

COLESLAW

5 c. shredded cabbage
1 c. shredded carrots
⅓ c. finely chopped green pepper
Dressing

Mix cabbage, carrots and green pepper in a bowl. Pour dressing over salad and toss. Serve chilled.

Dressing:

½ c. Hellmann's mayonnaise
1 T. lemon juice
1 tsp. sugar
¼ c. sour cream
2 tsp. celery seed
¼ tsp. salt
¼ tsp. black pepper

Mix together the mayonnaise, lemon juice, sugar, sour cream, celery seed, salt and pepper.

COUSCOUS SALAD

1 box couscous
⅓ c. shredded carrots
⅓ c. finely diced celery
½ c. cherry tomatoes, sliced in half
¼ c. extra virgin olive oil

2 T. lemon juice
1 tsp. ground turmeric
2 T. minced fresh Italian parsley
1 tsp. ground cumin
1 tsp. salt
½ tsp. pepper

Cook the couscous according to package directions, but do not add salt or butter. Fluff it up with a fork to cool. Mix in a bowl the olive oil, lemon juice, turmeric, parsley, cumin, salt and pepper. Add the carrots, celery and tomatoes to the couscous. Pour the dressing over and toss.

CRANBERRY ORANGE RELISH

1 I-lb. bag fresh cranberries
1 large naval orange

1 c. sugar

Wash the berries and drain. Wash and dry the orange. Cut the orange into 8 pieces. In the blender whirl the berries a bit, a few at a time, so that they are chopped. (Leave a few whole.) Transfer to a mixing bowl. Then put the orange pieces into the blender, a few at a time, chopping. Add the oranges to the bowl with the berries. Add 1 c. sugar and mix well. Chill in the refrigerator.

DANDELION SALAD

1 large bunch dandelion greens
¼ c. pecans, sautéed
2 T. butter
1 tsp. sugar
1 clove garlic, pressed
3 T. extra virgin olive oil

1 T. balsamic vinegar
1 tsp. oregano
1 T. fresh Italian parsley, minced
½ tsp. salt
½ tsp. black pepper

Wash and dry the dandelion greens. Break into small 2" pieces. Put into a salad bowl. Heat the butter in a small frying pan. Add the sugar and pecans. Sauté a few minutes until crisp. Set aside. In a bowl, mix together the garlic, oil, vinegar, oregano, parsley, salt and pepper. Pour the dressing over the dandelion greens. Toss. Add the pecans. Toss again and serve.

FROZEN GREEN SALAD

2 3-oz. pkg. cream cheese, softened
2 small cans crushed pineapple, drained, reserve juice
2 c. sugar
1 pt. whipping cream
2 3-oz. pkg. lime Jello
1 c. chopped walnuts

Add enough water to the reserved pineapple juice to make two cups. Boil the water mixture and add Jello. Stir to dissolve. Add the 2 cups sugar. Stir together to dissolve sugar. Put in refrigerator until consistency to beat. Whip until fluffy. Mix cream cheese and pineapple together. Fold into Jello mixture. Add walnuts. Whip the cream and fold in. Put into glass serving bowl. Refrigerate until set.

FRUIT COCKTAIL SALAD

2 3-oz. pkg. cream cheese, softened
1 c. Hellmann's mayonnaise
8 oz. heavy cream, whipped
1 large can fruit cocktail (3½ c.), drained
½ c. drained maraschino cherries, cut into fourths
2½ c. miniature marshmallows
2 tsp. maraschino cherry juice
lettuce leaves to put on serving platter
cherries and mint leaves for garnish

Blend softened cream cheese with mayonnaise. Fold in fruit cocktail, cherries, marshmallows and cherry juice. Then fold in whipped cream. Pour into a 2½-quart container. Cover and put into freezer overnight. To serve, let stand out of freezer a few minutes, then remove from container with a spatula. (If necessary, dip bottom of container in hot water for a few seconds to loosen up salad.) Place on platter which has been spread with some lettuce leaves. Slice through. Garnish with maraschino cherries and mint leaves.

FRUIT SALAD

1 c. fresh strawberries, cut in half if they are large
1 c. honeydew melon cut into chunks
1 c. cantaloupe cut into chunks
1 c. green seedless grapes
2 c. watermelon cut into chunks
1 c. blackberries

Prepare fruit. Place in a clear glass bowl (preferably). Serve with or without the dip.

(continued)

Fruit Dip:

1 8-oz. pkg. cream cheese, softened
1 7-oz. jar marshmallow cream
1 T. orange juice
2 drops red food coloring if desired

Blend together the cream cheese, marshmallow cream and orange juice. Add a few drops red food coloring and blend in if you would like color.

GREEK SALAD

4 c. romaine lettuce, shredded
1 c. cucumber, thinly sliced
2 tomatoes, seeded and drained and cut into 1" pieces
1 small red onion, halved and thinly sliced (½ c.)
½ red pepper, thinly sliced
½ green pepper, thinly sliced
16 kalamata or Greek black olives
6 to 8 flat anchovy fillets
1 c. crumbled feta cheese
1 lemon, thinly sliced

Place lettuce, cucumber, tomatoes, onion and peppers in a large salad bowl. Toss with Greek dressing and top with olives, anchovies and feta cheese. Garnish with lemon slices, if desired. Makes 6 to 8 servings.

Greek Salad Dressing:

¾ c. extra virgin olive oil
2 T. minced fresh Italian parsley
2 T. red wine vinegar
2 T. lemon juice
1 tsp. dried oregano, crushed
1 clove garlic, pressed
½ tsp. black pepper
¼ tsp. salt

HAM SALAD

½ lb. cooked and drained elbow macaroni
4 c. cooked cubed ham
½ c. minced onion
2 c. thinly sliced celery
⅔ c. chopped almonds
½ tsp. salt
½ tsp. white pepper
2 c. Hellmann's mayonnaise
½ c. extra virgin olive oil
2 T. wine vinegar
1 tsp. creamy yellow mustard
1 small clove garlic, pressed
½ c. half and half

Cook macaroni to al dente. In a large salad bowl, mix together cooked macaroni, ham, onion, celery, almonds, salt and pepper. In a small

(continued)

bowl, mix together the mayonnaise, oil, vinegar, mustard, garlic and half and half. Pour over salad ingredients and toss to mix.

ITALIAN SEAFOOD SALAD

1 lb. shrimp, peeled and deveined
1 lb. baby clams, shelled
2 lb. mussels, shelled
½ lb. scallops, cut in half if they are the large ones
½ lb. calamari, cut into rings (buy the one already cleaned)
½ lb. octopus, cut into chunks (optional)
3 stalks celery, sliced
2 red bell peppers, sliced and cut slices in half

½ c. pitted green olives
½ c. pitted large black olives
1 T. garlic, pressed
1 tsp. oregano
1 c. extra virgin olive oil
3 T. red wine vinegar
¼ c. minced fresh Italian parsley
1 tsp. chopped fresh mint (optional)
1 tsp. salt
1 tsp. black pepper

Wash the shrimp, clams, mussels, scallops, calamari and octopus (if you use it) in cold, salted water. Wash each one separately and steam each for about 5 minutes until done. As each different kind of seafood is steamed, drain and pat dry and put into a large mixing bowl. Do not overcook the seafood as it will be too tough. Add the celery, peppers, green and black olives to the seafood and toss. In a smaller bowl, mix together the garlic, oregano, oil, vinegar, parsley, mint, salt and pepper. Remove from bowl with a spatula, pouring over salad and toss. Marinate for at least one hour before serving. Garnish with extra springs of fresh parsley and mint.

KIWI TOMATO SALAD

3 fresh tomatoes, sliced ¼" thick
3 fresh kiwi, sliced ¼" thick
¼ c. extra virgin olive oil
1 tsp. wine vinegar
¼ tsp. oregano

½ small clove garlic, pressed
¼ tsp. salt
¼ tsp. black pepper
1 tsp. honey

Alternate the tomato slices and kiwi slices on a platter. Mix together the oil, vinegar, oregano, garlic, salt, pepper and honey. Pour over the salad and serve.

MACARONI SALAD

½ lb. elbow macaroni, cooked and drained
½ c. celery, thinly sliced
¼ c. minced green onions or fresh chives
1 c. chopped red pepper
1 medium tomato, seeded and diced
¼ c. black olives, sliced in half horizontally

½ c. shredded cheddar cheese
¼ c. grated Parmesan cheese
1 T. minced fresh Italian parsley
½ c. Hellmann's mayonnaise
1 tsp. salt
½ tsp. black pepper
½ tsp. sugar

Cook the macaroni to al dente. Mix the macaroni, celery, onions or fresh chives, red pepper, tomato, olives, cheddar and Parmesan cheeses in a salad bowl. In another bowl mix together the parsley, mayonnaise, salt, pepper, and sugar. Pour the dressing over the salad, toss and serve.

MARINATED VEGETABLE SALAD

2 c. cauliflower flowerets
2 c. broccoli flowerets
1 c. whole cherry tomatoes
½ lb. fresh mushrooms
1 medium zucchini, sliced
1 small cucumber, thinly sliced
3 T. scallions, sliced
1 16-oz. can green beans, rinsed and drained

¼ c. red wine vinegar
¾ c. extra virgin olive oil
1½ tsp. fresh basil, minced (or 1 tsp. dried)
1 T. minced fresh Italian parsley
1 tsp. salt
1½ tsp. pepper
2 cloves garlic, pressed

Place in a bowl the cauliflower, broccoli, cherry tomatoes, mushrooms, zucchini, cucumber, scallions and green beans. In another bowl, mix together the red wine vinegar, oil, basil, parsley, salt, pepper and garlic. Pour over the vegetables and let marinate in the refrigerator for at least 24 hours. Mix it now and then.

MIXED GREENS, PEAR AND PECAN SALAD

6 c. assorted greens (or pre-packaged mesclun)
1 ripe pear, cored and cubed
¼ c. pecans, toasted then broken into fourths
¼ c. currants or golden raisins
¼ c. crumbled blue cheese
¼ c. extra virgin olive oil
1 tsp. balsamic vinegar
1 tsp. lemon juice
½ tsp. salt
½ tsp. black pepper
1 tsp. honey

    Mix the greens, pear, pecans, currants or golden raisins and cheese in a salad bowl. In another bowl, mix together the oil, vinegar, lemon juice, salt, pepper and honey. Pour over the salad, toss and serve.

PASTA SALAD

½ lb. cooked and drained fusilli pasta
1 c. carrots steamed until crisp tender, drained and cooled
1 c. broccoli flowerets, steamed until crisp tender, drained and cooled
½ c. peas, cooked and drained
1 c. cherry tomatoes
½ c. red peppers thinly sliced and cut in half
½ c. green peppers thinly sliced and cut in half
½ c. black olives
2 T. fresh basil, minced or 2 tsp. dried
½ c. freshly grated Parmesan cheese
2 T. minced onion
1 T. red wine vinegar
1 tsp. balsamic vinegar
⅓ c. extra virgin olive oil
2 T. minced fresh Italian parsley
½ tsp. salt
½ tsp. black pepper
1 tsp. sugar

    Mix together the pasta, carrots, broccoli, peas, cherry tomatoes, red and green peppers and olives. In another bowl, mix together the basil, Parmesan cheese, minced onion, wine vinegar, balsamic vinegar, oil, parsley, salt, pepper and sugar. Pour salad dressing over pasta and vegetable mixture and toss.

PASTA SALAD WITH CHICKEN

2 lb. boned chicken breasts
2 T. olive oil
1 lb. shell macaroni cooked al dente, drained
1 c. toasted almonds
1 c. celery, sliced thinly
½ c. water chestnuts, drained and sliced
1 c. red seedless grapes
1 c. Ranch Dressing

Prepare Ranch Dressing and chill in refrigerator. Heat coals under grill. Wash and dry chicken. Coat chicken with the 2 tablespoons olive oil. Grill chicken over coals, turning, until done -- about 30 minutes. Cook pasta al dente and drain. Put pasta a a bowl. Slice grilled chicken at a diagonal and add to pasta. Add toasted almonds, celery, water chestnuts, grapes and dressing and toss.

Ranch Dressing:

1 pkg. Hidden Valley Ranch Salad Dressing Mix (Buttermilk Recipe)
1 c. buttermilk
1 c. mayonnaise

In a bowl, combine 1 cup buttermilk and 1 cup mayonnaise with entire contents of packet. Mix well. Cover and refrigerate. Chill 30 minutes to thicken. Stir before serving. Stays fresh 3-4 weeks.

PINEAPPLE BOATS

1 fresh ripe pineapple
1 apple
1 banana
1 c. strawberries
1 c. cottage cheese

Cut pineapple in half lengthwise. With a knife, cut pineapple in each half in fourths, but do not cut through shell. Carefully remove pineapple from each half. Remove core and dice pineapple into chunks. Spoon ½ cup cottage cheese into each pineapple shell. Core and dice apple. Slice banana. Slice strawberries. Arrange one-half pineapple chunks around cottage cheese in each shell. Then arrange one-half apple, one-half banana and one half strawberries alongside the pineapple. Serve.

PINEAPPLE CRANBERRY SALAD

1 14-oz. can crushed pineapple
2 3-oz. pkg. lemon Jello
½ c. lemon juice
3 T. shredded orange zest
1 16-oz. can whole cranberry sauce
1 c. chopped walnuts
water
pineapple slices for garnish
salad greens for garnish

Drain syrup from pineapple and add enough water to pineapple juice to make 1½ cups liquid. Put gelatin in a mixing bowl. Heat liquid to boiling point and pour over gelatin. Stir to dissolve gelatin. Stir in pineapple, lemon juice, orange zest, cranberry sauce and walnuts. Turn into a glass salad bowl. Chill until firm. Serve from bowl. Optional: Turn out onto a platter and garnish with pineapple slices and salad greens (and holly leaves if you make it for a Christmas salad). You may serve it with fruit dip on the side or serve plain.

Fruit Dip:

8-oz. pkg. cream cheese, softened
1 7-oz. jar marshmallow cream
1 T. orange juice
a couple of drops of red food coloring (if desired)

Blend cream cheese, marshmallow cream, orange juice and red food coloring.

POTATO SALAD

4 medium potatoes, boiled and peeled
3 hard-boiled eggs, cooled and diced small
1 rib celery, minced
3 T. minced onion
1 tsp. salt
½ tsp. white pepper
⅛ tsp. dill weed
½ c. Hellmann's mayonnaise
1 tsp. French's Classic Yellow mustard
¼ c. sour cream

When potatoes are cooled a little, dice them into a bowl. Add the diced eggs, celery and onion. In another bowl, mix together the salt, pepper, dill weed, mayonnaise, mustard and sour cream. Pour the dressing over the salad, toss and serve.

POTATO SALAD ROLL

3 medium potatoes
1/3 c. Hellmann's mayonnaise
1 tsp. salt
1 tsp. paprika
1/2 c. diced celery
3 hard-cooked eggs, chopped
2 T. minced onion

1 c. cream-style cottage cheese, drained
2 T. Hellmann's mayonnaise
2 T. finely chopped green pepper
2 T. diced red pepper
2 T. minced parsley

Pare, cook, drain and mash potatoes. Combine with 1/3 cup mayonnaise, salt, paprika, celery, eggs and onion. Chill. On waxed paper, shape mixture into 12" x 9" x 1/2" rectangle. In a bowl, combine cottage cheese, 2 tablespoons mayonnaise, green pepper and red pepper. Spread atop rectangle to within 1" of edges. Roll up from short side. Chill. When ready to serve, sprinkle with minced parsley. Have a slicing knife on hand for slicing portions. (For a meal, place in the center of a platter and surround with cooked shrimp, cherry tomatoes, zucchini and avocado slices.)

RED PEPPER SALAD

1 carrot, sliced at a diagonal
1 red pepper, cut into strips, then cut the strips in half
1 medium yellow squash, sliced
1/4 c. black pitted olives, sliced
1/2 medium red onion, sliced and slice the slices in half

3 T. extra virgin olive oil
2 T. minced fresh Italian parsley
1 T. red wine vinegar
1/4 tsp. salt
1 dash cayenne pepper

Put the vegetables into a salad bowl. Mix together the oil, parsley, vinegar, salt and cayenne pepper. Pour over salad and mix.

RICE SALAD

3 c. cooked rice (basmati is a good choice, but you can use whatever kind you like)
1 c. thin strips ham (or 1 c. cooked shrimp)
1/2 c. snow peas
2 tsp. olive oil

1/2 c. diced red peppers
2 T. finely chopped scallions
1 T. finely chopped fresh Italian parsley
1/2 tsp. salt
1/2 tsp. black pepper
French Dressing

(continued)

Cook the rice according to package directions. Cool. Heat a skillet. Add olive oil and heat. Sauté the snow peas for 3 minutes in the olive oil. Combine the rice, ham or shrimp, snow peas, peppers, scallions, parsley, salt and pepper. Pour over French Dressing (recipe follows) and mix.

French Dressing:

2 T. vinegar
½ tsp. salt
¼ tsp. freshly ground black pepper

½ c. extra virgin olive oil

SPINACH SALAD

1 lb. baby spinach leaves, washed and dried
½ c. crisp, fresh bean sprouts, or canned and drained bean sprouts
2 hard-boiled eggs, sliced
3 slices bacon, diced and fried crisp
1 c. fresh mushrooms, sliced
1 small can water chestnuts, sliced
1 lb. medium shrimp, peeled, deveined, cooked and chilled

½ c. toasted, slivered almonds
½ c. black olives, sliced in half
1 c. Hellmann's mayonnaise
½ c. sour cream
1 small clove garlic, pressed
2 T. minced fresh Italian parsley
2 T. crushed pineapple, drained
4 oz. blue cheese, crumbled
½ tsp. salt
½ tsp. black pepper

Mix together in a large salad bowl the spinach, bean sprouts, bacon, mushrooms, water chestnuts, shrimp, almonds and olives. In another bowl, mix together the mayonnaise, sour cream, garlic, parsley, pineapple, blue cheese, salt and pepper. Use as much dressing as you like on the salad and toss. Garnish with the sliced hard-boiled eggs.

STRAWBERRY CREAM SQUARES

2 3-oz. pkg. strawberry flavored gelatin
2 c. boiling water
2 10-oz. pkg. frozen strawberries

1 13½-oz. can crushed pineapple, drained
2 large ripe bananas, finely diced
1 c. sour cream

(continued)

Add the boiled water to the gelatin. Stir until dissolved. Add the 2 packages frozen strawberries. Stir occasionally until thawed. Add the drained pineapple and the diced bananas. Pour ½ of the mixture into an 8" x 8" x 2" pan. Chill until firm. (Keep the other half of the mixture out of the refrigerator until needed.) When the mixture is chilled, spread with the sour cream. Pour remainder of the gelatin mixture on top. Chill until firm. When ready to serve, cut into squares.

TACO SALAD

1 lb. ground beef chuck
2 cloves garlic, pressed
2 T. olive oil
1 16-oz. can red kidney beans, rinsed and drained
1 4-oz. can green chiles, drained and chopped
1 16-oz. can whole peeled tomatoes packed in juice, undrained
2 tsp. chili powder
1 tsp. cumin

1 tsp. salt
½ tsp. pepper
1 head iceberg lettuce
8 oz. shredded cheddar cheese
1 medium-sized tomato
1 bunch scallions with green tops
1 7-oz. pkg. tortilla chips
½ c. black olives, sliced in half
sour cream
sliced scallions (optional, for garnish)

In a medium-sized skillet, heat 2 tablespoons olive oil. Place ground chuck and minced garlic in skillet. Break up and brown meat. Transfer meat and garlic to a colander; drain off and discard fat. Return meat and garlic to skillet to heat. Add kidney beans. Stir and heat beans. Add chopped green chiles, undrained whole peeled tomatoes, chili powder, cumin, salt and pepper. Mix well with a wooden spoon and cook over low heat for about 30 minutes or until most of the moisture has evaporated from the meat. While meat is cooking, break apart and wash and dry lettuce (a salad spinner is best for this). Shred lettuce. Set aside into refrigerator. Cut out and discard core of tomato. Dice. Wash scallions. Dry. Trim off and discard root ends. Chop scallions finely to yield 1 cup. Save extra chopped scallions. Place lettuce in a large chilled bowl. Top lettuce with meat mixture. Arrange tortilla chips around outer edge. Sprinkle cheese, scallions, chopped tomato and sliced olives around meat mixture. Top with a dollop of sour cream and garnish with 2 tablespoons leftover scallions. Toss and serve.

TOMATO SALAD

4 fresh garden tomatoes, or vine-ripened tomatoes
1 small clove garlic, pressed
3 T. extra virgin olive oil
2 tsp. red wine vinegar
9 leaves fresh basil, minced
¼ tsp. salt
freshly ground black pepper
(you may add 2 T. chopped sweet red onion if you like)

Cut the tomatoes into slices and cut the slices in halves. Put into a salad bowl. (Add chopped sweet red onion if you like.) In a bowl, mix together the garlic, oil, vinegar, basil, salt and pepper. Pour over tomatoes.

TORTELLINI SALAD

1 lb. cheese-filled tortellini, cooked al dente and drained
1 8-oz. pkg. frozen artichoke hearts, cooked and drained
½ c. fresh broccoli flowerets, cooked crisp tender in boiling water
½ c. fresh carrots, sliced and cooked crisp tender in boiling water
½ c. black olives, sliced in half
¼ c. Parmesan cheese
¼ c. fresh basil, minced
¼ c. pine nuts
1 tsp. red wine vinegar
¼ c. extra virgin olive oil
½ tsp. salt
½ tsp. freshly ground pepper

Put the tortellini, artichoke hearts, broccoli, carrots and olives in a salad bowl. Mix together in another bowl the Parmesan cheese, basil, pine nuts, wine vinegar, olive oil, salt and pepper. Pour over salad and serve.

TUNA AND BEAN SALAD

2 c. dry cannellini beans
2 bay leaves
1 tsp. salt
3 T. extra virgin olive oil
1 tsp. salt
½ tsp. black pepper
2 6-oz. cans white tuna packed in oil
2 T. Italian parsley

Wash the beans, cover and soak overnight in water. To cook the beans, add more water to 2" above the beans. Bring water to a boil. Add the bay leaves and 1 teaspoon salt. Lower heat and simmer them

(continued)

for about two hours until tender. Drain. Discard bay leaves. If you prefer to use canned cannellini beans, use one 16-ounce can, rinsed and drained. Break up tuna in a salad bowl. Add the beans. Add the oil, salt, pepper and parsley. Mix and serve.

WALDORF SALAD

1½ c. diced apples
1½ c. finely sliced celery
1 c. coarsely chopped walnuts
¼ c. golden raisins
¾ c. Hellmann's mayonnaise

Mix all ingredients in a bowl and chill until cold.

BLUE CHEESE DRESSING

1 c. Hellmann's mayonnaise
½ c. sour cream
½ c. blue cheese, crumbled
¼ tsp. salt
½ tsp. black pepper
milk, if needed

Whisk mayonnaise, sour cream, salt and pepper together. Add a teaspoon of milk or so of milk if you want a thinner consistency. Mix in blue cheese and chill to develop flavor.

SESAME DRESSING

¾ c. corn oil
⅓ c. rice vinegar
3 T. sesame oil
1 tsp. salt
1 tsp. sugar
2 T. grated orange zest
1 tsp. black pepper
1 tsp. minced fresh ginger
1 small clove garlic, pressed
⅛ tsp. cayenne

Mix all ingredients together until smooth.

HERB DRESSING

1 tsp. Dijon mustard
1 T. fresh Italian parsley, minced
1 medium clove garlic, pressed
1 T. fresh basil, minced
½ tsp. dried tarragon
½ tsp. dried chervil (or ½ tsp. oregano)
2 T. lemon juice
2 T. wine vinegar
¾ c. extra virgin olive oil
1 dash tabasco sauce
½ tsp. salt
½ tsp. freshly ground black pepper

    Mix mustard, parsley, garlic, basil, tarragon and chervil or oregano together in a bowl. Add lemon juice and vinegar. Mix. Slowly add oil in a stream, all the while whisking in the same direction until oil is well blended. Add tabasco sauce, salt and pepper and whisk again.

VINAIGRETTE DRESSING

1 c. extra virgin olive oil
⅓ c. fresh lemon juice
1 tsp. sugar
1½ tsp. salt
¼ tsp. black pepper
½ tsp. paprika
½ tsp. dry mustard
1 clove garlic, pressed

    Mix together the lemon juice, sugar, salt, black pepper, paprika, mustard and garlic. Add the oil in a steady stream, whisking it in. Store in refrigerator in a glass-covered jar. Chill. Stir well before using.

ALMOND CHICKEN SALAD SANDWICH

¼ c. chopped, cooked chicken
1 T. finely chopped celery
2 T. Hellmann's mayonnaise
⅛ tsp. salt
dash pepper
2 T. chopped almonds
2 slices buttered white bread

    For one sandwich, mix together the chicken, celery, mayonnaise, salt, pepper and almonds. Spread on the buttered bread.

BAKED TOMATO CHEESE SANDWICHES

8 slices toast, without crust
8 slices crisp bacon, crumbled
8 slices tomatoes
½ lb. shredded cheddar cheese
2 c. Béchamel Sauce (see recipe in this book)
½ c. buttered bread crumbs

Heat oven to 350°. Place toast in 15" x 9" baking pan. Cover each slice with crumbled bacon, then with a slice of tomato and top with cheese. Pour white sauce over all and sprinkle with bread crumbs. Bake 25 minutes.

BEEF FAJITAS

10 8" flour tortillas
2½ lb. beef skirts
meat tenderizer
1 can beer
1 T. wine vinegar
¼ c. olive oil
1 tsp. salt

1 tsp. black pepper
1 clove garlic, pressed
2 T. dried onion flakes
½ tsp. oregano
½ tsp. basil
1 T. chili powder

Garnishments:

refried beans (recipe in this book)
1½ c. grated cheddar cheese
Pico de Gallo sauce (recipe in this book)

Tenderize beef skirts with the meat tenderizer. Mix together the beer, wine vinegar, olive oil, salt, pepper, garlic, onion flakes, oregano, basil and chili powder. Put the beef in a shallow pan and pour the marinade over. Cover and refrigerate overnight, turning once or twice. Prepare the Refried Beans and the Pico de Gallo Sauce. Fire up the charcoal and add mesquite wood, if you have some. When the charcoal is ready, remove the beef from the marinade and grill 10-15 minutes on each side. Put on a platter and slice thinly. Warm the tortillas in the oven. To prepare each sandwich, place 3 or 4 strips of beef on the top of the tortilla and top with some Pico de Gallo Sauce, refried beans and grated cheddar cheese. Wrap tortilla by folding one side over the other.

CHICKEN AND BACON SANDWICH

1 c. finely diced cooked chicken
½ c. crumbled crisp bacon
1 c. finely chopped tomato with seeds removed and drained
mayonnaise to moisten
Buttered bread

Mix together chicken, bacon, tomato and mayonnaise. Spread on bread.

CURRIED CHICKEN SANDWICHES

½ c. flaked coconut
½ c. chopped almonds
1 8-oz. pkg. cream cheese, softened
2 T. orange marmalade
1½ tsp. curry powder
¼ tsp. salt
¼ tsp. pepper
2 c. diced cooked chicken
3 T. finely diced green onions
12 buttered pumpernickel, wheat, or white bread slices

Bake coconut and almonds in shallow baking pans at 350, stirring occasionally, 5 to 8 minutes or until toasted. Stir together cream cheese, marmalade, curry powder, salt and pepper. Gently stir in chicken, coconut, almonds and green onions. Spread evenly on 6 bread slices and cover with the other six slices.

EGG AND OLIVE SANDWICHES

10 hard-cooked eggs, minced
¾ c. black olives, sliced thinly
½ c. mayonnaise
½ tsp. salt
8 slices buttered white bread

Mix together eggs, olives, mayonnaise and salt. Spread on 4 slices buttered bread. Cover with the other 4 slices buttered bread.

ITALIAN HERO SANDWICH

1 8" long hard roll
3 slices hard salami or soppressata
2 slices mortadella
3 slices capicola
2 slices provolone
½ c. shredded lettuce

3 slices tomato, ¼" thick
5 strips red and/or green pepper
3 thinly sliced pieces of red onion
2 T. extra virgin olive oil
dash of salt
dash of black pepper

Cut the bread in half lengthwise. Drizzle each half with a tablespoon of olive oil. Spread on one half the salami or soppressata, mortadella, capicola, provolone, lettuce, tomato, peppers and onion. Sprinkle with salt and pepper. Cover with other half.

LIVERWURST AND TOMATO SANDWICH

two slices buttered white bread
slice enough liverwurst to cover a slice of bread
slice one medium tomato into ¼" thick slices

Hellmann's mayonnaise
dash of salt and pepper

Spread mayonnaise over the buttered slices of bread. Then spread with the sliced liverwurst and sliced tomato. Sprinkle with a dash of salt and black pepper.

MEATBALL AND PROVOLONE SANDWICH

two meatballs
1 slice provolone

¼ c. tomato sauce
two slices Italian bread

Heat the meatballs and sauce. Slice the meatballs. Cover one slice of bread with the meatballs, provolone and sauce. Cover with the other slice of bread.

ORGANIC SANDWICH

1 slice Swiss cheese
½ Haas avocado, sliced
1 small tomato, sliced
¼ c. alfalfa sprouts

2 slices pumpernickel bread
1 T. extra virgin olive oil
salt and pepper

Sprinkle the oil on the pumpernickel bread. Spread one slice bread with the cheese, avocado, tomato and alfalfa sprouts. Sprinkle with salt and pepper.

PITA POCKETS THAI

1¼ lb. thinly sliced flank or sirloin steak
½ tsp. ground black pepper
2 tsp. salt
1 T. paprika
½ tsp. cumin
1 T. brown sugar
1 tsp. allspice
2 tsp. minced fresh ginger, plus 1 tsp.
1 T. finely chopped fresh Italian parsley

1 T. sesame oil
1 T. rice wine vinegar
2 T. soy sauce
1 T. sugar
1 finely minced jalapeño pepper
2 scallions, minced
8 c. Napa or Savoy cabbage, shredded
1 large carrot, shredded
½ c. fresh cilantro, minced
6 to 8 pita wraps, warmed

Partially freeze the meat for ease of slicing thinly. Marinate the flank or sirloin steak with a mixture of the black pepper, salt, paprika, cumin, brown sugar, allspice, 2 teaspoons ginger and the chopped parsley for 12 hours. Heat a frying pan and sauté the meat, with the mixture, for about 5 minutes. Remove from heat. Set aside. In a bowl, mix together the sesame oil, rice wine vinegar, soy sauce and sugar. Stir until sugar dissolves. Add the 1 teaspoon ginger and jalapeño. Combine in a frying pan with the scallions. Cook 1 to 2 minutes. Add cabbage and carrot and toss until heated through, about 3 to 4 minutes. Removed from heat and add cilantro. Combine with steak and serve on warm pita wraps.

ROAST BEEF CLUB SANDWICH

1 bun
2 slices roast beef
2 slices smoked turkey
1 slice cheddar cheese

1 slice Swiss cheese
caramelized onions with sweet pickles

(continued)

Heat oven to 350°. Put the beef, turkey, cheddar cheese and Swiss cheese on one side of the bun. To make caramelized onions with sweet pickles: Sauté two thin slices of onion and four slices of a pickle in 1 tablespoon butter, ½ teaspoon sugar and a dash of salt and pepper. When onion is tender, remove from heat. Put the bun, open-faced, on a baking sheet and put in oven. Bake until cheese is melted. Remove from oven and top with caramelized onions and pickles.

SAUSAGE AND PEPPERS SANDWICH

1 lb. Italian sausage (If you can't find good Italian sausage, use recipe for sausage in this book.)
2 red peppers
2 T. fresh Italian parsley, chopped

3 T. extra virgin olive oil
½ tsp. salt
¼ tsp. black pepper
1 baguette, cut into thirds and sliced lengthwise

Cook the sausage over low heat, covered, in ¼ cup water until browned on all sides. Turn from time to time. The water will evaporate and the sausage will emit its own juices. If it starts to become dry, add 2 tablespoons oil. The sausage should be cooked in about 30 minutes. Wash and slice the red peppers into strips. Heat a frying pan. Add 3 tablespoons oil. When the oil is heated, add the peppers and cook over medium heat for 10 minutes, turning. Lower the heat, add the parsley, cover and cook for 10-15 minutes longer, until done. Check and stir every five minutes. When done, sprinkle with the salt and pepper. Turn off heat. Slice the sausage lengthwise and place on 3 of the halves. Put some peppers on each. Cover with the other three slices of bread.

TOMATO SANDWICH

Garden fresh tomatoes, or vine-ripened tomatoes
Italian bread

extra virgin olive oil
salt & pepper
dash oregano

Sprinkle olive oil on the bread. Slice the tomatoes and place on bread. Sprinkle with salt, pepper and a dash of oregano.

TUNA MELT WITH TOMATO

1 6-oz. can water-packed tuna, drained
½ c. diced celery
¼ c. mayonnaise
⅛ tsp. salt
⅛ tsp. pepper

4 slices rye or white bread, toasted
4 oz. shredded Monterey Jack or cheddar cheese
4 slices tomato, ¼" thick

    Mix together the tuna, celery, mayonnaise, salt and pepper. Spread the mixture over two slices of the bread. Put half the cheese on each. Put two slices tomato on each. Place under broiler in baking pan for 1-2 minutes until cheese is melted and golden. Serve hot.

VEGETARIAN SANDWICH

½ zucchini, sliced
½ c. eggplant, diced
½ c. red peppers, diced

2 T. olive oil
salt & pepper
4 slices Italian bread

    Heat a frying pan. Put in the oil and heat the oil. Add the red peppers. Cook for 5 minutes. Add the eggplant. Cook 5 minutes longer. Add the zucchini. Cook 10 minutes, stirring now and then. Add the salt and pepper. Spread over two slices of bread. Cover with the other two slices of bread.

Recipe Favorites

Pasta

Rice

Casseroles

Main Dishes

Eggs

Sauces

Marinades

Stuffings

Vegetables

My Father and Mother

Helpful Hints

- When preparing a casserole, make an additional batch to freeze for when you're short on time. Use within 2 months.

- To keep hot oil from splattering, sprinkle a little salt or flour in the pan before frying.

- To prevent pasta from boiling over, place a wooden spoon or fork across the top of the pot while the pasta is boiling.

- Boil all vegetables that grow above ground without a cover.

- Never soak vegetables after slicing; they will lose much of their nutritional value.

- Green pepper may change the flavor of frozen casseroles. Clove, garlic, and pepper flavors get stronger when frozen, while sage, onion, and salt become more mild.

- For an easy no-mess side dish, grill vegetables along with your meat.

- Store dried pasta, rice (except brown rice), and whole grains in tightly covered containers in a cool, dry place. Refrigerate brown rice, and freeze grains if you will not use them within 5 months.

- A few drops of lemon juice added to simmering rice will keep the grains separated.

- When cooking greens, add a teaspoon of sugar to the water to help vegetables retain their fresh colors.

- To dress up buttered, cooked vegetables, sprinkle them with toasted sesame seeds, toasted chopped nuts, canned french-fried onions, grated cheese, or slightly crushed seasoned croutons.

- Soufflé dishes are designed with straight sides to help your soufflé rise. Ramekins work well for single-serve casseroles.

- A little vinegar or lemon juice added to potatoes before draining will make them extra white when mashed.

- To avoid toughened beans or corn, add salt midway through cooking.

- If your pasta sauce seems a little dry, add a few tablespoons of the pasta's cooking water.

- To prevent cheese from sticking to a grater, spray the grater with cooking spray before beginning.

Copyright © Morris Press Cookbooks

Pasta/Rice/Casseroles/Main Dishes/ Eggs/Sauces/Marinades/Stuffings/ Vegetables

AGNOLOTTI

Make recipe for Pasta Dough
1 egg mixed with 2 teaspoons water to seal dough

Filling:

2 lb. of fresh spinach, washed, dried, and stems removed and discarded
¾ c. water to steam spinach
2 c. ricotta cheese

3 egg yolks
½ c. Parmesan cheese
½ tsp. salt
½ tsp. white pepper
⅛ tsp. nutmeg

Sauce:

1½ c. heavy cream
½ c. butter

1 c. freshly grated Parmesan cheese

Prepare dough according to Pasta Dough recipe in this book. For filling, cook the spinach in the water for 10 minutes over medium heat, covered. Drain thoroughly (squeezing between the hands is best). Finely chop spinach and purée in a blender or food processor. Put the spinach in a bowl. Add the ricotta, the egg yolks, ½ cup grated Parmesan cheese, salt, pepper and nutmeg. Blend. Roll out the dough into two very large, thin sheets. Cut dough into 5 " circles. Fill the circles with 3 tablespoons filling. Moisten the outer edge of the dough with some egg mixed with 2 teaspoons of water. Fold the dough over in half and seal. Press edges of the agnolotti with the prongs of a fork to seal in stuffing and so that no water can enter. Repeat until all filling is used up. You can re-roll the dough scraps to make more circles if needed. As the agnolotti are cut and sealed, line them up on a lightly floured cloth. Heat a big pot of water to boiling. Cook the agnolotti. Do not crowd them, even if you have to make two batches. As they float to the surface, they are done. They take about 5 minutes to cook. Remove from the pot and drain. When all have been cooked, put them into a heated, shallow serving dish. Heat the cream with the butter. Pour the cream sauce over the agnolotti, and sprinkle with the Parmesan cheese. Serves 6.

ANGEL HAIR PASTA WITH OLIVE OIL & HERBS

1 lb. capellini or angel hair pasta
½ c. extra virgin olive oil
3 cloves garlic, pressed
1 tsp. salt
½ tsp. freshly grated black pepper

¼ tsp. hot red pepper flakes (optional)
15 fresh basil leaves, minced
2 T. fresh Italian parsley, minced

Bring a large pot of water to a boil. When the water reaches a boil, add 1 tablespoon salt, then the pasta. Stir the pasta. Cook until al dente, 5-6 minutes. Do not overcook. Meanwhile, heat the olive oil in a small saucepan over low heat. Add the parsley and garlic. Sauté gently for a minute or so, just until the garlic starts to brown. Then remove from heat immediately. Add the basil, salt, black pepper. Add hot pepper if desired. Remove the pasta from the pot when cooked. Drain and transfer it to a large serving platter. Pour the hot olive mixture over. Toss and serve.

BAKED ZITI

5 T. extra virgin olive oil
1 lb. Italian sausage
1 medium onion, sliced and then slice the slices in half
2 cloves garlic, pressed
1 28-oz. can peeled tomatoes (preferably San Marzano)
4 T. tomato paste
1 tsp. salt

½ tsp. crushed red pepper flakes
6 T. minced fresh Italian parsley
1 lb. ziti pasta
2 c. ricotta cheese
1 egg
1 c. shredded fresh mozzarella cheese
½ c. freshly grated Parmesan cheese

Heat oven to 350°. Grease a shallow 3-quart baking dish with olive oil. Set aside. Slice the sausage into 1" pieces at a diagonal. In heavy medium skillet heat 3 tablespoons oil over medium heat. Add sausage to skillet and brown. Add onion and garlic. Sauté 5 minutes. Add tomatoes, tomato paste, salt, pepper flakes and 4 tablespoons parsley. Heat to boiling. Reduce heat. Simmer gently 15 minutes. While the sauce is simmering, bring a large pot of water to a boil. Add 1 tablespoon salt. Add ziti and stir. Cook ziti until al dente. Drain. Put into a large mixing bowl. Set aside. In another bowl, mix ricotta and egg together. Stir the ricotta mixture, half the mozzarella and the tomato sauce into the ziti. Mix well until completely blended. Spread evenly in baking dish. Sprinkle with remaining mozzarella, the Parmesan cheese and remaining pars-

(continued)

ley. Drizzle with remaining oil. Bake 25 minutes or until hot and cheeses are lightly browned. Let sit 10 minutes before serving.

BEANS AND RICE

2 c. cooked rice
1 can red kidney beans, rinsed and drained
2 slices bacon, minced
2 T. extra virgin olive oil
½ onion, minced
½ c. celery, minced

1 clove garlic, pressed
½ c. finely chopped green peppers
½ tsp. salt
½ tsp. black pepper
⅛ tsp. thyme
2 T. fresh Italian parsley, minced

Cook rice according to package directions. In a frying pan, sauté the bacon until crisp. Remove from pan with a slotted spoon. Add 2 tablespoons oil to pan. Heat. Add onion, celery, garlic and peppers and sauté until cooked (about 10 minutes). Add beans, salt, pepper, thyme and parsley. When heated, add rice and cooked bacon. Mix together. Taste to see if you need more salt.

CANNELLONI

Tomato sauce: use 2 c. of Tomato Sauce without meat in this book
1 c. freshly grated Parmesan cheese for sprinkling and serving

Filling:

½ lb. mozzarella cheese, shredded
1 lb. ricotta cheese
½ c. grated Parmesan cheese

½ c. provolone cheese, shredded
½ tsp. white pepper
1 egg, slightly beaten

Béchamel Sauce:

4 T. butter
4 T. flour
1 c. milk
1 c. heavy cream

½ tsp. salt
½ tsp. white pepper
⅛ tsp. nutmeg

Make the crêpes. See recipe below. The batter should stand for at least one hour at room temperature. Make the recipe for tomato sauce

(continued)

without meat in this book. Heat the oven to 350°. While the tomato sauce is cooking, make the béchamel sauce: In a saucepan, melt the butter over medium heat. Stir in the flour. It will form a paste. Lower the heat and slowly stir in the milk, making sure the sauce is smooth. Then slowly stir in the cream. Add the salt, white pepper and nutmeg. The sauce will thicken a little. Set aside. In a bowl, mix together the mozzarella cheese, ricotta cheese, Parmesan cheese, provolone cheese, white pepper and the egg. Spread three tablespoons of filling on the browned side of each crêpe, rolling each up as it is filled. Line the crêpes in a single layer in a buttered, shallow 13" x 9" x 2" baking dish, seam side down. Pour the béchamel sauce over the filled crêpes. Pour two cups of the tomato sauce over the béchamel sauce. Sprinkle with a little grated Parmesan cheese. Heat for 20 minutes in the oven. Remove from oven and sprinkle with a little more Parmesan cheese.

Crêpes For Cannelloni:

1½ c. all-purpose flour
2¼ c. milk

4 eggs, slightly beaten
½ tsp. salt

Beat the eggs. Whisk together the flour, milk, eggs and salt. Batter should be fairly thin. Let batter stand for one hour. Place a nonstick 7" frying pan over medium heat. Oil pan ever so slightly. Stir the batter and pour about 2½ tablespoons batter in the frying pan, lifting the pan off the heat and tilting and rotating it so that the batter forms an even, thin layer. Cook until the top is set and the underside is golden. It is not necessary to turn them over. Remove the crêpe to a piece of wax paper. Continue cooking the rest of the crêpes, greasing the pan with a tiny bit of oil if necessary, and stirring the batter before starting each one. Stack the finished crêpes between sheets of wax paper.

COUSCOUS

1 c. couscous
1½ c. chicken broth
1 T. butter
1 T. minced Italian parsley

½ tsp. salt
¼ tsp. white pepper
1 T. extra virgin olive oil
¼ c. pine nuts

Bring the broth to a boil in a saucepan and immediately add the butter, parsley and couscous. Cover and lower heat to medium low. Remove the pan from the heat and let stand, covered, 5 minutes. While it is standing, heat the olive oil in a small saucepan, add the pine nuts. Sauté the nuts for a minute. Add the nuts, salt and pepper to the couscous.

CURRIED RICE

3 T. olive oil
1 onion, finely chopped
1 c. rice
2 tsp. curry powder
½ tsp. salt
2 T. butter
½ c. golden raisins
2 c. chicken broth

Heat oven to 375°. Butter a 1½-quart casserole. Heat oil in a skillet, add the onions and sauté until soft. Stir in the rice and cook, stirring, for 3-4 minutes. Add the curry powder, salt, butter and raisins and cook 1 minute more. Transfer to the buttered casserole, pour in the chicken broth. Stir. Cover and bake for 50 minutes. Check to see if the broth has evaporated. If not, cook a little longer.

DUMPLINGS

2 c. flour
1 T. baking powder
1 tsp. salt
¼ tsp. white pepper
2 T. minced Italian parsley
¼ tsp. thyme
¼ tsp. dill weed
4 T. butter, softened
¾-1 c. milk
1 c. chicken broth

Combine the flour, baking powder, salt, pepper, parsley, thyme and dill weed in a bowl. Cut in the butter with a fork until mixture resembles coarse meal. Add ¾ cup milk and stir gently with a fork. Add only enough the remaining ¼ cup milk to make the dough hold together. Heat broth to bubbly. Drop in dumplings by tablespoonfuls. Lower heat, cover and steam for 20 minutes without lifting cover.

FETTUCCINE WITH CREAM

1 lb. fettuccine
2 T. butter
2 c. heavy cream
salt to taste
freshly ground black pepper to taste
1 c. freshly grated Parmesan cheese
2 tsp. minced fresh Italian parsley

Bring water to boil in a large pot. Add 1 tablespoon salt. Cook the fettuccine, stirring, to al dente: 3-5 minutes if you make the fresh pasta; 5-8 minutes for packaged fettuccine. Drain. In a saucepan, melt butter, add cream. Heat until cream begins to bubble. Do not boil. Season with

(continued)

salt and pepper to taste. Turn off heat. Add Parmesan cheese and parsley. Stir. Put hot, cooked fettuccine in a warm serving dish. Add cream and toss.

FETTUCCINE WITH FOUR CHEESES

1 lb. fettuccine
¼ c. butter
1½ c. heavy cream
freshly ground black pepper to taste
2 T. Parmesan cheese, grated
2 T. fontina cheese, grated

2 T. Gruyère cheese, grated
2 T. provolone cheese, grated
¼ c. freshly grated Parmesan cheese for sprinkling
freshly grated pepper
2 tsp. fresh, minced Italian parsley

Bring a large pot of water to boiling. Add 1 tablespoon salt to the water. Add the fettuccine and stir. Cook fettuccine 3-5 minutes if you make the fresh pasta, 5-8 minutes for packaged fettuccine. Drain. For the sauce, melt the butter in a saucepan. Add cream and heat until the cream begins to bubble. Season with pepper only. Add the Parmesan, fontina, gruyère and provolone cheeses to sauce. Gently heat until melted. Do not boil. Put the hot, cooked fettuccine in a serving dish. Pour sauce over and toss. Sprinkle with the ¼ cup Parmesan cheese and the parsley and serve.

FETTUCCINE WITH LAMB SAUCE

Make recipe for Lamb Sauce in this book
1 lb. fettuccine

1 c. freshly grated Parmesan cheese

Prepare the lamb sauce. Bring a large pot of water to boiling. When the water is boiling, add 1 tablespoon salt. Add the fettuccine and stir. Cook the fettuccine al dente. Drain. Put into warmed serving dish. Pour some lamb sauce over and serve with Parmesan cheese. Put the remaining lamb sauce in a bowl on the table.

FETTUCCINE WITH PORCINI MUSHROOMS

1 lb. fettuccine
1 T. salt
6 T. butter
½ lb. fresh porcini mushrooms (or ½ c. dried)
¼ c. butter
1 tsp. salt
1 tsp. black pepper
⅔ c. freshly grated Parmesan cheese

    If you are using dried mushrooms, soak them in a cup of water until they have softened. Drain. Cut into ½" pieces. If you use fresh, brush any dirt off the mushrooms. Slice them into ½" dice. Put on a large pot of water to boil for the fettuccine. Put the ¼ cup butter in a medium-size skillet. Melt the butter and sauté the mushrooms for 3 to 5 minutes over medium heat. Lower the heat and cook until tender, about 5 more minutes. While the mushrooms are cooking, add 1 tablespoon salt to the boiling water and put in the fettuccine, stirring. Cook for 5-8 minutes. Drain. Put into a warm bowl. Add 6 tablespoons butter to the fettuccine and stir. Remove the mushrooms from the heat. Add the mushrooms to the fettuccine and toss. Add the salt, pepper and cheese and toss again.

FETTUCCINE PRIMAVERA

1 lb. fettuccine
⅓ c. pine nuts
1½ c. fresh broccoli flowerets
1½ c. fresh or frozen snow pea pods
1 c. sliced carrots
1 c. sliced zucchini
1 red pepper, sliced thinly
12 cherry tomatoes, halved
¼ c. butter
2 cloves garlic, pressed
2 c. heavy cream
¼ c. fresh Italian parsley, minced
1½ c. freshly grated Parmesan cheese
¼ c. fresh basil, minced
½ tsp. salt
½ tsp. black pepper

    Toast pine nuts in oven at 350° for a few minutes, until golden. Set aside. Cook broccoli, carrots, zucchini, red pepper and snow peas in boiling water 2-3 minutes until crisp tender. Drain. Keep covered to keep warm. Bring water to boil in a large pot. Add 1 tablespoon salt. Add fettuccine and stir. Boil pasta for 5-8 minutes. Drain. Put into large bowl. Melt butter in saucepan. Add garlic and sauté about 1 minute. Add parsley and basil, salt and pepper. Stir. Add heavy cream. Heat to just bubbly, but do not boil. Stir in cheese. Remove sauce from stove. Add cooked vegetables, pine nuts and tomatoes to pasta in a large bowl. Pour sauce over mixture and toss.

FRIED RICE

1 egg
2 c. cooked rice
1½ T. soy sauce
2 T. butter or oil
½ c. chopped onion

½ c. either cooked small shrimp, diced cooked bacon, minced boiled ham or diced cooked pork
½ c. frozen peas, cooked

Cook the rice following directions on package. Heat the butter or oil over medium heat. Sauté the onion for 3 minutes in the butter or oil. Add either the shrimp, bacon, ham or pork. Cook for 5-7 minutes. Add the cooked rice, soy sauce and peas. Beat the egg and add to the mixture. Stir and cook a few minutes longer.

GNOCCHI

3 lb. potatoes (russet or Yukon Gold are good to use)
1 tsp. salt
2½ c. flour
½ c. butter
recipe for Tomato Sauce With Meat in this book.

freshly grated Parmesan cheese for sprinkling if you use the Tomato Sauce with meat
Or use the Pesto Sauce in this book

Make tomato sauce with meat, or make the Pesto Sauce. While the sauce is cooking, prepare the gnocchi. Scrub potatoes. Put them in a pot with water enough to cover. Boil until cooked. Peel potatoes and put them through a ricer onto a lightly floured board. Sprinkle with the salt. While they are still warm, work the flour into them until they become a firm, but delicate and soft, dough. Divide the dough into pieces and roll these between well floured hands to form long cylinders about ½" in diameter. Cut these into pieces about 1" long and pinch the center of each lightly between the index finger and the thumb. Place them on a lightly floured cloth. Heat the oven to 375°. Put on a large pot of water to boil. When the water is boiling, drop in the gnocchi and remove them with a slotted spoon as soon as they float to the surface of the water. Put them in a colander to drain, then transfer them to a large ovenproof dish. Sprinkle with the butter, several tablespoons of grated Parmesan cheese, and with the meat sauce. Heat in the oven for 5 to 10 minutes and serve. Put some Parmesan cheese in a bowl and serve on the side and put some of the meat sauce in a bowl on the table. If you use the Pesto Sauce, toss the hot gnocchi with the Pesto Sauce. Do not serve the Parmesan cheese on the side.

LASAGNA

- 1 lb. bulk Italian sausage (store bought or use recipe in this book)
- 2 medium cloves garlic, pressed
- ½ c. chopped onion
- ½ c. minced celery
- ½ c. minced carrot
- 1 16-oz. can tomatoes put through blender
- 1 6-oz. can tomato paste
- 1 tsp. salt
- ½ tsp. dried oregano
- ½ tsp. pepper
- 3 T. extra virgin olive oil
- 10 oz. lasagna (8-10 pieces, depending upon the size of the lasagna you use)
- 1 lb. ricotta cheese
- ½ c. freshly grated Parmesan cheese
- 2 beaten eggs
- ¼ c. minced fresh Italian parsley
- ¼ tsp. pepper
- 1 lb. shredded mozzarella cheese
- some freshly grated Parmesan cheese for sprinkling

Heat oven to 350°. In a large skillet, cook sausage, breaking up, and the garlic, onion, celery and carrot until meat is lightly browned. Drain off excess fat. Stir in tomatoes, tomato paste, salt, oregano and the ½ teaspoon pepper. Simmer, uncovered, 30 minutes, stirring occasionally. When done, stir 3 tablespoons olive oil into the sauce. Cook lasagna according to package directions until al dente. Drain. Combine ricotta, Parmesan, eggs, parsley and the ¼ teaspoon pepper in a bowl. Place half the noodles in an oiled 13" x 9" x 2" baking dish. Spread with half the cheese filling. Add half the mozzarella and half the meat sauce. Repeat layers. Bake, uncovered, for 30 minutes. Let stand 15 minutes before serving. Cut into squares to serve. Makes 10 to 12 servings. Put some Parmesan cheese in a bowl for sprinkling.

LINGUINE WITH CLAM SAUCE

- Use recipe for Marinara Sauce in this book
- 1 lb. linguine
- 4 lbs. fresh clams (if you can't get fresh, use 3 15-oz. canned whole clams, drained)
- 2 T. tomato paste

To cook fresh clams:

- 2 c. water
- ¼ c. dry white wine
- ½ tsp. dried oregano
- 1 T. chopped fresh Italian parsley
- 1 bay leaf

Make the marinara sauce. If you use fresh clams, scrub them and simmer them in the water, wine, oregano, parsley and bay leaf until the shells open. Remove the clams from the broth, discarding any unopened

(continued)

ones, and shuck them, reserving any juice. Strain the broth and reserve. Add the clams, 2 tablespoons tomato paste and ½ cup of the reserved broth to the marinara sauce. Set sauce aside, keeping warm. Heat a pot of water to boiling. Add 1 tablespoon salt. Add the linguine and stir. Cook 5-8 minutes until al dente. Drain. Put linguine into a large serving dish. Add the heated sauce. Serve hot. (If you use canned clams, no need to cook them in the water and wine. Just add them to the marinara sauce with the tomato paste and ½ cup of the juice from the canned clams. Heat and add to linguine.)

LINGUINE WITH PROSCIUTTO AND MUSHROOMS

1 lb. mushrooms, sliced
¼ lb. butter
1 clove garlic, pressed
¼ c. minced fresh Italian parsley
½ lb. chopped prosciutto
1 tsp. salt
1 tsp. white pepper
1 c. heavy cream
1 c. freshly grated Parmesan cheese
I lb. linguine

Heat frying pan over medium heat. Melt butter. Add mushrooms and sauté for 3 minutes. Add garlic and parsley. Sauté 1 minute longer. Add prosciutto, salt, pepper and cream. Heat just until it begins to bubble. Do not boil. Boil a large pot of water. When boiling, add 1 tablespoon salt. Add linguine and stir. Cook linguine until al dente. Drain. Put into serving bowl. Pour sauce over and toss. Add ½ cup of the Parmesan. Toss again. Put the rest of the Parmesan cheese in a small bowl and serve alongside the linguine.

LINGUINE WITH SHRIMP AND SCALLOPS

1 lb. linguine
1 T. salt
¼ c. butter
½ lb. medium shrimp, cleaned, shelled and deveined
½ lb. scallops
2 T. minced fresh Italian parsley
¼ c. dry white wine (optional)
½ medium clove garlic, pressed
1 c. heavy cream
1 tsp. salt
½ tsp. white pepper
½ c. freshly grated Parmesan cheese

Bring a large pot of water to a boil. When boiling, add the 1 tablespoon salt to the water. Add the linguine and cook for 8 minutes until al dente,

(continued)

stirring occasionally. Drain and keep warm. While the pasta is cooking, heat a skillet. Put the butter into the skillet and melt. Add the shrimp, scallops, garlic and parsley. Sauté for 2-3 minutes, stirring, or until the shrimp turns pink. Add the wine and simmer for 2 minutes. Add the cream, salt and pepper. Cook over medium-low heat until the sauce begins to bubble. Do not boil. Put the linguine into a warm serving bowl. Add the sauce. Toss. Add the Parmesan cheese and toss again. Serve.

LINGUINE WITH ZUCCHINI

1 lb. linguine

Sauce:

2 c. zucchini, diced
1/4 c. extra virgin olive oil
2 cloves garlic, pressed
1/2 c. chicken broth
2 T. minced fresh Italian parsley
1 tsp. salt

1/2 tsp. white pepper
1 c. ricotta cheese
1/2 c. freshly grated Parmesan cheese
fresh chopped basil for garnish

Boil water in a large pot. When water is boiling, add 1 tablespoon salt. Add linguine, stir and cook 5-8 minutes until al dente. Drain and keep warm. Heat olive oil in skillet. Add zucchini and parsley and cook on medium heat for 6-7 minutes. Add garlic and cook 1 minute longer until zucchini is cooked, but not mushy. Heat chicken broth. Put ricotta in a large bowl. Add chicken broth to ricotta and stir until smooth and very creamy. Season with salt and pepper. Add cooked and drained linguine to the mixture. Then add zucchini mixture. Gradually add Parmesan cheese. Toss. Serve on warmed plates. Garnish with fresh chopped basil.

PASTA DOUGH

3 1/2 c. sifted all-purpose flour
5 eggs
1 T. olive oil

1 tsp. salt
extra flour for rolling pasta

Make a little mound of the flour on a pastry board and make a well in the center. Break the eggs into a deep bowl. Beat them with the tablespoon of olive oil and the salt, and pour them into the center of the well. Working with the fingers, mix the flour into the eggs a little at a time until it is all thoroughly combined. Then knead it with both hands until it is quite firm and very smooth to the touch. Dip a clean white

(continued)

cloth into warm water. Wring it out well. Place it over the dough to keep the dough from drying out, and set it aside to rest for a half hour. If you roll the dough by hand, flour the surface. Divide the dough into fourths and roll it into sheets with a rolling pin to a thickness suitable for the particular kind of pasta you intend to make. If you have a pasta machine, which is the easiest way, you can knead the dough by dividing the dough into fourths, flouring the dough and passing the dough through the rollers of the machine with the rollers at the widest setting, about 6 times, folding the dough over and flouring it before each pass. Then roll it out into sheets by passing the dough through the rollers, adjusting the knob on the machine to the next thinnest setting until it has passed through the thinnest setting. Lay the sheet on a lightly floured surface and roll out the next ball of dough.

PASTA WITH PEAS

1 lb. fusilli pasta
1 T. salt
2 T. extra virgin olive oil
1 medium onion, chopped
2 cloves garlic, pressed
1 14½-oz. can diced tomatoes
1 lb. green peas, frozen
⅓ c. chicken broth
1 tsp. basil
1 tsp. salt
1 tsp. black pepper
½ tsp. sugar
½ lb. bacon
1 c. freshly grated Parmesan cheese

    Heat a large skillet. Put in 2 tablespoons olive oil. Heat the oil. Add the onion and cook for 3 or 4 minutes, stirring. Add the garlic. Cook for 1 minute longer. Add the tomatoes, peas, chicken broth, basil, salt, pepper and sugar. Cover. Simmer over low heat for 20 minutes. Dice the bacon. Brown the bacon in another skillet. Drain off the fat, add to the mixture. While the sauce is cooking, bring a large pot of water to a boil. Add 1 tablespoon salt. Add the fusilli pasta and stir. Cook until al dente. Drain and toss with the sauce and then the Parmesan cheese.

PASTA WITH SEAFOOD SAUCE

1 lb. spaghetti
3 T. extra virgin olive oil
2 cloves garlic, pressed
2 28-oz. cans San Marzano
  tomatoes
¼ c. minced fresh Italian parsley
1 tsp. salt
1 tsp. pepper
¼ tsp. crushed red pepper flakes
3 T. butter

¾ lb. mushrooms
2 lb. mussels
1 lb. cleaned squid, sliced into ½"
  rings
1 lb. scallops
1 lb. shrimp, cleaned, shelled and
  deveined
½ lb. sea bass, cut into 1" pieces
1 c. dry white wine

Heat a large skillet. Put in the oil. Heat the oil and sauté the garlic and parsley in the oil for 1 minute. Add the tomatoes, salt, pepper and crushed red pepper flakes and simmer over a low heat for 15 minutes, mashing the tomatoes with a fork or a potato masher. In a saucepan, boil some water, add the mussels and discard any which do not open. Remove the remaining mussels from their shells and set aside. In a large saucepan over medium heat, put in the butter and sauté the mushrooms for 4 minutes. Add the wine. Heat to boiling, and add the shrimp, squid, sea bass and scallops. Lower the heat and simmer, stirring, for a few minutes until the shrimp turn pink. Add the cooked mussels. Add the tomato sauce to this mixture and keep warm. Put on a large pot of water to boil. When boiling, add 1 tablespoon salt. Add spaghetti and stir. Cook the spaghetti for 5 minutes until al dente. Drain. Put the drained spaghetti into a large serving dish. Pour the seafood sauce over the spaghetti and toss. Season with more salt and pepper if necessary.

PENNE PASTA WITH MARINARA SAUCE

1 lb. penne pasta
1 T. salt
1 recipe Marinara Sauce in this
  book

1 c. freshly grated Parmesan
  cheese

Prepare the marinara sauce. Bring a large pan of water to a boil. Add 1 tablespoon of salt to the boiling water. Add the pasta. Cook until al dente. Drain. Put into a warm serving dish. Pour the sauce over. Serve with the Parmesan cheese.

PENNE PASTA WITH MEAT SAUCE

1 Recipe Tomato Sauce or 1
Recipe Tomato Sauce With Meat
in this book

1 lb. penne pasta
1 c. freshly grated Parmesan cheese

    Prepare the Tomato Sauce With Meat and serve with the cooked penne pasta. Or prepare the Tomato Sauce without meat and prepare the meatballs and braciola and add to the sauce, and simmer over a low heat, covered, for 1 hour. If you use the sausage, fry the sausage until browned on all sides, add to the Tomato Sauce and simmer over a low heat for 30 minutes. Bring a large pot of water to a boil. Add 1 tablespoon of salt and add the pasta. Cook for 8 minutes, until al dente. Drain. Put some sauce over and serve the rest of the sauce with the meat in a bowl on the table. Put the grated Parmesan cheese in a bowl and put on the table.

POLENTA BROILED

For the polenta:

2 qt. boiling water, plus an extra qt. of boiling water in another pan

1 lb. cornmeal
2 tsp. salt
olive oil for broiling

    Bring the water to a boil. Add the salt. Stir and slowly add the cornmeal. Also bring another pan of water to a boil with the one quart of water to use in case the polenta gets dry and you have to add more water to it. (Keep it over a low heat.) When all the cornmeal is blended with the water, lower the heat and simmer for approximately 45 minutes, stirring occasionally with a whisk. As the polenta begins to thicken, stir with a wooden spoon. If the polenta gets too dry before it is done, add some boiling water from the other pan of boiling water, only as much as necessary. When the polenta is done, it will come away from the sides of the pan. Take as much polenta as you will need. Refrigerate the rest for another dish. Shape it into a loaf. Cut it into slices and brush lightly with olive oil. Place on foil-lined broiler pan under broiler until crisp and brown on each side. Serve with meat, poultry, or as an appetizer.

POLENTA WITH BUTTER AND CHEESE

Prepare polenta as for Polenta Broiled
softened butter
freshly grated Parmesan cheese or cheese slices

Take as much of the hot polenta as you will need. Refrigerate the rest. Shape it into an oval. Cut it into slices while still steaming hot. Spread with softened butter and sprinkle with grated cheese or top with cheese slices and heat.

POLENTA FRIED

Prepare Polenta as for Polenta Broiled
bread crumbs
extra virgin olive oil for frying

Make the polenta according to the recipe for polenta in Polenta Broiled. Shape it into a loaf. Cut it into ½" slices. Heat a medium size frying pan or an electric frying pan. Heat ¼ cup olive oil. Spread ½ cup of bread crumbs on a piece of wax paper. Dip the slices of polenta into the bread crumbs and fry until golden on each side. Repeat until you have as many fried slices as you need, adding oil to the pan and heating it and using more bread crumbs as necessary. Any leftover polenta may be covered and refrigerated.

POLENTA MARINARA

Use recipe for Polenta as in Polenta Broiled
Make 1 recipe Marinara Sauce in this book
1 6-oz. can tomato paste
1 c. freshly grated Parmesan cheese
1 lb. shredded mozzarella cheese

Make the polenta. Make the Marinara Sauce. Add the tomato paste to the Marinara Sauce and cook for 15 minutes. Set aside. Heat the oven to 350°. Oil a 13" x 9" x 2" glass baking dish. Turn the polenta onto a cutting board and shape it into a loaf. Slice it into ½" slices. Spread a layer of the slices in the bottom of the baking dish and cover with ⅓ of the sauce. Sprinkle ⅓ the Parmesan cheese on top, and then ⅓ of the shredded mozzarella cheese. Add another layer of the polenta slices, ⅓ of the sauce, ⅓ of the Parmesan cheese and ⅓ of the mozzarella cheese. Add another layer of the polenta slices, ⅓ of the sauce, ⅓ of the Parmesan cheese and ⅓ of the mozzarella cheese.

(continued)

Bake for 20 minutes. Let set for 10 minutes before serving. Cut into wedges or squares.

POLENTA WITH VEGETABLES

1 recipe for Polenta as in Polenta Broiled
2 cloves garlic, pressed
3 c. broccoli, cut up into small pieces
1 16-oz. can red kidney beans, rinsed and drained
¼ c. olive oil
1 tsp. salt
1 tsp. black pepper
½ c. freshly grated Parmesan cheese

Make the polenta as the recipe for Polenta broiled. While the polenta is cooking, heat a large skillet. Add the oil and heat. Sauté the broccoli in the hot oil until crisp-cooked. Add the garlic and cook 2 minutes longer. Add the beans, salt and pepper. Stir and set aside until polenta is cooked. Be sure polenta is not too dry. When polenta is cooked, add the vegetables to the polenta and serve warm with grated Parmesan cheese.

RAVIOLI WITH MEAT

Recipe for Tomato Sauce in this book

Recipe for Pasta Dough in this book

For the filling:

1 10-oz. pkg. frozen, chopped spinach, thawed
2 T. olive oil
2 more T. olive oil
1 lb. lean ground beef
1 clove garlic, pressed
1 tsp. salt
1 tsp. black pepper
½ tsp. oregano
½ c. freshly grated Parmesan cheese
2 eggs, lightly beaten
⅛ tsp. nutmeg
1 c. Parmesan cheese for sprinkling

Make the sauce. Make the pasta dough. While the dough is resting and the sauce is simmering, make the ravioli filling. Squeeze water out of the spinach. Heat 2 tablespoons oil in a skillet. sauté the spinach for 5 minutes and set aside. Reheat the same pan and add 2 more tablespoons olive oil. Heat and add ground beef. Cook, breaking up into

(continued)

small pieces. Add the garlic, salt, pepper and oregano. When the meat is cooked, put into a large mixing bowl. Add the cooked spinach and mix. Add the beaten eggs and mix. Add the ½ cup of grated Parmesan cheese and nutmeg. Mix well. Set aside. Roll out the pasta into 3"-wide sheets. Place 1 rounded tablespoon of mixture on the pasta sheets at intervals so that you will be able to cut in between the mounds with your pastry wheel, leaving 1" of dough on each side of the mound. (Each ravioli should be 3" x 3.") Cover the mounds with another sheet of dough. Cut in between the mounds with a pastry wheel. If you don't have a pastry wheel, use a sharp knife and press the edges of each ravioli with a fork to seal the edges. Put a large pot of water on to boil. When the water is boiling add the ravioli in batches so that they are not crowded. Cook for 5-7 minutes. Remove with a slotted spoon and keep warm until all the ravioli are cooked. Put the ravioli onto a shallow serving dish. Pour some sauce over. Put the remaining sauce in a bowl and put on the table. Put the Parmesan cheese in a serving bowl and put on the table.

RAVIOLI WITH SALMON

1 recipe Marinara Sauce in this book
1 recipe Pasta Dough in this book or 60 wonton skins
½ c. heavy cream
1 lb. salmon fillet, baked, skin removed
4 T. finely minced scallions
1 tsp. dill weed
2 T. lemon juice
2 T. extra virgin olive oil
1 tsp. salt
1 tsp. black pepper

Heat oven to 375°. Make Marinara Sauce. Make pasta dough. While sauce is cooking, bake salmon for 15 minutes. Remove from oven. Remove skin and discard. Put salmon in a large mixing bowl and mince. Add scallions, dill weed, lemon juice, olive oil, salt and pepper. Roll out pasta dough into 3"-wide strips or spread out wonton skins. Put 1 rounded tablespoonful of salmon mixture on the pasta dough at intervals so that you will be able to cut in between the mounds with your pastry wheel, leaving 1" of dough on each side of the mound. (Each ravioli should be 3" x 3.") Cover the mounds with another sheet of dough. Cut in between the mounds with a pastry wheel. If you don't have a pastry wheel, use a sharp knife and press the edges of each ravioli with a fork to seal the edges. Put a large pot of water on to boil. When the water is boiling, add the ravioli in batches so that they are not crowded. Cook for 5-7 minutes. Remove with a slotted spoon and keep warm until all the ravioli are cooked. Put the ravioli into a shallow serving dish. Pour

(continued)

the heavy cream into the marinara sauce. Stir. Pour some sauce over the ravioli. Pour the remaining sauce in a bowl and put on the table.

RIGATONI WITH SAUSAGE AND PEPPERS

1 lb. rigatoni
1 T. salt
¼ c. extra virgin olive oil
2 red peppers, sliced
2 green peppers, sliced
1 medium onion, sliced, then slice the slices in half
1 lb. Italian sausage
2 cloves garlic, pressed
¼ c. minced fresh Italian parsley

1 28-oz. can San Marzano tomatoes, mashed
½ tsp. oregano
1 bay leaf
2 tsp. salt
1 tsp. black pepper
¾ c. mozzarella cheese
½ c. freshly grated Parmesan cheese

Put the sausage in a skillet with ¼ cup water over medium heat. Cover and cook until the water evaporates. Lower the heat and cook for 15-20 minutes, turning the sausage until browned on all sides. Heat a large skillet. Put in ¼ c. extra virgin olive oil. Sauté the pepper strips and onions for 5 minutes. Add the garlic and parsley and sauté 1 minute longer. Add the tomatoes, oregano, bay leaf, salt and pepper and simmer, covered, for 20 minutes. When the sausage is cooked, slice it at a diagonal and add to the sauce. Bring a pot of water to boiling. Add 1 tablespoon salt and add the rigatoni and stir. Cook for 5-10 minutes until al dente. Drain and put into a shallow serving dish. Sprinkle the mozzarella cheese over. Pour the sauce over. Put the Parmesan cheese in a bowl and pass.

RISI E BISI (RICE AND PEAS)

1 c. rice (Basmati rice is a good choice)
2 c. chicken broth
2 T. butter
2 T. minced onion

1 T. minced fresh Italian parsley
1 c. frozen peas, cooked
¼ c. freshly grated Parmesan cheese

Heat a medium-sized saucepan. Put the butter in. Add the onion and parsley and sauté for 1 minute. Add the rice and sauté for 1 minute longer. Heat the chicken broth to boiling in another pan and add to rice. Cook, covered, until rice is cooked and broth is gone (about 15-20 minutes). Meanwhile, in another pan, cook the peas for five minutes in

(continued)

boiling water. Drain off the water and add the peas to the rice. Stir in the Parmesan cheese.

RISOTTO ALLA MILANESE

1 c. chopped onion
2 c. Arborio rice
½ c. butter
½ c. Marsala wine
3 c. chicken broth
½ tsp. saffron
½ c. freshly grated Parmesan cheese
1 tsp. salt
½ tsp. pepper

Melt the butter in a medium-sized saucepan over medium heat. Add the onions and sauté for 1 minute. Add the rice and stir for 2 minutes. Add the wine, chicken broth, saffron, salt and pepper. Simmer, covered, for 20 minutes, stirring occasionally. When cooked, add the Parmesan cheese and serve immediately. Risotto should be a little sticky.

SICHUAN NOODLE TOSS

½ lb. capellini
4 T. sesame oil
2 red peppers, sliced thinly
4 green onions, cut into ½" pieces
1 clove garlic, pressed
1 10-oz. pkg. fresh spinach, washed, dried and torn into bite-size pieces
2 c. cubed cooked chicken
1 8-oz. can sliced water chestnuts, drained
4 T. soy sauce
2 T. rice vinegar
1 tsp. minced fresh gingerroot
½ tsp. crushed red pepper (if desired)

Bring a pot of water to boiling. Cook capellini for 4-5 minutes until al dente. Drain. Place in a large salad bowl. Set aside. Heat 2 tablespoons sesame oil in a large skillet. Add red peppers, green onions and garlic. Sauté 2 minutes. Stir in spinach. Cover and cook over medium heat for 3 minutes. Remove from heat. Cool. With a rubber spatula, scrape into bowl with pasta. Mix. Add chicken and water chestnuts. Combine remaining 2 tablespoons sesame oil, soy sauce, vinegar and gingerroot. (Add crushed red pepper if desired.) Pour over salad and toss.

SPAGHETTI CARBONARA

¼ lb. bacon, diced
3 T. olive oil
1½ c. chopped onions
¼ c. minced fresh Italian parsley
1 c. diced fontina cheese
⅔ c. diced prosciutto or ham

hot red pepper flakes to taste (if desired)
1 lb. spaghetti
freshly ground pepper
1 c. freshly grated Parmesan cheese

Heat a pot of water to boiling. Meanwhile, heat the bacon in a skillet, stirring, until crisp. Transfer with a slotted spoon to a paper towel to drain. Add the olive oil to the skillet. Heat. Add onions. Cook onions until tender. Cook spaghetti in boiling water until al dente. Drain. Put into a large, warm bowl. Add the onions, bacon bits, parsley, fontina cheese, prosciutto, red pepper flakes (if desired) and toss. Add the Parmesan cheese and freshly ground pepper and toss again. Serve in hot pasta dishes.

SPAGHETTINI WITH SMOKED SALMON

1 lb. spaghettini
2 c. heavy cream
¼ c. butter
1 tsp. salt
1 tsp. freshly ground black pepper

8 oz. smoked salmon, diced
¼ oz. freshly grated Parmesan cheese
2 T. minced fresh Italian parsley

Bring water to a boil in a large pot. Melt butter in a large skillet. Add parsley and cook 3 minutes. Add cream and cook on medium heat until it begins to bubble. Add salt and pepper. Add smoked salmon and stir. Remove from heat and keep warm. Add 1 tablespoon salt to boiling water and cook spaghettini until al dente. Put spaghettini into a warm serving bowl. Pour sauce over and mix. Add Parmesan cheese and mix again.

SPANISH RICE

2 slices bacon, diced
3 T. olive oil
½ c. chopped onions
½ c. chopped green peppers
1 c. finely chopped celery
1 clove garlic, pressed
1 c. rice

1 c. chopped, drained, peeled, canned tomatoes
2 T. tomato paste
1¾ c. chicken stock
1 tsp. chili powder
⅛ tsp. red pepper
1 tsp. salt

(continued)

Heat oven to 350°. In heavy skillet, sauté bacon, onions, garlic, celery and peppers in olive oil. Cook until onions are golden, about 5 minutes. Add rice. Stir and heat well. Add tomatoes, tomato paste, chicken stock, chili powder, red pepper and salt. Mix well. Heat. Transfer to greased baking dish and cover. Cook for 30 minutes or until stock is absorbed and the rice is tender. Uncover and let stand for 5 minutes before serving.

TORTELLINI ALLA BOLOGNESE

Make Pasta Dough recipe in this book
Make Tomato Sauce recipe without meat in this book

½ c. heavy cream

Filling:

½ lb. cooked chicken
½ lb. cooked ham
½ c. minced mushrooms
2 T. butter
2 T. freshly grated Parmesan cheese

1 tsp. salt
½ tsp. pepper
1 egg, beaten
1 c. freshly grated Parmesan cheese for serving

Prepare the dough. Prepare sauce. While dough is resting and sauce is cooking, prepare filling. Put the chicken in a blender or food processor and mince. Put the chicken into a large mixing bowl. Put the ham into a blender or food processor and mince. Add the ham to the chicken. Heat a small skillet and sauté the mushrooms in the butter for 2 minutes. Add to the chicken and ham. Add the 2 tablespoons cheese, salt and pepper. Mix together. Add the beaten egg and mix again. Roll out the dough. Cut out the dough into 3" in diameter rounds. Put a small ball of filling in the center of each round. Dampen the edges of the rounds with water and fold the round in half to form a half moon, pressing them down well to seal the filling in firmly. As the tortellini are filled, set them out on a lightly floured cloth. Do not let them touch each other. Put on a large pot of water to boil. Cook them, a batch at a time, for about 5-7 minutes. Drain. Mix the heavy cream with the tomato sauce. Place the tortellini on a hot, lightly oiled serving platter, in layers, spreading each layer with the sauce. Serve with grated Parmesan cheese on the side.

VEGETARIAN LASAGNA

2 c. sliced zucchini
2 c. diced broccoli
1 red pepper, sliced
2 large tomatoes, sliced ¼" thick
1 egg, beaten
2 c. creamed cottage cheese
2 c. shredded mozzarella cheese
½ c. freshly grated Parmesan cheese
2 T. minced fresh Italian parsley
½ tsp. salt
10 lasagna noodles, cooked al dente
½ c. seasoned bread crumbs
1 recipe béchamel sauce

Heat oven to 350°. Bring two large pots of water to boiling. Add 1 tablespoon salt to one pot. Cook the lasagna and set aside. Put the zucchini, broccoli and red peppers in the boiling water in the other pot and cook to crisp tender. Remove from the water and drain. Set aside. In a bowl, mix egg with cottage cheese, the mozzarella, the Parmesan cheese, salt and parsley and set aside. Oil a 13" x 9" x 2" glass baking dish. Spread a layer of lasagna noodles over the bottom of the dish. Sprinkle with ¼ cup of the bread crumbs. Layer with half of the vegetable mixture. Spread with half the cheese mixture. Spread lasagna noodles over the cheese mixture. Sprinkle with the remaining bread crumbs. Then layer the rest of the vegetables over the noodles. Spread the tomatoes over the vegetables. Then layer the rest of the cheese mixture over the tomatoes. Pour the béchamel sauce over all. Cover with foil and bake for 20 minutes. Remove foil and bake for 10 minutes more. Let stand for 10 minutes before serving.

Béchamel Sauce:

4 T. butter
4 T. flour
1 c. milk
1 c. heavy cream
½ tsp. salt
½ tsp. white pepper
⅛ tsp. nutmeg

Melt the butter in a saucepan over medium heat. Add the flour and cook for one minute, making a paste. Slowly add the milk, stirring. The sauce will thicken. Add the cream, stirring. Add the salt, pepper and nutmeg. Cook just until it bubbles. Do not boil. Remove from heat.

BAKED CHICKEN AND RICE

1 c. rice, uncooked
1 can cream of mushroom soup
1 can cream of celery soup
1 can water
1 pkg. onion soup mix
1 3-4 lb. chicken, cut up

(continued)

Heat oven to 350°. Mix soups, rice and water in a bowl. Turn into a 9" x 13" baking dish. Place chicken pieces on top. Sprinkle with onion soup mix. Cover with foil. Bake for 2 hours.

BAKED STUFFED AVOCADOS

⅓ c. finely diced celery
⅓ c. soft bread crumbs, firmly packed
½ tsp. grated lemon zest
½ tsp. salt
⅛ tsp. pepper

⅛ tsp. ginger
¼ c. milk
2 ripe avocados (not too soft)
2 hard-cooked eggs, chopped
¼ c. buttered bread crumbs
1 T. butter

To make the bread crumbs, break up 2 slices of bread and whirl in blender. Sauté ¼ cup bread crumbs in 1 tablespoon melted butter in skillet. Set aside. Heat oven to 400°. Combine the celery, ⅓ cup bread crumbs, lemon zest, salt, pepper, ginger and milk. Cut avocados in half lengthwise. Remove seed. Scoop out enough of center to make a nest for the filling. Reserve the scooped-out portion. Cut a thin slice from bottoms of avocado halves to keep them upright during baking. Dice reserved scooped-out portion of avocado. Combine with eggs and bread crumb mixture. Spoon into avocado halves. Top with buttered crumbs. Bake until top is slightly browned, about 20 minutes. Serves 4.

BARLEY CASSEROLE

3 T. butter
1 c. barley
1 small onion, chopped
¼ c. finely chopped green pepper

½ c. chopped cashews
3 c. chicken broth, boiling
1 tsp. salt
½ tsp, pepper

Heat oven to 350°. Melt the butter in a saucepan. Add the onions and sauté for 3 minutes. Add the barley and sauté 2 minutes longer, stirring. Add the green pepper and cook 2 minutes more, stirring. Add the cashews, boiling chicken broth and salt and pepper. Pour into a covered 2-quart casserole. Cover and bake for 1 hour.

BURRITOS CON QUESO

2 T. butter
½ c. chopped onion
1 4-oz. can chopped green chilies, undrained
1 16-oz. can refried beans

8 8" flour tortillas
16 oz. Monterey Jack cheese, shredded
Salsa (see recipe in this book)

Heat oven to 350°. Make salsa and set aside. In skillet, sauté onion in butter 5 minutes. Remove from heat. Add green chilies and beans, mixing well. Spread each tortilla with ¼ cup bean mixture. Top each with 2 tablespoons shredded cheese and 2 tablespoons salsa. Fold burritos, overlapping ends in center. Place, folded side down, in one layer in a baking dish. Sprinkle with remaining cheese. Bake 15 minutes.

CHICKEN CHIP BAKE

2 c. cooked, cubed chicken
2 c. sliced celery
¾ c. Hellmann's mayonnaise
½ c. toasted slivered almonds
2 T. lemon juice

1 T. finely minced onion
½ tsp. salt
½ c. shredded cheddar cheese
1½ c. crushed potato chips

Heat oven to 400°. Combine chicken, celery, mayonnaise, almonds, lemon juice, onion and salt together. Put into an 8¼" x 1¾" round ovenware dish. Sprinkle with the cheese and top with the potato chips. Bake for 20 minutes. Serves 4-6.

CHICKEN CURRY

2 tsp. curry powder
1 T. butter
⅓ c. minced onion
⅓ c. diced celery
¼ c. sliced mushrooms
1 tsp. minced gingerroot
½ tsp. ground turmeric
½ tsp. ground cardamom
½ c. coconut milk

¼ c. chicken broth
1 T. cornstarch
1 T. cold water
2 c. cubed, cooked chicken
¼ tsp. salt
¼ c. sliced almonds
1 c. canned pineapple chunks
¼ c. heavy cream

Brown curry powder lightly in butter. Add onion, celery, mushrooms, gingerroot and mix well. Add turmeric and cardamom. Stir in coconut

(continued)

milk and broth. Bring to a boil. Combine cornstarch and cold water. Stir into hot mixture and cook and stir until sauce thickens. Add chicken, pineapple, salt and almonds. Heat through. Stir in cream. Serve with Basmati rice on the side.

Basmati Rice

2 c. water
1 T. salt

1 T. butter
1 c. Basmati rice

Bring water to a boil. Add salt, butter and rice. Lower heat and simmer for 15-20 minutes, until water is absorbed. Let the cooked rice sit, covered, for 15 minutes.

CHICKEN POT PIE

To Cook the Chicken:

1 3-lb. chicken
3 stalks celery
3 carrots
1 medium onion, sliced

2 bay leaves
½ tsp. thyme
1 tsp. salt
½ tsp. white pepper

Filling:

4 ribs celery, diced
4 carrots, sliced
1¾ c. potatoes, peeled and diced
1 10-oz. pkg. frozen peas
the cooked, diced chicken
½ c. butter

½ c. all-purpose flour
½ c. heavy cream
1 tsp. salt
1 tsp. pepper
2 c. strained chicken stock

Pie Crust:

2 c. flour
1 tsp. salt
¾ c. shortening

⅓ c. ice water
1 egg yolk mixed with 2 tsp. water

To prepare the chicken, put the chicken in a large pan and put in enough water to cover. Add 3 stalks of celery cut in half, the carrots cut in half, the sliced onion, bay leaves, thyme, salt and pepper. Bring the water to a boil. Lower the heat to a simmer and cook the chicken until tender, skimming the foam which forms on the surface. The chicken should be cooked in 1½ hours. Remove the chicken from the pot and let it cool. Strain the stock. To prepare the filling, Cook the diced celery, sliced carrots and diced potatoes in the stock about 10 minutes. After

(continued)

10 minutes, add the peas and cook 10 minutes longer. Remove the vegetables from the stock with a slotted spoon and place in a large mixing bowl. Set aside. Skin and bone the chicken and discard skin and bones. Dice the meat into 1" pieces and mix with the vegetables. Heat the oven to 375°. In a saucepan, melt the butter and stir in the flour. Cook 5 minutes, stirring constantly. Add enough chicken stock, slowly, about 2 cups, stirring constantly, to achieve a light and creamy consistency. Stir in 1 teaspoon salt and 1 tsp. pepper. Stir in the cream. Remove from heat and mix together with the vegetables and chicken. Make crust: Mix together the flour and salt. Cut in the shortening with a fork and mix until the mixture is like coarse crumbs. Stir in the water, a tablespoon at a time, until the dough holds together. Break the dough into 2 pieces, one a bit bigger than the other. Flour a surface and roll out the larger piece to fit the casserole dish. Pour in the mixture. Roll out the other piece of dough. Gently cover the casserole and seal edges and flute. Mix together the egg yolk and water. Brush the pastry with the egg mixture and puncture the crust with a fork in a few different places to allow steam to escape. Bake until crust is golden brown, about 35-40 minutes.

CHILI CON CARNE

3 T. olive oil
1 medium onion, chopped
2 cloves garlic, pressed
1 lb. lean ground beef
2 c. water
4 T. tomato paste
1 tsp. cumin powder
3 T. chili powder
1 15-oz. can tomatoes

2 tsp. paprika
1 tsp. salt
½ tsp. pepper
¼ tsp. crushed red pepper flakes (optional)
1 can red kidney beans, rinsed and drained
½ c. chopped onions
1 c. shredded cheddar cheese

Heat a large saucepan. Heat the oil and add the chopped onions. Sauté for 3 minutes. Add the garlic. Sauté 1 more minute. Add the beef. Brown for 5 minutes, breaking it up into large chunks. Add the water, tomato paste and cumin and simmer over a low heat for 45 minutes. Add chili powder, tomatoes, paprika, salt, pepper and beans, and optional crushed red pepper and simmer for one hour longer. Serve the ½ cup chopped onions and shredded cheddar cheese on the side.

CHOUCROUTE GARNIE

6 slices thick bacon
2 lb. sauerkraut, rinsed and drained
6 smoked pork chops
2 medium onions, sliced ½" thick
8-10 smoked, fresh or spiced sausages
½ tsp. ground cloves, mixed with ¼ c. water
2 c. dry, white wine
water
8 frankfurters

Heat oven to 325°. Line a large casserole or small covered roasting pan with the bacon. Spread the sauerkraut over the bacon. Place the smoked pork chops over the sauerkraut. Then layer the onion on top of the pork chops. Sprinkle cloves mixed with water over the onions. Lay the sausages over the onions. Pour the wine over the top and enough water to cover. Cover and put casserole in oven and bake for 2 hours. Put 8 frankfurters on top and bake, uncovered, for ½ hour longer. Serve with boiled potatoes.

Boiled Potatoes:

5 boiling potatoes
large pot with enough water to cover potatoes
1 tsp. salt
5 T. butter, melted
3 T. minced fresh Italian parsley

Boil the potatoes until cooked, about 20-30 minutes. (Test with a round toothpick to see if they are soft, but not mushy.) Remove from heat and drain. Peel potatoes. Cut into quarters. Put into a serving bowl. Sprinkle with salt. Drizzle with melted butter and sprinkle with parsley.

ENCHILADA CASSEROLE

2 T. olive oil
1 c. chopped onions
1 garlic clove, pressed
1 28-oz. can peeled tomatoes
½ tsp. cumin
1 tsp. salt
1 tsp. oregano
½ tsp. basil
12 canned whole green chiles
12 corn tortillas
3 c. grated cheddar cheese
1 8-oz. container sour cream

Make sauce: Heat oil in a large skillet. Add onions and garlic and sauté for 2 minutes. Add tomatoes and cumin, salt, oregano and basil. Mash tomatoes with a fork or a potato masher. Cook 20 minutes. Remove from heat. Keep hot. Heat oven to 325°. Dip tortillas in sauce. Place 1 chile on each tortilla. Place ¼ c. cheese on each tortilla. Roll up tortillas. Place tortillas as they are rolled, seam side down, in 13½"

(continued)

x 8¾" x 1¾" glass baking dish, making only one layer. Pour sour cream in remaining sauce. Mix together. Pour sauce over tortillas. Bake 20 minutes. Serve hot.

GREENS, BEANS AND SAUSAGE

½ c. water
1 lb. Italian sausage
2 T. extra virgin olive oil
1 can cannellini beans, rinsed and drained
1 clove garlic, pressed
½ c. chicken broth
1 head escarole, washed and broken into pieces
1 tsp. salt
1 tsp. black pepper

Heat a skillet. Put in the water and the sausage links. Cook the sausage, covered, first on medium heat until the water evaporates, then on low heat, for 30 minutes. As the sausage cooks, the water will evaporate and the sausage will begin to brown. Turn sausage so it browns on all sides. Remove from heat and slice ½" thick at a diagonal. Heat another skillet and put in the oil. Heat the oil a bit and cook the garlic over low heat for one minute. Add ½ cup chicken broth and heat. Add the escarole, salt and pepper. Cook for 5-7 minutes. Add the beans and sausage. Mix together and heat.

HUNGARIAN GOULASH WITH SPÄTZLE

¼ c. oil
2 medium onions, finely chopped
1 clove garlic, pressed
1 tsp. salt
½ tsp. caraway seeds
½ tsp. marjoram
½ tsp. cardamom
2 lb. lean beef, cut into ½" cubes
¼ c. flour
2 tsp. paprika
1 14½-oz. can diced tomatoes
1 c. water
1 c. sour cream

Put ¼ cup flour on waxed paper. Dredge the beef in it. Set aside. Heat the oil in a large saucepan. Sauté the onions for 5 minutes until they are soft. Add the garlic and sauté 1 minute longer. Add the beef and any remaining flour on the waxed paper. Mix and brown the beef. Add the salt, caraway seeds, marjoram, cardamom, paprika, tomatoes and 1 cup water. Simmer, covered, stirring occasionally, for 1½ hours or a little longer until the meat is tender. While the goulash is cooking, make the spätzle. Stir 1 cup sour cream into the goulash when it is done. Serve in a separate bowl from the spätzle. Put some spätzle on

(continued)

your plate and top with the goulash. (Put in a 200° oven to keep warm while you make the spätzle.)

Spätzle:

½ c. milk
½ c. water
2 c. flour
2 eggs, beaten lightly

¼ tsp. white pepper
2 tsp. salt
½ tsp. baking powder
¼ c. butter, melted

Bring a large pot of water to a boil. Mix water and milk together. Add eggs and mix. Add pepper, salt and baking powder. Gradually add flour, while mixing. Mix well. When water is boiling, drop batter by half teaspoonfuls into water. Push the batter off the spoon with your finger. Cook 5 minutes. You may have to cook them in two batches. Remove from water with a slotted spoon. Put in a bowl with a damp kitchen towel in it. When all the spätzle are cooked, transfer to a serving bowl. Be sure they are well drained. Add the melted butter. They will be light, but slightly chewy.

MACARONI WITH ARTICHOKES AND MOZZARELLA CHEESE

1 8-oz. pkg. frozen artichokes
1 small onion, finely chopped
3 oz. prosciutto, chopped
¼ c. butter
1 tsp. salt
½ tsp. pepper
½ c. chicken broth
1 T. minced fresh Italian parsley

1 lb. ditalini
¾ lb. shredded mozzarella cheese
1 tsp. oil
¼ c. breadcrumbs
½ c. freshly grated Parmesan cheese
½ c. half and half
½ c. minced sun dried tomatoes

Heat the oven to 375°. Cook the artichokes in salted water until tender. Drain. Slice in half. Heat the butter in a large pan, add the onion and prosciutto and cook over a medium heat until the onion is golden. Add the broth, artichokes, parsley, salt and pepper. Cook until bubbles appear. Set aside. Meanwhile, bring a large pot of water to a boil. Add 1 tablespoon salt and the ditalini. Cook until al dente. Drain the pasta, mix with the sauce, sun dried tomatoes, mozzarella cheese and the half and half. Oil a 13" x 9" x 2" baking dish with the 1 teaspoon oil. Pour the mixture into the baking dish. Sprinkle with the breadcrumbs and Parmesan cheese. Bake for about 15 minutes until the top has browned. Serve hot.

MACARONI AND CHEESE LAURINA

½ lb. small shell macaroni
2 c. New York State extra sharp cheddar cheese, grated
¼ c. freshly grated Parmesan cheese
1 tsp. salt
½ tsp. white pepper
½ tsp. paprika
1½ c. milk
3 T. flour
3 T. butter
1 fresh medium tomato, chopped, seeds removed
¼ c. fresh breadcrumbs
2 T. butter

Heat oven to 350°. Whirl a slice of bread in the blender to make the breadcrumbs. Bring a pot of water to a boil. Add 1 teaspoon salt. Add macaroni. Cook for 5-7 minutes until al dente. Drain. Put macaroni into a large bowl. Set aside. Melt 3 tablespoons butter in a saucepan. Add flour, stirring, until butter is golden. Add milk and stir until thickened. Add cheddar cheese. Add salt, pepper and paprika. Cook, stirring, until cheese melts. Add Parmesan cheese, stirring. Add chopped tomato to cooked macaroni. Pour sauce over macaroni and mix. Pour mixture into a 1½-quart buttered casserole. Sauté the breadcrumbs in a small pan with 2 tablespoons butter for two minutes. Sprinkle on top of casserole and bake for 20-25 minutes.

MACARONI AND CHEESE WITH ZUCCHINI

¼ c. butter
¼ c. flour
1 tsp. salt
½ tsp. pepper
1½ c. milk
2 T. olive oil
½ onion, minced
1 small carrot, minced
1 stalk celery, minced
1 lb. zucchini, thinly sliced
1 c. chicken broth
1 lb. penne pasta
2 tsp. chopped fresh basil
½ lb. mozzarella cheese, shredded
½ tsp. salt
½ tsp. white pepper
1 tsp. oil
3 T. dried breadcrumbs

Heat oven to 400°. Melt the butter in a small pan, stir in the flour and season with salt and pepper. Gradually add the milk and bring to a boil, stirring constantly, until thickened. Set aside. Heat a large pan. Add 2 tablespoons oil and heat. Add the onion, carrot and celery and cook and stir until the onion is golden. Add the zucchini to the pan, along with the broth. Cook for 15 minutes. Bring a large pot of water to a boil. Add 1 tablespoon salt. Put in the pasta. Cook until al dente. Drain. Mix with the vegetables and sprinkle with the basil, ½ teaspoon salt and ½ teaspoon pepper. Stir the mozzarella into the mixture. Brush

(continued)

a large ovenproof casserole with the teaspoon oil and sprinkle with the breadcrumbs. Pour in the pasta mixture, cover with the white sauce and put in the oven, uncovered, for 15 minutes or until bubbly. Serve hot.

MEXICAN CHEESE PUFF

3½ c. shredded Monterey Jack cheese
3½ c. shredded sharp cheddar cheese
2 7-oz. cans green chilies, drained, chopped
2 medium tomatoes, seeded and chopped
¼ c. black olives, sliced

½ c. flour
5 eggs, separated
1 5¼-oz. can evaporated milk
½ tsp. salt
½ tsp. oregano
½ tsp. cumin
½ tsp. white pepper
¼ tsp. cream of tartar

Heat oven to 300°. Stir together the jack and cheddar cheeses, the chilies, tomatoes, olives and 2 T. flour. Transfer to a greased, shallow 3-quart casserole. Beat egg yolks, adding remaining flour and milk. Stir in salt, oregano, cumin and pepper. In large bowl, beat egg whites with cream of tartar until stiff. Fold into the egg yolk mixture with a spatula. Spoon over the cheese mixture in the casserole. Bake for 60 minutes until firm. Let it stand 15 minutes before serving. Serves 10-12.

PAELLA

¼ c. olive oil
2½-lb. fryer chicken pieces
1 lb. chorizo sausage, cut into 1" slices
¾ c. chopped onion
2 cloves garlic, pressed
1½ c. uncooked rice
2 c. chicken broth
2 five-oz. cans whole baby clams, drained and juice reserved

¼ tsp. saffron
½ tsp. white pepper
2 tsp. salt
8-oz. pkg. frozen artichoke hearts, thawed
1 c. pimento-stuffed olives
1 lb. peeled, deveined shrimp, uncooked
1 14½-oz. can diced tomatoes

Heat oil in 18" in diameter skillet. Add chicken and chorizo and fry until brown on all sides. Pour off all but 2 tablespoons drippings. Push chicken and sausage to the side of pan. Stir in onion and garlic. Fry just until tender. Stir in chicken broth, clam juice, saffron and pepper and salt. Simmer, covered, for 45 minutes, stirring occasionally. If neces-

(continued)

sary add water. Stir in rice and cook, covered, 15 minutes longer. Add artichoke hearts, tomatoes and olives and cook, covered, for 10 minutes. Add shrimp and clams. Cover. Cook until shrimp turns pink and mixture is hot.

PIEROGI

1 recipe Pasta Dough in this book
2½ lb. potatoes
¾ lb. shredded cheddar cheese
3 T. butter
1 onion, minced
1 tsp. salt
1 tsp. pepper
1 tsp. savory
2 T. minced fresh Italian parsley
3 T. heavy cream
water for sealing Pierogi
Butter for frying

Make the Pasta Dough in this book. After the dough has rested for 30 minutes, divide it into 3 balls. Roll a ball out and cut out 3" circles. Keep circles covered with a damp towel so they won't dry out. Repeat with remaining balls of dough. Put on a pot of water to boil, enough to cover the potatoes. Cook the potatoes until done, about 20-30 minutes. While the potatoes are cooking, heat a small skillet and melt the 3 tablespoons butter. Put the chopped onions in and sauté until they are transparent. Add the parsley and cook for two minutes more. Set aside. Put another large pot of water on to boil. When the water boils, add 1 tablespoon salt. Peel the potatoes and put them through a ricer into a bowl. Add the onions and parsley mixture, salt, pepper, savory, and cream to the potatoes. Mix together. Add the cheddar cheese and mix. Put a rounded tablespoonful of filling on each 3" circle. Moisten the edges of the circles and fold one half over the other to form a half circle. Seal the edges. Line up the pierogi on a floured surface. Repeat until all are done. Drop several pierogi into the boiling water and cook until they rise to the top, at which time they are done. (About 5 minutes.) Remove the cooked pierogi with a slotted spoon and put in a colander to drain. To finish them, heat a skillet. Add ¼ cup of butter and fry them for 2-3 minutes on each side, until they are golden. Remove from the pan and add more to the pan until they are all cooked, adding more butter as needed. As they are cooked, place them on a warm platter and keep them warm.

RICE CASSEROLE

2 c. white rice
½ c. green onions chopped to ¼"
3 medium zucchini, chopped
¼ c. butter
¼ c. olive oil
7 eggs

2 c. freshly grated Parmesan cheese
1 tsp. salt
½ tsp. pepper
½ c. seasoned Italian bread crumbs

    Bring 4 cups of water to a boil in a large saucepan. Add the rice and stir. Cover and simmer at a medium-low heat for 20 minutes. Set aside to cool. (Cool it in the refrigerator.) Heat the oven to 350°. Heat a medium skillet. Add the oil and butter. Heat. Sauté the chopped onions and zucchini in the butter and olive oil until they are tender, about 10 minutes. Do not brown the onions. Put 6 eggs in a large mixing bowl. Whisk them until well beaten. Add the cooked rice and grated cheese. The rice must be cold. Mix. Stir in the sautéed vegetables, salt and pepper. Mix again. Lightly oil a large glass baking dish. Coat with the bread crumbs and spread the rice and vegetable mixture evenly in the dish. Whip an egg in a small mixing bowl and brush the rice evenly with the egg. Bake, uncovered, about 35-45 minutes, until golden brown. Cool for 30 minutes and serve.

SHEPHERD'S PIE

1½ lb. potatoes, peeled, quartered
2 T. butter
1 tsp. salt
2 T. olive oil
1 lb. lean ground beef
1 medium onion, chopped
1 stalk celery, thinly sliced
1 carrot, thinly sliced

1 T. flour
1 tsp. thyme
1 tsp. salt
½ tsp. black pepper
⅛ tsp. ground nutmeg
1 15-oz. can creamed corn
3 T. grated Parmesan cheese

    Heat oven to 350°. Boil the peeled and quartered potatoes for about 20 minutes. Mash and add the 2 tablespoons butter and 1 tsp. salt. Set aside. While the potatoes are cooking, heat 2 tablespoons olive oil in a skillet. Add the beef and cook for 15 minutes, breaking up and stirring. Push the meat aside and add the chopped onion, celery and carrot (add more oil if needed). Sauté for 10 minutes. Mix together with the meat. Add the flour and stir. Add the thyme, salt, pepper and nutmeg. Stir and remove from heat. Spread the mixture on the bottom of a 10" x 10" baking dish. Pour the creamed corn over. Spoon the mashed potatoes over the corn, making small peaks. Sprinkle with the Parmesan

(continued)

cheese. Bake until the potatoes are browned, about 25-30 minutes. Let set 10 minutes. Serve from baking dish.

SOUTHWESTERN CHILI CASSEROLE

¼ c. olive oil
3 lb. ground chuck
3 c. chopped onions
3 pkg. chili seasoning mix
3 cans (8-oz. size) tomato sauce
2 c. water
3 cans (1 lb. size) kidney beans, rinsed and drained

8 oz. corn chips
1 16-oz. can pitted black olives, drained and cut in half
1½ c. shredded sharp cheddar cheese

Heat oven to 325°. Cook meat in a large skillet in hot olive oil until it looses its color, breaking it up with a fork. Add the onions, chili seasoning mix, tomato sauce and water. Stir until it boils, lower the heat and simmer, covered, 15 minutes, stirring, now and then. In a large (4-quart) deep casserole, layer the meat mixture with the beans, corn chips, olives and cheese, ending with chips and cheese. Bake, covered, about 50 minutes. Uncover, bake 5 minutes longer. Serves 12.

STUFFED CABBAGE ROLLS

1 egg
2 tsp. salt
½ tsp. black pepper
1 tsp. Worcestershire sauce
½ c. chopped onion
½ c. milk
½ lb. ground beef

½ lb. ground pork
1½ c. cooked rice
1 head Savoy cabbage, or green cabbage
1 can condensed tomato soup
1 T. brown sugar

Heat oven to 350°. Cook rice and set aside. While rice is cooking, bring a pot of water to a boil. Break off the leaves from the head of cabbage and put them into the boiling water for 3-5 minutes, until they become limp. Drain the cabbage thoroughly in a colander. In a large mixing bowl, mix together the egg, salt, pepper, Worcestershire sauce, onion, milk, beef, pork and cooked rice. Lay out the cabbage leaves on a surface. Place ½ cup meat mixture on each leaf. Fold in sides and roll ends over meat. Place rolls in ungreased 11" x 7" x 2" baking dish,

(continued)

seam side down. Blend together soup, 1 soup can water and brown sugar. Pour over cabbage rolls. Bake, covered, for 1 hour until done.

STUFFED RED PEPPERS

3 c. Marinara Sauce recipe in this book
1 c. rice
6 large red bell peppers
1 c. chopped onion
1 clove garlic, pressed
1 lb. ground beef
¼ c. olive oil

1 14½-oz. can diced tomatoes
1 tsp. salt
½ tsp. pepper
1 c. freshly grated Parmesan cheese
½ c. black olives, drained and sliced
½ c. minced fresh Italian parsley

Make Marinara Sauce. Heat oven to 350°. Bring 2 cups of water to a boil in a medium saucepan. Add rice, turn down the heat and simmer, covered for 15-20 minutes. Set aside. While rice is simmering, cut off the tops of the peppers and remove seeds. Poke a few holes in the bottom of the peppers with a fork. Place the peppers upright in a baking dish, side by side. In a large skillet, sauté the onion, garlic and ground beef in the olive oil, breaking up the beef. When the beef begins to brown, add the can of tomatoes, salt and pepper and simmer, uncovered, for 10-15 minutes, stirring from time to time. Remove from heat and mix in the rice. Add the olives, parsley and cheese. Fill the peppers with the mixture. Pour the Marinara Sauce over the peppers, cover with foil and bake for 30 minutes. Uncover and cook for 15 minutes longer.

TUNA NOODLE CASSEROLE

8 oz. noodles
1 6½ or 7-oz. can white tuna packed in water, drained
½ c. Hellmann's mayonnaise
1 c. thinly sliced celery
⅓ c. chopped onion
¼ c. chopped green pepper
½ tsp. salt

1 10½-oz. can condensed cream of celery soup
½ c. milk
6 oz. shredded Monterey Jack cheese
¼ c. grated Parmesan cheese
½ c. sliced almonds
2 T. butter

Heat oven to 375°. Bring water to a boil in large saucepan. Add 1 tablespoon salt. Put in noodles and cook for 5 minutes. Drain. Flake tuna with a fork. Combine noodles with the tuna, mayonnaise, sliced celery, onion, chopped green pepper and salt in a large mixing bowl.

(continued)

In a smaller bowl, combine the cream of celery soup with the milk and mix. Pour over the tuna-noodle mixture and mix together. Add the Monterey Jack cheese and the Parmesan cheese and mix. Turn into a 2-quart buttered casserole dish. Bake, uncovered, for 25 minutes until bubbly. Sauté the almonds in the butter in a small skillet. Remove the casserole from oven and top with the almonds.

QUICHE LORRAINE

1 recipe for single Pie Crust in this book, unbaked
8 slices, bacon, diced
½ lb. shredded Swiss cheese
1 T. flour

½ tsp. salt
⅛ tsp. ground nutmeg
3 beaten eggs
1¾ c. milk
1 beaten egg white

Heat oven to 400°. Prepare Pie Crust. Put crust into a 10" pie pan. Pinch edges together to form an attractive edge. Brush a coating of the egg white on the bottom of the pie crust. Prick bottom and edges with a fork. Bake the crust for 6 minutes. Remove from oven. Reduce oven temperature to 325°. Fry bacon until crisp. Drain. Reserve 2 tablespoons of bacon for topping. Place remaining bacon in pie shell. Sprinkle cheese over. Combine flour, salt, nutmeg, eggs and milk. Whisk together. Pour over cheese. Sprinkle reserved bacon on top. Bake for 35 to 40 minutes or until set in the center. Let set 25 minutes before serving.

QUICHE WITH SPINACH AND MUSHROOMS

1 recipe for single Pie Crust in this book, unbaked
1 10-oz. pkg. frozen chopped spinach, thawed
¼ c. olive oil
¼ lb. fresh mushrooms, sliced
½ lb. shredded Swiss cheese

4 eggs
1½ c. half and half
1 tsp. salt
⅛ tsp. nutmeg
½ tsp. pepper
1 beaten egg white
½ tsp. paprika

Heat oven to 400°. Prepare pie crust. Put in pie pan and crimp edges so it looks attractive. Brush bottom of crust with egg white. Prick bottom and side of crust with a fork. Bake for 6 minutes. Remove from oven. Set aside. Lower temperature to 325°. Squeeze water out of spinach with your hands. Put oil in medium skillet on medium heat, add spinach and sauté for 7 minutes. Push spinach aside. Add mushrooms and sauté for 3 minutes. Mix together and set aside. Sprinkle bottom of

(continued)

pastry shell with half of the shredded cheese. Spread the spinach and mushrooms evenly over the cheese. Sprinkle with the rest of the cheese. In medium bowl, whisk the eggs together with the half and half, salt, nutmeg and pepper. Carefully pour mixture into the pie pan. Sprinkle paprika over top. Bake 50 minutes until golden. Let set for 25 minutes before serving.

BAKED CHILIES RELLENOS WITH CHEESE

3 7-oz. cans whole green chiles, drained
½ lb. shredded Monterey Jack
1 lb. shredded Colby cheese
5 eggs
½ c. milk
1 tsp. salt
1 tsp. white pepper
2 tsp. paprika

Heat oven to 350°. Butter deep casserole or soufflé dish. Mix shredded cheeses together. Place a layer of chilies on bottom of dish. Spread a layer of cheese. Repeat layers. Whisk together the milk, eggs, salt pepper and paprika. Pour over casserole. Bake for 50-60 minutes, until set. Test by piercing the middle with a round toothpick. If it comes out clean, the casserole is done.

BEEF AND EGGS

1 lb. lean ground beef
1 medium onion, chopped
3 T. olive oil
1 tsp. salt
1 tsp. black pepper
4 large eggs

Heat a large skillet. Add the olive oil and heat. Put in the beef and stir, breaking it up. Brown, push the beef aside and put in the onions, brown the onions. Mix together with the beef. Add the salt and pepper. Mix. In a bowl, whisk the eggs and pour over the meat. Mix together until the eggs are cooked.

CARIB BREAKFAST CASSEROLE

1 lb. breakfast sausage, cut into ½" pieces or 1 lb. bacon, diced into 1" pieces
6 eggs
2 c. milk
1 tsp. salt
1 tsp. French's creamy yellow mustard
4 slices bread, cubed
1 c. grated cheddar cheese

Brown sausage or bacon in a skillet. Remove from pan with a slotted spoon and set aside. Whisk eggs, milk, salt and mustard together. In bottom of greased 13" x 9" baking dish, arrange bread cubes. Top with sausage or bacon. Sprinkle cheese on top and pour egg mixture over all. Cover and refrigerate overnight. Heat oven to 350°. If using a glass baking dish, heat oven to 325°. Bake for 35-45 minutes.

CROQUE MONSIEUR

1 c. minced ham
2 T. finely minced onion
1 tsp. French's creamy yellow mustard
8 slices white bread
4 slices Swiss cheese
3 eggs
2 T. milk
3 T. butter

Combine ham, onion and mustard. Trim crusts from bread. Spread 4 slices of the bread with ham mixture. Arrange a slice of cheese on each. Top with 4 slices of bread. Whisk eggs and milk together in a shallow dish. Heat butter in a large skillet over medium heat or in an electric frying pan at 375°. Dip sandwiches in egg mixture and brown on both sides. Makes 4 sandwiches.

FRITTATA

¼ c. olive oil
1 medium onion, chopped
1 c. fresh mushrooms, sliced
2 medium zucchini, sliced
2 c. fresh spinach, washed, dried and chopped
2 T. minced fresh Italian parsley
½ c. grated Parmesan cheese
1 tsp. salt
½ tsp. pepper
6 eggs

Heat oil over medium heat in medium non-stick skillet. Add onions, mushrooms and zucchini and sauté, stirring, until limp. Add spinach and parsley. Stir for 3-4 minutes. In a bowl, whisk the eggs together

(continued)

with the Parmesan cheese, salt and pepper. Stir in vegetable mixture. Mix and return to the pan. Cook until eggs are set, about 7-10 minutes. Loosen edges with a spatula. Slide onto a plate. Place pan over plate. Flip plate over pan and cook other side for 2 minutes. Serve hot.

POTATOES AND EGGS

¼ c. olive oil
¼ c. butter
4 large potatoes, peeled and diced
1 medium onion, diced
1 tsp. salt
½ tsp. pepper
8 large eggs
½ c. freshly grated Parmesan cheese

In a large non-stick skillet, heat the olive oil and butter. Add the potatoes and cook over medium-low heat for 15 minutes, turning. Then add the onions and cook until the potatoes and the onions are golden brown, stirring now and then. Add the salt and pepper. Mix. In a bowl, whisk the eggs until the mixture is frothy. Add the cheese and stir. Add the eggs to the potatoes and onions. Cook over low heat on one side. You may either scramble it together with a spatula, or loosen the edges of the omelet, turn it over and brown the other side by sliding it onto a plate. Place pan over plate. Flip plate over pan and cook other side for 2 minutes. Serve immediately.

POTATOES AND EGGS WITH PEPPERS

½ c. olive oil
4 large potatoes, diced
1 large green pepper, diced
1 large red pepper, diced
¼ c. minced fresh Italian parsley
1 tsp. salt
½ tsp. pepper
8 large eggs
½ c. grated Parmesan cheese

In a large, non-stick skillet, heat the olive oil and brown the potatoes and peppers over medium low heat. Add the salt, pepper and parsley. Cook until the potatoes and peppers are tender and the potatoes are golden brown. In a mixing bowl, whisk the eggs with the Parmesan until frothy. Pour over the vegetables. Cook over low heat, covered until eggs are done. Loosen the edges. When the egg is cooked, slide the mixture onto a large plate and cover the plate with the pan. Flip the plate over, turning the mixture into the pan and cook for 2 minutes longer. Serve immediately.

SCALLOPED HAM AND EGGS

6 hard-boiled eggs, sliced lengthwise
2 c. finely diced ham
½ lb. bacon, diced
1 can cream of celery soup
2 T. butter
⅔ c. milk
8 oz. cream cheese, cubed
1 c. buttered bread crumbs
1 tsp. paprika
Wheat Chex

Heat oven to 375°. Lay out the egg halves in a buttered 11½" x 7½" x 2" baking dish. Fry the bacon until crisp. Drain on paper towels. Mix the soup with the milk and add the ham to the mixture. Sprinkle the bacon on the eggs. Pour the ham and soup mixture over the bacon. Spread the cubed cream cheese over. In a skillet, melt the butter and put in the bread crumbs. Stir in the paprika and mix. Sprinkle over the cream cheese. Bake 25 minutes. Bring to the table in the baking dish. Put a bowl of Wheat Chex alongside the baking dish. Put some Wheat Chex on your plate and top with a helping of the casserole.

BÉCHAMEL SAUCE

4 T. butter
4 T. flour
1 c. milk
1 c. heavy cream
½ tsp. salt
½ tsp. white pepper
⅛ tsp. nutmeg

Melt the butter in a saucepan and stir in the flour. Cook, stirring, to blend. Slowly add the milk, stirring. The sauce will thicken. Add the cream, salt, pepper and nutmeg, stirring. Cook just until it bubbles. do not boil. Remove from heat.

CHIMICHURRI SAUCE

½ c. minced fresh Italian parsley
¾ c. olive oil
3 T. red wine vinegar
2 T. dried oregano
½ tsp. ground cumin
1 tsp. salt
2 cloves garlic, pressed
¼ tsp. dried crushed red pepper

Mix together the parsley, olive oil, wine vinegar, oregano, cumin, salt, garlic and red pepper. Let stand 2-3 hours before using to let flavors blend. Good to marinate beef in.

CHINESE SAUCE

2 T. olive oil
1 clove garlic, pressed
1 tsp. fresh, grated gingerroot
3 T. soy sauce
2 T. molasses

3 T. dry sherry or white wine
½ tsp. salt
½ c. jellied cranberry sauce
¼ tsp. ground allspice
1 T. honey

Heat the olive oil in a saucepan over medium heat. Add the garlic and gingerroot and sauté for 1 minute. Add the soy sauce, molasses, sherry, salt, cranberry sauce, allspice and honey, stirring. Heat and remove from stove. Good for basting duck, spareribs.

HOLLANDAISE SAUCE

3 egg yolks
1 T. fresh lemon juice
¼ lb. melted butter

2 T. hot water
dash of cayenne pepper
½ tsp. salt

Heat water in a double boiler. In the top of the double boiler put the egg yolks, and with a wire whisk beat until smooth. Add the lemon juice and gradually whisk in the melted butter, pouring in a thin stream. Slowly stir in 2 tablespoons hot water, the cayenne and the salt. Continue to mix for 1 minute. The sauce should be thickened. Serve immediately.

HORSERADISH SAUCE

3 T. horseradish
½ c. Hellmann's mayonnaise
½ c. sour cream

⅛ tsp. salt
⅛ tsp. pepper

Mix all ingredients together. Chill. Excellent with roast beef.

HOT MUSTARD SAUCE

2 T. cold water
¼ c. dry mustard
½ tsp. turmeric

¼ tsp. salt
1 T. salad oil

(continued)

Gradually add 2 tablespoons cold water to ¼ cup dry mustard, stirring. Then add the turmeric, salt and oil. Stir again. For egg rolls, sliced pork, shrimp, cheese or ham.

MARINADE

½ c. soy sauce
6 T. sherry
2 T. brown sugar

1 tsp. fresh ginger, minced
1 garlic clove, pressed
¼ c. olive oil

Combine the soy sauce, sherry, brown sugar, ginger, pressed garlic and olive oil. Use as much of the mixture you need to marinate spareribs, shrimp, beef kabobs or chicken for broiling or grilling. Mixture keeps for one month in the refrigerator.

MARINARA SAUCE

¼ c. extra virgin olive oil
2 medium cloves garlic, pressed
¼ c. minced fresh Italian parsley
1 tsp. oregano
1 tsp. dried, or 3 T. fresh, minced basil

1 36-oz. can San Marzano tomatoes
1½ tsp. salt
1 tsp. black pepper
½ tsp. sugar

Heat a saucepan. Add the olive oil and heat. Add parsley and garlic. Sauté about 1 minute over medium low heat. Do not let the garlic brown. Add tomatoes. Mash with a fork or a potato masher. Add the oregano, basil, sugar, salt and pepper. Simmer gently for 20 minutes over medium heat, uncovered. Lower the heat if it bubbles too fast. It should bubble gently.

PESTO ALLA GENOVESE

1 c. fresh basil leaves, washed, dried and chopped
¼ c. minced fresh Italian parsley
½ c. pine nuts
3 cloves garlic, pressed

⅔ c. freshly grated Parmesan cheese
¾ c. extra virgin olive oil
¼ tsp. salt
2 T. butter, melted

(continued)

Put the basil, parsley, pine nuts and garlic in a food processor. Whirl briefly. Scrape into a mixing bowl. Stir in the olive oil, butter, Parmesan cheese and salt. Heat and serve with Gnocchi or Linguine.

PICO DE GALLO SAUCE

½ c. finely chopped jalapeño peppers
½ c. finely chopped onions
½ c. seeded, diced tomatoes
⅓ c. finely diced avocado
3 T. finely chopped fresh coriander

2 T. lime juice
1 tsp. olive oil
½ tsp. salt
½ tsp. pepper

Combine all ingredients together. Serve with Mexican or Tex Mex food.

PLUM SAUCE

2 T. oil
1 small onion, minced
1 clove garlic, pressed
1 tsp. grated, fresh gingerroot
1 30-oz. can whole purple plums, pitted and drained
½ c. brown sugar

1 T. cornstarch
¼ c. orange juice
¼ c. dry sherry
1 T. rice wine vinegar
¼ tsp. anise seeds
1 tsp. salt
¼ tsp. pepper

Purée the plums in the blender. Blend orange juice with cornstarch. Set aside. Heat a skillet. Put in oil and heat. Add onion and garlic. Sauté for 4 minutes over medium low heat. Add gingerroot. Cook 1 minute longer. Add plums, sugar, cornstarch blended with orange juice, sherry, wine vinegar, anise seeds, salt and pepper. Simmer, uncovered, 20 minutes stirring now and then. Use on ribs, chops or chicken, brushing on the last 10 minutes of baking, broiling or grilling.

RED CLAM SAUCE

(if you can't get fresh clams, use 3 15-oz. canned whole clams, drained)

Fresh Clams:

4 lb. fresh clams	½ tsp. dried oregano
2 c. water	1 T. chopped fresh Italian parsley
¼ c. dry white wine	1 bay leaf

Marinara Sauce:

¼ c. extra virgin olive oil	1 36-oz. can San Marzano tomatoes
2 medium cloves garlic, pressed	1½ tsp. salt
¼ c. minced fresh Italian parsley	1 tsp. black pepper
1 tsp. oregano	2 T. tomato paste
1 tsp. dried, or 3 T. fresh, minced basil	

Make the Marinara sauce. Heat a saucepan. Add the olive oil and heat. add parsley and garlic. Sauté about 1 minute over medium low heat. Do not let the garlic brown. Add tomatoes. Mash with a fork or a potato masher. Add the oregano, basil, salt and pepper. Simmer gently for 20 minutes over a medium heat. Lower the heat if it bubbles too fast. It should bubble gently. While the sauce is cooking, prepare the clams. Scrub the clams and simmer them in the water, wine, oregano, parsley and bay leaf until the shells open. Remove the clams from the broth, discarding any unopened ones, and shuck them, reserving any juice. Strain the broth and reserve. Add the clams, 2 tablespoons tomato paste and ½ cup of the reserved broth to the marinara sauce. If you use canned clams, it is not necessary to cook them in the water and wine. Just drain them. Reserve ½ cup of the juice. Strain the ½ cup of the juice. Add the canned clams to the marinara sauce with the tomato paste and ½ cup of the juice from the canned clams. Heat to boiling. Turn off heat.

RED WINE SAUCE

3 T. butter
3 T. flour
1 c. beef broth
1 T. carrot
1 T. onion
1 T. celery
pinch thyme
½ bay leaf or 1 small bay leaf

4 T. butter
2 T. finely chopped onion
1⅔ c. dry red wine
1 bay leaf
2 T. fresh mushrooms, minced
1 tsp. fresh Italian parsley, minced
¼ tsp. salt
¼ tsp. pepper

Put the carrot, onion and celery in a food processor and purée. Make a roux by melting 3 tablespoons butter in a small saucepan over medium low heat. Stir in the flour. Mixture will be like paste. Slowly stir in the beef broth. When it boils, turn heat to low and add the puréed vegetables and the thyme and bay leaf. Cover and simmer slowly for 15 minutes. In another saucepan, sauté the 2 tablespoons finely chopped onion in 1 tablespoon of butter over low heat until the onion is golden. Add the wine, mushrooms, bay leaf, parsley, salt and pepper. Cook over medium heat until only ⅓ of the liquid remains. Stir in the beef broth mixture. Just before serving, beat in the remaining 3 tablespoons of the butter, bit by bit. Makes 1 cup.

SEAFOOD COCKTAIL SAUCE

1 c. tomato ketchup
2 T. prepared horseradish
¼ tsp. Tabasco sauce
2 tsp. very finely minced celery

¼ tsp. salt
¼ tsp. pepper
1 tsp. fresh lemon juice

Mix all ingredients together and chill. For shrimp, crab, lobster, oysters on the half shell.

SAUSAGE STUFFING

1 lb. Italian sausage, purchased or use ½ recipe for Sausage in this book
1 T. olive oil
¼ c. chopped onion
¼ c. finely minced celery
½ green bell pepper, diced
4 c. bread cubes
3 T. minced fresh Italian parsley
1 8-oz. can sliced water chestnuts, drained
1 15-oz. can chicken broth
2 tsp. rubbed sage
1 tsp. salt
½ tsp. black pepper
2 T. butter, melted

Heat oven to 375°. Toast bread cubes in oven for 10 minutes, until lightly browned. Remove from oven and set aside. Remove casing from sausage if using purchased sausage. Put 1 tablespoon olive oil in skillet. Brown sausage, breaking it up, about 15 minutes. Remove from skillet with a slotted spoon to a large bowl. Sauté onion, celery and green pepper in drippings for 3-4 minutes. Add to sausage meat and mix together. Add the parsley, water chestnuts, sage, salt and pepper. Mix. Add the bread cubes and mix. Transfer to a buttered, deep casserole. Pour in the chicken broth and mix. Sprinkle melted butter over the top. Bake for 30 minutes, uncovered.

STUFFING

6 T. butter
2 medium onions, chopped
1 c. chopped celery
5 c. toasted bread cubes
½ c. chicken broth
½ tsp. rubbed sage or poultry seasoning
¼ c. minced fresh Italian parsley
¼ tsp. thyme
½ tsp. oregano
½ tsp. salt
½ tsp. pepper
½ tsp. savory
2 T. butter
¼ c. chicken broth

Heat oven to 350°. Heat butter in a large skillet. Sauté onions and celery until soft. Put in a bowl and mix with ½ cup broth, rubbed sage or poultry seasoning, parsley, thyme, oregano, salt, pepper and savory. Mix well. Add toasted bread cubes. Transfer to a buttered, deep casserole. Melt 2 tablespoons butter in the skillet which was used for the celery and onions, add ¼ cup broth. Heat and pour over casserole and bake for 25 minutes. It should be moist on the inside and crispy on top.

STUFFING WITH OYSTERS

**Make one recipe Stuffing
2 8-oz. cans whole oysters,
 drained**

Heat oven to 350°. Follow the directions for Stuffing. After all the ingredients have been mixed together, gently stir in the oysters. Put in a buttered, deep casserole, heat the 2 tablespoons butter with the ¼ cup broth. Pour over the stuffing and bake for 25 minutes.

SWEET AND SOUR SAUCE

**1 T. oil
1 clove garlic, pressed
1 tsp. grated gingerroot
1 T. cornstarch
½ c. pineapple juice**

**3 T. brown sugar
¼ c. cider vinegar
¼ c. ketchup
1½ tsp. soy sauce**

Mix the cornstarch and pineapple juice in a small bowl. Set aside. Heat a skillet. Add the oil. Sauté the garlic and gingerroot for one minute. Pour pineapple juice mixture into the skillet, stirring. Add the sugar, vinegar, ketchup and soy sauce. Stir and heat until bubbly. Serve with egg rolls.

TARTAR SAUCE

**1⅓ c. mayonnaise
1 T. capers
2 T. sweet pickle relish**

**1 T. finely minced onion
½ tsp. tarragon**

Mix all ingredients together and chill. Good for shrimp, scallops, fish.

TOMATO SAUCE

¼ c. extra virgin olive oil
1 medium onion, finely chopped
2 cloves garlic, pressed
1 36-oz. can San Marzano
  tomatoes
1 6-oz. can tomato paste
1 6-oz. can water

1 tsp. oregano
2 T. chopped fresh basil
¼ c. minced fresh Italian parsley
1 tsp. sugar
2 tsp. salt
1 tsp. black pepper
1 T. extra virgin olive oil

Heat a saucepan. Put the olive oil in and heat over medium heat. Add the onions. Cook for 4 minutes. Add the garlic. Cook 1 minute longer. Add the tomatoes and mash with a potato masher. Add the tomato paste, water, oregano, basil, parsley, sugar, salt and pepper. Stir and bring to a boil. Lower the heat and simmer for 30 minutes. Turn off heat and drizzle 1 tablespoon oil on top. This sauce can be frozen. It will keep in the refrigerator for up to 7-10 days.

TOMATO SAUCE WITH BEEF

Make one recipe Tomato Sauce in this book

1½ lb. lean ground beef
2 T. olive oil

Heat a skillet. Heat the oil. Brown the beef in the oil, breaking up. Make the Tomato Sauce up to the simmer point. Add the beef to the sauce and simmer, covered, over a low heat for 45 minutes, stirring occasionally.

TOMATO SAUCE WITH LAMB

Recipe for Tomato Sauce in this book
1½ lb. boneless lamb shoulder, cut into 1" chunks

3 T. olive oil

Heat 3 tablespoons olive oil. Add the lamb and brown on all sides. Make the Tomato Sauce, up to the simmer point. Add the lamb to the tomato sauce and simmer the sauce, covered, over a low heat for 1 hour, or until the lamb is tender, stirring occasionally.

TOMATO SAUCE WITH PORK

Recipe for Tomato Sauce in this book
2-3 lb. pork shoulder butt, cut into four pieces
3 T. olive oil

Brown the pork pieces in the olive oil. Make the Tomato Sauce up to the simmer point. Add the browned pork to the tomato sauce and simmer on low heat, covered, for 1 to 1½ hours. Stir occasionally.

ARTICHOKES PIZZAIOLA

2 8-oz. pkgs. frozen artichokes
⅓ c. extra virgin olive oil
1 clove garlic, minced
1 14½-oz. can diced tomatoes
¼ tsp. oregano

1 T. minced fresh Italian parsley
1 tsp. salt
½ tsp. pepper
¼ c. chicken broth
¼ c. grated Parmesan cheese

Heat the oil in a deep saucepan. Sauté the garlic for one minute over low heat. Add the artichokes, tomatoes, oregano, parsley salt, pepper and broth. Simmer gently, uncovered, for about 25 minutes, until the artichokes are cooked. Put into a serving platter and sprinkle with the Parmesan cheese.

ARTICHOKES WITH STUFFING

6 large artichokes
2 c. freshly made bread crumbs from 3 slices bread
¾ c. freshly grated Parmesan cheese
¼ c. minced fresh Italian parsley

1 clove garlic, pressed
½ c. extra virgin olive oil
1 T. olive oil
½ tsp. black pepper
½ tsp. salt

Wash the artichokes. Cut off ½" of the tips of the leaves and discard. Cut off the stems and slice a thin layer from the bottom so the artichokes will sit level in the pan. Spread the leaves apart, opening them up. Put 3 slices bread in the blender to make fresh bread crumbs. In a mixing bowl, combine the bread crumbs with the cheese, parsley, garlic ½ cup olive oil, pepper and salt. The stuffing should be crumbly. Loosely stuff each artichoke leaf with some of the stuffing. Fill, but do not overload. Fill a large pan with 2 inches of water. Add 1 tablespoon olive oil. Stand the artichokes up in the pan. Do not get water on the stuffing.

(continued)

Bring the water to a boil, cover, then turn down heat so that the artichokes will simmer. Cook for 60 minutes. If the water should evaporate, add a little hot water. Test a leaf to see if it is tender. If not, cook longer. Serve hot as an appetizer or a vegetable side dish.

ASPARAGUS

2 lb. asparagus, washed
½ c. olive oil
2 T. lemon juice
1 T. minced fresh Italian parsley
½ tsp. salt
¼ tsp. black pepper

Break off the tough, lower part of the stems of the asparagus and discard. Cook the asparagus in an enamel or a steel pan, or an asparagus cooker with a removable rack. Lay the asparagus in the pan. Add 2 cups of water. Bring to a boil. Add 1 teaspoon salt. Lower the heat and simmer for about 12 minutes to cook until al dente. They should not be mushy, but they should have a bite to them. Test with a fork to see if they are easily pierced, but firm. Remove from water when they are cooked and drain on a cloth. Transfer to a hot serving platter. While the asparagus is cooking, mix the oil, lemon juice, parsley, salt and pepper thoroughly. Pour the sauce over them.

BAKED ACORN SQUASH

2 medium-size acorn squash
2 T. butter
2 T. brown sugar
¼ tsp. salt
¼ tsp. black pepper

Heat the oven to 375°. Wash the squash and split them in half. Remove the seeds and discard. Place the halves in a baking dish, cut side down, with ¼" water. Cover loosely with foil. Bake for 45 minutes. Turn squash right side up. Heat the butter and sugar in a saucepan or microwave until butter is melted. Add salt and pepper and pour over squash halves. Return to the oven for 15 minutes longer or until tender. Pierce with a fork to test for doneness.

BAKED BEANS

1 lb. navy beans
6 c. water
1 medium onion, chopped
½ lb. bacon, diced
¼ c. molasses
¼ c. dark brown sugar

½ c. ketchup
½ c. water
1 tsp. salt
¼ tsp. dry mustard
⅛ tsp. pepper

Wash the beans. Soak the beans in a large pot in enough water to cover overnight. The beans will have absorbed some of the water. Add more water to cover and simmer for 1-2 hours until tender. Do not boil. Heat oven to 300°. Sauté the diced bacon in a skillet until crisp. Remove bacon and add to beans. Sauté the onion in the same skillet for 4-5 minutes. Add to the pan with the beans. Mix together the molasses, brown sugar, ketchup, salt, mustard and pepper and ½ cup water. Pour over the beans and mix. Put into a 4-quart baking dish or a 10" x 13" x 2" baking pan. There should be enough water to just cover the top of the beans. If not, add some. Bake, covered, for 5 hours, stirring occasionally, and adding a little hot water if they get dry before they are done. When they are tender and the liquid is thickened, remove from oven.

BAKED VEGETABLES

3 carrots, pared
1 medium-size eggplant
2 medium-size zucchini
½ lb. asparagus
2 medium yellow squash
2 c. seasoned Italian bread crumbs
½ c. extra virgin olive oil

¼ c. minced fresh Italian parsley
½ c. freshly grated Parmesan cheese
1 tsp. oregano
2 cloves garlic, pressed
½ tsp. pepper
½ tsp. salt
2 eggs

Wash and dry the vegetables. Cut into 3" spears (leave skins on squash, zucchini and eggplant). Bring a large pot of water to a boil. Drop the vegetable spears into the water. Parboil for 3 minutes. Drain on paper towels. Heat the oven to 400°. Beat the eggs until frothy. In a mixing bowl, combine the bread crumbs, olive oil, oregano, parsley, garlic, grated cheese, salt, pepper and eggs. Lay the vegetables on an oiled baking sheet. Spread the crumb mixture over them. Bake for 15 minutes. Serve hot.

BEANS ALLA TOSCANO

1 lb. dried cannellini, pinto or navy beans
1 celery stalk
2 bay leaves
4 slices bacon
3 T. finely minced onion
4 T. extra virgin olive oil
1 tsp. sage
1 clove garlic, pressed
1 tsp. salt
1 tsp. pepper

Wash the beans. Put the beans in a large pot and cover with water. Soak overnight. To cook, add enough water to cover the beans, plus about 3". Add the celery stalk, cut in half, and the bay leaves. Simmer the beans for 1-1½ hours, until tender. Do not boil. Drain the beans. Put into a bowl. Discard the celery and bay leaves. Chop the bacon and sauté until crisp in a medium-size skillet. Add the bacon to the beans. In the same skillet, sauté the onion until golden. Add the garlic and sauté one minute more. Add to the beans, along with the sage, salt and pepper. Add the olive oil. Season with more salt and pepper if necessary.

BEETS

2 lbs. beets, washed and trimmed
6 T. butter
salt

Bring a pot of water to a boil. Add 1 tsp. salt. Drop in the beets. Simmer for 30 minutes, or until they are tender. Drain, peel and cut into thick slices. Put them into a vegetable dish. Add the butter and sprinkle with salt. Stir.

BLACK-EYED PEAS

1 10-oz. pkg. frozen black-eyed peas
1 medium tomato, seeded and chopped
¼ c. Vidalia onion, diced
¼ c. diced green pepper
¼ c. celery, diced
½ tsp. cumin
½ tsp. salt
½ tsp. pepper
½ c. Hellmann's mayonnaise

(continued)

Cook the black-eyed peas according to package directions. Drain. Mix the peas with the tomato, onion, diced green pepper, celery, cumin, salt and pepper. Fold in mayonnaise.

BROCCOLI

3 c. broccoli flowerets
1 clove garlic, pressed
3 T. extra virgin olive oil

½ tsp. turmeric
½ tsp. salt
½ tsp. pepper

    Heat a medium-size skillet. Heat the oil. Drop in the broccoli and cook, covered, to crisp tender, over medium-low heat, about 5-7 minutes. Add the garlic and cook two minutes more, stirring with a wooden spoon. Add the turmeric, salt and pepper.

BUTTERNUT SQUASH

1 medium butternut squash
3 T. butter

½ tsp. salt
½ tsp. pepper

    Peel the squash (I use a potato peeler). Cut in half lengthwise. Remove the seeds and discard. Cut it into chunks. Put the squash in a pot of water, enough to cover it. Bring water to a boil, lower heat and simmer until the squash is cooked, about 15-20 minutes. Drain the squash. Mash with a potato masher or a fork. Stir in the butter, salt and pepper. Add more salt and pepper if you like.

CABBAGE WITH CANNELLINI BEANS

½ half head Savoy cabbage
1 can cannellini beans, rinsed and drained
2 cloves garlic, pressed

½ tsp. salt
¼ tsp. black pepper
3 T. olive oil

    Remove the core of the cabbage and discard. Slice the cabbage thinly. Put into a skillet with the garlic and add ½ cup water. Bring to a boil, lower the heat and simmer for 10 minutes, until just tender. It should be crisp-tender. Add the beans, salt and pepper. Cover and heat

(continued)

for a few minutes. If any water remains, pour it off. Drizzle the olive oil over and stir.

CANDIED SWEET POTATOES

4 lb. sweet potatoes
½ c. brown sugar
½ tsp. cinnamon
¼ tsp. nutmeg
¼ tsp. allspice
½ tsp. salt
¼ c. melted butter
½ c. orange juice
¾ c. broken pecans

Cook the potatoes in boiling water about 25 minutes until tender. Peel and mash with a fork. Combine ¼ cup of the brown sugar, the cinnamon, melted butter and broken pecans. Set aside. Combine ¼ cup brown sugar, nutmeg, allspice, salt, orange juice. Mix together with the mashed potatoes. Pour into a buttered baking dish. Sprinkle the pecan mixture evenly over top. Bake at 350° for 20 minutes until bubbly.

CARROTS WITH BRANDY

2 lbs. carrots
6 T. butter
½ tsp. salt
½ tsp. pepper
1 tsp. sugar
2 T. minced fresh Italian parsley
⅓ c. brandy

Wash and scrape the carrots. Slice ½" thick at a diagonal. Heat the butter in a skillet over moderate heat and add the sliced carrots. Season with salt, pepper and the sugar. Add the parsley on top of the carrots. Lower the heat, cover the pan, and cook them slowly for about 30 minutes, or until they are tender, stirring them frequently. If they start to dry, add a few teaspoons water. Remove the cover, add the brandy, heat for a few seconds, ignite, and shake the pan until flames subside. Turn carrots out into a hot vegetable dish.

CAULIFLOWER WITH BÉCHAMEL

1 head cauliflower
1 recipe béchamel sauce in this book
½ c. fresh bread crumbs
1 T. butter
2 T. freshly grated Parmesan cheese

(continued)

Whirl 1 slice bread in blender to make bread crumbs. Heat the oven to 400°. Break up the cauliflower into flowerets. Cook it in boiling, salted water for 12 minutes, or until it is tender. Drain in a colander. While it is cooking, make the béchamel sauce. In a small skillet, heat the butter and sauté the bread crumbs. Set aside. Arrange the cauliflower in a baking dish, piled two deep. Pour over the béchamel sauce. Sprinkle with the bread crumbs and then the Parmesan cheese. Bake for 6-8 minutes, until the crumbs are crisp.

CELERY AMANDINE

⅓ c. whole, salted almonds
2 T. butter
¼ c. chicken broth
4 c. sliced celery
1 T. finely minced onion

½ tsp. sugar
½ tsp. salt
½ tsp. ginger
½ clove garlic, pressed

Sauté the celery, onion and garlic in the butter for 3 minutes. Add the broth, sugar, salt and ginger. Cook about ten minutes. Add the almonds. Stir and put into serving dish.

CHICK PEAS

2 cans chick peas, rinsed and drained
¾ c. extra virgin olive oil
2 T. lemon juice
2 T. red wine vinegar

2 T. finely chopped scallions
1 clove garlic, pressed
1 T. minced fresh Italian parsley
¼ tsp. salt
¼ tsp. black pepper

Put the chick peas in a bowl. Combine the olive oil, lemon juice vinegar, scallions, garlic, parsley, salt and pepper. Pour over the chick peas and mix.

CHINESE GREEN BEANS

1 lb. fresh green beans
1 T. chopped scallions
1 garlic clove, pressed
1 tsp. fresh gingerroot, minced
3 T. sesame oil

1 T. brown sugar
½ tsp. salt
2 T. soy sauce
1 T. water

(continued)

Wash and snip the ends off of the beans. Bring a pot of water to boil, enough to cover beans. Cook in boiling water 4 to 6 minutes. Drain. Heat a skillet. Add the sesame oil. Sauté scallions, garlic and gingerroot 1 minute. Add sugar, salt and soy sauce. Cook until sugar dissolves. Add beans and water. Put heat on medium and stir-fry 3 minutes. Serve immediately.

CORN SOUFFLÉ

1 T. butter
1 T. flour
½ c. milk
½ tsp. salt

⅛ tsp. paprika
½ tsp. Tabasco
2 c. canned corn, drained
2 eggs, separated

Preheat oven to 350°. Butter a 1½ quart casserole. Heat the butter in a skillet. Stir in the flour. Slowly add the milk. Cook for 2 minutes, stirring. Stir the egg yolks in a small bowl, then add a little of the milk mixture, stirring briskly. Add the yolk mixture to the milk mixture in the pan. Stir for 1 minute, then remove from the heat and add the corn, salt, paprika and Tabasco. Set aside. Beat the egg whites until stiff. Fold a fourth of the whites into the corn mixture and blend. Then gently fold in the remaining whites. Spoon into the prepared casserole and bake for about 30-35 minutes.

CREAMED SPINACH

2 lbs. fresh spinach
6 T. butter, softened
½ tsp. salt
1 T. flour

½ tsp. black pepper
⅛ tsp. nutmeg
1 c. heavy cream

Wash the spinach. Bring a pot of water to boiling. Add the spinach and cook for 3 minutes. Drain. Press to remove excess water. Finely chop and set aside. Melt the butter in a saucepan. Add the spinach, salt pepper and nutmeg. Stir over very low heat for about 5 minutes or until the butter has been almost absorbed by the spinach. Sprinkle with one tablespoon flour. Stir. Add cream. Cook for 4-5 minutes longer.

EGGPLANT PARMIGIANA

1 recipe Marinara Sauce in this book
4 T. tomato paste
1½ lb. eggplant
1½ c. seasoned Italian bread crumbs
2 eggs, slightly beaten
¼ c. extra virgin olive oil
1 c. freshly grated Parmesan cheese
8 oz. shredded mozzarella cheese

Make the Marinara Sauce. Add the tomato paste to the marinara sauce and stir. Heat oven to 350°. Lightly oil a 13" x 9" x 2" baking dish. Wash eggplant. Do not peel. Cut crosswise into slices ½" thick. In a pie plate, combine beaten eggs and 1 tablespoon water. Mix well. On a sheet of waxed paper, combine bread crumbs with ½ cup Parmesan cheese. Mix well. Heat a skillet. Heat oil in skillet. Dip eggplant slices into egg mixture, coating well. Then dip into crumb mixture, coating evenly. Sauté slices in oil until crisp on both sides. Arrange half the slices in the baking dish. Sprinkle with ¼ cup Parmesan cheese. Top with half the mozzarella cheese. Cover with half tomato sauce. Repeat layers. Bake 25 minutes.

GREEN BEANS AND POTATOES

2 lbs. potatoes, peeled and diced
1 lb. fresh or frozen green beans
1 14½-oz. can diced tomatoes
½ c. chicken broth
1 clove garlic, pressed
3 T. extra virgin olive oil
½ tsp. basil
1 tsp. salt
1 tsp. black pepper
1 T. extra virgin olive oil

If you use fresh beans, wash and snip off the ends. Bring the broth and tomatoes to a boil in a saucepan. Add the basil, salt, pepper and potatoes and simmer for 15 minutes. Add the garlic, 3 tablespoons olive oil and green beans, return to a boil, lower heat and simmer until the beans are tender. Sprinkle 1 tablespoon olive oil on top.

KALE

1 lb. kale
1 clove garlic, pressed
¼ c. extra virgin olive oil
½ tsp. salt
½ tsp. pepper

Strip the leaves from the stems. Discard the stems. Wash and break the leaves into small pieces. Put the kale in a pot, add the garlic and

(continued)

1 cup water. Bring to a boil. Lower heat and simmer until tender, about 15-20 minutes. It should be crisp tender. Drain. Add salt, pepper and olive oil. Put the kale in a bowl.

LENTILS

1 lb. lentils
1 c. finely chopped ham
2 bay leaves
2 carrots, sliced
3 T. olive oil
2 stalks celery, with leaves, sliced

½ c. chopped onion
1 clove garlic, pressed
1 tsp. salt
1 tsp. pepper
4 c. beef broth
1 T. olive oil for drizzling

Clean the lentils. Soak them overnight in a pan with enough water to cover. Drain. Heat a large pot. Add the olive oil and heat. Sauté the carrots, celery, onions and garlic for 8 minutes. Add the ham and stir. Put in the bay leaves, salt pepper, lentils and beef broth. There should be enough broth to cover the lentils. If not, add more. Bring to a boil. Cover, reduce heat and simmer for one hour. Remove the cover and cook until the lentils are tender and most of the liquid has evaporated. Drizzle 1 tablespoon olive oil over.

MARINATED VEGETABLES

1 c. extra virgin olive oil
⅓ c. wine vinegar
3 cloves garlic, pressed
1 tsp. salt
½ tsp. black pepper
1 tsp. oregano
2 tsp. sugar
1 c. green pepper strips

1 c. red pepper strips
1 c. carrot sticks
1 c. celery
1 red onion, cut into chunks
½ head cauliflower, broken into flowerets
2 c. broccoli flowerets
1 c. drained, pitted black olives

Bring a large pot of water to a boil. Drop in all the vegetables, except the onions and olives. Return to a boil. Cover and simmer 5 minutes. Vegetables should be crisp-tender. Drain. Cool slightly. Transfer to a bowl. Add onions and olives. Mix together the oil, wine vinegar, garlic, salt, pepper, oregano and sugar. Pour over vegetables and toss. Marinate in the refrigerator for at least an hour. Marinating overnight will develop the flavor more.

ONION STRINGS

3 medium onions
1 c. flour
1 c. seltzer water
salt
fat for deep frying: ½ olive oil, ½ corn oil

Slice the onions ⅛" thick or as thinly as possible. Separate into rings. Heat 2" of oil in deep fat fryer or a deep saucepan to 375° or use an electric frying pan. Whisk together the flour and seltzer water. Dip onion rings into batter. Shake off excess. Drop into hot oil, cooking a batch at a time, without crowding, turning once. Just cook until golden. Be sure the oil has heated to 375° before dropping the next batch in. As you remove the batches from the oil, drain them briefly on paper towels and keep warm in 200° oven. When they are all cooked, lightly salt, then heap them onto a hot serving platter.

POTATO CASSEROLE

1 c. chopped onion
1 10¾-oz. can cream of chicken soup
2 c. sour cream
¼ c. butter, melted
1 tsp. salt
1 2-lb. bag of frozen hash brown potatoes, thawed
2 c. shredded cheddar cheese
1 tsp. paprika
1 c. crushed potato chips

Heat oven to 350°. Mix together the chopped onion, cream of chicken soup, sour cream, butter and salt in a large bowl. Add the thawed potatoes and cheddar cheese. Mix. Pour into a 9" x 13" greased baking dish. Sprinkle with paprika. Top with potato chips. Bake for 45 minutes to 1 hour, uncovered, until bubbly.

POTATO CHIPS

6 Idaho potatoes
peanut oil, sunflower oil or canola oil for deep frying
salt

Wash and peel potatoes. Slice the potatoes paper thin with a vegetable slicer. Soak them in ice water for 1 hour, changing the water a couple of times. Drain and dry them thoroughly on paper towels. Drop them, a batch at a time, in 2" of fat which has been heated to 375°, until they are crisp and golden. Do not let them stick together. Drain on

(continued)

paper towels, salt lightly, and transfer to a serving dish. Repeat with the next batch, making sure the oil is heated to 375°. Proceed until all are cooked.

POTATO NESTS

3 large potatoes
Oil for cooking
½ tsp. salt for sprinkling

Heat oven to 400°. Peel potatoes. Cut lengthwise into tiny strips. Heat 2 tablespoons oil in a large skillet. Cook potatoes until nearly tender but not brown, stirring and turning with a spatula. Remove from skillet. Sprinkle with salt and arrange potatoes against sides and bottom of large, deep, muffin pans, pressing firmly into place. Bake 15 minutes, or until golden. Serve hot filled with any creamed fish, meat or poultry, such as the following recipe. Makes 6 nests.

Creamed Chicken:

2 T. butter
3 T. flour
1 c. milk
⅓ c. heavy cream
⅛ tsp. pepper
1½ c. cubed cooked chicken
1 tsp. salt
½ c. cooked peas, optional

Melt the butter in a saucepan and stir in the flour. Cook for 2-3 minutes over medium heat, stirring constantly, until well blended. Gradually add the milk and cream and stir for 5 minutes until thickened and smooth. Add the pepper, chicken and salt (and the peas if you like). Simmer 5 minutes more.

POTATOES AU GRATIN

¼ c. butter
¼ c. sifted all-purpose flour
1 tsp. salt
⅛ tsp. pepper
2 c. milk
1 c. shredded sharp cheddar cheese
2 lb. cooked potatoes
2 T. butter, melted
¼ c. unseasoned bread crumbs
1 T. minced fresh Italian parsley

Cook, peel and dice the potatoes. Put them in a mixing bowl. Heat oven to 375°. Grease a 1½-quart casserole. Combine ¼ cup melted butter, ¼ cup flour, salt and pepper in a saucepan. Cook over low heat,

(continued)

stirring until smooth. Add milk gradually, stirring constantly. Add cheese. Cook about 5 minutes or until sauce thickens, stirring occasionally. Combine sauce with diced potatoes in the mixing bowl. Place in prepared casserole. Mix 2 tablespoons melted butter, bread crumbs and parsley. Sprinkle on top of potatoes. Bake 20 minutes or until browned and bubbly.

RED CABBAGE AU CARAMEL

2 lb. red cabbage
2/3 c. sugar
1/3 c. water
1/4 c. red wine vinegar
water to cover
1 tsp. salt
1 T. kümmel

Heat oven to 350°. Bring a large pot of water to boil. Wash cabbage. Remove center core and discard. Slice the cabbage very fine (this can be done in food processor). Put cabbage in boiling water for 15 minutes. Drain. Put into a mixing bowl. In a skillet, make a caramel of the sugar and 1/3 cup water, stirring. It should be very brown, but it must not burn. Add vinegar and cook 5 minutes. Pour over cabbage and mix. Pour mixture into a casserole with a cover. Add some boiling hot water to cover cabbage. Cover and bake for 60 minutes. Season with salt and kümmel, stirring.

REFRIED BEANS

1 lb. dried pinto beans
6 slices bacon
1/4 c. finely minced onion
1/4 c. finely minced green pepper
1 clove garlic, pressed
2 tsp. salt
1 tsp. chili powder

Wash beans. Put into a large bowl. Cover with 6 cups cold water. Refrigerate, covered, overnight. Turn beans and liquid into a large saucepan. Add enough water to cover beans, plus 1". Bring to boiling. Reduce heat and simmer, covered, about 1 1/2 hours, or until tender. Drain beans, reserving liquid. Add water to liquid, if necessary, to make 1 cup. Finely dice bacon. In a large skillet, sauté bacon until crisp. Remove from pan and set aside. In bacon drippings in skillet, sauté onion, green pepper and garlic until tender, about 5-8 minutes. With a wooden spoon, stir in beans, bacon, salt and chili powder. Cook over medium low heat, stirring in reserved bean liquid, a little at a time, and

(continued)

mashing beans until all are mashed and mixture is creamy. Turn into a serving dish. If desired, sprinkle with shredded cheese.

ROASTED POTATOES

4 medium-size baking potatoes
1 tsp. oregano
1 tsp. salt
2 T. extra virgin olive oil

    Heat oven to 375°. Peel and dice potatoes into a large dice. Put into a 13" x 9" x 2" baking pan. Sprinkle with olive oil and toss with a spatula. Sprinkle with oregano and salt. After a half hour, lift and turn with a spatula so they brown on all sides. Turn again until done. This should take 45 minutes.

ROASTED RED PEPPERS

12 red bell peppers
4 cloves garlic, pressed
1/3 c. minced fresh Italian parsley
1/2 tsp. salt
1/2 tsp. pepper
1/2 c. extra virgin olive oil

    Heat oven to 350°. Wash the peppers and leave the moisture on them. Lay them on a large baking sheet with sides so they won't roll off. Bake the peppers until they begin to blister, turning them every 10 minutes so that all sides will get roasted. When the skins are puffed up on all sides, they are done. This takes around 30 minutes. They should be soft, but not mushy. When they cool a little, peel the skins off and discard. Pull out the stem and remove the seeds and discard. Slice the peppers into 1/2" strips and place them in a large bowl. Drain off any liquid. Mix together the garlic, parsley, salt, pepper and oil. Pour over peppers, mix and marinate in the refrigerator a few hours or longer. Serve as a side dish, in an antipasto, on salads, in sandwiches or on pizza. For a sandwich, do not use mayonnaise, they already have oil on them. You may also freeze the roasted peppers in a plastic bag, but do not freeze with the marinade on them. When you take them out of the freezer, thaw. Make the marinade and put it on them.

SCALLOPED POTATOES

4 medium baking potatoes
1 tsp. salt
1 tsp. pepper

4 T. melted butter
1½ c. half and half
1 tsp. paprika

Heat oven to 325°. Butter a 9½" x 13½" x 2" baking dish. Peel the potatoes, cut in half lengthwise, and slice ¼" thick. Put them into a large mixing bowl. Add the salt and pepper to the half and half and pour the half and half mixture into the bowl. Mix and turn into the baking dish. Drizzle the butter over. Sprinkle with paprika. Cover lightly with foil. Bake for 40 minutes. Remove the foil and bake 10-15 minutes longer. Prick with a fork to see that they are soft. If not, bake a little longer. Let them sit for 10 minutes before serving.

SMASHED RED POTATOES

4 medium red-skinned potatoes
3 slices bacon, diced
4 scallions, minced
1 c. shredded cheddar cheese

½ c. heavy cream
1 tsp. salt
1 tsp. pepper

Wash the potatoes. Cover with water in a saucepan. Boil until cooked, about 30 minutes. Remove from heat when done. Drain. While the potatoes are cooking, sauté the bacon in a skillet until crisp. Remove from pan and set aside. In the same pan, sauté the scallions until limp. Pour the cream into the pan and heat, but do not let it boil. Put the potatoes into a large bowl. Mash with a fork. Add the bacon, scallions and cream mixture, cheese, salt and pepper. Mix all together.

SPINACH SAUTÉ

1 lb. fresh spinach
2 T. extra virgin olive oil
1 clove garlic, pressed

½ tsp. salt
½ tsp. pepper

Wash spinach thoroughly. Remove rough stems and discard. Break leaves up in to pieces. Put spinach into a pot with the moisture left on and add ¼ cup water. Add the garlic. Bring to a boil. Lower heat and simmer, uncovered, for 5 minutes, stirring. If any water remains, drain. Add 2 tablespoons oil, salt and pepper. Sauté one minute.

STUFFED BAKED ONIONS

3 large Spanish onions, 3" in diameter or larger
12 tiny white onions, cooked
2 T. butter
½ tsp. salt

½ tsp. pepper
½ c. fresh bread crumbs
2 c. Béchamel Sauce recipe in this book

Peel large onions. Gently boil in salted water for 25 minutes. Do not overcook. Drain and cut each in half crosswise. Remove center rings to make a 2" wide hole. Peel excess layer from small white onions to reduce size to ½" in diameter or less. Cook in boiling water for 10 minutes. Melt butter in skillet, add crumbs, salt and pepper and toss. Place small onions in béchamel sauce and heat. Arrange the six Spanish onion halves in baking dish. Fill centers first with small onions and then with sauce. Pour remaining sauce over. Sprinkle with crumbs and brown under broiler. Serves 6.

STUFFED BAKED POTATOES

4 large Idaho baking potatoes
4 slices bacon, diced
1 tsp. salt
1 tsp. white pepper

4 T. butter
1 c. sour cream
8 oz. shredded cheddar cheese
2 T. minced scallions

Heat oven to 400°. Bake the potatoes for 45 minutes. Squeeze to see if they are done. Remove from oven. Set aside to cool a little. Lower oven to 350°. Sauté the bacon in a skillet until crisp. Remove and drain on paper towels. Cut the potatoes lengthwise. Scoop out the pulp and put through a potato ricer into a mixing bowl. If you don't have a ricer, mix with a mixer. Add the bacon, butter, sour cream, half of the cheese, the scallions, salt and pepper to the potatoes. Mix well. Spoon the potato mixture back into the potato shells. Top the potatoes with the remaining cheese. Place on a baking sheet and bake until the cheese melts, about 10 minutes.

TOMATOES, OVEN DRIED

3 lb. plum tomatoes
salt

extra virgin olive oil

Heat oven to 200°. Halve tomatoes lengthwise and place on cake rack on baking sheet, cut side up. Sprinkle with salt, and bake until dry

(continued)

and pliable, 8 to 10 hours. Check after 8 hours. Don't let them darken as they should be red. Turn once or twice during baking. Store in refrigerator in sealed container, with olive oil to cover.

VEGETABLE STIR FRY

3 T. peanut oil
2 garlic cloves, pressed
1 lb. fresh green beans
4 large carrots, cut diagonally into ¼" thick slices
½ small head red cabbage, shredded into ¼" thick slices
2 ribs celery, cut diagonally into ½" slices
1 red pepper, cut into thin strips
2 tsp. fresh gingerroot, minced
⅓ c. chicken broth
½ tsp. salt
2 T. lime juice
1 tsp. sugar
2 tsp. balsamic vinegar
1 T. sesame oil
¼ c. peanuts

Heat peanut oil in a large skillet over medium-high heat until hot. Add garlic and stir-fry 1 minute. Add gingerroot, green beans, carrots, celery and pepper and stir-fry until crisp tender. Add cabbage, chicken broth, salt, lime juice, sugar, vinegar and sesame oil. Stir fry 5 minutes. Pour into a serving dish and garnish with peanuts.

YELLOW SQUASH

2 medium squash, sliced at a diagonal ¼" inch
2 T. minced onion
1 T. minced fresh Italian parsley
1 T. extra virgin olive oil
2 T. butter
½ tsp. salt
½ tsp. pepper

Heat butter and oil in a skillet. Add the squash and minced onion. Sprinkle with parsley. Cook for 15 minutes, covered. Stir occasionally so that all pieces get cooked and browned. Sprinkle with salt and pepper.

ZUCCHINI SAUTÉ

2 medium zucchini, sliced at a diagonal ¼" thick
1 T. minced fresh Italian parsley
3 T. extra virgin olive oil
½ tsp. salt

(continued)

Heat the oil in a medium skillet. Add the zucchini and sprinkle with the parsley. Cover and cook over medium heat for 15 minutes, stirring and turning occasionally, so that all the pieces get cooked and a little browned. It's done when it is tender. Sprinkle with salt and serve.

Recipe Favorites

Meats
Poultry

My Brother Rudy

Helpful Hints

- Certain meats, like ribs and pot roast, can be parboiled before grilling to reduce the fat content.

- Pound meat lightly with a mallet or rolling pin, pierce with a fork, sprinkle lightly with meat tenderizer, and add marinade. Refrigerate for 20 minutes and cook or grill for a quick and succulent meat.

- Marinating is a cinch if you use a plastic bag. The meat stays in the marinade and it's easy to turn. Cleanup is easy; just toss the bag.

- It's easier to thinly slice meat if it's partially frozen.

- Adding tomatoes to roasts helps to naturally tenderize the meat. Tomatoes contain an acid that works well to break down meats.

- Whenever possible, cut meat across the grain; this will make it easier to eat and also give it a more attractive appearance.

- When frying meat, sprinkle paprika on the meat to turn it golden brown.

- Thaw all meats in the refrigerator for maximum safety.

- Refrigerate poultry promptly after purchasing. Keep it in the coldest part of your refrigerator for up to 2 days. Freeze poultry for longer storage. Never leave poultry at room temperature for over 2 hours.

- When frying chicken, canola oil provides a milder taste, and it contains healthier amounts of saturated and polyunsaturated fats. Do not cover the chicken once it has finished cooking, because covering will cause the coating to loose its crispness.

- One pound of boneless chicken equals approximately 3 cups of cubed chicken.

- Generally, red meats should reach 160° and poultry should reach 180° before serving. If preparing fish, the surface of the fish should flake off with a fork.

- Rub lemon juice on fish before cooking to enhance the flavor and help maintain a good color.

- Scaling a fish is easier if vinegar is rubbed on the scales first.

- When grilling fish, the rule of thumb is to cook 5 minutes on each side per inch of thickness. For example, cook a 2-inch thick fillet for 10 minutes per side. Before grilling, rub with oil to seal in moisture.

Meats And Poultry

BEEF BRACIOLA

8 slices beef steak cut ¼" thick (3" wide by 6" long)
3 T. minced Italian parsley
1 c. soft bread crumbs
¼ c. prosciutto, pancetta or bacon, minced
3 T. freshly grated Parmesan cheese
1 clove garlic, pressed
1 tsp. salt
1 tsp. pepper
5 T. olive oil
toothpicks for holding together
½ c. beef broth

Whirl 2 slices bread in blender to make bread crumbs. Combine parsley, bread crumbs, prosciutto, grated cheese, garlic, 2 tablespoons olive oil, salt and pepper. Divide and spread the mixture among the 8 slices of beef. Roll up each slice of beef and secure with two toothpicks. Heat a skillet. Add 3 tablespoons oil and heat. Brown the meat on all sides over medium heat. Add the beef broth. Lower the heat and simmer for one hour, or until tender. Add more broth, heated, if necessary.

BEEF BURGUNDY

2½ lb. boneless beef chuck, cut into 1½" cubes
3 T. brandy
½ lb. small white onions, peeled (about 12)
½ lb. small fresh mushrooms
4 T. olive oil
1 medium onion, chopped
2½ T. flour
1 tsp. salt
⅛ tsp. pepper
2 T. meat extract paste
2 T. tomato paste
1½ c. Burgundy wine
1 10½-oz. can beef broth
1 bay leaf
¼ tsp. thyme

Heat the oven to 350°. Heat 2 tablespoons of the oil in a large skillet. Put in chopped onions and slowly brown until they are golden. Remove and put into a 4-quart Dutch oven or baking dish. Add 2 tablespoons oil to the same skillet and heat. Put the flour on a sheet of waxed paper. Roll the beef in it. Brown the beef in the skillet. Cook in two or more batches and remove the browned meat to the Dutch oven or baking dish as it is done. Pour the brandy over the beef. Stir. Add the mushrooms, small white onions, thyme, salt, pepper, bay leaf and beef broth to the beef. Mix the tomato paste and the meat extract paste with the

(continued)

wine. Add to the beef and stir well. Bake, covered, stirring occasionally for 1½ to 2 hours, until meat is fork tender.

BEEF GRILL

a 3-lb. piece of thick sirloin steak
¼ c. soy sauce
2 T. sherry
1 T. sugar

1 T. sesame oil or salad oil
1 clove garlic, pressed
2 T. minced scallions

If you put the meat in the freezer and partially freeze, it is easier to slice. Cut the sirloin across the grain into ¼" thick slices (or have the butcher do it for you). Combine the soy sauce, sherry, sugar, oil, garlic and scallions together. Place the slices of meat into the mixture turning, to coat, and let stand for an hour. In the meantime, heat charcoal grill. Thread the beef on skewers. Cook the meat on both sides for a few minutes to your likeness.

BEEF TACOS

2 T. oil
1 lb. ground chuck
1 medium onion, chopped
1 clove garlic, pressed
1 tsp. salt
½ tsp. pepper
1 6-oz. can tomato sauce

Taco shells
1 c. fresh tomato, coarsely chopped
1 c. shredded lettuce
1 c. grated Monterey Jack or sharp cheddar cheese
Salsa (see recipe in this book)

Heat oven to 400°. In heated skillet, sauté the chuck in the oil until browned, breaking up. Push aside. Add onions. Sauté until golden and add garlic. Cook one minute longer. Add salt, pepper and tomato sauce. Cook ten minutes longer, covered, stirring once or twice. Remove from heat. Fill taco shells with meat mixture, top with grated cheese. Bake until cheese melts. Remove from oven. Serve with bowls of lettuce, tomato and salsa.

BEEF TERIYAKI

1½ lb. sirloin, cut into 1½" cubes
2 T. brown sugar
½ c. soy sauce
6 T. sherry
¼ T. olive oil
1 tsp. fresh ginger, minced
¼ tsp. pepper
1 clove garlic, pressed
1 can whole water chestnuts, drained
1 can pineapple chunks, drained
1 green pepper cut into 1½" x 1½" pieces
½ lb. small mushrooms

Mix together the brown sugar, soy sauce, sherry, olive oil, ginger, pepper and garlic in a bowl. Add the cubes of meat and stir to coat. Let stand 2 hours at room temperature. Alternate meat, pineapple, peppers and mushrooms on skewers. Place a water chestnut at the tip of each skewer. Prepare charcoal grill. Cook over coals 10-12 minutes. Serves 4.

BEEF WITH CREAM

1½ lb. round steak
¼ c. flour
½ tsp. pepper
1 tsp. salt
¼ c. butter
¼ lb. fresh mushrooms, sliced
½ c. chopped onion
1 clove garlic, pressed
1 can beef broth
1 c. sour cream
3 c. cooked noodles, mixed with 1 T. butter

The meat will be easier to slice if you partially freeze it. Cut steak into thin strips, about ¼" thick. Put the flour on waxed paper and dust meat with flour. Heat the butter in a large skillet. Brown meat. Add the mushrooms, onions, garlic and brown. Stir in the beef broth. Add the salt and pepper. Cover, lower heat and simmer for 1 hour until meat is tender. Stir now and then. Gradually stir in sour cream. Cook over low heat 5 minutes to heat sour cream. Do not boil. Just before meat is done, bring a pot of water to a boil. Add 1 tablespoon salt and add the noodles. Cook to al dente. Drain and coat with 1 tablespoon butter. Serve beef over cooked and buttered noodles.

CARBONADE OF BEEF FLAMANDE

3 T. butter
2 T. oil
3 lb. chuck or rump of beef cut into slices, ½" thick
1½ lb. onions, thinly sliced
1 tsp. salt
1 tsp. pepper
2 cloves garlic, pressed

1 12-oz. bottle beer
1 c. beef stock
1 T. brown sugar
bay leaf
½ tsp. thyme
2 T. minced fresh Italian parsley
2 T. cornstarch
2 T. vinegar

Heat oven to 350°. Heat 2 tablespoons butter and 2 tablespoons oil together in a large skillet. Brown beef slices well over high heat. Remove them as they are browned. You may have to do this in two batches. Reduce heat, add 1 more tablespoon butter and heat. Add the sliced onions. Remove when golden brown. Stir in garlic for one minute. Add stock to pan and heat. Turn off heat and set pan aside. Layer beef and onions in a large casserole. Pour beer into skillet with stock. Add sugar, salt, pepper, bay leaf, thyme and parsley and stir. Pour over beef. Cover casserole and bake 2½ hours, or until meat is fork tender. Discard bay leaf. Put a cup of the juice from the casserole into skillet. Add cornstarch and vinegar and stir to thicken. Add the remaining juice. Heat. Stir. Pour over meat. Serves 6 to 8.

CORNED BEEF AND CABBAGE

1 4-5 lb. piece of corned beef
2 bay leaves
10 black peppercorns

1 medium onion, sliced
1 large head green cabbage

Put corned beef in a large pot and add water to cover plus 3". Drop in the bay leaves, peppercorns and onion slices. Bring water to boil. Lower heat and simmer, covered, 3-4 hours until meat is tender. During the last 15-20 minutes of cooking, add cabbage, cut into wedges, and cook (uncovered) until cabbage is tender. Serve with caraway potatoes and horseradish sauce. (Recipe is in this book.)

Caraway Potatoes:

5 potatoes
1 T. caraway seed
6 T. butter

1 tsp. salt
½ tsp. pepper

Scrub and boil potatoes until tender when pierced with a round toothpick, about 20-25 minutes. Peel the potatoes. Cut into quarters and

(continued)

place in serving dish. Melt the butter. Stir in the caraway seed, salt and pepper and pour over potatoes.

GRILLED BEEFBURGERS

2 lb. ground chuck
6 T. chopped onions
1 tsp. salt
1 tsp. pepper
2 T. olive oil
2 tsp. Kitchen Bouquet

8 Kaiser rolls
lettuce
8 slices tomato
8 slices crisply cooked bacon
8 slices cheddar or provolone cheese

Prepare the charcoal grill. Put ground chuck in a mixing bowl. Stir in the chopped onions, salt and pepper. Shape into 8 patties. Mix the oil and Kitchen Bouquet together. Brush on each side of patty and grill for 5 minutes on each side, or longer if desired. Put on buns and add lettuce, tomato, bacon and cheese, as desired.

KUNG PAO BEEF

1 beaten egg white
2 tsp. cornstarch
½ tsp. salt
2 lb. boneless beef sirloin, cut into 1" cubes
2 T. soy sauce
2 T. sesame oil
1 T. rice wine or sherry
½ tsp. salt
1 red pepper, sliced thinly
3 T. peanut oil
1 tsp. crushed red pepper

2 cloves garlic, pressed
1 tsp. minced fresh gingerroot
3 scallions, cut into ½" pieces
2 T. soy sauce
3 T. rice wine
1 tsp. sugar
1 c. chicken broth
1 T. cornstarch, mixed with 2 T. water
½ c. peanuts
4 c. cooked rice

Cook the rice following package directions. Mix together the egg white, 2 teaspoons cornstarch and ½ teaspoon salt. Combine with the beef. Refrigerate for 30 minutes. Mix together the 2 tablespoons soy sauce, 2 tablespoons sesame oil, 1 tablespoon rice wine or sherry and ½ teaspoon salt in a large mixing bowl. Set aside. While rice is cooking, in a large skillet or wok, heat 2 tablespoons peanut oil over high heat. Stir-fry the beef for 3-5 minutes, until brown. Remove and put into warm dish, keeping warm. Add 1 tablespoon peanut oil to the skillet. Heat. Add crushed red pepper, garlic, gingerroot, sliced red pepper, scallions

(continued)

and stir-fry for 3 minutes. Add the soy sauce, rice wine, sugar, chicken broth and cornstarch mixed with 2 tablespoons water. Stir the sauce to thicken. Return the meat to the pan, heat, and sprinkle in the peanuts. Stir. Put into a serving bowl. Put the rice in another serving bowl. Take some rice and spoon some beef over the rice.

LIVER AND ONIONS

1 lb. calves liver, cut into ¼" thick slices
½ c. flour
½ tsp. salt
½ tsp. pepper

3 T. olive oil
4 slices bacon, cooked crisply
1 recipe Onion Strings in this book

Prepare the Onion Strings and keep warm in a 200° oven. Cook the bacon. Put into the oven. Mix together the flour, salt and pepper. Put on a piece of waxed paper. Coat the slices of liver with the flour. Heat a large skillet. Put in the oil. Heat on medium high heat. Fry the liver until crisp. About 2 minutes each side. Put on serving platter. Lay bacon over the liver and top with the onion strings.

MEATBALLS

1 lb. lean ground round
1 egg
2 large cloves garlic, pressed
¼ c. chopped fresh Italian parsley
¼ c. freshly grated Parmesan cheese

1½ tsp. salt
1 tsp. pepper
2 slices bread which have been soaked in water briefly and the water has been squeezed out
4 T. olive oil

Mix all ingredients thoroughly in a bowl. Shape into 12 balls. Heat frying pan. Add 4 tablespoons olive oil. When oil is heated add meatballs. Brown on all sides over medium heat, turning over. Lower the heat to low, cover and cook for 25 more minutes, turning now and then.

MEAT LOAF

1½ lb. ground round
1 T. oil
1 c. chopped onion
1 clove garlic, pressed
1 T. minced fresh Italian parsley
4 slices white bread, soaked in ¼ c. milk briefly and the milk squeezed out
½ tsp. basil
¼ tsp. thyme
¼ tsp. chervil
2 eggs
⅛ tsp. cloves
1 tsp. salt
1 tsp. pepper

Heat oven to 350°. Mix all ingredients together thoroughly. Put into a 9" x 5" x 4" loaf pan. Put into oven and bake one hour. Pour off any liquid. Let set for 20 minutes, put onto serving platter and slice.

MONGOLIAN BARBEQUE

Meats, Turkey and Vegetables:

1 lb. fresh pork loin, sliced thinly
1 lb. beef sirloin, sliced thinly
1 lb. turkey breast, sliced thinly
2 green peppers, thinly sliced
1 bunch scallions cut into ¼" pieces
1 large onion, thinly sliced
3 carrots, thinly sliced
3 stalks celery, thinly sliced
2 c. fresh bean sprouts
½ head white cabbage, shredded
8 c. cooked rice

Condiments:

½ c. vinegar
½ c. cooking sherry
3 tsp. tabasco sauce diluted with ½ c. water
¼ c. lemon juice diluted with ¼ c. water
½ c. rice wine
½ c. soy sauce
1 c. oil

It is easier to slice the meats and turkey when they are partially frozen. Using a sharp knife, slice the meats and put each one on a separate dish. Refrigerate each one after slicing. Prepare the vegetables and put each kind in a separate dish. Put each of the condiments into separate bowls, labeling what is in each. Heat the grill with lots of charcoal as the fire should be very hot. While the grill is heating, cook the rice and put into a large serving bowl. Arrange the meats, vegetables and bowls of condiments attractively on a table. Each guest takes a plate and makes selections of meats, vegetables and teaspoons of desired sauces, which are sprinkled over the meats and vegetables.

(continued)

The filled plates are taken to the grill and put into a pan set over the coals. First, the meats are stir-fried for a few minutes, with the condiments, then the vegetables are added to the meat and stir-fried a little longer. The cooked food is returned to the plate to which rice has been added.

PEPPER STEAK

1½ lb. boneless sirloin cut into 2½" x ¼" slices

3 c. cooked rice

Marinade:

1½ tsp. salt
1 T. blended whiskey
1 tsp. finely minced gingerroot
1 tsp. sugar
1 tsp. soy sauce

1 T. oyster sauce
1 T. cornstarch
1 tsp. sesame oil
½ tsp. white pepper

For Cooking:

4 T. peanut oil
1 slice fresh gingerroot
3 large green peppers, thinly sliced

4 T. black beans, mashed with 4 cloves garlic, pressed

Sauce:

2 T. cornstarch
1 T. oyster sauce
2 tsp. dark soy sauce
½ clove garlic, pressed

½ tsp. sugar
½ tsp. salt
¼ tsp. white pepper
1 c. water

Meat will be easier to slice if it is partially frozen. For marinade, combine salt, whiskey, gingerroot, sugar, soy sauce, oyster sauce, cornstarch, oil and pepper in a large pie plate or shallow glass dish. Add steak slices, coat and let the meat stand 1 hour. Heat 1 tablespoon peanut oil with slice of gingerroot in wok or large skillet. Add pepper strips and stir-fry one minute. Remove peppers to small bowl. Heat wok or skillet with remaining 3 tablespoons peanut oil and black bean/garlic paste and cook until lightly browned. Add marinated beef in a thin layer. Cook, stirring from side to side to brown meat. Remove meat. Set aside. For the sauce, combine the cornstarch, oyster sauce, dark soy sauce, garlic, sugar, salt, white pepper and water. Stir well. Pour into wok,

(continued)

stirring continuously until mixture comes to a boil. Return beef and peppers to wok. Mix well, heat until piping hot. Serve with rice.

POT ROAST

4-5 lbs. boneless chuck or rump roast
2 T. flour
4 T. olive oil
3 cloves garlic, pressed
1 medium onion, chopped
2 carrots, cut into thirds
1 stalk celery, cut into fourths
1 tsp. thyme
1½ tsp. salt
½ tsp. pepper
½ c. dry, red wine
1 c. tomato juice

Heat oven to 325°. Heat a skillet. Put 2 tablespoons oil into the skillet and heat. Rub the flour all over the roast. Brown the roast on all sides and put into a baking casserole with a cover. Put the onion and garlic in the skillet and brown. Add the 2 tablespoons oil and the carrots, celery, thyme, salt, pepper, wine and tomato juice. Cook for 10 minutes. Pour over the roast and cover the roast. Put into the oven and bake for three to four hours, until tender. Serve with mashed potatoes.

ROAST BEEF

1 standing rib roast, at least 4 lbs.
2 T. Kosher salt
2 tsp. black pepper

Heat oven to 500°. Sprinkle Kosher salt mixed with the black pepper on on a sheet of waxed paper. Roll the roast in it to coat with the salt and pepper. Insert a meat thermometer into the meatiest part of the meat, but don't let it touch the bone. Put the roast, standing on its ribs, fat side up, in an open roasting pan. Roast, uncovered, in oven for 15 minutes to seal in the juices. Lower the heat to 325°. The meat thermometer will register 140° for rare; 160° for medium; 170° for well done. The meat will continue cooking when removed from the oven for a few minutes, so don't let it cook longer than you would like. Let it rest for 15 minutes before slicing. Serve with Roasted Potatoes (recipe in this book).

SAUERBRATEN

5-6 lb. bottom round of beef
3 garlic cloves, cut into slivers
1 medium onion, thinly sliced
2 c. water
2 c. wine vinegar
½ lemon, sliced and seeded
6 peppercorns
2 bay leaves
4 whole cloves
2 chopped onions
½ c. butter
1 carrot, finely chopped
2 T. tomato paste
¼ c. sugar
dash of paprika
¼ c. flour
1 c. sour cream
⅛ tsp. ground ginger
2 T. molasses

With a knife, make several ½" slits in the beef. Insert slivers of garlic into the slits. Put the meat into a large bowl and cover with onion slices. In a sauce pan, boil the water, wine vinegar, lemon slices, peppercorns, bay leaves and cloves. Pour over meat. Cover meat and refrigerate at least 24 hours, turning as it marinates. Heat oven to 325°. In a skillet, sauté 2 chopped onions in ¼ cup butter. Remove meat from marinade, and dust meat with flour. Push onions aside and brown meat. Put the meat into a baking dish with a cover. In the skillet, add marinade, 1 carrot, finely chopped, 2 tablespoons tomato paste, ¼ cup sugar and a dash of paprika. Pour over meat. Cover and bake 3-4 hours or until tender. Remove to heated platter. In a skillet melt ¼ cup butter and add the flour. Make a roux by stirring with a whisk. Slowly add 2 cups of the juices, stirring. Add ⅛ teaspoon ground ginger and 2 tablespoons molasses. Heat and stir until thickened. Add 1 cup sour cream. Heat, but do not boil. Season with salt and pepper and serve with meat. Serve with Dumplings. (Recipe is in this book.)

SAVORY SPANAKOPITAS

¾ c. butter
1 c. chopped onions
2 T. butter
1½ lb. ground beef
1 pkg. (10 oz.) frozen chopped spinach, thawed and drained
⅓ c. minced fresh Italian parsley
⅓ c. chopped fresh dill or 1 tsp. dried
½ tsp. pepper
½ tsp. grated lemon zest
¼ tsp. salt
½ lb. crumbled feta cheese
2 eggs, beaten
16 sheets filo dough

Heat oven to 375°. Squeeze water out of spinach. Sauté onion in 2 tablespoons butter. Add beef, breaking up, and brown. Add spinach,

(continued)

parsley, dill, pepper, lemon peel and salt. Simmer 2-3 minutes. Remove from heat. Add eggs and mix. Add feta and mix again. Butter a 13" x 9" baking dish. Melt the ¾ cup butter. Place a sheet of filo in baking dish. Brush with butter. Stack 7 more sheets on top, brushing each with butter. Spoon in mixture. Cover with remaining filo, brushing each sheet with butter. Tuck edges of filo under. Brush top with butter. Gently cut through top layers to mark pieces, first by drawing horizontal lines, and then crossing between the lines with diagonal lines. Bake 40-45 minutes. Cut all the way through the scored lines.

SESAME BEEF

1½ lb. sirloin steak, sliced into ⅛" thick slices
2 cloves garlic, pressed
1 T. peanut oil
1 T. rice wine vinegar
½ tsp. salt
½ tsp. pepper
2 T. sesame seeds
1 T. sugar
1 T. peanut oil
1 T. cornstarch
¼ c. soy sauce
¼ c. rice wine
1 T. sesame oil
¼ c. peanut oil for cooking
2 red peppers, thinly sliced
½ lb. asparagus, tough ends removed and cut the asparagus in half
½ tsp. crushed red pepper
5 scallions, chopped
1 T. minced fresh gingerroot
3 c. cooked rice

Put beef into freezer for 45 minutes first. It's easier to slice. Put the sliced steak in a bowl. Mix together the garlic, 1 tablespoon peanut oil and 1 tablespoon rice wine vinegar. Pour over beef and toss. Marinate overnight in refrigerator. Remove from refrigerator. Cook the rice following the directions on the package. Add sesame seeds, sugar and 1 tablespoon peanut oil to the beef. Toss. In a small bowl, combine 1 tablespoon cornstarch, ¼ cup soy sauce, salt, pepper, ¼ cup rice wine and sesame oil. Set aside. Heat a wok or a large skillet. Put in 2 tablespoons peanut oil and heat over high heat. Add the beef in two batches, stir-frying quickly and turning to brown. Remove the first batch and put into a warmed platter. Add the second batch and stir-fry quickly, turning to brown. Remove and put onto platter. Add 2 tablespoons peanut oil to the pan. Heat and fry the peppers and asparagus 2 minutes. Stir the small bowl of cornstarch, soy sauce salt and pepper, rice wine and sesame oil. Add to the hot pan, lower the heat and add the red pepper, scallions and gingerroot. Cook until bubbly. Return the beef to the pan. Cook 2 minutes and serve in a bowl alongside the rice.

SHORT RIBS ROGER

8 short ribs, approximately 4" long
¼ c. flour
1 tsp. salt
1 tsp. black pepper

¼ c. oil
1 large onion, chopped
1 bay leaf
½ c. water
1 tsp. Kitchen Bouquet

Heat the oven to 350°. Heat a large skillet. Put in ¼ cup oil. Heat the oil. Put the flour in a brown paper bag. Shake the ribs, 2 at a time, in the flour and put into the hot oil. Brown on all sides. Put into a casserole or a baking pan. Sprinkle with salt and pepper. Sauté the onion in the same skillet until golden. Add the water and Kitchen Bouquet. Stir and pour over meat. Add the bay leaf. Cover and cook 2 hours. Take the cover off and cook 15 minutes longer.

STEAK AUDREE

¼ lb. butter
¼ c. minced onion
⅛ tsp. pepper
1 clove garlic, minced
¼ c. dry, white wine
1 T. minced fresh Italian parsley
2 T. olive oil

4 3-oz. slices of beef tenderloin
1 8-oz. pkg. frozen artichoke hearts, cooked
8 large shrimp, peeled, deveined and cooked
1 baguette (purchased or use recipe in this book)

Melt butter in heated skillet. Add onion and sauté until transparent. Add pepper, garlic, wine and parsley. Cook over moderate heat, stirring, 2 minutes. Refrigerate for 24 hours. When you are ready to assemble dish, Cook the artichoke hearts according to package directions. Drain and set aside. Peel, devein and cook shrimp in boiling water until it turns pink. Drain and set aside. Turn on oven broiler. Heat refrigerated sauce in a small skillet. Set aside. Coat beef with olive oil. Put on broiling pan and broil for 7 minutes per side. Lower oven to 350°. Arrange the meat in two ovenproof serving dishes. Arrange 4 shrimp around the meat in each and split the artichoke hearts between the two dishes. Pour half the sauce over each. Bake, uncovered, for five minutes. Serve with bread to dunk in sauce. Serves 2.

STEAK DIANE

To make sauce:

2 T. butter
2 tsp. shallots, chopped
6 large mushrooms, sliced
¼ c. brown sauce
½ c. heavy cream

1 T. minced fresh Italian parsley
½ tsp. salt
½ tsp. pepper
¼ c. Madeira Wine

To prepare meat:

4 filets of tenderloin
a few grains salt
freshly ground black pepper

2 T. butter
2 oz. brandy
Kitchen Bouquet

Make Brown Sauce. Melt butter in a skillet. Add shallots and mushrooms. Cook until mushrooms are soft. Add Brown Sauce and cream. Cook until bubbly. Add parsley, salt and pepper. Set aside. Just before serving, add ¼ cup Madeira Wine. To prepare meat, brush meat with Kitchen Bouquet and allow to dry 10 minutes. Melt butter and sauté meat on both sides over high heat. Sprinkle with brandy and ignite. Sprinkle with a few grains salt and freshly ground black pepper. Cover with sauce.

Brown Sauce:

¼ c. butter
3 T. flour
2 chopped medium onions
2 finely chopped carrots
1 leek, minced (optional)
2 stalks celery, finely sliced
¼ tsp. thyme

4 c. beef stock
2 T. tomato paste
½ tsp. salt
½ tsp. pepper
1 bay leaf
¼ tsp. savory

Melt the butter in a skillet. Heat and add the onions, carrots, leek and the celery. Sauté until tender, about 10 minutes. Add the flour and stir. Add the thyme, beef stock, tomato paste, salt, pepper, bay leaf and savory. Simmer for 30 minutes over low heat. (Leftover Brown Sauce may be frozen.)

STEAK WITH OYSTERS

4 8-oz. tenderloin steaks
12 medium fresh oysters
½ tsp. salt
½ tsp. pepper

4 T. butter
1 T. minced shallots
1 T. minced fresh Italian parsley
4 slices bacon

Insert a sharp knife into the side of each steak and make a pocket. Heat 2 tablespoons butter in a skillet. Sauté the oysters with the salt and pepper and some of the oyster liquid only until the edges begin to curl. Drain. Stuff each steak with three oysters, wrap each steak around the edges with a slice of bacon and secure with a toothpick. Broil in the oven for about 7 minutes each side. Heat 2 tablespoons butter in another skillet. Add the shallots and parsley. Sauté until the shallots are soft. Pour over the cooked steaks. Serves 4.

STUFFED FLANK STEAK

1½ c. toasted bread cubes
½ c. finely sliced celery
½ c. chopped onions
¼ lb. fresh mushrooms, sliced
1 tsp. salt
½ tsp. pepper

2 T. butter, melted
1 T. olive oil
1 2-lb. flank steak, scored
  diagonally on both sides
½ c. beef broth

Heat oven to to 450°. Heat a skillet. Melt 2 tablespoons butter and heat. Add the celery, onions, and mushrooms. Cook, stirring, until onions are tender, about 5 minutes. Put into a mixing bowl. Add the bread cubes, salt, pepper and 1 tablespoon olive oil. Mix. Heap the mixture onto the flank steak. Fold the edges, one over the other, secure with toothpicks and tie with kitchen string. Put the steak, folded side down, in a baking pan. Add ½ cup beef broth or 1 bouillon cube dissolved in ½ cup water to the pan. Put flank steak in the oven and bake, uncovered, for 10 minutes. Lower the heat to 350°, cover and bake for 2 hours. Uncover, baste with the juices and cook 10 minutes longer.

SUKIYAKI

1 lb. beef tenderloin, sliced very thin
½ c. soy sauce
¾ c. canned chicken broth
3 T. sugar
2 T. vegetable oil
3 c. Chinese cabbage (about ½ head), shredded
12 scallions, cut into ½" lengths
2 medium Spanish onions, cut in half lengthwise, then into ¼" slices
1 c. sliced fresh mushrooms
4 stalks celery, sliced diagonally in thin strips
1 5-oz. can bamboo shoots, drained
1 6-oz. can water chestnuts, drained and halved
½ lb. tofu, cut into cubes
1 can bean sprouts, drained or 1 lb. fresh
3 c. spinach, washed and dried, then sliced thinly
3 c. cooked rice

Cook rice following instructions on package directions. Combine soy sauce, broth and sugar. Mix well and set aside. Heat 2 tablespoons oil in heavy skillet. Add cabbage, scallions, onions, mushrooms, celery, bamboo shoots, water chestnuts, tofu and bean sprouts. Stir together. Pour soy sauce mixture over vegetables. Cook over high heat 8 minutes. Push vegetables to side of pan. Add meat and spinach. Simmer 2 minutes, stirring and browning meat. Mix everything together and cook 2 minutes longer. Serve with cooked rice. Serves 6.

OSSO BUCO ALLA MILANESE

6 meaty veal shanks
⅓ c. flour
½ c. olive oil
1 c. chopped onions
1 c. sliced carrots
1 T. minced fresh Italian parsley
2 stalks celery, sliced
1 clove garlic, pressed
1 c. dry white wine
1 tsp. dried basil
½ tsp. thyme
1 bay leaf
1 tsp. sugar
1½ tsp. salt
½ tsp. black pepper
1 15-oz. can chicken broth
1 28-oz. can San Marzano tomatoes
1 6-oz. can tomato paste
Gremolata
1 recipe Risotto Alla Milanese in this book

Heat the oven to 325°. Rub the veal shanks with flour. Heat a large skillet. Put in the olive oil and heat. Put in the veal shanks and brown on all sides, about 20 minutes. Remove them as they are browned and put into a baking dish in one layer. Add the onions, carrots, parsley, celery and garlic to the skillet. Sauté until the onions are tender, about

(continued)

5 minutes. Add the tomatoes. Crush the tomatoes with a fork or a potato masher. Add the tomato paste and stir. Add the white wine, basil, thyme, bay leaf, sugar, salt, pepper and the chicken broth. Bring to a boil. Turn off heat. Pour mixture over veal shanks. Bake, covered, for 2 hours, turning the shanks over after one hour. Transfer osso buco to serving dish, spreading sauce over top. Sprinkle with Gremolata if you like. Serve with Risotto Alla Milanese recipe in this book.

Gremolata:

1 clove garlic, pressed
1 T. minced fresh Italian parsley
1 tsp. grated orange zest
1 tsp. grated lemon zest

2 T. toasted pine nuts
⅛ tsp. salt
½ tsp. freshly ground pepper

Toast the pine nuts in the oven at 350° for 5 minutes. Mix together the garlic, parsley, orange zest, lemon zest, toasted pine nuts, salt and pepper.

ROAST VEAL

1 3-lb. veal rump roast
2 cloves garlic, slivered
2 T. olive oil

1 T. Kosher salt
black pepper
1 tsp. rosemary

Sauce (optional):

⅓ c. dry white wine

⅓ c. chicken broth

Heat the oven to 450°. Sprinkle the salt on wax paper. Rub the olive oil over the veal. Roll the veal in the Kosher salt. With a sharp knife, make ½" deep slits in several places on the surface of the veal. Push slivers of garlic in the slits. Sprinkle with pepper and rosemary. Insert a meat thermometer into the thickest part of the meat. Put in the oven for 15 minutes at 450°. Lower heat to 325°. Roast until the thermometer registers 165°. Remove the roast to a platter. Cover loosely with aluminum foil and let stand for 15 minutes before slicing. Serve with or without sauce. To make the sauce, set the roasting pan over high heat and pour in the wine and broth. Bring to a boil, scraping up the browned bits with metal spatula. Cook for 1 minute. Season with salt and pepper to taste. Serve in a bowl alongside the roast.

SALTIMBOCCA

12 slices of veal, ½" thick
6 slices thinly sliced prosciutto
6 slices mozzarella cheese, sliced ¼" thick
2 tsp. rubbed sage
½ tsp. salt

½ tsp. black pepper
⅓ c. flour
2 T. butter
2 T. olive oil
½ c. Marsala wine
toothpicks for securing

Put the veal slices between sheets of wax paper and pound them with the flat side of a meat mallet until they are about ¼" thick. Sprinkle some rubbed sage, salt and pepper on six of the slices of veal. Lay one slice prosciutto on the seasoned slices of veal and one slice of mozzarella on top of the the prosciutto. Top each one with the remaining slices of veal and skewer with 4 round toothpicks on the edges and roll in the flour, shaking excess off. Heat the butter and olive oil in a large skillet. Sauté the veal over medium-high heat on both sides until brown, about 8 minutes per side. Remove from pan and place on a warm serving dish. Remove the toothpicks and discard. Add the Marsala wine to drippings in pan, lower heat and simmer until heated, stirring and scraping the bottom of the pan. Pour sauce over veal and serve immediately.

STUFFED VEAL

1 2-lb. boneless veal roast
2 slices white bread
¼ c. milk
1 lb. zucchini
½ c. chopped onion
3 T. olive oil
½ tsp. salt
½ tsp. pepper

2 lightly beaten eggs
¼ c. freshly grated Parmesan cheese
2 T. minced fresh Italian parsley
¼ c. flour
¼ c. butter
¼ c. dry white wine
½ c. chicken broth

Heat the oven to 350°. Slit the veal part way through horizontally so as to form a bag. Soak the bread in the milk. Squeeze and set aside. Cut the zucchini into slices. Heat the oil in a large skillet. Add the onion and sauté over a medium heat until golden. Add the zucchini, season with the salt and pepper, mix well and cook for 15 minutes, stirring and turning now and then. Beat the eggs in a bowl. Scrape the zucchini and onions into the eggs. Stir. Stir in the Parmesan cheese and parsley. Mix in the bread. Stuff the mixture into the pocket in the veal and tie with kitchen string so that no openings remain. Dust the meat with the flour. Melt the butter in a skillet. Add the meat and brown all over. Pour

(continued)

the wine over the veal and simmer until the wine evaporates. Put the veal in a baking dish. Pour the chicken broth in the skillet. Heat the broth and scrape the skillet. Pour over the meat. Cover and bake for 2 hours, until tender.

VEAL BIRDS

1½ lb. veal cutlets
celery stuffing
2 T. butter
1 T. olive oil
½ tsp. salt

½ tsp. black pepper
1 15-oz. can chicken broth
½ c. heavy cream
round toothpicks for securing

Heat oven to 350°. Pound the veal with the flat side of a meat mallet until it is ¼" thick. Spread some of the celery stuffing down the middle of each piece and roll lengthwise. Secure with toothpicks. Melt the butter and oil in a skillet and brown the veal birds on all sides, a few at a time. Transfer to a baking dish, sprinkle with the salt and pepper, and pour the chicken broth over them. Put them in the oven, cover and bake 1 hour. Stir in the cream and bake, uncovered for 20-30 minutes more.

Celery Stuffing:

4 T. butter
1 c. finely sliced celery
4 T. finely chopped onion
4 T. minced fresh Italian parsley

4 c. dry bread crumbs
¼ tsp. black pepper
½ tsp. salt
¼ c. chicken broth

Melt the butter in a skillet. Stir in the celery and onion and sauté for 5 minutes. Remove from the heat and blend in the parsley, bread crumbs, pepper, salt and chicken broth.

VEAL CHOPS

6 loin or rib veal chops, cut 1" thick
2 T. olive oil

2 T. butter, melted
salt
pepper

Turn on the broiler. Mix together the butter and olive oil. Brush the chops with the mixture. Brown the chops quickly near the heat of the broiler. Move them further away from the heat and broil them for 8 minutes on each side. Season with salt and pepper.

VEAL CORDON BLEU

4 slices veal ½" thick
4 thin slices Canadian bacon or baked ham
4 thin slices Muenster cheese
½ c. flour
½ tsp. salt
½ tsp. white pepper

⅛ tsp. thyme
½ tsp. paprika
1 egg, beaten
2 T. milk
1 c. dry bread crumbs
¼ c. olive oil

Pound the veal with the flat side of a meat mallet to ¼" thick. Place a slice of ham and a slice of cheese on top of each piece of veal. Roll up and secure with toothpicks. Mix the flour with the salt, pepper, thyme and paprika. Put into a shallow dish. Mix the beaten egg with the milk. Put into a shallow dish. Put the bread crumbs on wax paper. Dredge the veal rolls in the flour, dip into the egg mixture and roll in the bread crumbs. Heat a skillet. Add the olive oil and heat. Brown veal rolls in hot oil on all sides over medium-high heat. Lower heat to medium and cook, turning, for about 20 minutes.

VEAL MARSALA

1 lb. veal loin, cut into scallops ½" thick
1 tsp. salt
1 tsp. pepper
¼ c. flour

2 T. olive oil
2 T. butter
½ c. dry Marsala wine
½ c. chicken broth

Pound veal with the flat side of a meat mallet to flatten to ¼" thick. Put the flour on wax paper. Dredge the veal in the flour, shaking off excess flour. Heat the oil and butter in a large skillet. Sauté veal on both sides in the hot oil and butter over medium heat. Remove the veal from the skillet and keep warm. Pour the Marsala wine into the skillet. Scrape the skillet and add the chicken broth and stir. Simmer on medium heat for 7 minutes. Add the salt and pepper. Put veal on a warm serving platter and pour sauce over.

VEAL PARMIGIANA

1 recipe Marinara Sauce in this book
1 lb. ¼" thick veal scallopine
¼ c. flour
2 eggs, beaten

1 c. seasoned dry bread crumbs
¼ c. olive oil
8 oz. shredded mozzarella cheese
¼ c. freshly grated Parmesan cheese

Make the Marinara Sauce. Heat oven to 350°. While the sauce is cooking, put the flour on wax paper. Put the beaten eggs in a shallow dish. Put the bread crumbs in a shallow dish. Dip the veal scallopine first in the flour, shaking off excess, then in the eggs, then in the bread crumbs. Lay on the wax paper. Heat a large skillet. Put in ¼ cup olive oil. Heat the oil. Add veal slices, a few at a time, and cook on medium-high heat until golden brown on both sides, 2-3 minutes for each side. Add more oil as needed. Place the veal in a 10" x 6½" x 2" baking dish in a single layer. Add half the Marinara Sauce and half the mozzarella and Parmesan cheeses. Repeat the layers, ending with Parmesan cheese. Cover baking dish with foil. Bake 30 minutes or until bubbly. Makes 4-6 servings.

VEAL PICCATA

1 lb. veal scallopine
¼ c. flour
¼ c. olive oil
½ lb. fresh mushrooms, sliced
1 8-oz. pkg. frozen artichoke hearts

2 T. butter
1 clove garlic, pressed
1 tsp. rubbed sage
⅓ c. brandy
1 tsp. salt
½ tsp. black pepper

Cook the artichoke hearts in boiling water according to package directions. Drain. Heat a skillet. Put 2 tablespoons butter in the skillet and sauté the artichokes for 8-10 minutes. Remove and keep warm. Put the veal slices between sheets of wax paper and pound them with the flat side of a meal mallet until they are about ¼" thick. Put the flour on wax paper and coat the veal, shaking off any excess flour. Add 2 tablespoons oil to the skillet and sauté the veal until golden on each side, about 2 minutes each side. Remove from pan and keep warm. Add 2 tablespoons oil to the pan. Heat the oil and add the mushrooms, garlic, sage, salt and pepper. Sauté over moderate heat for 5 minutes. Add the brandy. Simmer for 4 minutes. Remove the pan from the heat. Put the veal on a hot serving platter. Arrange the artichokes around the veal. Pour the mushroom sauce over all.

VEAL STEW

2 lb. veal shoulder, cubed into 1½" pieces
¼ c. flour
¼ c. butter
2 T. olive oil
1 medium onion, chopped
1 clove garlic, pressed
2 carrots sliced 2" long
2 large potatoes, cubed
1 stalk celery, sliced
¼ c. dry white wine
1 15-oz. can chicken broth
1 tsp. salt
½ tsp. black pepper
2 T. minced fresh Italian parsley
1 bay leaf
½ c. heavy cream

Put the flour on wax paper. Roll the cubed veal in the flour. Heat a large pot. Put in the butter and heat. Add the veal cubes and brown on all sides. Add any remaining flour and stir in. Pour in the chicken broth. Put the heat on low and simmer. In another skillet, put in 2 tablespoons olive oil and heat. Add the onions and garlic. Cook, stirring for 5 minutes. Add the white wine and stir. Cook for 4 minutes. Add to the veal. Add the carrots, celery, potatoes, salt, pepper, parsley and bay leaf to the veal. Simmer, covered, over low heat for 1 hour and 15 minutes, stirring often. Check to see if the veal is tender. If not, cook until tender. Stir in the cream. Bring to a simmer again just to heat the cream. Do not boil.

VITELLO TONNATO

1 4-lb. boned leg of veal, rolled and tied
1 large carrot, pared and sliced
1 celery stalk, sliced
1 T. minced fresh Italian parsley
1 medium onion, peeled and stuck with 2 whole cloves
1 clove garlic, slit in half
1 tsp. salt
Tuna Sauce

Day before serving: In 8-quart kettle, combine the veal, carrot, celery, parsley, onion, garlic and salt with 3½ quarts water and bring to a boil. Reduce heat, and simmer the veal, covered, 1½ hours, or until the meat is tender. Remove the veal from the stock. Let the meat cool, then refrigerate until well chilled. Strain veal stock. Refrigerate and reserve for Tuna Sauce. To serve: Slice veal thinly, Arrange the slices in a row, overlapping each other, in center of a shallow dish. Pour Tuna Sauce over the veal slices. If desired, garnish with anchovy fillets and capers. Makes 12 servings.

(continued)

Tuna Sauce for Vitello Tonnato:

3 7-oz. cans Italian tuna, packed in oil
2 2-oz. cans flat anchovy fillets, drained
1 3¼-oz. jar capers, drained, for garnish
½ c. reserved veal stock
2 c. Hellmann's mayonnaise

Put tuna and anchovies in a mixing bowl. Break up with a fork until the mixture is minced. Dilute with ½ cup veal stock. Put into food processor, half at a time, to purée. If the mixture is too thick, add more stock. Scrape into a bowl. Stir in the mayonnaise, a little at a time. Refrigerate until needed.

BROILED MARINATED LAMB CHOPS

6 loin lamb chops, 1" thick
1 clove garlic, pressed
2 T. fresh lemon juice
½ tsp. paprika
½ tsp. black pepper
½ tsp. salt
1 c. yogurt
¼ c. finely minced onions

Trim fat from chops. Put in a glass baking dish. Sprinkle with lemon juice on both sides. In a small bowl, mix together the garlic, paprika, pepper, salt, yogurt and onions. Pour over lamb chops, turning chops so that they are completed coated. Refrigerate 8 hours or overnight. Broil or grill for 8 minutes on each side.

LAMB CURRY

2½ lb. lamb shoulder
1 medium onion, chopped
1 clove garlic, pressed
4 T. oil
4 tsp. chopped gingerroot
2 tsp. turmeric
2 T. coriander
½ tsp. sugar
½ tsp. pepper
2 tsp. salt
½ tsp. crushed red pepper
2 T. curry powder
1 14½-oz. can diced tomatoes
1 c. cream of coconut
½ c. heavy cream

Cut the lamb into 1" cubes, removing any fat. Heat a large pot and put 2 tablespoons olive oil in the pan. Heat the oil and brown the meat in batches. As the batches are browned, transfer them to a bowl. If necessary, add more oil to the pan. When all the meat is browned, add 2 more tablespoons of oil to the pan and heat. Add the onion and brown. Add the garlic and gingerroot. Fry for another minute. Add the turmeric,

(continued)

coriander, sugar, salt, pepper, red pepper and curry powder. Fry for another minute, stirring with a wooden spoon. Add the tomatoes and cream of coconut. Bring to a boil, reduce heat and return the lamb to the pot. Cover and simmer for 1½ hours, stirring a couple of times. Check to see if meat is tender, if not simmer longer. When the lamb is tender, add the cream to the pot and stir. Heat, but do not boil.

LAMB SHISH KABOBS (SOUVLAKIA)

4 c. cooked Basmati rice
4 lb. leg of lamb, cut into 1½" cubes, and trimmed of fat

Lamb Marinade:

¼ c. olive oil
¼ c. wine vinegar
¼ c. lemon juice
1 garlic clove, pressed

1 tsp. oregano
2 tsp. salt
¼ tsp. black pepper

Vegetables and Marinade:

¼ c. olive oil
1 tsp. salt
½ tsp. pepper
½ tsp. oregano
1 tsp. sugar
3 green peppers, cut into squares

12 mushrooms
3 medium zucchini, cut in half lengthwise and then into large chunks
1 red onion, cut in half, cut each half into fourths

Cook rice following package directions. Prepare marinade by mixing together in a bowl the olive oil, vinegar, lemon juice, garlic, oregano, salt and pepper. Put the lamb cubes in a shallow glass baking dish and pour over the marinade. Toss to coat well. Cover and refrigerate overnight. When you are ready to grill, prepare the charcoal. While the charcoal is heating, prepare the vegetables by mixing together the olive oil, sugar, salt, pepper and oregano in a large bowl. Add the vegetables and toss to coat. Place the vegetables on one set of skewers. Place the lamb on the other set. The lamb will take longer to cook. Grill the lamb for about 7 minutes on each side. Grill the vegetables for about 4 minutes on each side, as desired. Serve on a bed of rice. Place the cooked rice in the center of a large platter. Remove the lamb from the skewers and place on the rice. Remove the vegetables from the skewers and surround the rice with the grilled vegetables.

ROAST LEG OF LAMB

1 6-lb. leg of lamb
2 T. olive oil
2 cloves garlic, slivered
3 T. Kosher salt
1 tsp. pepper
1 T. rosemary

Heat oven to 450°. Coat the lamb with the olive oil. Put the Kosher salt on wax paper. Roll the lamb in the salt and coat well. Sprinkle the lamb with the pepper. With a sharp knife, make ½" slits in several places all over the lamb. Insert slivers of garlic into the slits. Place the lamb in a shallow roasting pan. Sprinkle the lamb with rosemary. Insert a meat thermometer into the meat, but do not let it touch the bone. Roast for 15 minutes, then lower the heat to 350° and roast for two hours more, or until the thermometer reaches 180°.

ROAST RACK OF LAMB

2 3-lb. racks of lamb, trimmed
1 tsp. salt
⅔ c. dry red wine
⅓ c. chicken broth
3 T. honey
½ tsp. dried thyme
¼ tsp. salt
2 tsp. cornstarch
2 T. balsamic vinegar
1 c. dried cherries
1 c. chopped walnuts, toasted

Heat oven to 450°. Wrap exposed bone with aluminum foil to protect from burning and remove foil before serving. Place lamb racks in shallow roasting pan. Sprinkle with 1 teaspoon salt. Insert meat thermometer into thickest part of meat, being sure that it does not touch the bone. Bake for 15 minutes. Lower temperature to 325° and bake for 1 hour, or until the meat thermometer registers 125° for rare, 145° for medium or 175° for well done. Put the lamb on a warm serving platter and keep warm. Let the lamb rest for 10 minutes, covered with foil. Toast the chopped walnuts in the oven for 5 minutes. While the lamb is resting, prepare the sauce by combining the wine, chicken broth, honey, thyme, dried cherries and salt in a saucepan. Bring to a boil. Boil 5 minutes. Combine the cornstarch with the balsamic vinegar, stirring well. Add to the wine mixture. Boil 1 minute. Remove from heat. Add the walnuts to the sauce and serve with the lamb.

BARBECUED SPARERIBS

4 lb. fresh pork spareribs, cut into serving-size pieces

Barbecue Sauce:

¾ c. molasses
¾ c. catsup
¾ c. chopped onion
2 cloves garlic, pressed
⅓ c. orange juice
2 T. olive oil

1 T. salt

1 T. vinegar
½ tsp. dry mustard
½ tsp. salt
½ tsp. pepper
1 tsp. Worcestershire sauce
Dash Tabasco

Use Plum Sauce recipe or Chinese Sauce recipe in this book or use the following recipe: Put 2 tablespoons olive oil in a saucepan. Heat the oil and add the chopped onion. Sauté onion until golden. Add the garlic and cook one minute longer. Add the molasses, catsup, orange juice, vinegar, mustard, salt, pepper, Worcestershire sauce and Tabasco. Bring to a boil. Reduce heat and simmer, uncovered, for 10 minutes. Turn off heat and set sauce aside. Place pork spareribs in large pot with 1 tablespoon salt. Add enough water to cover spareribs. Cover pan and heat to boiling. Reduce heat. Keep covered and simmer for 45 minutes. Drain. Heat oven to 325°. Transfer pork spareribs in a single layer to a shallow roasting pan, meat side up. Spread with 1 cup of the barbecue sauce. Cover and roast for 1 hour. Spread the rest of the sauce on the spareribs and roast, uncovered, 15 minutes longer.

CURRIED LOIN OF PORK

1 3-lb. boned loin of pork
¼ c. olive oil
Mirepoix: 1 large carrot, finely minced, 1 medium onion, finely chopped
Bouquet Garni: 1 bay leaf, ¼ tsp. dried sage

1 tsp. Kosher salt
¼ c. dry white wine
½ c. beef stock
4 T. curry powder

Heat oven to 350°. Heat a large skillet. Put oil in skillet and heat. Brown meat on all sides. Put meat in baking pan. Add mirepoix to skillet and brown vegetables, stirring. Add white wine, beef stock and bouquet garni to vegetables. Heat. Pour vegetable mixture over meat. Sprinkle meat with 1 teaspoon Kosher salt. Put into oven and cook, uncovered, for 2¼ hours, sprinkling the meat with 1 tablespoon curry powder 4

(continued)

times during cooking. Remove meat to serving platter. Mash sauce in baking pan and pour over meat. Serves 6.

GIAMBOTTE (ITALIAN SAUSAGE AND PEPPERS)

2 lb. Italian sausage
¼ c. water
1 14½-oz. can diced tomatoes
1 medium red onion, sliced in half, slice halves into quarters
1 green bell pepper, sliced, then slice the slices in half
2 red bell peppers, sliced, then slice the slices in half
3 T. olive oil
2 T. minced fresh Italian parsley
1 tsp. salt
1 tsp. black pepper
1 tsp. sugar
1 tsp. oregano
½ tsp. crushed red pepper (optional)
½ lb. fresh mushrooms, sliced

Put the sausage and water in a large skillet over medium heat. When the water evaporates, turn the heat down to low and sauté the sausage, turning to brown on all sides. Remove the sausage and set aside. Add 3 tablespoons olive oil to the pan and heat the oil. Add the peppers. Break apart the onions and add, and sauté until browned. Stir in the parsley, salt, pepper, sugar, oregano and crushed red pepper. Slice the browned sausages into 1" pieces at a diagonal. Add the sausage and tomatoes. Simmer, covered, for 20 minutes over medium heat. Stir and add the mushrooms and simmer for 10 minutes longer.

KUNG PAO PORK

1 lb. lean pork tenderloin
½ egg white (beat egg white, then divide in half)
2 tsp. cornstarch
½ tsp. salt
1 red bell pepper
1 green bell pepper
½ small onion
¼ c. soy sauce
⅓ c. chicken broth
½ tsp. salt
1 T. fresh lemon juice
1 tsp. sugar
2 tsp. cornstarch
¼ tsp. crushed red pepper
2 T. olive oil
2 cloves garlic, pressed
¾ c. cashews
2 c. cooked rice

Cook rice following instructions on package and keep warm. Cut pork into ½" cubes. Mix together the egg white, 2 teaspoons cornstarch and

(continued)

salt. Combine with the pork. Refrigerate for 30 minutes. Cut red and green bell peppers and onion into 1" pieces. Combine the soy sauce, chicken broth, salt, lemon juice, sugar and 2 teaspoons cornstarch. Stir until blended and set aside. Pour olive oil into a wok or large skillet, coating sides. Heat to medium-high heat. Add pork and garlic. Stir-fry 3 minutes, browning. Add peppers, onion and crushed red pepper. Stir-fry 3 minutes or until vegetables are tender. Stir soy sauce mixture again. Add to skillet. Stir-fry until thickened, about 3-4 minutes. Stir in cashews. Serve over rice.

MOO SHU PORK

2 T. soy sauce
1 T. dry sherry or rice wine
1 tsp. sesame oil
1½ lb. boneless lean pork, cut into ½" cubes
10 shiitake mushrooms
3 c. shredded Napa cabbage
2 carrots, cut into thin strips 2" long
½ c. scallions, cut into ½" pieces
1 15-oz. can bean sprouts, drained
2 T. peanut oil

2 eggs, lightly beaten with ½ tsp. salt
3 cloves garlic, pressed
3 T. grated gingerroot
¼ c. chicken stock
1 tsp. cornstarch
2 T. soy sauce
1 T. dry sherry or rice wine
2 tsp. sesame oil
Hoisin sauce
1 tsp. sugar
16 6" flour tortillas

Combine the 2 tablespoons soy sauce, 1 tablespoon sherry or rice wine and 1 teaspoon sesame oil in a bowl. Add the pork. Toss to coat evenly. Cover and refrigerate for 30 minutes, turning once. Soak the mushrooms in enough hot water to cover for 20 minutes. Drain and slice thinly. Set aside on a platter with the cabbage, carrots and scallions. Mix together the ¼ cup chicken stock with the 1 teaspoon cornstarch. Set aside. Heat a wok or large skillet over high heat. Add 2 tablespoons peanut oil and swirl to coat the pan. Put in the pork and stir-fry until browned, about 2 minutes. Add the garlic and gingerroot and stir-fry one minute. Add the mushrooms, cabbage, carrots, bean sprouts and scallions. Stir-fry 2 minutes. Add the eggs and stir-fry until the eggs are done. Stir the ¼ cup chicken stock/cornstarch mixture and add. Stir-fry 2 minutes until mixture thickens a little. Stir in the 2 tablespoons soy sauce, 1 tablespoon sherry or rice wine, 2 teaspoons sesame oil, and 1 teaspoon sugar and cook, stirring until sauce boils, about 1 minute. To serve, spread a small amount of Hoisin sauce on a warm flour tortilla.

(continued)

Spoon about ½ cup moo shu mixture in center of tortilla, wrap, folding the ends to close and serve.

PORK SATAY

¼ c. ground almonds
1 clove garlic, pressed
¼ c. soy sauce
3 T. fresh lemon juice
2 T. ground coriander
2 T. finely minced onions
1 T. brown sugar
1 tsp. salt
¼ tsp. pepper
⅛ tsp. cayenne
1½ lb. lean pork
olive oil

The almonds can be ground in a food processor or blender. Mix together the almonds with the garlic, soy sauce, lemon juice, coriander, onions, brown sugar, salt, pepper and cayenne. Cut the pork into 1½" cubes and add to the marinade. Mix well and let stand 3 hours, turning a couple of times. Prepare the charcoal. String the meat on skewers and grill over the charcoal, turning to brown on all sides for 20-25 minutes, or until meat is well done. Baste with a little olive oil.

PULLED PORK

1 4-lb. boneless Boston butt or pork shoulder blade roast
3 cloves garlic, slivered
1 c. lemon juice
½ c. olive oil
3 tsp. Tabasco sauce
1 T. sugar
1 tsp. salt
1 tsp. pepper

Heat oven to 425°. With a sharp knife, make ½" slits in the pork all around at 2" intervals. Push a sliver of garlic in each slit. Heat a large skillet. Add 3 tablespoons olive oil and heat. Brown the pork on all sides. Put on rack in a roaster and roast for 20 minutes. Mix together the lemon juice, remaining olive oil, Tabasco sauce, sugar, salt and pepper. Lower temperature to 325°. Pour ¼ cup of the sauce over the pork. Put ¼ cup water in the roaster. Cover with roaster cover or cover tightly with foil. Baste after two hours with ¼ cup of the sauce. Bake 3-3½ hours, or until meat is tender enough to be shredded easily with a fork. Skim the fat from the pan juices and discard. Mix the remaining sauce with the pan juices. Heat through. Shred the meat into strings with a fork and serve with the sauce made with the pan juices.

ROAST PORK ALLA TOSCANA

1 5-lb. rib or loin roast of pork
3 cloves garlic, halved
1 T. rosemary
1 c. dry white wine

1 c. beef broth
1 T. Kosher salt
1 tsp. pepper

    Heat the oven to 425°. Make slits in the pork with a sharp knife at 2" intervals and insert half cloves of garlic in the slits. Rub the pork with the Kosher salt and pepper. Put the meat thermometer in the thickest part of the pork, but do not let it touch the bone. Put the pork in a roasting pan and sprinkle it with the rosemary. Cook the pork for 15 minutes and reduce the heat to 325°. After the first hour of cooking, add the wine to the juices in the pan, and then baste every 10 minutes. Cook until the meat thermometer reads 185°. Transfer the pork to a hot serving platter and keep warm. Place the roasting pan over medium heat and boil off some of the liquid, being careful not to burn the drippings. Skim off the fat, and add the beef broth. De-glaze the pan by scraping the bottom with a spatula and reduce the stock by $1/4$. Cut the pork into slices on the platter and spoon the sauce over the slices.

ROASTED FRESH HAM

1 bone-in fresh ham with skin left on
1 c. dry white wine
2 cloves garlic, pressed
½ tsp. freshly ground black pepper

1 c. olive oil
⅓ c. wine vinegar
¼ c. fresh lime juice
1 tsp. salt

    Heat oven to 425°. Put a meat thermometer in the ham, but do not let it touch the bone. Roast the ham for 30 minutes and lower the heat to 325°. Roast 1 hour more and baste with ½ cup dry white wine. Roast 30 minutes more and baste with ½ cup dry white wine. Continue roasting and basting with pan drippings, until the thermometer reaches 185°. When the ham is done, remove to a large serving platter, cover loosely with foil and let it sit for 30 minutes before carving. Sauce for Ham: Mix together the garlic, pepper, oil, vinegar, lime juice and salt. Serve the sauce in a bowl alongside the ham.

SAUSAGE

2 lbs. coarsely ground fresh pork butt
3 T. fresh Italian parsley, minced
1 T. fennel seeds
2 tsp. salt
1 tsp. coarsely ground black pepper
2 cloves garlic, pressed
¼ tsp. thyme
3 T. olive oil

In a bowl, combine the ground pork butt, parsley, fennel, salt, pepper, garlic and thyme. Shape into 10-12 patties. Put the oil in a large skillet and add the patties. Fry over moderate heat, browning on each side, for 20 minutes. If you prefer to put the sausage in casings, you will need a meat grinder with a sausage stuffer and sausage casings. Using a yard of casing at a time, work all but a few inches of casing onto the sausage stuffer. Tie a knot at the end of the casing. Feed the meat through the grinder and into the casing. Twist into links and tie with kitchen string. Keep sausage refrigerated until ready to cook. To cook the sausage with casing, put the sausage in a skillet, add ¼ cup of water and cook until the water evaporates. Lower the heat and simmer, turning to brown, for 30 minutes.

STUFFED PORK CHOPS

4 bone-in, center-cut pork loin chops, 1" to 1½" thick
2 T. butter
½ c. chopped onion
¼ c. chopped celery
1 c. toasted bread crumbs
¼ tsp. rubbed sage
1 T. minced fresh Italian parsley
⅛ tsp. thyme
¼ tsp. salt
¼ tsp. pepper
1 T. olive oil
round toothpicks to secure chops
1 T. butter
1 T. olive oil

Heat oven to 350°. Whirl 2 slices of bread in blender and toast crumbs in oven for 10 minutes. Make a pocket in the pork chops by cutting to the bone. Melt the butter in a skillet. Add the onion and celery. Sauté for 5 minutes. Put the onion and celery in a bowl and add the toasted bread crumbs and toss. Mix together in another small bowl the sage, parsley, thyme, salt and pepper. Pour the seasonings over the stuffing mixture. Toss. Add 1 tablespoon olive oil and mix together. Put one fourth of the stuffing in each chop. Close the openings with toothpicks. Heat 1 tablespoon butter and 1 tablespoon olive oil in a large skillet. Add the chops and brown on both sides. Lower the heat and simmer slowly for one hour, adding water to the pan if necessary so

(continued)

they do not get dry, and turning now and then. Cook longer if they are not tender, adding water if necessary.

CHICKEN AMANDINE

2 c. finely sliced raw breast of chicken
¼ c. peanut oil
3 5-oz. cans bamboo shoots, drained
2 c. diced celery
1 c. diced bok choy
2 5-oz. cans water chestnuts, drained and sliced
1 tsp. minced gingerroot
½ c. slivered almonds
2 T. soy sauce
3 c. chicken broth
¼ c. cornstarch
½ c. cold water
¼ c. whole toasted almonds
4 c. hot cooked rice

Cook rice following instructions on package. Heat a large skillet. Put ¼ cup peanut oil in the pan and heat. Add the chicken and cook, stirring, about 10 minutes. Add the bamboo shoots, celery, bok choy, water chestnuts, gingerroot and slivered almonds. Cook and stir 1 minute. Stir in broth and soy sauce and reduce heat. Cover and cook until vegetables are crisp-tender, about 5 minutes. Stir cold water and cornstarch together and gradually stir into chicken mixture. Heat to boiling, stirring constantly until mixture thickens. Put into serving dish and top with whole toasted almonds. Serve alongside a bowl of rice.

CHICKEN BAKED WITH PARMESAN CHEESE

1 3-lb. broiler-fryer chicken, cut up, with breast cut into fourths
½ c. flour
1 c. freshly grated Parmesan cheese
½ c. seasoned bread crumbs
1 tsp. salt
1 tsp. paprika
1 tsp. oregano
½ tsp. pepper
2 eggs, beaten with 2 tsp. water
2 T. olive oil

Heat oven to 375°. Put the ½ cup of the flour into a brown paper bag. Shake the chicken pieces in the bag, a few at a time, and shake off excess flour. Lay the pieces on wax paper as they are coated with flour. Mix together the bread crumbs, Parmesan cheese, salt, paprika, oregano and pepper. Dip the floured chicken pieces in egg mixture, then in the Parmesan mixture. Put on a rack in a roasting pan. Sprinkle with the olive oil. Bake for 1 hour.

CHICKEN CACCIATORE WITH POLENTA

5 lbs. broiler-fryer chicken, cut up, with breast cut into fourths
½ c. flour
3 T. olive oil
2 T. butter
1½ c. chopped onion
½ c. dry red wine
1 28-oz. can tomatoes
1 6-oz. can tomato paste
¼ c. minced fresh Italian parsley
1½ tsp. salt
1 tsp. oregano
½ tsp. basil
½ tsp. pepper
2 cloves garlic, pressed
1 bay leaf
½ c. fresh mushrooms, sliced
2 carrots, each cut into fourths
1 green pepper, sliced
1 red pepper, sliced
1 recipe Polenta in this book

Heat oven to 350°. Put the flour in a brown paper bag. Shake the chicken pieces in the bag to coat, shaking off excess flour. Lay the chicken pieces on wax paper. Heat a large skillet or Dutch oven on top of the stove. Put in the oil and butter and heat. Brown the chicken pieces on all sides until golden, about 20 minutes. Remove from skillet. Add the onion, mushrooms, carrots, garlic and peppers to the same skillet and sauté for 10 minutes. Mash the tomatoes in a shallow dish and add to the vegetables. Stir in the tomato paste, wine, parsley, salt, oregano, basil, pepper and bay leaf. Cook, stirring, until the mixture comes to a boil. Add the chicken pieces, mixing in. Turn the heat down to low, cover the pan and simmer for 10 minutes. Keep covered and bake for 1½ hours. Check to see if the chicken is tender. While the chicken is cooking, prepare the Polenta. Serve the chicken in a large serving bowl and the polenta in another. Spoon some of the polenta onto dinner plates and spoon some chicken and sauce over the polenta.

CHICKEN IN CREAMED COCONUT SAUCE

2 whole boneless chicken breasts, each cut into 4 pieces
½ c. olive oil
½ c. finely chopped onions
3 garlic cloves, pressed
4 tsp. finely chopped gingerroot
2 tsp. ground cardamom
¼ tsp. ground cloves
1 cinnamon stick, 3" long
½ c. slivered almonds
½ c. cream of coconut
¼ tsp. turmeric
½ tsp. crushed red pepper
2 tsp. Kosher salt
¼ c. heavy cream
1 T. ground coriander
2 c. cooked Basmati rice

Heat the oil in a large skillet on medium heat. Add the onions and cook until limp. Add the garlic and gingerroot. Cook for 1 minute more.

(continued)

Add the cardamom, cloves, and cinnamon stick and cook about 4 minutes. Add almonds and cook, stirring, for 2 minutes. Push this mixture aside and add chicken to the pan. Cook on both sides, for about 2 minutes. Add cream of coconut, turmeric, red pepper and salt and bring to a boil. Reduce heat, add coriander, and simmer, covered, until the chicken pieces are thoroughly cooked and tender, about 30 minutes. Stir and turn the chicken now and then. Stir in the cream and turn off the heat. Let the dish rest, covered, for 1 hour. Heat before serving, but do not boil. Transfer to serving dish. Put the cooked Basmati rice in a bowl and serve alongside the chicken.

CHICKEN WITH CREAMY SWISS CHEESE SAUCE

¼ c. flour
2 tsp. salt
1 tsp. paprika
12 half chicken breasts, skinned and boned
¼ c. butter
2 T. olive oil
¼ c. water

2 tsp. cornstarch
¼ c. cream
1 c. sour cream
¼ c. dry sherry
1 tsp. lemon zest
1 tsp. lemon juice
1 c. shredded Swiss cheese

On a piece of wax paper, mix together the flour, salt and paprika. Roll the chicken in the mixture. Heat a large skillet. Add the butter and olive oil and heat. Lightly brown the chicken on both sides. Add ¼ cup water to the skillet, lower the heat and simmer, covered, 35 minutes until tender, turning to cook evenly. Test chicken with a fork to see if it is tender. Heat oven to 350°. Put chicken on a shallow glass baking dish. Mix together the cornstarch with ¼ cup cream. Stir into drippings in skillet. Cook, stirring, over low heat. Gradually stir in sour cream, sherry, lemon zest and lemon juice, stirring until thickened. Pour over chicken. Sprinkle with the cheese. Put into oven until cheese melts.

CHICKEN CREOLE

1 3½-lb. broiler-fryer chicken, cut up
¼ c. all-purpose flour
¼ c. olive oil
1 T. olive oil
1 green pepper, chopped
1 c. chopped onion
1 clove garlic, pressed
1 bay leaf
1 tsp. thyme
1 16-oz. can tomatoes, mashed
1 6-oz. can tomato paste
¼ lb. cooked ham, cubed
1 tsp. salt
1 tsp. Tabasco sauce
½ lb. smoked sausage, sliced
3 c. cooked rice

Heat oven to 325°. Put the flour in a brown paper bag. Shake the chicken pieces in the bag, a few at a time, and shake off excess flour. Heat a large skillet. Put the ¼ cup olive oil in the skillet and heat. Brown the chicken on all sides and put the chicken in a baking pan. Add 1 tablespoon olive oil to the skillet and heat. Sauté the pepper, onion and garlic for 5 minutes. Add the bay leaf, thyme, mashed tomatoes, tomato paste, ham, salt and Tabasco sauce. Heat, stirring. Pour over the chicken. Cover the chicken and bake for 2 hours. Cook the rice following instructions on package. Slice the sausage into ½" pieces. Add the sausage and cooked rice and bake, covered, for 30 minutes longer.

CHICKEN CROQUETTES

¼ c. butter
¼ c. flour
1 tsp. salt
1 c. milk
2 c. finely diced cooked chicken
½ c. grated onion
2 tsp. fresh lemon juice
2 T. minced fresh Italian parsley
½ tsp. white pepper
½ tsp. savory
1 egg, beaten with 1 tsp. water
⅔ c. dry bread crumbs
⅓ c. vegetable oil

Melt butter and blend in flour and salt. Stir in milk gradually and cook, stirring, until mixture thickens. Cook over low heat 3 minutes. Cool. Stir in chicken, onion, lemon juice, parsley, white pepper and savory. Chill for 1 hour. Roll mixture into 8 balls. Dip first in egg beaten with water and then in bread crumbs. Heat oil in skillet or electric frying pan to 375°. Fry croquettes, turning, until brown on all sides.

CHICKEN FRIED

3½ lb. cut-up chicken, the breast cut into fourths
1½ c. buttermilk
1 tsp. salt
½ tsp. black pepper

2 c. all-purpose flour
2 tsp. salt
1 tsp. black pepper
Crisco shortening for frying

Mix together the buttermilk, teaspoon salt and ½ teaspoon black pepper in a large bowl. Put the chicken pieces in the mixture and toss to coat well. Cover the bowl and refrigerate overnight, or at least 2 hours. Mix together the 2 cups flour, 2 teaspoons salt and 1 teaspoon black pepper. Put into a brown paper bag. Shake the chicken pieces in the bag, a few at a time, to coat and shake off the excess. Put chicken on a rack to dry about 20 minutes. Put 1" of shortening into 2 cast iron pans or a large electric skillet. Heat to 350°. Lay the pieces of chicken in the fat, skin side down, and cover. Cook for 10 minutes. Turn the chicken pieces with tongs and cook on the other side 10 minutes more. Turn again and cook 5 more minutes each side. Remove the chicken to a rack to drain.

CHICKEN KIEV

½ lb. butter softened
2 T. fresh lemon juice, strained
1 tsp. tarragon
½ tsp. salt
¼ tsp. pepper
8 boneless chicken breast halves
round toothpicks for securing
2 c. unseasoned dry bread crumbs

1 tsp. salt
1 tsp. black pepper
2 large eggs beaten with 2 tsp. water
½ c. all-purpose flour
½ c. vegetable or olive oil
Pam for spraying

Cream together in a bowl the butter, lemon juice, tarragon, ½ teaspoon salt and ¼ teaspoon pepper. Shape the butter into a rope, 8" long, on a piece of wax paper. Roll up the wax paper around the roll and refrigerate for 2 hours. Pound each piece of chicken breast with the flat side of a meat mallet until all pieces are ¼" thick. Season each with salt and pepper. Cut the butter into 8 pieces, 1" each. Lay each piece of chicken on a work surface. Place one piece of butter on each piece. Roll up and wrap the chicken around the butter and secure with toothpicks, being sure there is no opening. Mix together the bread crumbs, salt and pepper and put into a shallow dish. Put the flour on wax paper. Put the egg mixture in a shallow dish. Roll the chicken first

(continued)

into the flour, shaking off any excess, then into the egg mixture and then into the bread crumbs. Put the chicken on a plate and refrigerate for 2 hours, or overnight if you want to prepare it to this point a day ahead. Heat oven to 350°. Heat a large skillet. Put in ½ c. vegetable or olive oil. Heat the oil and sauté the chicken for 3 minutes on each side. Transfer to a baking sheet which has been sprayed with Pam and bake for 25-30 minutes. Serve immediately.

CHICKEN QUESADILLA

6 6" flour tortillas
½ c. shredded Monterey Jack cheese
½ c. shredded Colby cheese
1 16-oz. can refried beans (or use Refried Beans recipe in this book)
1 c. finely chopped, cooked chicken
2 T. finely sliced scallions
2 T. oil
8 oz. sour cream
2 ripe avocados, mashed with 1 tsp. lemon juice

Heat the refried beans in a skillet. Spread each tortilla with some of the beans. Mix chicken with the scallions. Divide mixture among the tortillas. Mix the Monterey Jack and Colby cheeses together. Divide among the tortillas. Heat a skillet. Heat 1 tablespoon oil. Cook quesadillas, one at a time, over medium heat about 4 minutes, until the cheese begins to melt and the bottom of the tortilla is lightly browned. Add more oil to pan as needed and heat oil before adding tortillas. Put tortillas on a plate. Top with mashed avocado mixture and then sour cream.

CHICKEN AND SAUSAGE

¼ c. olive oil
1 c. chopped onion
1 red pepper, sliced
1 tsp. oregano
4 boneless chicken breasts, sliced in half
2 lb. hot Italian sausage links
2 c. dry white wine
½ lb. fresh mushrooms, sliced
1 tsp. salt
1 T. flour
¼ c. chicken broth

Heat a large skillet. Add ¼ cup olive oil and heat. Brown sausage and chicken, turning, to brown on all sides. Stir in wine, bring to a boil and lower heat. Cover and simmer until the chicken pieces are tender, about 1 hour. Transfer to a bowl and keep warm. In the same skillet, add the peppers, onions and oregano. Brown the vegetables over low heat for 10 minutes. Mix together the flour and chicken broth. Add to

(continued)

the mixture, stirring. Add the sliced mushrooms. Cook 10 minutes longer. When the vegetables are tender, season with salt. Return the browned sausages and chicken, heat through. Arrange chicken, sausage and vegetables on platter. Pour sauce over.

CHICKEN SCALLOPS

12 boneless, skinned chicken breast halves
1 tsp. salt
1 tsp. pepper
3 eggs, beaten with 3 tsp. water
½ c. butter
½ c. olive oil
½ c. flour
1 c. unseasoned dry bread crumbs
lemon wedges

Place chicken on sheets of waxed paper. Sprinkle with a few drops of water and cover with another sheet of waxed paper. Pound chicken with flat side of a meat mallet until each piece is about ¼" thick. Remove paper. Sprinkle with salt and pepper. Put flour on wax paper. Put beaten egg mixture in a shallow dish. Put bread crumbs in a shallow dish. Dip chicken in flour, then egg mixture, then bread crumbs. Heat half of the butter and half of the olive oil in a large skillet over medium heat. Sauté chicken pieces in butter and oil until golden brown on both sides. Add more butter and oil if necessary. Serve with lemon wedges.

CHICKEN TANDOORI

1 3-4 lb. chicken, cut into pieces, the breast cut into fourths
1½ tsp. ginger
⅛ tsp. coriander
¼ tsp. pepper
½ tsp. cinnamon
½ tsp. ground cardamom
1 T. ground turmeric
1½ tsp. salt
1 tsp. ground cumin
⅛ tsp. cayenne
2 cloves garlic, pressed
1 c. grated onion
½ pt. yogurt
½ c. heavy cream

Combine the ginger, coriander and pepper. Rub into the chicken pieces. Place chicken in shallow open roasting pan. Combine the cinnamon, cardamom, turmeric, salt, cumin, cayenne, garlic, onion, yogurt and cream. Pour the marinade over the chicken and allow to marinate, covered and refrigerated, for several hours or overnight. Heat oven to

(continued)

375°. Roast the chicken 1 hour, uncovered, basting often, with the sauce in the pan.

CHICKEN TENDERS WITH HONEY MUSTARD

4 skinless, boneless chicken breasts
1 c. all-purpose flour
½ tsp. salt
¼ tsp. pepper

1 c. buttermilk
oil for frying
1 c. honey
¼ c. Dijon mustard

Cut the chicken into ½" x 2" strips. Blend honey and mustard in a small bowl and set aside. Place the buttermilk in a shallow dish. Mix together the flour, salt and pepper in a shallow dish. Dip chicken in buttermilk, shaking off excess. Roll chicken in flour mixture to coat well. Place chicken on wax paper. Heat a skillet or an electric frying pan. Pour 1" of the oil in the skillet or electric frying pan. Heat to 375°. Fry the chicken in batches by placing a layer of chicken in the skillet at a time. Fry, turning once, for about 4 minutes on each side or until golden brown and crisp. Drain on paper towels. Add more oil as needed and heat to 375° before cooking next batch. Serve with the honey mustard sauce.

CHICKEN WITH TOMATO/SOUR CREAM SAUCE

1 3½-lb. fryer-broiler, cut up, the breast cut into fourths
¼ c. olive oil
½ c. chopped onion
2 cloves garlic, pressed
¼ c. minced fresh Italian parsley
2 T. flour

2 tsp. salt
1 tsp. pepper
1 14½-oz. can diced tomatoes
1 c. sour cream
½ c. freshly grated Parmesan cheese

Heat oven to 350°. Heat a large skillet. Put in the olive oil and heat. Add the chicken pieces and brown. Remove chicken and transfer to a baking dish. Cook onion, garlic and parsley in drippings for 5 minutes. Blend in flour, pepper and salt. Stir. Add tomatoes and mix well. Pour sauce over chicken and bake, covered, 1½ hours. Stir in the sour cream and Parmesan cheese. Serve hot.

CHICKEN AND WALNUTS

2 c. shredded Chinese cabbage
1 c. celery, diced
1 c. sliced onions
1 7-oz. can sliced water chestnuts, drained
3 T. peanut oil
1¾ c. walnuts, broken
1½ lb. skinless, boneless chicken breasts

1 tsp. salt
2 T. cornstarch
2 T. soy sauce
1 tsp. sugar
2 T. dry sherry
3 T. peanut oil
½ c. chicken broth
3 c. cooked rice

Cook rice following instructions on package. Cut chicken into ½" thin strips, 3" long. Mix together salt, cornstarch, soy sauce, sugar and sherry. Set aside. Heat a large skillet or wok. Put in 3 tablespoons peanut oil and heat. Sauté the cabbage, celery, onions and water chestnuts to crisp-tender. Remove to a bowl. Brown walnuts and add to vegetables. Add 3 more tablespoons peanut oil to skillet or wok and heat. Sauté chicken until tender. Push chicken aside, stir cornstarch mixture again and add to pan. Cook a minute and gradually add chicken broth. Heat, stirring, until thickened. Return vegetables and walnuts to skillet or wok. Stir. Serve with rice.

HONEY-BASTED CHICKEN BREASTS

3 whole chicken breasts, boned, with skin on, cut in half
½ c. honey
¼ c. fresh lime juice
¼ c. salad oil

1 medium-size onion, finely diced
1 tsp. salt
1 tsp. pepper
Pam for spraying

Mix honey, lime juice and oil until well blended. Add onion and pour over chicken. Marinate ½ hour. Remove chicken from marinade and place on a broiler rack sprayed with Pam. Sprinkle with salt and pepper. Broil 7" from broiler to avoid scorching, turning frequently. Baste with honey mixture several times during broiling. Broil for 10 minutes each side and pierce with a fork to check to see if chicken is tender. Serve with Curried Avocado Dip.

Curried Avocado Dip:

2 c. diced ripe Haas avocados
2 tsp. fresh lime juice
2 tsp. sugar
⅛ tsp. salt

⅛ tsp. Tabasco sauce
¼ c. heavy cream
¼ c. pineapple juice
½ tsp. curry powder

(continued)

Mash avocados to a fine paste. Add lime juice, sugar, salt, Tabasco sauce, cream, curry powder and pineapple juice. Mix until well blended. Chill.

KUNG PAO CHICKEN

Main Ingredients:

- 4 chicken breast halves, boned, skin removed
- ½ egg white (beat egg white lightly, then divide it in half)
- 2 tsp. cornstarch
- ½ tsp. salt

- 4 T. peanut oil
- 2 medium carrots, sliced
- 1 medium green pepper, sliced
- 1 medium onion, sliced
- 1 10-oz. pkg. snow peas, thawed

Sauce and Condiments:

- 2 T. bean sauce
- 1 T. hoisin sauce
- 2 cloves garlic, pressed
- 1 tsp. chile paste with garlic
- 1 T. minced fresh gingerroot
- 1½ tsp. sugar
- 1 T. dry sherry
- 1 tsp. sesame oil

- 1 T. red wine vinegar
- 3 T. oyster sauce
- ½ c. chicken broth
- 2 T. soy sauce
- 2 tsp. cornstarch
- 6 dried, hot red chiles
- 1 c. shelled, unsalted peanuts
- 3 c. cooked rice

Cook rice following instructions on package. Cut the chicken into ½" cubes. Mix together the egg white, cornstarch and salt. Combine with the chicken. Refrigerate for 30 minutes. Combine the bean sauce, hoisin, garlic, chili paste with garlic, gingerroot, sugar, sherry, sesame oil, wine vinegar, oyster sauce, chicken broth, soy sauce and cornstarch in a small bowl. Set aside. Heat 2 tablespoons of the oil in a wok or skillet. Add the peanuts. Sauté the peanuts until they are light golden brown. Remove with slotted spoon and drain on paper towels. Add the chicken mixture. Cook about 5 minutes, stirring, until the chicken becomes translucent. Do not brown. Remove the chicken and drain well. Add 2 more tablespoons of the peanut oil to the skillet and heat. Add the carrots, green peppers, onion and snow peas to the wok or skillet and cook until crisp tender, about 3 minutes. Add the sauce, hot red chiles and the chicken and cook until it bubbles. Pour into a serving bowl. Sprinkle with the peanuts. Put the cooked rice in a bowl alongside the chicken.

PARTY CHICKEN BREASTS

8 chicken breasts, skinned and boned
8 slices bacon
1 jar dried sliced beef
1 10¾-oz. can cream of mushroom soup

16 oz. sour cream
½ lb. sliced fresh mushrooms
round toothpicks for securing

Heat oven to 325°. Mix together the mushroom soup, sour cream and mushrooms. Pour on bottom of 15" x 9" x 2" baking dish. Lay out the chicken breasts on a work surface. Lay 3 or 4 slices of beef on each breast. Roll up and wrap a slice of bacon around chicken breast and secure with a toothpick. Place chicken breasts on sauce and bake for 2 hours, uncovered. Baste occasionally.

ROAST CHICKEN

1 3½ lb. broiler-fryer
2 cloves garlic, sliced
salt and pepper for sprinkling

1 T. Kosher salt
1 T. olive oil
1½ tsp. rosemary

Heat oven to 350°. Spread the slices of garlic around the cavity of the chicken. Sprinkle the cavity with salt and pepper. Rub the olive oil all over the chicken. Sprinkle the chicken with Kosher salt and then with rosemary. Put into a roasting pan, cover and bake for 1½ hours. Uncover and bake ½ hour longer, basting with pan juices a few times. Let the chicken rest for 10 minutes before carving.

SESAME CHICKEN

1 lb. chicken breasts, skinned and boned
1 tsp. salt
2 T. soy sauce
2 T. maple syrup

2 T. dry sherry
½ tsp. finely minced gingerroot
½ tsp. Chinese five-spice powder
2 T. vegetable oil
2 T. sesame seeds

Cut each breast in half lengthwise and thinly slice crosswise into ½" strips. In a shallow baking dish, stir together salt, soy sauce, maple syrup, sherry, gingerroot, five-spice powder and oil. Add chicken pieces and turn to coat evenly. Cover and refrigerate at least 2 hours, or up to 8 hours, turning occasionally. Preheat oven to 400°. Sprinkle chicken

(continued)

pieces with sesame seeds. Bake, uncovered, about 20-25 minutes, or until chicken is cooked. Baste occasionally with marinade. Remove from oven and serve on a platter.

STUFFED CHICKEN BREASTS

4 whole chicken breasts
2 c. toasted bread cubes
1/3 c. chopped celery
1/3 c. chopped onion
2 T. butter
1/2 tsp. rubbed sage

1/2 tsp. salt
1/2 tsp. pepper
2 T. minced fresh Italian parsley
4 T. olive oil
Kosher salt for sprinkling
Pam for spraying

Heat oven to 350°. In a skillet, melt the butter. Add the celery and onions and sauté for 5 minutes. Put the toasted bread cubes, celery and onion mixture, rubbed sage, salt, pepper and parsley in a bowl with 2 tablespoons olive oil. Toss. Fill each chicken breast cavity with 1/4 of the mixture. Spray a baking dish with Pam. Put the chicken breasts, stuffed side down, in the baking dish. Rub some olive oil on each chicken breast and sprinkle some Kosher salt on each one. Bake, uncovered, for 1 1/2 hours.

ROAST DUCK

1 5-6 lb. duck
1/2 tsp. salt

1/2 tsp. pepper
water

Heat oven to 450°. Rub the inside of the duck with salt and pepper. Prick the skin of the duck all over, at an angle, so as not to pierce the meat. This allows the fat to run out as the duck cooks. Place the duck breast side up on a rack in a shallow roasting pan and roast for 45 minutes. Turn the duck breast side down and roast for 45 minutes longer. Pour off fat. Turn the duck breast side up again after the second 45 minutes of roasting and insert a meat thermometer into the thigh, but do not let it touch the bone. Roast the duck for 1 hour, basting every 15 minutes, and then spray ice water on the duck and roast another 15 minutes. When the meat thermometer reads 180° in the thigh, it is done. The duck will be crispy. Eat without sauce if you like. If you like an orange sauce, use the following recipe. Or you may use the recipe for Chinese Sauce in this book. The Chinese Sauce is basted on during last hour of cooking.

(continued)

Orange Sauce:

1 tsp. butter	**zest of ½ orange**
2 tsp. brown sugar	**¼ tsp. salt**
¼ c. orange juice	**¼ tsp. black pepper**
1 c. chicken broth	
2 T. Grand Marnier or any sweet orange liqueur	

Melt butter in a skillet on medium heat, then add sugar and stir until well blended. Add orange juice, chicken broth, Grand Marnier and orange zest to mixture, stirring until well blended. Reduce by simmering on medium heat until sauce is thick enough to coat duck. Season with salt and pepper.

Recipe Favorites

Recipe Favorites

Fish
Seafood

My Brother Nello

Helpful Hints

- Never overcook foods that are to be frozen. Foods will finish cooking when reheated. Don't refreeze cooked, thawed foods.
- When freezing foods, label each container with its contents and the date it was put into the freezer. Always use frozen, cooked foods within 1–2 months.
- To avoid teary eyes when cutting onions, cut them under cold running water or briefly place them in the freezer before cutting.
- Fresh lemon juice will remove onion scent from hands.
- To get the most juice out of fresh lemons, bring them to room temperature, and roll them under your palm against the kitchen counter before cutting and squeezing.
- Add raw rice to the salt shaker to keep the salt free flowing.
- Transfer jelly and salad dressings to a small plastic squeeze bottle – no more messy, sticky jars!
- Ice cubes will help sharpen garbage disposal blades.
- Separate stuck-together glasses by filling the inside glass with cold water and setting both in hot water.
- Clean Corning Ware® by filling it with water and dropping in two denture cleaning tablets. Let stand for 30–45 minutes.
- Always spray your grill with nonstick cooking spray before grilling to avoid sticking.
- To make a simple polish for copper bottom cookware, mix equal parts of flour and salt with vinegar to create a paste.
- Purchase a new coffee grinder and mark it "spices." It can be used to grind most spices. However, cinnamon bark, nutmeg, and others must be broken up a little first. Clean the grinder after each use.
- In a large shaker, combine 6 parts salt and 1 part pepper for quick and easy seasoning.
- Save your store-bought-bread bags and ties—they make perfect storage bags for homemade bread.
- Next time you need a quick ice pack, grab a bag of frozen peas or other vegetables out of the freezer.

Fish/Seafood

BAKED SNAPPER

1 2-lb. whole red snapper, cleaned, boned and head removed
1 tsp. ground ginger
1 tsp. salt
1 tsp. black pepper
1 onion, sliced into rings
1 T. rice wine
1 T. soy sauce
1 tsp. brown sugar
2 T. peanut oil

Heat oven to 350°. Score the fish on both sides diagonally in one direction, then in the opposite direction to give a diamond pattern. In a small bowl, mix together the ginger, salt and pepper. Rub into both sides of fish and sprinkle a little on the inside of fish. Place a piece of foil large enough to enclose the fish on a baking sheet. Arrange the onion on the foil and top with the fish. Mix together the rice wine, soy sauce, brown sugar and oil and pour over the fish. Seal seams tightly. Bake for 30 minutes. Check to see if fish flakes when pierced with a fork. If so, it's done. Put the fish on a serving platter and pour over the cooking juices.

BAKED STUFFED SEA BASS

1 8-lb. striped bass, cleaned and deboned
½ c. melted butter
¼ c. lemon juice
1 c. chopped onions
¼ c. butter
2 c. toasted bread cubes
1 c. shredded carrot
¼ lb. fresh mushrooms, chopped
½ green pepper, chopped
2 T. minced fresh Italian parsley
1 clove garlic, pressed
2 tsp. salt
½ tsp. pepper
½ tsp. marjoram
2 T. olive oil
Pam for spraying
skewers or round toothpicks
kitchen string

Heat oven to 350°. Rub cavity of fish with salt and pepper. Heat ¼ cup butter in a skillet. Sauté the onions, carrot, mushrooms, peppers, parsley and garlic for 5 minutes. Mix together in a bowl with the bread cubes, salt, pepper, marjoram and oil. Stuff the cavity of the fish. Close the opening with skewers or round toothpicks and lace the skewers or toothpicks with kitchen string. Spray baking pan with Pam. Put fish in baking pan. Brush fish with oil. Spoon any extra stuffing in baking dish. Mix ½ cup melted butter and ¼ cup lemon juice. Cook fish, uncovered,

(continued)

brushing occasionally with butter mixture, until fish flakes easily with a fork, about 1½ hours.

BROILED SALMON

2 lb. salmon fillet
2 T. butter, melted
2 T. lemon juice
½ tsp. dill weed
salt
pepper
Pam for spraying

    Heat the broiler. Place the salmon, skin side down, on a broiler pan sprayed with Pam. Brush the salmon with the butter and sprinkle with lemon juice. Sprinkle the dill weed over. Put 7" inches under broiler and broil for 10 minutes. Check thickest part to see if it is flaky. If it is, then it's done. Sprinkle with salt and pepper. Serve plain or with Hollandaise Sauce or Tartar Sauce (recipes in this book).

COD

2 lb. cod
2 c. water
2 T. dry white wine
2 T. lemon juice
2 T. olive oil
1 clove garlic, pressed
2 T. minced fresh Italian parsley
2 T. dry white wine
1 14½-oz. can diced tomatoes
1 tsp. basil
1 tsp. oregano
1 tsp. salt
1 tsp. pepper
1 T. black olives, sliced

    Slice the cod across the fillet into 3" pieces. Put water, 2 tablespoons wine and lemon juice in a skillet and bring to a boil on high heat. Reduce heat and add the cod. Simmer, covered, for 6 minutes. Remove cod from skillet and keep warm. Pour off liquid from skillet and discard. Put the olive oil in skillet and sauté the garlic and parsley for one minute. Add 2 tablespoons wine, tomatoes, basil, oregano, salt and pepper. Simmer for 15 minutes. Add the cod and cook 4 minutes longer. Put the cod on a serving dish. Pour the sauce over and top with the olives.

CRAB CAKES

2 lb. crabmeat
4 slices bread
1 T. Old Bay seasoning
¼ c. minced fresh Italian parsley
2 eggs, beaten
½ tsp. Tabasco sauce
½ c. Hellmann's mayonnaise
2 T. fresh lemon juice
¼ tsp. salt
¼ tsp. pepper
¼ c. olive oil

Whirl the bread in blender to make crumbs. Mix together the Old Bay seasoning, parsley, Tabasco sauce, mayonnaise, lemon juice, salt and pepper. Beat the eggs and stir in. Break the crab into lumps about half the size of a walnut and add to the mixture. Mix together. Stir in the bread crumbs. Form into patties. Cover and refrigerate a few hours. Heat a skillet. Add 2 tablespoons olive oil and heat. Fry the patties, in batches, for 4 minutes on each side so they become golden brown. Add more olive oil if necessary, but be sure oil is heated before adding more patties.

DOVER SOLE IN LEMON BUTTER

2 lb. Dover sole fillets
½ tsp. pepper
½ tsp. salt
¼ c. flour
¼ c. corn oil
2 T. butter
¼ c. butter
juice of ½ lemon

Lightly flour fish, shaking off excess. Heat a skillet. Heat the corn oil and 2 tablespoons butter. Sauté fish over medium heat, turning, for about 3 minutes per side. You may have to cook in two batches, add more butter, if necessary. Heat the butter before you put the fish in. Put sole onto a serving platter, keeping platter warm in 200° oven. For the lemon butter, melt the ¼ cup butter, stir in the lemon juice, salt and pepper, heat slightly, and blend well. Pour over sole.

FRIED CALAMARI WITH SAUCE

1½ lb. calamari, cleaned
1½ c. all-purpose flour
1 lemon
2 tsp. salt

1 c. corn oil for cooking
1 c. olive oil for cooking
3 eggs, beaten until frothy

For the tomato sauce:

1 36-oz. can San Marzano tomatoes
¼ c. extra virgin olive oil
2 cloves garlic, pressed
½ c. chopped onion

½ tsp. sugar
1 tsp. salt
1 tsp. pepper
2 T. minced fresh Italian parsley
½ tsp. crushed red pepper flakes

Cut the calamari into ½" thick rings. Squeeze the lemon into a bowl of cold water, add the 2 teaspoons salt and the calamari, and soak for ½ hour. Meanwhile, prepare the sauce. Heat the olive oil in a saucepan. Sauté the onion for 3 minutes. Add the garlic and sauté the onion and garlic 1 minute. Add the tomatoes and mash with a fork or a potato masher. Add the salt, pepper, sugar, parsley and crushed red pepper flakes. Lower the heat and simmer for 20 minutes, uncovered. Remove the calamari from the water and drain, rinse under cold water and pat dry thoroughly with paper towels. Heat 1" of the vegetable oil and olive oil in a deep fryer or a skillet or electric frying pan to 375° (medium heat). Beat the eggs in a small bowl until frothy. When the oil is hot, put the calamari in a large colander, pour the flour over the calamari. Toss, coating thoroughly, and shake off excess flour. Dip in the beaten eggs, shake, then add to the hot oil. Add enough calamari to the pan so there is only one layer. Cook on one side for 1 minute, turn and cook on the other side for about 3 minutes. Use a slotted spoon to transfer them to a platter lined with paper towels. Keep warm in a 200° oven until all are done. Be sure to bring the oil to 375° before adding the next batch. Add more oil to the pan if necessary, but heat to 375°. When the tomato sauce is cooked, put into a serving bowl. Set the platter of fried calamari beside it. Serve hot.

FRIED SMELT

2 lb. fresh smelt
1 c. olive oil for frying
1 c. vegetable oil for frying

batter for dipping
salt for sprinkling
lemon slices, if desired

Prepare the batter. Heat 1" of the olive oil and the vegetable oil in a skillet or electric frying pan to 375°. Dip the smelt in the batter, shaking

(continued)

off excess and fry the smelt in the hot oil in one layer for about 3 minutes per side, until batter is golden. Be sure to bring oil to 375° before adding next batch. Add more oil if necessary, but be sure to bring it to 375° before adding fish. Transfer to a platter lined with paper towels and sprinkle with salt. Serve with lemon slices.

Batter:

1 c. all-purpose flour
¼ tsp. salt
¼ tsp. ground pepper
2 T. olive oil

3 egg yolks
1 c. water
1 tsp. baking soda
3 egg whites, stiffly beaten

Beat the egg whites until stiff and set aside. Mix together the egg yolks, oil, water, salt, pepper, baking soda and flour. Fold in egg whites.

FRITTO MISTO

¼ lb. orange roughy, cut into ½" strips
¼ lb. shrimp, cleaned, shelled and deveined
¼ lb. calamari, cleaned and cut across body into ½" circles
¼ lb. scallops
2 medium zucchini, cut into 3" x ½" strips

1 c. broccoli flowerets
¼ lb. mushroom caps
1 green or red bell pepper, cut into strips
1 8-oz. pkg. frozen artichoke hearts, thawed
oil, for frying (½ olive oil, ½ vegetable oil)
lemon wedges

Prepare the batter. Heat oil 2" deep in a skillet or electric frying pan to 375°. Dip the assorted seafood and vegetables in the prepared batter and shake off any excess batter. Cook in batches, turning, until crisp and golden. Lift out with a slotted spoon and drain on paper towels. Be sure oil is heated to 375° before putting in next batch. Keep warm in 200° oven until everything is cooked. If you need to add more oil, be sure it heats to 375°. Serve with lemon wedges.

Batter:

1 c. all-purpose flour
¼ tsp. salt
¼ tsp. ground pepper
2 T. olive oil

3 egg yolks
1 c. water
1 tsp. baking soda
3 egg whites, stiffly beaten

Beat the egg whites until stiff and set aside. Mix together the egg yolks, oil, water, salt, pepper, baking soda and flour. Fold in egg whites.

HALIBUT FLORENTINE

4 halibut steaks
2 10-oz. pkgs. frozen chopped spinach
1 tsp. grated lemon zest
2 slices onion
2 tsp. minced onion
2 slices lemon
pinch salt
6 peppercorns
1 bay leaf

5 T. butter
3 T. flour
½ tsp. salt
⅛ tsp. white pepper
⅛ tsp. dry mustard
1 c. milk
½ c. reserved fish stock
2 hard-cooked eggs, diced
freshly grated Parmesan cheese for sprinkling

Heat oven to 350°. Put the halibut In a large skillet with enough water to cover the halibut and add 2 slices of lemon, 2 slices of onion, 1 bay leaf, a pinch of salt and 6 peppercorns. Bring water to a boil. Lower heat and simmer, covered, until halibut is opaque through when flaked, about 8 minutes. Remove halibut steaks. Strain the stock through cheesecloth and reserve ½ cup. Cook spinach according to package directions and drain. Press out excess water. Add lemon zest, 2 teaspoons minced onion and 2 tablespoons butter to a skillet, along with the spinach, and heat gently, stirring, until butter melts. Set aside. In a 1-quart saucepan, melt remaining butter. Stir in flour, salt and pepper and mustard until blended. Gradually stir in milk and reserved fish stock with a whisk, keeping smooth. Cook until bubbly and thickened. Stir in hard-cooked eggs. Divide spinach mixture among 4 individual ovenproof serving dishes, or you may bake everything in one baking dish. Place halibut over spinach. Spoon egg sauce over halibut. Sprinkle with Parmesan cheese. Tightly cover each oven-proof serving dish or the baking dish with foil. Bake for 15 to 20 minutes. Uncover and brown briefly under broiler. Serves 4.

JAMBALAYA

- ¼ c. olive oil
- 1 lb. andouille sausage, cut into slices
- 1 3-lb. chicken, cut into pieces, with the breast cut into 4 pieces
- 1 lb. shrimp, peeled and deveined
- 1 dozen shucked oysters, with their juices
- 2 c. chopped onion
- 3 ribs celery, sliced
- 1 large green bell pepper, chopped
- 3 cloves garlic, pressed
- 1 15-oz. can diced tomatoes
- 2 T. tomato paste
- 2 bay leaves
- ¾ c. chopped green onions
- ¼ c. minced fresh Italian parsley
- ¼ tsp. cayenne pepper
- 2 tsp. salt
- 1 tsp. black pepper
- 2 tsp. thyme
- 1 T. basil
- 1 T. oregano
- 2 T. paprika
- 2 T. dried onion flakes
- 2 c. uncooked rice
- 6 c. water

Heat the oil in a large saucepan. Sauté the chicken, turning to brown, and cook over low heat, covered, for 30 minutes. Add the sausage and sauté the sausage for about 15 minutes, turning, and stirring now and then. Remove the chicken and sausage with a slotted spoon and set aside. Add the onion, celery, green pepper and sauté for 15 minutes, stirring now and then. Push the vegetables aside and add the garlic. Sauté for one minute. Add the diced tomatoes, tomato paste, bay leaves, chopped green onions, parsley, cayenne pepper, salt, black pepper, thyme, basil, oregano, paprika and dried onion flakes and cook for 10 minutes. Return the chicken and sausage to the pan. Stir. Add the shrimp, rice and water and stir well. Simmer, covered, until the rice is cooked. Add the oysters, cover, and cook for 5 minutes. Turn the heat off. Keeping the cover on, let it sit for 10 minutes.

KUNG PAO SHRIMP WITH CASHEWS

- 1½ lb. shrimp, shelled and deveined
- ¼ c. orange juice
- 3 T. red wine vinegar
- 2 T. soy sauce
- 2 tsp. sugar
- 2 tsp. cornstarch
- 2 T. corn oil
- 1 small onion, cut in half and then quartered
- 2 tsp. grated gingerroot
- 2 cloves garlic, pressed
- ½ tsp. crushed red pepper flakes
- 1 tsp. salt
- 1 red bell pepper, cut into strips
- 1 c. roasted cashews
- 1 tsp. sesame oil
- 2 cups cooked rice

(continued)

Cook rice following instructions on package. In a small bowl, mix together the orange juice, vinegar, soy sauce, sugar and cornstarch. Set aside. Heat a wok or large skillet, add the 2 tablespoons corn oil and heat over medium-high heat. Add the onion, gingerroot, garlic, crushed red pepper flakes and and salt and stir-fry 30 seconds. Add the red bell pepper strips and cook until crisp-tender, about 1-2 minutes. Add the shrimp and stir-fry until it turns pink, about 5 minutes. Stir the orange juice mixture and add to the wok or skillet. Stir until slightly thickened, about 1 minute. Stir in the cashews and sesame oil. Put into serving bowl and put alongside bowl of rice. Serves 4.

LOBSTER IN THE MOON

1 2-lb. lobster, extracted from its shell by splitting it lengthwise and removing the meat, and cut into chunks
½ tsp. salt
½ tsp. pepper
1 T. extra virgin olive oil
1 T. butter
1 T. finely chopped shallots or fresh chives
½ clove garlic, pressed

½ c. cognac
½ c. dry white wine
1 14½-oz. can diced tomatoes, drained
1 T. minced fresh Italian parsley
⅛ tsp. cayenne
1 T. butter
1 T. flour
½ c. cream
10 sheets phyllo pastry sheets
½ c. melted butter for brushing

Heat oven to 400°. In a 7" x 10" baking dish, layer 5 sheets of phyllo pastry, brushing each one with butter. In a large skillet, heat the 1 tablespoon olive oil and 1 tablespoon butter. Sauté the lobster, shallots, parsley and garlic for 2 minutes. Add the cognac and wine. Add the diced tomatoes, cayenne, salt and pepper. Turn heat down and simmer for 15 minutes. Remove the lobster with a slotted spoon and put into the baking dish (the "moon") which has been lined with the phyllo sheets. In a small saucepan, melt 1 tablespoon butter and add 1 tablespoon flour to the butter, stirring until it forms a paste. Add the sauce from the saucepan in which the lobster was cooked and stir until bubbly and slightly thickened. Add ½ cup cream and stir. Pour over lobster and cover with 5 sheets of phyllo pastry, brushing each one with butter. Turn in the edges of the phyllo pastry and brush with butter. Put into the oven and bake for 10 minutes.

LOBSTER THERMIDOR

2 1½ or 2-lb. lobsters, boiled
¼ c. butter
1 c. sliced mushrooms
½ tsp. paprika
½ tsp. salt
½ tsp. pepper
½ c. sherry

2 T. flour
2 c. cream
2 egg yolks
¼ c. soft breadcrumbs
¼ c. freshly grated Parmesan cheese

Whirl 1 slice bread in blender to make soft bread crumbs. Fill a pot with enough water to cover the lobsters. Bring the water to a boil and then drop in the lobsters. Cook for 12 minutes. Remove from pot and drain. Split the boiled lobsters lengthwise of shell and remove all lobster meat. Cut the lobster meat into chunks. Rinse out shell and dry. Set aside. Heat oven to 400°. Heat the butter and sauté the mushrooms for 3 minutes. Add the salt, pepper and flour, stirring, to form a paste. Add the sherry, stirring with a whisk until smooth. Add the egg yolks and stir. Slowly stir in the cream. Add the lobster meat. Mix well. Put the lobster shells in a shallow pan. Fill the lobster shells with the mixture, sprinkle with the breadcrumbs and Parmesan cheese. Then sprinkle with paprika. Bake 15 minutes. Serve immediately.

LUTEFISK

2 lb. lutefisk
½ tsp. salt

½ tsp. pepper
½ c. melted butter

Soak lutefisk in cold water overnight in the refrigerator. Rinse and drain. Cut in serving-size pieces and place in cheesecloth. Tie the cloth together. Bring a large pot of water to a boil. Put the lutefisk in the boiling water and cook for 5 minutes or until fish is tender. Drain water. Remove lutefisk from cheesecloth and put on paper towels until water is absorbed, then put on a serving platter. Pour hot butter over and sprinkle with salt and pepper.

NORWEGIAN CREAMED HERRING

12 small salt herring fillets
1½ c. milk
2 T. finely chopped onion
½ c. sour cream

½ c. mayonnaise
2 bay leaves
6 peppercorns
¼ tsp. salt

(continued)

Soak the herring in milk for 4 hours. Drain, dry the herring and remove the bones and discard. Blend together the onion, sour cream, mayonnaise, bay leaves, peppercorns and salt. Fold in the herring. Marinate in the refrigerator overnight.

OYSTER FRITTERS

36 oysters, rinsed and shucked
3 lemons, quartered
oil for frying
1 c. all-purpose flour
¼ tsp. salt
¼ tsp. ground pepper

1 T. corn oil
3 egg yolks
1 c. water
1 tsp. baking soda
3 egg whites, stiffly beaten

Make the batter: Beat the egg whites until stiff and set aside. Mix together the egg yolks, oil, water, salt, pepper, baking soda and flour. Fold in the beaten egg whites. Set aside. Put the shucked oysters and their liquid into a saucepan and add ¼ cup water. Bring to a boil over medium heat, and remove from the stove. Allow them to cool in the cooking liquid. Drain and pat dry with paper towels. Pour oil to 1" deep in a skillet or an electric frying pan and heat to 375°. Dip oysters in batter, shaking off excess, and fry, turning, until golden brown. Keep them warm in a 200° oven until all are done. If you are frying them in batches, be sure the oil heats to 375° until you put in the next batch. Put them on a serving platter and garnish with the lemon quarters.

SALMON PIE

1 recipe Pie Crust for two-crust pie in this book
1 16-oz. can red salmon, drained and bones removed
2 medium-size potatoes, boiled, peeled and diced
1 tsp. salt

1 tsp. pepper
½ c. heavy cream
¼ c. chopped onion
3 T. butter
1 egg yolk mixed with 2 tsp. water
1 egg white

Heat oven to 375°. Melt the butter in a small skillet. Add the onion and sauté for 5 minutes. Mix together the diced boiled potatoes, salt, pepper, heavy cream and onion. Flake the salmon and fold into the mixture. Roll out bottom pie crust and place into a 9" pie plate. Brush bottom crust with egg white. Spread mixture over pie crust. Roll out top pie crust and place over mixture. Trim ends and seal by fluting between

(continued)

your fingers and thumb. Mix egg yolk and water together. Brush some over top of pie. Prick top of pie with a fork to let air escape. Put into oven and bake for 40-50 minutes, or until crust is golden.

SALMON, POACHED

1 3-lb. piece of salmon fillet
1 carrot, sliced in half
½ medium onion, sliced
1 bay leaf
6 peppercorns
1 tsp. salt
2 sprigs fresh Italian parsley

Rinse fish and dry. Combine the carrot, onion slices, bay leaf, peppercorns, salt and parsley in an oval fish cooker or frying pan large enough to accommodate fish. Add 4 cups water and bring to a boil. Lower heat and simmer 15 minutes. Add fish and cover. Simmer 25 minutes or until fish flakes easily. Serve with Tartar Sauce recipe or Hollandaise Sauce recipe in this book.

SAUTÉED SHRIMP

2 T. butter
3 T. extra virgin olive oil
2 lb. large shrimp, shelled and deveined
½ tsp. salt
¼ tsp. black pepper
2 cloves garlic, pressed
¼ c. minced fresh Italian parsley
¼ c. dry white wine

Heat butter and 2 tablespoons oil in a skillet. Sauté shrimp over medium heat about 5 minutes, stirring and turning over until the shrimp turn pink. Sprinkle shrimp with salt and pepper and place on a hot serving plate. Add 1 tablespoon olive oil to the skillet and heat. Add garlic and parsley to skillet. Sauté for about 1-2 minutes. Do not let garlic get brown. Add wine and cook for 5 minutes. Pour over shrimp.

SHRIMP CREOLE

5 lb. shrimp, shelled and deveined
½ lb. diced bacon
3 green peppers, finely chopped
3 onions, finely chopped
2 cloves garlic, pressed
3 c. celery finely chopped
½ c. minced Italian parsley
1 36-oz. can San Marzano tomatoes
1 6-oz. can tomato paste
1 tsp. sugar
1 tsp. black pepper
1 tsp. salt
1 bay leaf
1 tsp. curry powder
1 tsp. thyme
1 tsp. crushed red pepper flakes
5 cups cooked rice

Cook rice following instructions on package. Cook diced bacon in a skillet until crisp. Remove from pan and set aside. Sauté peppers, onions, garlic, celery and parsley in bacon drippings. Add tomatoes, tomato paste, sugar, pepper, salt, bay leaf, curry powder, thyme and red pepper flakes, stirring and mashing tomatoes with a fork or a potato masher. Cook, covered, for 20 minutes. Add shrimp and cook, stirring, now and then, 20 minutes more. Serve with rice.

SHRIMP CURRY

2 lb. shrimp, shelled and deveined
2 medium onions, chopped
½ c. finely diced celery
1 green bell pepper, chopped
2 cloves garlic, pressed
2 T. olive oil
2 T. butter
2 T. flour
1 tsp. salt
1 tsp. black pepper
2 T. minced fresh cilantro
1 T. cumin
1 tsp. ground coriander
1 tsp. ground turmeric
1 tsp. curry powder
½ tsp. crushed red pepper flakes
1 14½-oz. can diced tomatoes
½ c. heavy cream
5 cups cooked rice

Cook rice following instructions on package. Heat the oil and butter in a large skillet. Add the onions, garlic, celery and bell pepper. Sauté over low heat, covered, about 15 minutes, stirring now and then. Add the flour and stir. Add the salt, pepper, cilantro, cumin, ground coriander, ground turmeric, curry power and red pepper flakes. Add the tomatoes and cook over low heat, covered, stirring now and then, until the tomatoes are very soft, about 15-20 minutes. Add the shrimp and cook until shrimp is pink. Stir in the heavy cream. Add more salt if necessary. Serve over hot rice.

SHRIMP ÉTOUFFÉE

2 lb. shrimp, peeled and deveined
½ c. sliced andouille or smoked sausage
1 tsp. salt
½ tsp. black pepper
½ tsp. crushed red pepper flakes
1 large onion, chopped
½ c. finely chopped celery
¼ c. finely chopped green bell pepper
¼ c. finely chopped red bell pepper
1 tsp. dried thyme
½ tsp. basil
2 cloves garlic, pressed
¼ c. olive oil
1 16-oz. can chicken broth
3 T. tomato paste
1 T. cornstarch
3 cups cooked rice

Cook rice following instructions on package. Heat the olive oil in a large saucepan. Add the onion, celery, green and red peppers and sauté for 20 minutes over low heat, stirring. Push the vegetables aside and add the garlic and sauté one minute longer. Mix the cornstarch with ¼ cup chicken broth and add to the vegetables. Stir. Add the remaining chicken broth, stirring until mixture gets a little thickened. Add the thyme, basil, tomato paste, salt, pepper and red pepper flakes. Stir. Add the sausage and simmer for 25 minutes. Add the shrimp and simmer, uncovered, stirring, until shrimp is pink. Serve with the cooked rice. Serves 4.

STIR-FRY SHRIMP AND VEGETABLES

1 lb. shrimp, peeled and deveined
4 T. olive oil
¼ lb. fresh mushrooms, sliced
¼ lb. fresh snow peas (or use frozen, thawed)
2 c. broccoli flowerets
1 c. sliced celery
½ red pepper, cut into ¼" strips
½ c. chicken broth
2 tsp. cornstarch
½ c. sliced water chestnuts, drained
3 green onions, cut into ½" pieces
3 T. soy sauce

Heat 2 tablespoons olive oil in a wok or large skillet. Add shrimp and stir-fry about 5 minutes, or until pink. Remove shrimp and set aside. Add 1 tablespoon oil and stir-fry mushrooms 2 minutes. Remove mushrooms. Set aside. Add 1 tablespoon oil, heat and stir-fry snow peas, broccoli, celery and red pepper about 3 minutes. Add the water chestnuts and onions to the skillet. Mix the cornstarch, soy sauce and the chicken broth together and add to the skillet. Add the shrimp and mush-

(continued)

rooms back to the skillet, stirring constantly. Stir-fry 2 minutes or until thoroughly heated and sauce thickens.

STUFFED BAKED CALAMARI

1 recipe Marinara Sauce in this book
8 large squid, cleaned, tentacles removed and chopped
2 c. fresh bread crumbs
2 cloves garlic, pressed
¼ c. minced fresh Italian parsley
½ c. freshly grated Parmesan cheese
½ tsp. salt
½ tsp. black pepper
3 T. olive oil
toothpicks for securing

Heat oven to 350°. Whirl 4 slices bread in blender to make bread crumbs. Prepare the Marinara Sauce. Add the chopped tentacles to the Marinara Sauce. While the sauce is cooking, combine the bread crumbs, garlic, parsley, grated cheese, salt, pepper and olive oil. (The mixture will be a bit crumbly, but if you squeezed it in your hand it would hold together.) Divide the mixture among the calamari and stuff each one. Don't overstuff or they will break open and the stuffing will spill out, so leave a little bit of room. Close each opening with a round toothpick. Line up the stuffed calamari in a baking dish and pour the sauce over them. Cover tightly with foil and bake for 45 minutes.

STUFFED FLOUNDER

8 flounder fillets
½ c. butter
1 c. shrimp, peeled and deveined
3 T. minced green pepper
3 T. minced onions
2 T. minced fresh Italian parsley
1 T. fresh lemon juice
½ tsp. salt
½ tsp. pepper
¼ c. fresh bread crumbs
round toothpicks for securing

Whirl 1 slice bread in blender to make bread crumbs. Heat the oven to 350°. Bring ½ cup water to a boil in a saucepan. Add shrimp and cook just until pink. Remove from pan and drain. Pat dry with paper towels. Chop. Heat ¼ cup butter in a skillet. Add the green pepper and onions and cook until the onions are transparent. Add chopped shrimp, parsley, salt, pepper and bread crumbs. Mix well. Divide the filling among the 8 fillets, roll up, and secure with a round toothpick. Arrange the fish on a buttered baking pan and pour ¼ cup melted butter mixed

(continued)

with 1 tablespoon lemon juice over the fish. Sprinkle with salt and pepper. Bake for 25 minutes, basting frequently.

STUFFED SHRIMP WITH CRAB

12 large shrimp, peeled, deveined and butterflied
½ lb. crabmeat, picked over well to remove any bits of shell or cartilage
1 T. minced onions
1 T. minced fresh Italian parsley
1 T. minced celery
6 T. butter, melted
⅓ c. cracker crumbs
1 beaten egg
½ tsp. salt
½ tsp. white pepper
round toothpicks for securing

Heat the oven to 350°. Heat 2 tablespoons butter. Sauté onions, parsley and celery in the butter until tender. Remove from heat. Add the cracker crumbs, crabmeat and egg. Mix well and season with salt and pepper. Place 6 of the butterflied (or flattened) shrimp in a buttered baking pan. Divide the stuffing among the 6 shrimp. Top the shrimp with 6 more shrimp and poke each one with two round toothpicks to hold together. Melt 4 tablespoons butter and pour over shrimp. Bake for 20 minutes, basting with the butter in the baking pan.

TROUT AMANDINE

4 rainbow trout, boned and which have had heads removed
1 T. olive oil
1 T. lemon juice
¼ c. butter
½ c. sliced almonds

Heat oven to 350°. Grease a baking pan with the olive oil. Put the fish, skin side down in the baking dish. Melt the butter and mix together with the lemon juice. Pour over the fish. Sprinkle with almonds. Bake for 15 minutes. The fish should flake easily with a fork if it is done.

Recipe Favorites

Breads

Rolls

Pancakes

Muffins

Cakes

Frostings

Candy

Cookies

Bars

My Sister Arlinda

Helpful Hints

- When baking bread, a small dish of water in the oven will help keep the crust from getting too hard or brown.

- Use shortening, not margarine or oil, to grease pans when baking bread. Margarine and oil absorb more readily into the dough.

- To make self-rising flour, mix 4 cups flour, 2 teaspoons salt, and 2 tablespoons baking powder. Store in a tightly covered container.

- One scant tablespoon of bulk yeast is equal to one packet of yeast.

- Hot water kills yeast. One way to tell the correct temperature is to pour the water over your forearm. If you cannot feel hot or cold, the temperature is just right.

- When in doubt, always sift flour before measuring.

- Use bread flour for baking heavier breads, such as mixed grain, pizza doughs, bagels, etc.

- When baking in a glass pan, reduce the oven temperature by 25°.

- When baking bread, you can achieve a finer texture if you use milk. Water makes a coarser bread.

- Nuts, shelled or unshelled, keep best and longest when stored in the freezer. Unshelled nuts crack more easily when frozen. Nuts can be used directly from the freezer.

- Enhance the flavor of nuts, such as almonds, walnuts, and pecans, by toasting them before using in recipes. Place nuts on a baking sheet and bake at 300° for 5–8 minutes or until slightly browned.

- Dust a bread pan or work surface with flour by filling an empty salt shaker with flour.

- For successful quick breads, do not overmix the dough. Mix only until combined. An overmixed batter creates tough and rubbery muffins, biscuits, and quick breads.

- Muffins can be eaten warm. Most other quick breads taste better the next day. Nut breads are better if stored 24 hours before serving.

- Over-ripe bananas can be frozen until it's time to bake. Store them unpeeled in a plastic bag.

- The freshness of eggs can be tested by placing them in a large bowl of cold water; if they float, do not use them.

Bread/Rolls/Pancakes/Muffins/Cakes/ Frostings/Candy/Cookies/Bars

APPLE BRAN MUFFINS

1½ c. bran cereal with raisins
⅔ c. milk
2 eggs
1 c. sugar
¼ c. vegetable oil
1 tsp. vanilla
1½ c. flour

2½ tsp. baking powder
½ tsp. salt
¼ tsp. nutmeg
¾ tsp. cinnamon
¼ tsp. cloves
1 c. finely chopped apples
¼ c. raisins

Heat oven to 375°. Combine milk, eggs, sugar, oil and vanilla in a bowl. Stir together. Stir in bran cereal. Sift together flour, baking powder, salt, nutmeg, cinnamon, and cloves and add to the batter. Fold in apples and raisins with a spatula. If you use non-stick muffin cups, very lightly wipe them with shortening. If you use aluminum muffin cups, use more shortening and coat them with flour, or you can use paper liners. Put batter into muffin cups, filling about ⅔ full. Bake for 25 minutes for large muffins, 20 minutes for small. Check to see if they are done by sticking a muffin with a round toothpick that comes out clean.

APPLE FRITTERS

1 c. flour
½ tsp. salt
1½ tsp. baking powder
1 T. sugar
1 egg, beaten
½ c. milk

1 tsp. oil
shortening for cooking
1 c. chopped apples
syrup or confectioners' sugar for sprinkling

Sift together in a large mixing bowl the flour, salt, baking powder and sugar. Combine beaten egg, milk and oil. Add to dry ingredients, stirring to moisten. Stir in the apples. Heat shortening to 2" in a saucepan, electric frying pan or deep fat fryer to 375°. Drop batter by well rounded tablespoonfuls into hot fat. Cook on both sides until brown. Serve with syrup or sprinkle with sifted confectioners' sugar. Makes 8 small fritters.

AVOCADO BREAD

1 egg, beaten
1 mashed, ripened Haas avocado
½ c. buttermilk
⅓ c. oil
2 c. flour
¾ c. sugar

½ tsp. baking soda
½ tsp. baking powder
¼ tsp. salt
1 c. chopped pecans
softened butter for spreading

Heat oven to 350°. Grease and flour a 9" x 5" loaf pan. Mix beaten egg, mashed avocado, buttermilk and oil together. Add flour, sugar, baking soda, baking powder and salt. Stir thoroughly. Add pecans and mix until blended. Pour into baking pan. Bake 1 hour. Insert a round toothpick in top to see if it comes out clean. If it does, the bread is done. Cool 10 minutes in pan. Turn out of pan onto a serving plate. Slice and serve warm with butter.

BAGUETTES

1 recipe Bread Dough in this book
cornmeal for sprinkling baking sheet

water to put in oven while bread is baking

After dough has risen to rim of bowl, sprinkle with enough flour so that dough doesn't stick to your hands and punch down dough. Turn dough onto a floured surface. Divide dough into 4 portions. Cover and let rest for 10 minutes. Take one portion of dough and roll into an 8" x 10 " rectangle on lightly floured surface, pressing out air bubbles. Roll up tightly beginning with the long side. Pinch the edges together to close the seam and tuck underneath. Sprinkle 2 baking sheets with cornmeal. Place the baguette on baking sheet and prepare remaining 3 portions of dough in the same manner. Place two baguettes on each baking sheet 4" apart. Slash tops of baguettes diagonally with a sharp knife about ¼" deep and 2" apart. Heat oven to 400°. Cover with clean white cloth and let rise until double in size. When baguettes have risen to nearly double in size, place in the oven on a rack in the middle position. On the lower rack, place a shallow pan with 1 cup of water. Bake for 25 minutes, or until loaves are golden and sound hollow when tapped. Cool on wire racks. Let cool and serve within 12 hours.

BANANA BREAD

½ c. granulated sugar
½ c. brown sugar
3 T. vegetable oil
1 egg
1¼ c. mashed bananas (2-3 medium)
3½ tsp. baking powder
1 tsp. salt
2 tsp. vanilla
⅓ c. milk
2½ c. flour
1½ c. chopped walnuts

    Heat oven to 350°. Grease and flour bottom of 9" x 5" x 3" loaf pan. Whirl together the granulated sugar, brown sugar, oil, and egg in mixer. Add the mashed banana and mix. Add the baking powder, salt, vanilla and milk, stirring slowly. Add the flour. Mix. Add the walnuts and mix well. Pour into pan. Bake until round toothpick comes out clean, about 60 minutes. Cool slightly. Loosen sides of loaf from pan. Remove from pan. Cool completely before slicing. You may wrap with cellophane wrap and store in refrigerator no longer than one week.

BLUEBERRY STREUSEL MUFFINS

¼ c. chopped almonds
¼ c. brown sugar
1 T. all-purpose flour
2 T. butter, softened
½ c. oats
2 c. all-purpose flour
2 tsp. baking powder
¼ tsp. baking soda
¼ tsp. salt
½ tsp. sugar
2 tsp. grated lemon zest
1½ c. fresh or frozen blueberries
¾ c. buttermilk
¼ c. vegetable oil
1 egg, beaten

    Heat oven to 375°. Mix together 1 tablespoon flour and brown sugar. Cut in butter until mixture is crumbly. Stir in almonds and oats. Mix together and set aside. Combine 2 cups flour, baking powder, baking soda, salt, sugar and grated lemon zest in a bowl. Add blueberries, tossing gently. Make a well in center of mixture. Whisk together buttermilk, oil and egg. Fold into flour mixture, stirring just until moistened. Spoon batter into muffin pans which are well greased and floured or lined with paper liners, filling ⅔ full. If you use non-stick muffin pans, grease very lightly. Sprinkle with oat mixture. Bake 20 minutes, or until golden. Prick with round toothpick in center of muffin to see if it comes out clean. Remove from pans and cool on wire racks.

BREAD DOUGH

2 yeast cakes or 2 pkgs. dry yeast
2 c. warm water
2 tsp. salt
1 tsp. sugar

$4\frac{1}{2}$ c. unbleached, all-purpose flour
2 T. extra virgin olive oil

Use a bowl with a 12-cup capacity. Put yeast in bowl. Pour water over yeast. Add salt and sugar. Let stand for about 10 minutes until yeast is melted and a bit frothy. Add 2 cups flour and stir with a fork until batter is smooth and well mixed. Add 1 cup flour and stir, blending. Add 1 more cup flour, stirring. Then add $\frac{1}{2}$ cup flour. When blended, add 2 tablespoons oil, kneading with your hands. Knead for 5 minutes. Add more oil if dough sticks to your hands. Put a clean white cloth cloth over bowl and let dough rise to rim of bowl in non-drafty place, away from cold. This makes three 12" in diameter pizzas, or two loaves bread, or four baguettes. For bread, turn dough onto a floured surface and divide into two portions. Roll each portion into an 8" x 15" rectangle. Roll up from the 8" side and pinch the ends to seal. Lightly grease two 9" x 5" x 3" loaf pans. Put a portion into each pan. Cover and let rise until almost double in size. Heat oven to 375° while bread is rising. Put bread into oven on the middle rack. On the bottom rack, place a shallow pan with one cup of water in it. Bake for 45 minutes until golden, and sounds hollow when tapped. Remove from pans and cool on wire racks, if you have them, or let them cool resting on their sides.

BREAD STICKS WITH SESAME SEEDS

$2\frac{1}{2}$ c. unbleached, all-purpose flour
1 cake yeast or 1 pkg. dry yeast
2 tsp. salt

1 tsp. sugar
1 c. warm water
sesame seeds
1 egg, beaten with 2 tsp. water

In a large bowl, mix together the yeast, salt, sugar and water. Let stand for 10 minutes until yeast dissolves. Stir in 1 cup flour with a fork until batter is smooth. Stir in another cup of flour and stir. Pour $\frac{1}{2}$ cup flour over dough and knead for 5 to 10 minutes, until the dough is smooth and elastic. Cover with a clean white cloth and let the dough rise in a warm place until it is double in size. Divide the dough into pieces and roll into long thin 10" sticks, $\frac{1}{2}$" in diameter. Sprinkle sesame seeds on wax paper. Brush a bit of egg mixture on each stick and roll the sticks in the sesame seed. Put the sticks on baking sheet. Sprinkle more sesame seed on the wax paper as it is used up. Cover with a

(continued)

clean white cloth and let rise until almost double in size. While they are rising, heat oven to 400°. Bake until crisp and golden for 20 minutes.

BUCCELLATO (ITALIAN EASTER BREAD)

½ tsp. salt
¼ c. warm water
1 yeast cake or 1 pkg. dry yeast
3 T. sugar
zest of 1 orange, grated

3 beaten eggs
1 c. golden raisins, which are soft
1 T. olive oil
2 c. flour

Mix together in a large bowl the salt, warm water and yeast. Let stand for 10 minutes. Add 3 tablespoons sugar and stir with a fork. Add orange zest. Add the eggs and mix. Stir in 1 tablespoon olive oil. Add the raisins to the flour and mix and add to the batter. Let it rise until double in bulk. Punch the dough down. Roll out into an 8" x 10" rectangle and roll up beginning with the 8" side. Pinch the ends together to seal. Put into a greased 9" x 5" x 3" loaf pan. While the bread is rising, heat the oven to 375°. When the bread has almost doubled in size, put into the oven and bake for 25-35 minutes. Frost with a powdered sugar icing if you like, or serve without the icing.

Icing:

2 T. melted butter
2 T. cream or milk

½ tsp. vanilla
1½ c. confectioners' sugar

Mix the butter, cream or milk and vanilla together in a bowl. Slowly beat in the sugar until thick and creamy.

BUTTERMILK BISCUITS

2 c. sifted all-purpose flour
2¼ tsp. baking powder
1 tsp. salt

¼ tsp. baking soda
6 T. butter, softened
¾ c. buttermilk

Heat oven to 450°. Sift together flour, baking powder, salt and baking soda. Cut in butter with a fork or pastry blender until mixture is crumbly. Add buttermilk and mix quickly, but thoroughly. Turn onto floured surface. Knead lightly for a few seconds. Divide dough into pieces the size of a golf ball. Shape into a ball. Place on a baking sheet 3" apart and

(continued)

press down to ½" thickness. Brush with milk. Bake for 12 to 15 minutes, or until golden brown.

CHEESE BREAD

1 pkg. dry yeast
1 c. scalded milk
1 T. sugar
2 tsp. salt
1 tsp. thyme
½ tsp. marjoram
2 T. butter, melted
2½ c. flour
1 c. shredded cheddar cheese

Heat the milk until tiny bubbles appear and quickly remove from heat. Let it cool to lukewarm. In a large bowl, mix together the yeast, lukewarm milk, sugar and salt. Let it sit for 10 minutes. Stir in the thyme, marjoram and butter. Stir in 1 cup flour with a fork and blend well. Add 1 more cup of flour and blend. Pour ½ cup flour over the dough and knead the dough for 5 minutes, until it is smooth and elastic. Cover the dough with a clean white cloth and let it rise in a warm place until it is double in size. Grease a 9" x 5" x 3" loaf pan. Lightly flour a surface and roll the dough out to an 8" x 15" rectangle. Spread the cheese over the rectangle and roll up the rectangle from the 8" side. Twist the dough a half turn and fit it into the loaf pan, tucking the ends under. Cover with a clean, white cloth. Leave in a warm place until the dough almost doubles in size. Heat the oven to 375°. When the dough has risen, put in the oven and bake for 45 minutes, or until golden and it sounds hollow when tapped. Let it sit for five minutes and then remove from pan. Let the bread cool on a rack or turn it on its side to cool.

CINNAMON BUNS

2¼ c. unbleached, all-purpose
  flour
1 pkg. dry yeast
1 tsp. salt
1 tsp. sugar
1 c. warm water
½ c. confectioners' sugar
½ c. heavy cream
¾ c. pecans, chopped
3 T. melted butter
⅓ c. brown sugar
1½ tsp. ground cinnamon
½ tsp. nutmeg

Put yeast in a large bowl. Pour warm water over yeast. Add salt and sugar. Let stand for about 10 minutes until yeast is melted and a bit frothy. Add 1 cup flour and stir with a fork until batter is smooth and well mixed. Add 1 cup flour and stir, blending. Then add ¼ cup flour

(continued)

and knead with your hands for 5-10 minutes. Put a clean white cloth cloth over bowl and let dough rise in a warm place until it is double in bulk. On a floured surface, roll out dough into a 8" x 10" rectangle. Brush with melted butter. Mix together the brown sugar, cinnamon and nutmeg. Sprinkle over rectangle. Roll up from the 10" side. Cut into 9 slices. Mix together the confectioners' sugar, heavy cream and chopped pecans. Spread into a 9" x 9" baking pan. Place the slices, cut side down, on the mixture. Cover with the cloth and let rise to almost double in size. While the buns are rising, heat oven to 375°. Bake for 25 minutes, or until golden. Cool for 5 minutes and invert onto serving platter. Makes 9 buns.

CRANBERRY FRUIT NUT BREAD

2 c. flour
2 tsp. baking powder
½ tsp. baking soda
1 tsp. salt
1 c. sugar
¼ c. shortening

½ c. orange juice
1 T. grated orange zest
1 egg, well beaten
¾ c. chopped nuts
1½ c. fresh cranberries, chopped

Heat the oven to 350°. Sift together flour, baking powder, baking soda and salt. Set aside. Beat the shortening and sugar together in the mixer and add the egg and the orange zest. Add the flour mixture alternately with the orange juice. Put the cranberries through a food processor or blender and coarsely chop. Mix into the dough. Add the nuts and mix. Pour into a greased and floured 9" x 5" x 3" loaf pan. Bake for 1 hour. Insert a round toothpick in the top to see if it comes out clean. If not, bake a little longer. Cool in pan for 10 minutes, and then turn out on a cake rack to cool completely.

CRÊPE BATTER

1½ c. all-purpose flour
2¼ c. milk

4 eggs, slightly beaten
½ tsp. salt

Whisk together the flour, milk, eggs and salt. Batter should be fairly thin. Let batter stand for one hour. Place a nonstick 7" frying pan over medium heat. Oil pan ever so slightly. Stir the batter and pour about 2½ tablespoonfuls batter in the frying pan, lifting the pan off the heat and tilting and rotating it so that the batter forms an even, thin layer. Cook until the top is set and the underside is golden. It is not necessary

(continued)

to turn them over. Remove the crêpe to a piece of wax paper. Continue cooking the rest of the crêpes, greasing the pan with a tiny bit of oil if necessary, and stirring the batter before starting each one. Stack the finished crêpes between sheets of wax paper.

DATE LOAF

2 c. sifted all-purpose flour
1 tsp. baking powder
¼ tsp. salt
½ c. butter
1 c. brown sugar
2 eggs, beaten

½ tsp. baking soda
½ c. milk
2 tsp. vanilla
1 lb. pitted dates, chopped
½ c. chopped pecans
1 c. heavy cream

Heat oven to 350°. Line the bottom of a 9" x 5" x 3" loaf pan with waxed paper. Sift flour, baking powder and salt together. In mixing bowl, cream butter with brown sugar until light and fluffy. Add beaten eggs and mix. Dissolve baking soda in milk and add with vanilla to creamed mixture. Add chopped dates and nuts to flour mixture. Stir into creamed mixture. Mix well. Turn batter into prepared pan. Bake 60 minutes, or until done. Test for doneness by pricking with a round toothpick to see if it comes out clean. If not, bake a little longer. Cool in pan 5 minutes. Remove from pan. Remove waxed paper and cool on rack. When cake is cool, turn out onto serving plate. Whip cream. Slice and serve with whipped cream.

DILLY CASSEROLE BREAD

1 pkg. dry yeast
¼ c. warm water
1 c. creamed cottage cheese, room temperature
2 T. sugar
1 T. butter

2 T. minced onion
1½ tsp. dill weed
1 tsp. salt
¼ tsp. baking soda
1 egg
2¼ c. flour

Heat oven to 350°. Combine yeast with water, butter, sugar and salt. Let stand for 10 minutes. Add cottage cheese, minced onion, dill weed and egg. Mix well. Add 1 cup flour and mix. Add baking soda and 1¼ cups flour and mix. Put in greased bowl, turning to grease top. Cover and let rise in a warm place, free from draft, until double in size, about 1 hour. Punch dough down and place in greased 8" casserole. Bake

(continued)

for 40 to 50 minutes until done. Remove from oven. Pour 1 tablespoon melted butter over and sprinkle with a little salt.

DINNER ROLLS

1 pkg. dry yeast
½ c. warm water
2 T. shortening
1 T. sugar
2 tsp. salt
½ c. scalded milk
2 eggs, beaten
3 c. flour

Put yeast in a large bowl. Add the warm water and let stand 10 minutes. Scald milk by heating in saucepan over medium heat until tiny bubbles appear. Blend shortening, sugar and salt into scalded milk. Cool to lukewarm. Add to bowl with yeast. Stir in beaten eggs. Stir in 1 cup flour with a fork and mix batter well. Add 1 more cup flour and mix. Add 1 more cup of flour and mix in well. Sprinkle with 2 tablespoons flour and turn onto a floured surface and knead for 5 minutes until smooth. Place in greased bowl, turning to coat top with grease. Let rise until doubled. Punch down. Shape into rolls. Place in 9" x 13" greased baking dish. Cover and let rise until doubled. Heat oven to 400°. Bake for 15-20 minutes, until golden.

DOUGHNUTS, BAKED

Doughnuts:

¾ c. milk, scalded
⅓ c. sugar
1 tsp. salt
1 pkg. dry yeast
¼ c. warm water
4 c. sifted flour

½ tsp. cinnamon
¼ tsp. nutmeg
⅛ tsp. mace
⅓ c. soft shortening
2 eggs, well beaten
¼ c. butter, melted

Cinnamon Sugar:

Mix together
½ c. sugar

1 tsp. cinnamon

Creamy Glaze:

Beat together
⅓ c. butter
2 c. confectioners' sugar

1½ tsp. vanilla
4-8 tsp. water

Chocolate Glaze:

Beat together
4 oz. semi-sweet chocolate, melted
⅓ c. butter

2 c. confectioners' sugar
1½ tsp. vanilla
4-6 T. hot water

To scald milk, heat until tiny bubbles appear. Remove from heat. Combine milk, sugar and salt. Cool to lukewarm. Stir. Dissolve yeast in warm water. Let sit for 10 minutes. Add cooled milk mixture to yeast. Add shortening and eggs to mixture and beat. Add cinnamon, nutmeg and mace. Add 2 cups flour to liquids and beat well. Add remaining flour to make a soft dough. Knead on floured surface for 5 minutes. Place in greased bowl. Turn dough over to grease top. Cover with a clean cloth and let rise until doubled. Roll out dough to ¼" thick. Cut into rounds with a round biscuit cutter or an inverted glass 3" in diameter. Re-roll the scraps to make more rounds. Lift with a spatula onto greased baking sheets. Cover with a cloth and let rise until very light. Heat oven to 375°. Bake 10-15 minutes. Brush with melted butter and shake in cinnamon sugar or spread with creamy glaze or chocolate glaze. For chocolate doughnuts, omit nutmeg and cinnamon. Stir in ½ c. cocoa with first addition of flour. After baking, shake in confectioners' sugar or spread with chocolate glaze.

DOUGHNUTS FILLED WITH JELLY

¾ c. milk, scalded
⅓ c. sugar
1 tsp. salt
1 pkg. dry yeast
¼ c. warm water
4 c. sifted flour
½ tsp. cinnamon
¼ tsp. nutmeg
⅛ tsp. mace
⅓ c. soft shortening
2 eggs, well beaten
Vegetable oil for deep frying
16 oz. raspberry or jam of your choice
2 c. sifted confectioners' sugar for rolling doughnuts in

To scald milk, heat until tiny bubbles appear. Remove from heat. Combine milk, sugar and salt. Cool to lukewarm. Stir. Dissolve yeast in warm water. Let sit for 10 minutes. Add cooled milk mixture to yeast. Add shortening and eggs to mixture and beat. Add cinnamon, nutmeg and mace. Add 2 cups flour to liquids and beat well. Add remaining flour to make a soft dough. Knead on floured surface for 5 minutes. Place in greased bowl. Turn dough over to grease top. Cover with a clean cloth and let rise until doubled. Roll out dough to ¼" thick. Cut into rounds with a round biscuit cutter or an inverted glass 3" in diameter. Re-roll the scraps to make more rounds. Put rounds on a lightly floured surface. Cover with a cloth and let rise until very light. While doughnuts are rising, sift confectioner's sugar into a shallow dish. Set aside. Fit a pastry bag with a small tip and fill pastry bag with the jam. Set aside. Heat 3" of vegetable oil in a deep pot or deep fryer to 360°. Fry the doughnuts, a few at a time, until golden and puffed, turning to cook on both sides, about 5-7 minutes. Lift out with a slotted spoon. Drain on paper towels. Fill doughnuts with about 2 teaspoons jam with the pastry bag. Roll in confectioners' sugar while still warm. Makes about 2 dozen doughnuts.

FRIED BREAD

1 recipe Bread Dough in this book
olive oil for frying
salt or confectioners' sugar

Take a piece of dough the size of a golf ball. Shape dough into 3" rounds, ½" thick. Lay on a lightly floured surface. Repeat until all dough is used up. Cover with a clean white cloth. Let rise until almost double in size. Heat oil 1" deep in a skillet to 375°. Fry the rounds until golden, turning to fry on both sides. Put on paper towels to drain. Sprinkle with salt or confectioners' sugar, whichever you prefer. Serve immediately.

GERMAN STOLLEN

1 pkg. dry yeast
¼ c. warm water
½ c. butter
1 c. milk, scalded
¼ c. sugar
1 tsp. salt
¼ tsp. ground cardamom
2 tsp. vanilla
3 c. flour
1 egg

1 c. raisins
½ c. currents
¼ c. chopped candied fruits
½ c. chopped almonds
2 T. grated orange zest
1 T. grated lemon zest
melted butter to spread
confectioners' sugar for sifting on top

Soften yeast in water. To scald milk, heat in saucepan over medium heat until tiny bubbles appear. Melt butter in hot milk. Add sugar, salt and cardamom. Cool. Put into a large bowl and stir in 1 cup flour. Add egg and beat well. Stir in yeast mixture, vanilla, raisins, currents, candied fruits, almonds, orange zest and lemon zest. Mix in 1 more cup of flour and blend well. Add another cup of flour and blend in. Turn out onto floured surface and shape into a ball. If it sticks to your hands, add a little more flour, as needed. Let it rest 10 minutes, covered. Knead 5-8 minutes until smooth and satiny. Place in a greased bowl, turning so the top gets greased. Cover and let rise until double. Heat oven to 350°. Punch down dough and form into an oval, ½" thick by 12". Brush with melted butter. Fold long side over to within 1" of opposite side, and turn 1" of shorter edges underneath the loaf. Place on a greased cookie sheet. Cover and let rise until almost double and bake for 40-50 minutes, until golden and a round toothpick inserted in center comes out clean. Brush top with melted butter and sprinkle with confectioners' sugar

JULE KAGE

1 c. scalded milk
¼ c. shortening
½ c. sugar
1 tsp. salt
¼ tsp. ground cardamom
½ tsp. cinnamon
1 pkg. dry yeast
¼ c. warm water

1 beaten egg
3 c. flour
½ c. raisins
½ c. candied fruit
½ c. chopped maraschino cherries
1 egg yolk mixed with 2 teaspoons water

Scald milk by heating until tiny bubbles form. Add shortening, sugar, salt, cardamom and cinnamon to scalded milk. Cool to lukewarm. Add yeast to warm water in a large mixing bowl and let it sit for 10 minutes.

(continued)

Add egg and mix. Add cooled milk mixture and blend. Add 2 cups flour and mix. Blend in raisins, candied fruit and cherries. Add 1 cup flour and mix well. Knead for 5 minutes. Divide dough into thirds. Form into 3 16" ropes and braid together. Place on greased cookie sheet. Cover and let rise until double in bulk. Brush some egg yolk onto top. Heat oven to 350°. Bake 40-50 minutes, until golden, or if a round toothpick inserted in center comes out clean.

LEFSE

3 c. boiled and riced potatoes
2 T. melted butter
2 T. cream
1 T. sugar
1 tsp. salt
½ tsp. baking powder
1 c. flour
confectioners' sugar for sprinkling

Heat a lefse griddle or a pancake griddle to 375°. Mix together the melted butter, cream, sugar and salt. Pour over hot riced potatoes and mix. Stir the baking powder into the flour. Then mix the flour into the dough. Divide the dough into 3 pieces if you have a lefse griddle, or 4 pieces for a pancake griddle. Roll out on a floured surface, about ⅛" thick. It is important to roll the dough thin. Bake until lightly brown on both sides. Serve with butter and confectioners' sugar.

NORWEGIAN CHRISTMAS BREAD

1 pkg. dry yeast
¼ c. warm water
1 c. milk, scalded
⅓ c. shortening
½ c. sugar
1 tsp. salt
1 tsp. ground cardamom
1 egg, beaten
3 c. flour
¾ c. raisins
¼ c. candied diced citron
1 egg yolk mixed with 2 tsp. water
½ c. slivered almonds

Grease a 9" x 5" loaf pan. Add yeast to warm water in a large bowl and let it sit for 10 minutes. Scald milk by heating until tiny bubbles form. Remove from heat and add shortening, sugar, salt and cardamom. Let it cool to lukewarm. When cool, add to yeast. Add egg and stir. Add 1 cup flour, beating until smooth. Stir in raisins and citron. Add 1 more cup of flour and blend. Add remaining cup of flour and mix well. Grease bowl and turn dough around in bowl so the top gets greased. Cover and let rise until double in bulk. Punch down and turn onto a floured

(continued)

surface. Shape into a loaf. Place in 9" x 5" loaf pan. Cover with a clean cloth and let rise until almost double in size. Heat oven to 350°. Brush with egg yolk mixture. sprinkle with slivered almonds. Bake for 50-60 minutes, until golden and when a round toothpick inserted in center comes out clean.

OLIVE BREAD

1 c. warm water
1 pkg. yeast
3 T. extra virgin olive oil
1 tsp. salt
1 tsp. sugar
2¼ c. unbleached all-purpose flour
½ c. Spanish stuffed olives, cut in half lengthwise
½ c. pitted black olives, cut in half lengthwise
cornmeal for sprinkling

    Put water into a 12-cup mixing bowl. Add yeast, sugar and salt and let it sit for 10 minutes. Stir in 1 cup flour and mix with a fork until smooth. Add 1¼ cups of flour, blending well. Add the olive oil, 1 tablespoon at a time, kneading dough for 5-8 minutes. Let dough rise until double in size. Put dough on a floured surface and roll out into a 10" x 13" rectangle. Mix the olives together and spread the olives on the dough. Roll the dough up from the 10" side. Put onto a baking sheet, seam side down, which has been sprinkled with cornmeal. Cover and let rise until almost double in bulk. Heat the oven to 400°. Put a pie plate on the bottom shelf of the oven and fill it half full with hot water. With a sharp knife, score the top of the loaf ¼" deep in three places. Bake for 15 minutes. Lower the heat to 375° and bake for 30 minutes more, or until the bottom is golden and sounds hollow when tapped.

PANCAKES - LAURINA'S

2 eggs, separated
1 T. corn or canola oil
1 c. buttermilk
½ tsp. baking soda
½ tsp. salt
1 c. all-purpose flour
2 tsp. baking powder
2 T. sugar
1 tsp. vanilla
butter and syrup or jam for serving

    Heat griddle to 375°. When griddle is heated, very lightly smear with shortening, using a paper towel. Wipe off excess. Mix together the egg yolks, oil, vanilla, sugar, salt and buttermilk with a rubber spatula. Add

(continued)

baking soda, baking powder and flour. Blend. Beat egg whites until stiff. Fold into batter with rubber spatula. Drop 3 tablespoons of batter on griddle for each pancake, spacing so that they do not run together. When air bubbles form on the tops, flip over with a pancake spatula and cook underside until golden. Serve hot with butter and syrup or jam.

PIZZA WITH ANCHOVIES

1 recipe Bread Dough in this book
1 tin anchovies (use 3 tins for 3 pizzas)
cornmeal for sprinkling

Bread Dough in this book makes enough dough for 3 12" pizzas. For anchovy pizza, divide dough into thirds for a 12" pizza. Roll out the third of dough on a floured surface to 12". If it shrinks a bit, let it rest for 10 minutes and resume rolling it out. Sprinkle pizza pan with cornmeal and place dough on pan. Cover and let rise until almost double in size. Heat oven to 375°. Break anchovies into thirds. Spread over dough. Bake for 20 minutes or until golden. (Freeze the other two thirds dough in two oiled freezer bags if you are making one pizza.)

PIZZA WITH TOMATO AND CHEESE

1 recipe Bread Dough in this book
1 recipe Marinara Sauce in this book
1½ c. shredded mozzarella cheese
¼ c. freshly grated Parmesan cheese
¼ c. black olives, sliced in half lengthwise (optional)
cornmeal for sprinkling
(Triple topping recipe for 3 pizzas)

Bread Dough in this book makes enough dough for 3 12" pizzas. For tomato and cheese pizza, divide dough into thirds for a 12" pizza. Roll out the third of dough on a floured surface to 13". If it shrinks a bit, let it rest for 10 minutes and resume rolling it out. Sprinkle pizza pan with cornmeal and place dough on pan, bringing up the edge of the dough to form a little collar so the sauce won't run off the edge. Cover and let rise until almost double in size. Make the Marinara Sauce. Heat oven to 375°. Spread 2 cups of the sauce over the dough to the collar and sprinkle with the olives if you like. Bake for 20 minutes, remove from oven and spread the mozzarella cheese over and return to the oven for 5 minutes until the cheese melts and the bottom is golden. Remove

(continued)

from oven and sprinkle with the Parmesan cheese. (Freeze the other two thirds dough in 2 oiled freezer bags if you are making one pizza.)

PIZZA VEGETARIAN

1 recipe Pizza Dough in this book
1 recipe Marinara Sauce in this book
1 8-oz. pkg. frozen artichokes, cooked
1 c. broccoli flowerets, crisp cooked
½ c. sun dried tomatoes
1½ c. mozzarella cheese
¼ c. freshly grated Parmesan cheese
(Triple topping recipe for 3 pizzas)

Bread Dough in this book makes enough dough for 3 12" pizzas. For vegetarian pizza, divide dough into thirds for a 12" pizza. Roll out the third of dough on a floured surface to 13". If it shrinks a bit, let it rest for 10 minutes and resume rolling it out. Sprinkle pizza pan with cornmeal and place dough on pan, bringing up the edge of the dough to form a little collar so the sauce won't run off the edge. Cover and let rise until almost double in size. Heat oven to 375°. Prepare the Marinara Sauce. Bring water to a boil in a saucepan. Drop in the broccoli. Cook for 4 minutes. Remove with a slotted spoon and place on paper towel to drain. Drop the artichokes in the water and cook for 10 minutes. Remove with a slotted spoon and set on paper towels to drain. Spread the crisp-cooked broccoli, cooked artichokes and sun dried tomatoes on the dough. Spread 2 cups sauce over the vegetables. Bake for 20 minutes. Remove from oven and sprinkle the mozzarella cheese on the pizza and return to the oven for 5 minutes longer, or until the bottom is golden. Sprinkle with Parmesan cheese. (Freeze the other two thirds dough in 2 oiled freezer bags if you are making one pizza.)

PIZZA WITH MEAT

1 recipe Bread Dough in this book
1 recipe Marinara Sauce in this book
½ lb. cooked Italian sausage (2 links), casing removed
1 small onion, sliced thinly
1 green pepper, sliced thinly
25 slices pepperoni
1½ c. shredded mozzarella cheese
¼ c. grated Parmesan
(Triple topping recipe for 3 pizzas)

Bread Dough in this book makes enough dough for 3 12" pizzas. For meat pizza, divide dough into thirds for a 12" pizza. Roll out the third

(continued)

of dough on a floured surface to 13". If it shrinks a bit, let it rest for 10 minutes and resume rolling it out. Sprinkle pizza pan with cornmeal and place dough on pan, bringing up the edge of the dough to form a little collar so the sauce won't run off the edge. Cover and let rise until almost double in size. Make the Marinara Sauce. Heat oven to 375°. Remove the casings from the sausage and sauté the sausage, breaking the meat up, for 10 minutes. Spread the meat over the pizza. Spread the sliced onion and sliced green pepper strips over the pizza, then spread the pepperoni over the pizza. Spread 2 cups sauce over the toppings. Bake for 20 minutes and remove from oven. Sprinkle the mozzarella cheese over and return to the oven. Bake 5 minutes longer, or until bottom of crust is golden. Sprinkle with the grated Parmesan cheese. (Freeze the other two thirds dough in 2 oiled freezer bags if you are making one pizza.)

PRETZELS - AMY JO

1 pkg. dry yeast
¾ c. warm water
1 tsp. sugar
½ tsp. salt

1¾ c. flour
1 egg mixed with 2 tsp. water, beaten
¼ c. Kosher salt

Put yeast, sugar, salt and warm water in a large bowl. Let stand 10 minutes. Add 1 cup flour and stir with a fork until mixture is smooth. Add ¾ cup flour and stir. Turn dough out onto a lightly floured surface, and knead for 5 minutes, until smooth and satiny. Cut dough into 18 pieces. Roll each piece on a lightly floured surface into a 9" rope. Grease a baking sheet. Sprinkle some Kosher salt on a long sheet of wax paper. Brush a bit of egg on each rope. Roll the ropes into salt. Leave each rope long or form into a pretzel shape. Place on baking sheet. Heat oven to 400°. Let rise until double in size. Bake for 15 minutes until golden brown.

PUMPKIN BREAD

1⅓ c. sugar
⅓ c. oil
1 c. canned pumpkin
2 eggs
1⅔ c. flour
½ tsp. salt
1 tsp. baking soda
½ tsp. nutmeg

¼ tsp. ginger
½ tsp. cinnamon
¼ tsp. ground cloves
1 tsp. baking powder
2 tsp. vanilla
2 T. water
½ c. raisins
1 c. chopped nuts

Heat oven to 350°. Beat sugar and oil together. Beat in eggs. Add pumpkin and mix. Add salt, baking soda, nutmeg, ginger, cinnamon, ground cloves, baking powder, vanilla and water. Mix well. Add flour and mix. Add raisins and nuts and mix. Grease and flour a 9" x 5" x 3" loaf pan. Pour batter into the pan. Bake for 1 hour. Prick with a round toothpick. If it comes out clean the bread is done. If not, bake a few minutes longer. Let sit for 5 minutes. Remove to a cake rack and let cool completely.

RAISIN NUT BREAD

½ c. boiling water
2 T. sugar
1½ tsp. salt
3 T. shortening
½ c. milk
1 pkg. dry yeast
2 T. warm water
1 egg

3 c. flour
½ c. raisins
½ c. chopped walnuts
3 T. brown sugar
2 tsp. cinnamon
1 T. melted butter
2 T. milk
1 c. confectioners' sugar

Mix together the yeast and 2 tablespoons warm water in a large mixing bowl. Let sit for 10 minutes. Pour boiling water over sugar, salt and shortening in a bowl. Add milk. Cool to lukewarm. Add to yeast mixture. Beat in egg. Gradually add flour, 1 cup at a time, beating after each addition. Turn onto floured surface. Knead for 5 minutes until smooth and elastic. Place in greased bowl. Cover and let rise until doubled. Punch down. On floured surface roll into a 9" x 12" rectangle. Brush the dough with 1 tablespoon melted butter. Mix together the raisins, chopped walnuts, brown sugar and cinnamon. Sprinkle the mixture over the dough. Roll up from the 9" side. Place in a greased 9" x 5" x 3" loaf pan. Cover and let rise until double. Heat oven to 375°. Bake for 40-45 minutes, until the crust is golden. Remove from the pan

(continued)

and cool on a rack. When cool, Mix together the milk and confectioners' sugar and spread over top. Topping is optional.

SAUSAGE BREAD

½ recipe for Sausage in this book or 1 lb. purchased Italian sausage	1½ c. shredded mozzarella cheese
2 T. olive oil	¼ c. grated Parmesan cheese
½ recipe Bread Dough in this book	1 egg, beaten
	cornmeal for sprinkling

Prepare bread dough and let rise until double in bulk. Prepare ½ recipe for Sausage in this book or purchase 1 pound Italian sausage. Remove the casing if you use purchased sausage. Brown the sausage for 15 minutes in hot oil, breaking up and stirring. Remove from heat and pour off liquid. Set aside to cool. After the bread dough has risen, turn onto a floured surface and roll into a 12" x 12" square. Brush beaten egg on dough to within 1" of edges. Spread the crumbled sausage to within ½" of the edges of the square. Sprinkle with the mozzarella cheese, then sprinkle with the grated Parmesan cheese. Roll up and pinch edges together to seal and turn under. Sprinkle cornmeal on a baking sheet. Put the bread on the baking sheet, seam side down, and cover and let rise until double in bulk. Heat oven to 350°. When the bread has risen, put in oven and bake for 40-45 minutes until golden on top and underneath. Serve hot.

SOURDOUGH STARTER

2 c. warm water	¼ c. powdered milk
1 pkg. dry yeast	⅓ c. plain yogurt
1 T. sugar or honey	2 c. sifted all-purpose flour

Dissolve yeast in ½ cup warm water. Stir in remaining water, sugar or honey, powdered milk, yogurt and flour. Whisk ingredients together. Cover with cheesecloth. Let stand at room temperature 48 hours. It should have tripled in volume. Whisk two times a day. Cover tightly and put into refrigerator until ready to use. Bring to room temperature before using. To keep starter going after using, add ¾ cup water, ¾ c. sifted all-purpose flour and 1 teaspoon sugar to remaining starter. Let stand at room temperature until bubbly and fermented, at least one day. Cover and refrigerate until ready to use again. If not used with 10 days, add

(continued)

1 teaspoon sugar. Repeat adding 1 teaspoon sugar every 10 days. If starter should start to turn pink, discard and start all over again.

SOURDOUGH BREAD

2 pkg. dry yeast
1½ c. warm water
1 c. sourdough starter (recipe in this book)
2 tsp. salt

2 tsp. sugar
4½ to 5 c. flour
½ tsp. baking soda
cornmeal for sprinkling
butter for brushing

Sourdough starter must be brought to room temperature before using. Soften yeast in warm water. Let stand 10 minutes. Blend in starter, salt and sugar. Add 2¼ cups flour and beat until well blended and smooth. Cover. Let rise until light and bubbly, about 1½ hours. Combine baking soda and 2¼ cups flour. Stir into dough. Add enough additional flour to make a nice, smooth, but not sticky dough. Turn out to floured surface and knead 5-8 minutes. Divide dough in half. Cover and let rest 10 minutes. Shape into two round loaves. Sprinkle cornmeal on 2 round cake pans. With sharp knife, make 3 diagonal slashes ¼" deep across top of loaves. Cover and let rise until double. Heat oven to 375°. When dough has risen, bake 40-45 minutes, until golden. Brush with butter.

SOURDOUGH ENGLISH MUFFINS

1 c. sourdough starter (recipe in this book)
¾ c. buttermilk
2¾ to 3 c. flour

1 tsp. baking soda
¼ tsp. salt
6 T. cornmeal

Sourdough starter must be brought to room temperature before using. Mix starter and buttermilk. Add baking soda and salt to buttermilk mixture. Stir to combine. Add 1 cup of flour and mix well. Add 1¾ cup flour and mix with your hands so that dough holds together, but is not sticky. Turn onto lightly floured surface and knead 5-7 minutes until smooth, adding more flour, if necessary. Roll dough to ¾" thickness. Let rest a few minutes. Cut into 3" rounds. Put scraps together and make more muffins. Sprinkle wax paper with 6 tablespoons cornmeal. Put muffins on top of cornmeal and press slightly. Turn over and press lightly, so that the muffins are well coated with the cornmeal. Cover and let rise until very light. Heat a griddle to 375°. Lightly grease with a paper towel, wiping off any excess. Bake about 15 minutes each side, turning after

(continued)

the first ten minutes and then turning to bake for 10 minutes on the other side. Turn to bake 5 minutes more each side. If they don't appear to be done, bake 5 minutes more each side. Cool. Split with a fork and toast. Serve with butter and jam. Makes 12-14.

STUFFED CALZONE

1 recipe Bread Dough in this book
cornmeal for sprinkling on baking sheets

olive oil for brushing
1 egg beaten with 2 tsp. water

Filling 1:

1 lb. salami or prosciutto, diced

1 lb. mozzarella cheese, sliced

Filling 2:

1 lb. Italian sausage, casing removed and cooked until brown
1 medium onion, chopped and sautéed with the green pepper

1 green pepper, finely diced
¾ c. grated Parmesan cheese

Filling 3:

2 chicken breasts, sautéed in olive oil until cooked, then diced
1 can black olives, drained and sliced lengthwise
8 oz. sun dried tomatoes, thinly sliced

½ tsp. basil
½ tsp. oregano
1 tsp. salt
1 tsp. pepper

After the dough has risen, split the dough into 8 portions. Roll each portion into 8" to 10" circles, about ¼" thick. Brush them with olive oil and select a filling of your choice, dividing the filling among the 8 calzones. Moisten the edges with the egg mixture. Fold one half over the other and seal well so that the filling does not escape during baking. Brush the outside tops with water. Sprinkle cornmeal on a 2 baking sheets and line them up on the baking sheets, spacing 2" apart. Cover with a clean white cloth and let rise for 1 hour. Heat the oven to 375°. After they have risen to almost double, bake for 30 minutes until golden.

WHEAT BREAD

1 pkg. dry yeast
1⅓ c. skim milk
1¼ tsp. salt
¼ c. vegetable oil

¼ c. honey
3½ c. unsifted coarse whole-wheat flour
oil

Put yeast and 2 tablespoons warm water in bowl of electric mixer. When yeast is melted, add milk, salt, oil and honey. Mix together. On low speed, stir in 1 cup wheat flour and mix. Stir in the remainder of the wheat flour to make a smooth dough. Put oil on your hands and knead dough for 5-8 minutes and shape into a ball. Grease the bowl and the top of the dough with oil. Cover with a clean white towel and let rise until double in size. Turn dough onto a lightly floured surface and shape into an 8" long loaf. Grease a 9" x 5" x 4" loaf pan and put the dough in. Cover with a clean kitchen towel and let rise until double in bulk, about 1½ hours. Heat oven to 350°. Place loaf on middle shelf of oven. Bake for 1 hour. Turn out onto cake rack and cool.

ZUCCHINI BREAD

3 eggs
1 c. oil
2 c. sugar
2 c. grated zucchini
3 tsp. vanilla
3 c. flour

¼ tsp. baking powder
3 tsp. cinnamon
1 tsp. baking soda
1 tsp. salt
1 c. chopped nuts

Heat oven to 350°. Beat eggs until light and thick. Mix in oil, sugar, vanilla and zucchini. Add baking powder, cinnamon, baking soda, salt and one cup flour. Mix. Add 2 more cups flour and mix. Stir in nuts. Grease and flour 2 9" x 5" x 4" loaf pans. Divide the mixture between the loaf pans. Bake for 60 minutes. Insert a round toothpick in center to see if it comes out clean. Cool for 5 minutes in pans. Remove and cool completely on cake racks.

ANGEL CUSTARD CAKE

2 angel food cakes

Custard:

1 pt. milk
1 c. sugar
2 T. flour
1½ tsp. almond flavoring
4 eggs, separated
1 pkg. Knox gelatin

½ c. cold water
1 pt. whipping cream
½ pt. whipping cream for frosting
½ c. flaked coconut for sprinkling
6 maraschino cherries for garnish

Mix together the gelatin and cold water, stirring to dissolve. Set aside. Whisk together 1 pint milk, 1 cup sugar, 2 T. flour, 1½ tsp. almond and 4 egg yolks. Put the milk mixture in a saucepan and cook over low heat, stirring constantly until thickened. Stir the gelatin mixture and add to the milk mixture. Set aside. Beat the egg whites until stiff. Beat 1 pint whipping cream. Fold the whipped cream into the egg whites. Fold into the custard mixture. Break up the two angel food cakes into chunks. Layer ¼ of broken up cake on the bottom of a 10" tube pan. Pour ¼ of the custard mixture over cake. Repeat layers until the pan is full. Refrigerate 24 hours. Turn the cake over onto a serving plate and frost with ½ pint whipped cream. Sprinkle with coconut. Garnish with cherries.

APPLE CAKE

3 c. sifted all-purpose flour
1 tsp. baking soda
1 tsp. baking powder
1 tsp. salt
1½ c. oil

2 c. sugar
3 eggs
2 tsp. vanilla
2 c. finely chopped apples
1 c. chopped pecans

Frosting:

½ c. butter
½ c. brown sugar

2 tsp. milk

Heat oven to 325°. Grease and flour a bundt pan or a 10" tube pan. Stir together the flour, baking soda, baking powder and salt. In a large bowl at medium speed with an electric mixture, beat together oil, sugar, eggs and vanilla until combined. Gradually beat in flour mixture until smooth. Fold in apples and pecans. Turn into prepared pan. Bake 1 hour and 20 minutes, until a round toothpick inserted in center comes out clean. Let cool for 5 minutes and turn out onto a serving plate. Mix

(continued)

together the butter, brown sugar and milk. Boil for 2 minutes. Spoon hot mixture over cake.

BANANA PINEAPPLE CAKE WITH PECANS

3 c. all-purpose flour
1 tsp. baking soda
1 tsp. baking powder
1 tsp. cinnamon
1 tsp. salt
1¾ c. sugar
4 eggs

1½ c. vegetable oil
2 tsp. vanilla
2 c. ripe bananas, diced
1 8-oz. can crushed pineapple, with juice
1 c. chopped pecans

Heat oven to 350°. Grease and flour a 10" tube pan. In a medium-size bowl, mix together flour, baking soda, baking powder, cinnamon and salt. In mixer, stir together the sugar, eggs, oil, vanilla and pineapple, with juice. Gradually add the flour mixture, stirring at low speed. By hand, with a rubber spatula, fold in the bananas and pecans and blend well. Scrape with the spatula into the prepared tube pan. Bake for 1 hour and 10 minutes, or until a round toothpick inserted in center comes out clean. The cake will be cracked on top. Cool for 10 minutes in pan. Remove from pan and cool thoroughly on cake rack. Frost with Cream Cheese Frosting.

Cream Cheese Frosting:

3 oz. cream cheese, softened
5 T. butter, softened

½ tsp. vanilla
2 c. confectioners' sugar

In electric mixer, whip together the cream cheese, vanilla and butter. Gradually add the confectioners' sugar and whip until fluffy, about 5 minutes.

BANANA POUND CAKE

1 c. shortening
½ c. butter, softened
3 c. sugar
5 large eggs
3 ripe bananas, mashed
3 T. milk

2 tsp. vanilla
3 c. all-purpose flour
½ tsp. salt
1 tsp. baking powder
confectioners' sugar for sprinkling

(continued)

Heat oven to 350°. Grease and flour a 10" tube pan. Beat shortening and butter at medium speed with an electric mixture about 2 minutes or until creamy. Gradually add sugar, beating 5 to 7 minutes. Add eggs, one at a time, beating just until yellow disappears. Combine mashed bananas, milk and vanilla. Combine flour, salt and baking powder. Add to shortening mixture alternately with banana mixture, beginning and ending with flour mixture. Beat at low speed just until blended after each addition. Pour batter into prepared tube pan. Bake for 1 hour and 10 minutes or until a round toothpick inserted in center of cake comes out clean. Cool in pan for 10 minutes. Remove cake from pan and let cool completely on cake rack. Sprinkle with sifted confectioners' sugar.

BLUEBERRY CITRUS CAKE

1 pkg. 2-layer-size lemon cake mix
½ c. orange juice
½ c. water
⅓ c. oil
3 eggs

1½ c. fresh or frozen blueberries
1 T. finely shredded orange zest
1 T. finely shredded lemon zest
1 recipe Citrus Frosting

Heat oven to 350°. Grease and flour two 9" x 1½" round baking pans. Set aside. In a large mixing bowl, combine cake mix, orange juice, water, oil and eggs. Beat with an electric mixer on low speed for 1 minute. Increase speed to medium and beat for 2 minutes. With a spatula, gently fold in blueberries, orange zest and lemon zest. Pour batter into prepared pans. Bake for 30 to 35 minutes or until a round toothpick inserted in center comes out clean. Cool layers in pans for 10 minutes. Remove cakes from pans and cool thoroughly on cake racks. Frost with Citrus Frosting. Store frosted cake in refrigerator.

Citrus Frosting

3-oz. pkg. softened cream cheese
¼ c. softened butter
3 c. sifted confectioners' sugar
2 T. orange juice

1 c. heavy cream
2 T. finely shredded orange zest
1 T. finely shredded lemon zest

In medium bowl, beat together cream cheese and butter until fluffy. Add the confectioners' sugar and orange juice. Beat until combined. In another bowl, beat the cream into soft peaks. Fold into the cream cheese mixture. Fold in the orange zest and the lemon zest.

CANNOLI CAKE

Sponge Cake:

6 eggs, separated
1 c. sugar, divided
1 c. plus 2 T. cake flour
½ tsp. cream of tartar
½ tsp. salt
1 tsp. vanilla

Filling:

3 T. rum
2 lb. ricotta cheese
1 c. confectioners' sugar
8 oz. cream cheese, softened
1 tsp. vanilla
¼ c. heavy cream
¼ c. semi-sweet mini chocolate chips
¼ c. chopped citron

Frosting:

2 c. whipping cream
½ tsp. vanilla

Heat oven to 325°. Line two 9" round cake pans with wax paper. Grease and flour the wax paper. Set aside. In large mixing bowl with electric mixer, beat 6 egg yolks on high speed until thick and pale yellow. Add ½ cup sugar, ½ teaspoon salt and 1 teaspoon vanilla and mix. Sift the flour evenly over the top and stir in with a spatula. In another large bowl, beat 6 egg whites and ½ teaspoon cream of tartar until soft peaks form. Gradually beat in ½ cup sugar. Fold ⅓ of the egg whites into the egg yolk mixture with a rubber spatula. Then fold in the remaining whites. Scrape the batter into the prepared pans with a rubber spatula and spread evenly. Bake about 25 minutes, until the top springs back when lightly pressed and a round toothpick inserted in the center comes out clean. Let cool in the pans for 10 minutes. Slide a thin knife around the sides of the cakes to detach them from the side of the pans. Invert them on cake racks to cool. Peel off the wax paper and discard. When cool, slice each cake horizontally in half, so you have four layers. To prepare the filling, beat the ricotta, confectioners' sugar, cream cheese, vanilla and heavy cream until smooth. Fold in chocolate chips and citron. Place one cake layer on cake plate. Sprinkle with 1 tablespoon rum. Spread with ⅓ of the filling. Place a second cake layer on top and sprinkle with one tablespoon rum. Spread with ⅓ of the filling. Place a third cake layer on top and sprinkle with one tablespoon rum. Spread with ⅓ of the filling. Place the fourth cake layer on top. Whip the 1 cup whipping cream, adding the vanilla. Spread the top and sides of the cake with the whipped cream. Keep refrigerated.

CARROT CAKE

4 eggs
1½ c. sugar
¾ c. vegetable oil
2 c. grated raw peeled carrots
1¾ c. unbleached flour
½ c. wheat germ

2 tsp. cinnamon
2 tsp. baking powder
2 tsp. baking soda
½ tsp. salt
1 c. chopped nuts
1 c. raisins

Heat oven to 350°. Beat eggs in an electric mixture. Add sugar and beat. Add oil and grated carrots. Mix together. Mix together flour, wheat germ, cinnamon, baking powder, baking soda and salt. Add the flour mixture to batter. Beat for 3 minutes. Mix in nuts and raisins. Grease and flour two 9" cake pans. Pour batter in the two pans. Bake for 35 minutes. Or you can bake in a greased and floured oblong 9" x 13" x 2" pan for 45 minutes. Frost with cream cheese frosting.

Cream Cheese Frosting:

6 oz. cream cheese, softened
6 T. butter, softened
2½ c. to 3 c. sifted confectioners' sugar

2 tsp. vanilla

Beat together the cream cheese, butter and vanilla. Gradually beat in the sugar, a cup at a time.

CASSATA ALLA SICILIANA

Sponge Cake:

6 eggs, separated
1 c. sugar, divided
1 c. plus 2 T. cake flour

½ tsp. cream of tartar
½ tsp. salt
1 tsp. vanilla

Rum Syrup:

1¼ c. sugar
1 c. water
4 orange slices

2 lemon slices
⅔ c. golden rum

Cheese Filling:

1 lb. ricotta cheese
½ c. confectioners' sugar
½ c. mini semi-sweet chocolate pieces
4 oz. mixed candied fruit, finely chopped

1 T. golden rum
2 T. semi-sweet chocolate pieces, melted
½ c. raspberry jam

Frosting:

2 c. heavy cream
2 T. confectioners' sugar

candied cherries

Heat oven to 325°. Line two 9" round cake pans with wax paper. Grease and flour the wax paper. Set aside. In large mixing bowl with electric mixer, beat 6 egg yolks on high speed until thick and pale yellow. Add ½ cup sugar, ½ teaspoon salt and 1 teaspoon vanilla and mix. Sift the flour evenly over the top and stir in with a spatula. In another large bowl, beat 6 egg whites and ½ teaspoon cream of tartar until soft peaks form. Gradually beat in ½ cup sugar. Fold ⅓ of the egg whites into the egg yolk mixture with a rubber spatula. Then fold in the remaining whites. Scrape the batter into the prepared pans with a rubber spatula and spread evenly. Bake about 25 minutes, until the top springs back when lightly pressed and a round toothpick inserted in the center comes out clean. Let cool in the pans for 10 minutes. Slide a thin knife around the sides of the cakes to detach them from the side of the pans. Invert them on cake racks to cool. Peel off the wax paper and discard. When cool, slice each cake horizontally in half, so you have four layers. While the cake is baking, make the Rum Syrup: In small saucepan, combine granulated sugar, 1 cup water and the orange and lemon slices. Bring to boiling, stirring until sugar is dissolved. Boil gently, uncovered, 20 minutes. Discard fruit slices. Stir in ⅔ cup rum. Set aside. Make Cheese Filling: In medium bowl, combine ricotta and ½ cup confectioners' sugar.

(continued)

Beat with mixer until well combined, about 3 minutes. Stir in ½ cup semi-sweet chocolate mini pieces, the candied fruit and 1 tablespoon golden rum. For chocolate-cheese filling: Remove 1 cup cheese filling to a small bowl, and stir in melted chocolate pieces until well blended. To assemble cake: Place one of the four cake layers, cut side up, on serving plate. Drizzle with ½ cup rum syrup. Spread with ½ the plain cheese filling. Spread cut side of second layer with half of the raspberry jam. Place, jam side down, over cheese layer. Drizzle with ½ cup rum syrup. Spread with all the chocolate-cheese filling. Add third layer, cut side up. Drizzle with ½ cup rum syrup. Spread with remaining plain cheese filling. Spread remaining jam over cut side of fourth layer. Place, jam side down, over cheese layer. Drizzle on remaining rum syrup. Beat cream with 2 tablespoons confectioners' sugar until creamy stiff. Do not overbeat. Use to frost sides and top of cake. If desired, place some of the cream in pastry bag with rosette tip, and use to decorate cake. Garnish with candied cherries. Refrigerate at least 4 hours.

CHEESECAKE

Crust:

1½ c. zwieback or graham cracker crumbs (9 whole graham crackers)

5 T. melted butter
2 T. sugar
¼ tsp. cinnamon

First Layer Filling:

3 8-oz. pkg. cream cheese, softened
1 c. sugar

1 tsp. vanilla
3 eggs

Second Layer Filling:

2 c. sour cream
2 T. sugar

½ tsp. vanilla

Topping:

1 10-oz. pkg. frozen strawberries, thawed

1½ T. cornstarch

Heat oven to 350°. Prepare crust: Crush graham crackers, two at a time, by rolling out between two sheets of wax paper with a rolling pin. Combine the zwieback or graham cracker crumbs with the melted butter, sugar and cinnamon in a bowl and mix well. Pat the crumb mixture over the bottom and 1 inch up the sides of a 9" springform pan. Bake in the

(continued)

oven for 8 minutes. Set aside to cool. Beat together in an electric mixer the softened cream cheese, sugar, vanilla and eggs until creamy. Pour over the crust and bake for 15 minutes. While it is baking, whisk together the sour cream, sugar and vanilla until creamy. Pour over the top of cream cheese mixture and bake 5 minutes. Turn oven off and let set for 25 minutes. For the topping, strain the berries and set aside. Pour the juice in a saucepan with the cornstarch and heat over medium heat, stirring, until thick. Add the berries. When cool, pour over the cake. Let the cake set overnight in the refrigerator.

CHOCOLATE CHEESECAKE

Crust:

1½ c. zwieback or graham cracker crumbs (9 whole graham crackers)
5 T. melted butter
2 T. sugar
¼ tsp. cinnamon

Filling:

8 oz. sweet cooking chocolate
1¼ lb. cream cheese, softened
¼ tsp. salt
2 tsp. vanilla
⅔ c. sugar
4 eggs
1 c. heavy cream
½ c. flour

Heat oven to 325°. Crush the graham crackers by rolling out, two at a time, between two sheets of wax paper. Mix the crumbs with the butter, 2 tablespoons sugar and the cinnamon. Lightly grease the bottom and sides of a 9" springform pan. Press the mixture over the bottom and 1" up the sides. Bake in the oven for 8 minutes. Set aside. Melt the chocolate in the top part of a double boiler over hot water or in the microwave oven. Remove from heat and cool slightly. With an electric mixer, over medium speed, mix the cream cheese with the salt, vanilla and sugar. Beat in the eggs until mixture is creamy, scraping sides and bottom of bowl with spatula. Stir in the melted chocolate. Stir in the flour. Stir in the cream. Pour the mixture over the crumb crust. Set the pan on top of a baking sheet in case some of the mixture should spill over. Bake for 1 hour. Do not open the oven door. Turn off oven and leave in the oven for 1 hour. (The top will be cracked, but this does not harm the flavor of the cake.) Remove from oven and let sit for 1 hour, then chill in refrigerator for 4 hours. Run a metal spatula around the sides of the pan and remove sides.

CHOCOLATE CAKE

Chocolate Cake:

1 c. cocoa	½ tsp. salt
2 c. boiling water	1 c. butter, softened
2¾ c. all-purpose flour	2½ c. sugar
2 tsp. baking soda	4 large eggs
½ tsp. baking powder	2 tsp. vanilla

Filling:

8 oz. white baking chocolate	2 c. heavy cream

Frosting:

½ c. cocoa, sifted	1 lb. confectioners' sugar
⅓ c. milk	2 tsp. vanilla
½ c. butter, softened	dash salt

Heat oven to 350°. Grease and flour three 9" round cake pans. Place cocoa in medium bowl. Gradually stir in boiling water until blended. Set aside to cool completely. In another bowl, mix together flour, baking soda, baking powder and salt. In large bowl of electric mixer, beat 1 cup butter with granulated sugar until light and fluffy. Add eggs, one at a time, beating well after each addition. Beat in vanilla. Alternately add ¼ flour mixture with ⅓ cocoa mixture until well blended. Repeat with remaining flour and cocoa mixture until all is used up and mix well. Pour batter into the three prepared cake pans, dividing equally. Bake 25 minutes, or until round toothpick pricked into center comes out clean. Cool layers in pans 10 minutes, then remove from pans and cool thoroughly on cake racks. Make filling: In top of double boiler placed over hot water, combine white chocolate and ¼ cup heavy cream. Heat, covered, until chocolate melts and stir until mixture is smooth. Remove from heat and cool. Scrape into large bowl of electric mixer with rubber spatula. Stir in remaining 1¾ cups of heavy cream. With mixer at high speed, beat until thick. Spread between cooled cake layers, dividing evenly. Make frosting: Combine softened butter, confectioners' sugar, dash salt, vanilla, milk and sifted cocoa in bowl of electric mixer. Beat until fluffy, about 5 minutes. With spatula, cover top and sides of cake with frosting. Refrigerate cake for a couple of hours.

CHOCOLATE ROLL

¾ c. cake flour
¼ c. cocoa
1 c. sugar
1 tsp. baking powder
4 eggs, separated
¼ tsp. salt

¼ c. water
1 tsp. vanilla
ice cream or whipped cream for filling
confectioners' sugar for sprinkling

Heat oven to 375°. Sift flour with cocoa, ½ cup of the sugar and baking powder. Beat egg whites with salt until foamy. Add ½ cup sugar, a little at a time, beating after each addition. Continue beating until stiff peaks are formed. Beat egg yolks until light and lemon colored, gradually adding water and vanilla. Fold dry ingredients into yolks until well blended, then fold yolk mixture into beaten whites. Grease bottom of a 15½" x 10½" x 1" jelly roll pan. Line with waxed paper and grease wax paper. Turn batter into pan, spreading to corners. Bake 15 minutes, or until cake springs back when pressed lightly with fingers. Remove from oven and invert pan over clean, smooth kitchen towel which has been dusted with confectioners' sugar. Remove pan and peel off paper. Cut crisp edges from cake and discard. Cool cake 5 minutes. Start with long end and roll cake lengthwise, rolling with towel inside the roll. Cool thoroughly. When ready to serve, unroll and spread surface of cake with softened ice cream or whipped cream. Re-roll, without the towel inside. Sprinkle top with confectioners' sugar and slice with a knife that has a serrated edge and serve. If you fill with ice cream and are not going to serve right away, put into freezer. Let set at room temperature 5 minutes before slicing and serving. If you fill with whipped cream, refrigerate until ready to serve.

CUPCAKES WITH FILLING

Cupcakes:

2 c. cake flour
3 oz. unsweetened chocolate, melted
1 tsp. baking soda
¾ tsp. salt

½ c. vegetable shortening
1½ c. light brown sugar
2 eggs
1 c. buttermilk
2 tsp. vanilla

Vanilla Cream Filling:

3 T. shortening
3 T. butter
1 c. confectioners' sugar

1 tsp. vanilla
1 c. corn syrup

Frosting:

½ c. butter, softened
3 c. confectioners' sugar
2 tsp. vanilla

½ c. cocoa, sifted
⅓ c. milk
dash salt

Melt chocolate in microwave or in top of double boiler with hot water in pan underneath over medium heat. Cool. Heat oven to 350°. In a medium bowl, sift together the flour, baking soda and salt. In a mixing bowl, beat together the shortening and sugar until fluffy. Add the eggs, one at a time, beating after each addition. Stir in melted chocolate. Add vanilla and mix together. Alternately add the flour mixture with the buttermilk and mix well. Generously grease and flour muffin tins. Fill the muffin tins ⅔ full and bake for 15 minutes, or until the centers spring back when lightly pressed and a round toothpick pricked into the center of a cupcake comes out clean. Set the pan on a rack to cool. Fill with the vanilla cream filling. For the filling: With an electric mixer, beat together the shortening and butter until blended. Turn mixer speed down and add the vanilla. Gradually add the confectioners' sugar. Turn mixer speed up and beat until light and fluffy, about 5 minutes. Gradually drizzle in the corn syrup until the filling is light and fluffy. Scrape the filling into a pastry bag fitted with a plain tip and force filling into top of cupcakes. Frosting: Beat together in electric mixer the butter, sugar, vanilla, cocoa, salt and milk for 5 minutes. Frost cupcakes.

FRUIT CAKE

8 T. butter
1 c. dark-brown sugar
1 tsp. lemon extract
1 tsp. vanilla
2 eggs
½ c. molasses
2 c. flour
½ tsp. baking soda
1 tsp. cinnamon
½ allspice

½ tsp. mace
¼ tsp. ground cloves
¼ tsp. nutmeg
½ tsp. salt
½ c. milk
2 c. mixed candied fruit, diced
½ c. candied citron, diced
1 c. golden raisins
1 c. chopped pecans
1 c. chopped walnuts

Heat oven to 325°. Butter two 9" x 5" x 3" loaf pans. Line them with foil, then butter the foil. Cream the butter with an electric mixer. Add the brown sugar and beat until light. Add the lemon and vanilla extracts and eggs and beat well. Stir in the molasses and blend. Mix together the flour, baking soda, cinnamon, allspice, mace, cloves, nutmeg and salt. Add to the mixture and blend. Add the milk and blend. Stir in the candied fruit, citron, raisins, pecans and walnuts and mix well. Spoon into the pans and bake for 1¼ hours, until a toothpick inserted in the center comes out clean. Turn out onto racks to cool. Remove the foil. When completely cool, wrap first with plastic wrap, then with foil. Store in an airtight container. If you want a Brandied Fruit Cake, soak two large pieces of cheesecloth in brandy. Wrap each fruit cake in the cheesecloth, covering all sides, then wrap well in the plastic wrap, and then in the foil. Moisten the cheesecloth with additional brandy every few days for about a week. The brandy will flavor and preserve the cake.

GERMAN SWEET CHOCOLATE CAKE

Cake:

1 4-oz. pkg. Baker's German Sweet Chocolate
½ c. boiling water
1 c. butter
4 eggs, separated
2½ c. sifted all-purpose flour
½ tsp. salt
2 c. sugar
1 tsp. vanilla
1 c. buttermilk
1 tsp. baking soda

Coconut Pecan Frosting:

1 c. evaporated milk
1 c. sugar
3 egg yolks
½ c. butter
1 tsp. vanilla
1⅓ c. flaked coconut
1 c. chopped pecans

Buttercream Frosting:

4 T. butter, softened
2 c. confectioners' sugar
2 T. cream or milk

Heat oven to 350°. Grease and flour 3 9" round cake pans. Melt chocolate in boiling water. Cool. Cream butter and sugar until fluffy. Add egg yolks, one at a time, and beat well after each. Add melted chocolate and vanilla. Mix well. Sift together flour, salt and baking soda. Add the flour mixture alternately with the buttermilk to the mixture, beating after each addition until smooth. Beat egg whites until stiff. Fold egg whites into mixture. Pour mixture into the 3 prepared pans. Bake for 30 to 40 minutes. Cool for 5 minutes and turn out onto cake racks. Prepare Coconut Pecan Frosting: Combine 1 cup evaporated milk, 1 cup sugar, 3 egg yolks, ½ cup butter and 1 teaspoon vanilla. Cook and stir over medium heat until thickened, about 12 minutes. Add 1⅓ cup flaked coconut and 1 cup chopped pecans. Beat until thick enough to spread. Place first cake on plate and frost with with ⅓ of the Coconut Pecan Frosting. Place second cake on top and frost with ⅓ of the frosting. Place third cake on top and frost with ⅓ of the frosting. Prepare Buttercream Frosting: Cream butter and cream or milk in electric mixer. Slowly add confectioners' sugar. When blended, put mixer speed on high and whip for 5 minutes. Frost sides of cake with Buttercream Frosting.

HEATH BAR CAKE

2 c. brown sugar
2 c. flour
1 c. butter, softened
2 eggs, beaten
1 c. buttermilk

1 tsp. baking soda
¼ tsp. salt
1 tsp. vanilla
1 c. chopped nuts
4 Heath bars, chopped finely

Heat oven to 350°. Grease and flour a 9" x 12" baking pan. Mix together the brown sugar and flour. Cut in the butter with a fork, until crumbly. Reserve 1 cup and set aside. Add the eggs, buttermilk, baking soda, salt and vanilla to the remaining flour mixture. Blend well with a mixer. Pour batter into the prepared pan. Mix the chopped nuts, chopped Heath bars and reserved cup of flour mixture together. Sprinkle over top of cake. Bake for 30 minutes.

LEMON RASPBERRY CAKE

1 c. Crisco shortening
2 c. sugar
4 large eggs
3 c. cake flour
2½ tsp. baking powder

½ tsp. salt
1 c. milk
1 tsp. almond extract
1 tsp. vanilla extract
1 10-oz. jar raspberry preserves

Heat oven to 350°. Grease and flour 3 9" round cake pans and line with wax paper. Grease and flour wax paper. Set pans aside. Beat shortening and sugar at medium speed of an electric mixer until creamy. Add eggs, one at a time, beating well after each addition. Add almond and vanilla extracts. Combine flour, baking powder and salt. Add to shortening mixture alternately with milk, beginning and ending with flour mixture. Mix after each addition. Pour into prepared pans. Bake 25-30 minutes, or until a round toothpick inserted in center comes out clean. Cool in pans for 10 minutes. Remove from pans, and let cool completely on wire cake racks. Slice layers in half horizontally to make 6 layers. Place 1 layer, cut side up, on a cake plate. Spread with 3 tablespoons raspberry preserves. Do the same thing with with the 2nd, 3rd, 4th and 5th layers. Top with 6th layer, cut side down. Frost top and sides of cake with Lemon Buttercream Frosting. Store in refrigerator.

Lemon Buttercream Frosting

1¼ c. butter
2 tsp. grated lemon zest

3 tsp. lemon juice
3 c. sifted confectioners' sugar

(continued)

In bowl of electric mixer, beat together butter, lemon zest, and lemon juice. On low speed, gradually add sifted confectioners' sugar. When added, raise speed to high and whip for 5 minutes.

ORANGE TORTE

1 c. butter, softened
1 c. sugar
3 eggs
2½ c. sifted all-purpose flour
1 tsp. baking soda
½ tsp. baking powder
½ tsp. salt
1½ c. walnuts, chopped
1 c. buttermilk
2 T. grated orange zest
½ c. orange juice

Heat oven to 350°. Grease and flour a 10" tube pan. Cream butter in mixing bowl. Add sugar gradually, beating until fluffy. Add eggs, one at a time, beating after each addition. Sift together the flour, baking soda, baking powder and salt. Combine buttermilk, orange zest and orange juice. Add dry ingredients to the creamed mixture alternately with the buttermilk mixture. Mix in nuts. Pour into prepared pan and bake 1 hour, or until round toothpick inserted in center comes out clean. Let torte stand in pan 30 minutes after removing from oven. Remove cake from pan to cake rack to cool thoroughly. Put cake onto cake platter. Frost top and sides of cake.

Frosting

1½ c. confectioners' sugar
3 T. softened butter
½ tsp. vanilla
pinch salt
2 T. milk

Mix together the confectioners' sugar, butter, vanilla, salt and milk on low speed of electric mixer. When mixed, raise speed to high and beat for 5 minutes.

PANETTONE (ITALIAN CHRISTMAS BREAD)

⅓ c. scalded milk
1 pkg. dry yeast
¼ c. warm water
2 eggs, beaten
½ tsp. salt
1 tsp. vanilla
8 T. butter, softened
½ c. sugar
2½ c. flour
½ c. candied fruit, diced small
¼ c. citron, diced small
½ c. golden raisins

(continued)

Heat oven to 350°. Scald milk by heating it until tiny bubbles appear. Set aside to cool. Put the yeast and warm water in a small mixing bowl. Let sit for 10 minutes until yeast is softened. Beat the butter and sugar together until fluffy with electric mixer. Beat in the eggs. Add the softened yeast, salt and vanilla and beat. With the mixer on stir, alternately add the flour and milk. On a floured surface, knead the dough 5-8 minutes until smooth. Roll out with a rolling pin. Sprinkle with the candied fruit, citron and raisins. Fold over and roll out again. Repeat two or three times, until the fruits are blended into the dough. Transfer to a large, greased bowl. Cover with a clean cloth. Place in a warm place and let rise until double in bulk. Return to the floured board. Grease a 10" tube pan. Knead the dough until smooth and form into a circle. Put into the pan and brush with melted butter. Cover with a cloth, and let rise until double. Heat oven to 350°. When dough has risen, bake for 45 minutes, or until the top has browned. Turn out onto a cake rack and cool.

POUND CAKE

½ lb. butter, softened
1⅔ c. sugar
5 eggs
2 c. cake flour
½ tsp. salt

2 tsp. vanilla or ½ tsp. ground mace
confectioners' sugar for sprinkling

Heat oven to 325°. Grease and flour a 9" x 5" loaf pan. With electric mixer on medium speed, cream the butter with the sugar and vanilla (or mace) and beat until fluffy. Add the eggs, one at a time, beating after each addition. Put the speed on low and add 1 cup flour and salt and combine well. Add 1 more cup flour and mix well, but do not overbeat. Scrape into the prepared pan and and bake for 1¼ hours. Insert a round toothpick in the center to see if it comes out clean. If not, bake 5-10 minutes longer and check again. Cool in the pan for 5 minutes, and then turn out onto a cake rack. Cool thoroughly. Sift confectioners' sugar over the top. Slice thinly.

SOUR CREAM PEAR COFFEE CAKE

⅔ c. light brown sugar
½ c. all-purpose flour
1 tsp. cinnamon
4 T. butter, softened
⅔ c. walnuts, toasted and
  chopped
2½ c. all-purpose flour
1½ tsp. baking powder
½ tsp. baking soda

½ tsp. salt
1¼ c. sugar
6 T. butter, softened
2 large eggs
2 tsp. vanilla
1⅓ c. sour cream
3 firm, but ripe Bosc pears,
  peeled, cored, and cut into 1"
  pieces

Heat oven to 350°. Grease and flour 13" x 9" x 2" metal baking pan. Prepare Streusel: In medium bowl, mix together brown sugar, the ½ cup flour and cinnamon. With a fork, cut in the butter until mixture is crumbly. Mix in walnuts. Set aside. For cake, mix together flour, baking powder, baking soda and salt. Set aside. In a large bowl, with mixer at medium speed, beat sugar with butter until fluffy. Add eggs, one at a time and beat in vanilla. With mixer at low speed, alternately add flour mixture and sour cream, beginning and ending with flour mixture, until batter is smooth, occasionally scraping bowl. With rubber spatula, fold in pears. Spoon batter into pan. Spread evenly. Sprinkle top with streusel mixture. Bake 35 to 45 minutes, until round toothpick inserted in center comes out clean. Cool cake in pan on wire rack for 1 hour to serve warm, or cool completely.

STRAWBERRY CAKE

6 eggs, separated
1 c. sugar, divided
½ tsp. cream of tartar
½ tsp. salt
2 T. fresh lemon juice
2 tsp. grated lemon zest
1 c. plus 2 T. cake flour

2 pt. strawberries, washed and
  hulled
2 c. heavy cream
½ c. confectioners' sugar
½ tsp. vanilla
¼ c. strawberry jelly, melted

Heat oven to 350°. Blot berries dry with paper towels. Beat egg whites together with the cream of tartar until soft peaks form. Gradually beat in ½ cup sugar until egg whites are stiff. Set aside. In another, larger bowl, with electric mixer, beat 6 egg yolks on high speed until thick and pale yellow. Add ½ cup sugar, ½ tsp. salt, lemon juice and lemon zest and beat. Sift the flour evenly over the top and stir in with a rubber spatula. Mix well. Fold ⅓ of the beaten egg whites into the egg yolk mixture with a rubber spatula. Then fold in the remaining

(continued)

whites. Pour the batter into an ungreased 10" tube pan. Bake 40 minutes, or until top springs back when gently pressed with fingertip. Invert pan over cake rack. Let cake cool completely. With metal spatula, carefully loosen cake from edges of pan and around tube. Push up bottom of pan to remove from sides. Slide spatula underneath cake to loosen from bottom and put cake on wax paper. Mark the side of cake into thirds with toothpicks. With these as a guide, slice cake into three equal layers. Place bottom layer, cut side up, on plate. Slice 1 pint berries. In medium bowl, beat cream and slowly add confectioners' sugar. Add vanilla. Spread bottom layer with ¾ cup cream and half of the sliced berries. Repeat with second layer. Top with third layer, cut side down. Frost top and sides with remainder of whipped cream. Slice the second pint of berries and toss with the melted jelly. Arrange the berries on top of the cake. Refrigerate 1 hour.

WHITE CAKE/WEDDING CAKE

Batter for a two-layer cake:

2½ c. cake flour
2½ tsp. baking powder
½ tsp. salt
½ c. Crisco shortening
1½ c. sugar

1 tsp. vanilla
¼ tsp. almond extract
1 c. skim milk
5 egg whites

Heat oven to 350°. Grease and flour 2 9" round cake pans. Sift together flour, baking powder and salt. With electric mixer, cream shortening with sugar, vanilla and almond extracts. Add sifted dry ingredients and milk alternately in small amounts, beginning and ending with dry ingredients. Beat egg whites until stiff peaks are formed. Fold into batter with a rubber spatula. Turn into prepared pans. Bake for 30 minutes. Cool in pans for 5 minutes, then remove to cake racks to cool thoroughly. Frost. For a multi-layer wedding cake, or layers of graduated proportions, increase the amount of batter and icing accordingly.

Icing for White Cake/Wedding Cake

4 tsp. meringue powder
⅓ c. warm water
1 lb. confectioners' sugar

½ c. Crisco shortening
¾ tsp. vanilla

(continued)

Soak meringue powder in 1/3 cup warm water for 20 minutes. Beat until fluffy. Add powdered sugar, vanilla and Crisco. Beat until smooth and fluffy. Hand mixer: 15 minutes; electric mixer: 7 minutes.

ALMOND CARAMEL CANDY

1 1/2 c. sugar
1/4 c. cold water
3/4 c. light corn syrup
1/4 c. butter
3 oz. unsweetened chocolate, melted
1 c. light cream, warmed, but not boiled
1 c. roasted almonds
2 tsp. vanilla
1/8 tsp. salt

Butter a baking sheet with sides. Set aside. Melt chocolate in microwave or in top pan of double boiler with hot water in the pan underneath over medium heat. Combine sugar, cold water, corn syrup and butter in a saucepan. Bring to a boil. Stir in the melted chocolate. Cook over medium heat to 240° on the candy thermometer, stirring occasionally. Add hot cream, a little at a time, stirring constantly. Cook to 246°. Remove from heat and cool to 220°. Stir in the almonds, vanilla and salt. Pour onto buttered baking sheet. When cool enough to handle, form into rolls and cool. Cut crosswise into 2" pieces and wrap individually in plastic wrap or wax paper and twist the ends to close.

ALMOND CRUNCH

1 c. butter
1 1/4 c. sugar
2 T. corn syrup
2 T. water
1 c. slivered almonds, toasted
2 c. milk chocolate chips

Line a 15" x 10" x 1" pan with foil. Set aside. In heavy saucepan, combine butter, sugar, corn syrup and water. Heat, stirring constantly, until mixture boils and sugar is dissolved. Boil to brittle state (300°) on candy thermometer. Remove from heat. Stir in almonds. Pour mixture into foil-lined pan. Sprinkle milk chocolate chips over brittle. Allow to stand until morsels become shiny. Spread the chocolate with a metal spatula. Let cool and refrigerate 1 hour. Break into pieces. Makes 2 lbs. candy.

BAKED CARAMEL CORN

6 qt. popped popcorn (about 1 c. unpopped)
1 c. almonds
1 c. peanuts
1 c. butter
2 c. brown sugar
½ c. light or dark corn syrup
1 tsp. salt
1 tsp. vanilla
½ tsp. baking soda

Heat oven to 300°. Spray a large roasting pan with just a bit of non-stick coating. Pop corn and put only popped corn in roasting pan. Discard unpopped kernels. Add nuts and stir. Keep hot in oven. In a saucepan, melt butter. Stir in brown sugar, corn syrup and salt. Bring to a boil, stirring constantly. Boil, without stirring, for 5 minutes. Temperature would be 244° on a candy thermometer. Remove from heat and stir in baking soda and vanilla. Pour over popped corn and nut mixture, stirring to coat popcorn and nuts. Lower heat to 250°. Bake for 45 minutes, stirring every 15 minutes. Cool. Store in an airtight container. Makes about 6 quarts.

CANDIED APPLES

5 medium red apples
2 c. sugar
1 c. water
⅔ c. light corn syrup
1 2" cinnamon stick
3-4 drops red food coloring
wooden skewers or wooden ice cream sticks

Set a frying pan with 2" of water to boil. Turn off heat and cover. Wash and dry the apples. Remove the stems and insert wooden sticks in place of the stems. In a saucepan, combine 2 cups sugar, 1 cup water, ⅔ cup corn syrup and one cinnamon stick. Stir until the sugar is dissolved. Bring to a boil. Boil without stirring until syrup reaches 290° on a candy thermometer, the soft-crack stage. Remove the cinnamon stick. Add the food coloring. Set the saucepan in the frying pan of hot water. Quickly dip apples in the syrup, one at a time, and swirl to coat evenly. Twirl the apple at the end so the extra syrup drips off. Set each apple on wax paper to harden. Best eaten within 24 hours.

CANDIED CITRUS PEEL

zest from 6 oranges (or a mixture of lemons, oranges and grapefruit to equal same)
1 tsp. salt
½ c. light corn syrup
2 c. sugar
1 c. water
sugar for rolling in

Wash and dry fruit. With potato peeler, remove zest only from each piece of fruit, no white part. Cut the peel into ½" strips. Put in a saucepan the corn syrup, 2 cups sugar, 1 teaspoon salt and 1 cup water. Cook over medium heat, stirring constantly, until sugar is dissolved. Add the citrus pieces. Bring to boiling, then reduce heat and simmer gently 45 minutes, until most of the syrup is absorbed. Drain. Spread 1 cup or more of sugar on wax paper. Roll peel in sugar, a few pieces at a time. Arrange in a single layer on trays. Let dry 48 hours. Store in covered container between layers of wax paper.

CARAMEL APPLES

5 medium red apples
1 lb. vanilla caramels, unwrapped
2 T. water
5 wooden skewers or ice cream sticks
1 c. chopped peanuts

Wash and dry apples. Remove stems and insert wooden sticks in place of the stems. Spread out some wax paper and sprinkle the chopped peanuts on the wax paper. Combine in the top of a double boiler the caramels and 2 tablespoons water. Heat over boiling water until melted, stirring frequently. Dip the apples, one at a time, in the caramel mixture, turning until coated. Scrape sauce from bottoms of apples and roll bottoms of apples in chopped nuts. Place on wax paper. Chill until firm.

CARAMEL CRUSHES

1 lb. vanilla caramels, unwrapped
4 T. cream
1 tsp. vanilla
1 c. corn flakes
1 c. Rice Krispies
½ c. chopped pecans

Spread out some wax paper. Melt caramels, cream and vanilla in the top of a double boiler over boiling water. Mix together the corn flakes, Rice Krispies and pecans in a large bowl. Remove the caramel

(continued)

mixture from heat when melted and and pour over the cereal and nuts. Stir together and shape into small balls. Place on wax paper to harden.

CARAMEL PECAN LOGS

Nougat Center:

3 c. sugar
1⅓ c. light corn syrup
1 c. water
2 egg whites, stiffly beaten

¼ c. melted butter
1 tsp. vanilla
⅛ tsp. salt

Caramel Coating:

2 c. sugar
1¼ c. light corn syrup
1½ c. light cream

1 tsp. vanilla
¼ tsp. salt

Pecan Coating:

6 c. pecans, coarsely chopped

Beat the egg whites until stiff. Set aside. Put the chopped nuts in a shallow dish and set aside. To make nougat center, combine ¾ cup sugar, ⅔ cup corn syrup and ¼ cup water in 1½-quart heavy saucepan. Stir over medium heat until sugar dissolves, then boil to soft ball stage (238°). Pour syrup over beaten egg whites, beating constantly until slightly cool. This takes about 5 minutes. Spoon into well buttered bowl and make a well in center. Let stand while you make second syrup. Combine remaining 2¼ cup sugar, ⅔ cup corn syrup and ¾ cup water. Cook over medium heat, stirring, until sugar is dissolved. Continue cooking to hard ball stage (258°). Pour syrup immediately into center of egg white mixture in bowl. Beat vigorously with wooden spoon until mixed thoroughly. Stir in butter, vanilla and salt. Let stand, beating occasionally, until mixture is very stiff and holds its shape. Transfer from bowl into wax paper-lined 8" square pan. With buttered fingers, press it into pan. Keep in refrigerator until very firm - 2 or 3 hours. Turn the firm candy onto cutting board and remove wax paper. Cut in half, and half again, making 4 squares. Cut each square into 4 logs of equal size. You'll have 16 small logs. You are now ready to make caramel coating. To make carmel coating, combine sugar, corn syrup and ½ cup cream in 2-quart heavy saucepan. Stir over medium heat until sugar dissolves. Cook to soft ball stage (236°). Slowly add ½ cup cream and again cook to soft ball stage (236°). Add remaining ½ cup cream and cook to firm ball stage (242°). Stir often as caramel mixture thickens.

(continued)

Remove from heat and stir in vanilla and salt. Pour mixture into top of double boiler, scraping pan with rubber spatula, and set over hot water. Gently drop nougat logs, one at a time, into caramel (work quickly with two forks), coating thoroughly. Hold log over caramel to drain. Drop logs into shallow dish containing nuts and roll to coat. As they are coated with nuts, transfer to wax paper. When cool, wrap logs, individually, in aluminum foil and store in refrigerator at least 5 hours, or for weeks. When ready to serve, cut in ½" slices. Makes 4¾ pounds or about 128 slices.

CHOCOLATE ALMOND BARK

1 11½-oz. pkg. milk chocolate chips
1 T. shortening
½ c. raisins
½ c. chopped toasted almonds, divided

Spread wax paper in a 13" x 9" x 2" baking pan, with some overlapping the ends. Combine in the top of a double boiler over boiling water the chocolate chips and vegetable shortening. Heat until chips are melted and mixture is smooth. Remove from heat and stir in raisins and half the almonds. Spread into baking pan. Sprinkle remaining almonds on top. Chill in refrigerator until ready to serve, at least 1 hour. Before serving, break into pieces.

CHOCOLATE NUT CARAMELS

2 oz. unsweetened chocolate
1⅛ c. sugar
⅛ tsp. salt
1 c. cream, warmed
1 c. light corn syrup
¼ c. butter, softened
1 tsp. vanilla
1 c. pecan halves

Grate chocolate in food processor into granules and set aside. Lightly butter an 8" square pan. Warm cream (do not boil) and set aside. In a 2-quart saucepan, stir sugar, salt and ⅓ cup cream. Bring to boil and add corn syrup and cook, stirring, to 248° on candy thermometer (firm ball stage). Add ¼ cup cream and cook to 230°. Add the rest of the cream and cook to 230°. Add butter. With wooden spoon, paddle constantly while cooking to 248°. Set pan on cake rack and sprinkle chocolate on top. Cool to 220°. Stir chocolate and stir in vanilla and pecans. Turn into buttered pan. When firm, cut into 1" squares and wrap.

CHOCOLATE TRUFFLES

10 oz. semi-sweet chocolate pieces
2 T. water
1 c. confectioners' sugar
2 T. golden rum or Grand Marnier or Cointreau
⅓ c. heavy cream
2 T. sifted cocoa or chocolate sprinkles

In top of double boiler, combine chocolate pieces and 2 T. water. Place over hot, not boiling, water, stirring occasionally, until chocolate is melted. Scrape chocolate into medium bowl with rubber spatula. Add sugar, cream and rum or other liquor. Stir until combined, then beat well. Place sheet of plastic wrap directly on surface of chocolate. Refrigerate 1 hour. Spread cocoa or chocolate sprinkles on a sheet of wax paper. Drop rounded teaspoonfuls of chocolate mixture onto cocoa. Roll with palm of hand into balls, covering completely with cocoa or chocolate sprinkles. Refrigerate, covered, to store. Makes about 3 dozen.

GORP

1 c. quick-cooking rolled oats
1 c. shelled peanuts
¼ c. wheat germ
½ c. honey
½ c. pecans or walnuts
2 T. vegetable oil
1 c. M&M candies
½ c. chopped, mixed dried fruit
½ c. raisins
Optional: ½ c. coconut and/or ½ c. dates

Heat oven to 300°. In a large bowl, combine oats, peanuts, wheat germ and nuts. In a small bowl, combine honey and oil and stir into mixture. Spread out in a 9" x 9" x 2" pan. Bake for 30 to 40 minutes until light brown, stirring every 10-15 minutes. Remove from oven and transfer to another lightly greased pan to cool. Break up into large pieces. Stir in candy, fruit and raisins. Store in tightly covered container or plastic bag.

MARSHMALLOW CREAM FUDGE

3 c. sugar
12 T. butter
⅔ c. evaporated milk
12 oz. semi-sweet chocolate chips
7 oz. marshmallow cream
1½ c. chopped walnuts
1 tsp. vanilla

(continued)

Butter a 13" x 9" x 2" glass dish. Mix sugar, butter and milk in large saucepan. Stir together until well blended and sugar is dissolved. Bring to 234° on candy thermometer, stirring now and then. Remove from heat and add chocolate chips. Blend. Add marshmallow cream and blend. Add vanilla and nuts and mix nuts in. Pour into prepared glass baking dish and cool. When cool, cut into squares.

MINTS

2 oz. cream cheese, softened
¼ tsp. mint flavoring
1⅔ c. confectioners' sugar
2 drops green food coloring
granulated sugar for rolling in

For molded mints, you will need rose molds and leaf molds. Stir cheese. Add flavoring and color. Mix in sugar. Knead with hands until it is like a dough. Break off pieces and roll into marble-size balls and dip in granulated sugar. (If it's too soft to work with, refrigerate for a half hour.) Press sugared side into molds and unmold onto wax paper. For round mints, just roll into marble-size balls and put on wax paper. For chocolate mints: Stir 3 tsp. cocoa and ½ tsp. vanilla into the cream cheese before mixing in sugar.

PEANUT BRITTLE

2 c. sugar
1 c. white corn syrup
½ c. water
½ c. butter
2 c. raw peanuts
1 tsp. baking soda

Butter 2 cookie sheets and set aside. In 3-quart saucepan, heat together sugar, corn syrup and water, stirring until sugar dissolves. When syrup boils, blend in butter. Stir frequently after temperature reaches 230°. Add peanuts when temperature reaches 280°. Stir constantly to hard crack stage (305°). Remove from heat, quickly stir in baking soda. Mix well and pour on prepared cookie sheets. Loosen from sheets when candy hardens. Break into pieces. Makes 2½ pounds. Store in a tin, covered.

PEANUT BUTTER CHEWIES

½ c. crunchy peanut butter
3 T. honey
1 tsp. vanilla
¾ c. instant nonfat dry milk

pinch of salt
3 T. confectioners' sugar
½ c. finely chopped unsalted peanuts

Mix together the peanut butter, honey, vanilla, dry milk, salt and sugar in a bowl. Using your hands, blend until very well mixed. Shape the mixture into 1" balls and roll them in the peanuts. Store in refrigerator.

TORRONE (NOUGAT CANDY)

1 c. blanched filberts
½ lb. blanched whole almonds
¼ tsp. salt
2 c. sugar
1 c. light corn syrup
¼ c. water
½ c. honey

2 egg whites
2 tsp. vanilla
¼ c. butter, softened
Optional: 2 squares edible rice paper (available from certain Italian confectioners or Oriental food shops)

Preheat oven to 350°. Line an 11" x 7" by 1¼" pan or glass baking dish with edible sheets of rice paper or foil. If you use the foil, butter. Spread filberts and almonds on cookie sheet. Toast in oven 8-10 minutes, just until golden. Set aside. In large bowl of mixer, at high speed, beat egg whites until stiff peaks form when beater is slowly raised. Set aside. In heavy 3-quart saucepan, combine sugar, corn syrup, honey, salt and ¼ cup water. Stir over medium heat until sugar is dissolved. Continue cooking to 252° on candy thermometer, without stirring. In a thin stream, pour about ¼ of hot syrup over egg whites, beating constantly, at high speed, until mixture is stiff enough to hold its shape, about 3 to 5 minutes. Continue cooking the rest of the syrup to 318° on candy thermometer. In a thin stream, pour hot syrup over meringue, beating constantly, at high speed, until mixture is stiff enough to hold its shape. Add vanilla and butter, beating until thickened again, about 5 minutes. With wooden spoon, stir in toasted nuts. Turn mixture into prepared baking dish. Smooth top with rubber spatula. Top with another sheet of edible rice paper or with sugared foil. Refrigerate until firm. Loosen edge of candy all around. Turn out on large block. Peel off foil, but keep edible rice paper on candy if you use it. With sharp knife, cut into 1½" by 1" pieces. Wrap each piece individually in wax paper. Store in refrigerator. Makes about 2½ pounds.

TURTLES

1 lb. vanilla caramels, unwrapped
2 T. butter
1 T. water
1 11½-oz. pkg. milk chocolate chips
½ c. light corn syrup
2 T. water
2 c. pecan halves

Grease and line 2 cookie sheets with wax paper. Combine in the top of a double boiler, over boiling water, caramels, butter and water. Heat until carmels melt and mixture is smooth. Keep over boiling water. Combine in another double boiler, over hot (not boiling) water, milk chocolate chips, corn syrup and water. Heat until mixture is smooth. Keep warm over hot water. Drop caramel mixture by rounded teaspoonfuls onto greased, wax paper-lined cookie sheets. Place 3 pecan halves on top of each caramel to make head and legs. Drop chocolate mixture over caramel-nut piece by slightly rounded measuring teaspoonfuls. Chill in refrigerator until set (about 30 minutes). Remove from wax paper onto serving platter. Refrigerate until ready to serve. Makes about 4 dozen turtles.

ALMOND BISCOTTI

2½ c. flour
2 tsp. baking powder
¼ tsp. salt
2 tsp. almond extract
¼ c. butter, softened
1 c. sugar
3 eggs
1 c. slivered almonds

Heat oven to 350°. Grease 2 aluminum cookie sheets. Sift flour with baking powder and salt 3 times. Set aside. In medium bowl, with mixer at medium speed, beat butter with sugar until very light. Add eggs, one at a time, beating well after each addition. Beat in almond extract. Add flour mixture, beating at low speed, until blended. Blend in almonds at low speed. Remove from bowl onto a lightly floured surface. Divide mixture in half. Shape each half into an 11" x 5" oval. Place on prepared cookie sheets. Bake 15 to 20 minutes, or until pale golden-brown. Remove from oven. Cut each loaf into 1" thick slices. Turn each slice on its side. Bake on one side 8 minutes, then turn over on the other side and bake 5 minutes more or until lightly browned. Remove slices to wire rack and let cool completely. Makes 18 to 20 slices.

ANISE COOKIES

8 T. butter
⅓ c. sugar
1 tsp. baking powder
1 tsp. vanilla
1 tsp. anise flavoring

2 tsp. anise seed
2 eggs
3 T. milk
2 c. flour
½ tsp. salt

Heat oven to 350°. Blend sugar and butter. Add eggs and beat until fluffy. Add flavorings, anise seed, milk, baking powder and salt. Then add flour and beat. Turn out onto a lightly floured surface. Break off pieces of dough the size of a walnut and shape them into the letter S and place on greased aluminum cookie sheet. Bake for 10-12 minutes.

BAKLAVA

Baklava:

2 c. chopped almonds
2 c. chopped walnuts
½ c. sugar
grated zest of one lemon

1 tsp. cinnamon
1 pound purchased phyllo sheets
1 c. melted butter

Syrup:

1½ c. sugar
1 c. water
grated zest of ½ lemon
1 c. honey

1 tsp. cinnamon
4 T. lemon juice
2 T. rum or brandy (optional)

Heat oven to 350°. Butter the bottom and sides of a 13" x 9" baking pan. Mix together the chopped almonds, chopped walnuts, ½ cup sugar, grated zest of one lemon and 1 teaspoon cinnamon and set aside. Arrange 1 sheet phyllo dough on the bottom of the pan, letting it hang over the edges an inch or two. Brush with melted butter and top with six more sheets of phyllo dough, each brushed with melted butter, each lapping over the edges of the pan. Sprinkle with ¼ of the nut mixture. Fold in one layer of the overlapping sides. Top with 3 more layers of phyllo dough which have been cut down to 13" x 9" to fit the pan, brushing each one with melted butter. Sprinkle ¼ of the nut mixture on top. Fold in one layer of the overlapping sides. Top with 3 more layers of phyllo dough which have been cut down to 13" x 9", brushing each one with melted butter. Add ¼ of the nut mixture. Fold in one layer of the overlapping sides. Top with three more sheets of phyllo dough which have been cut down to 13" x 9", brushing each one with melted butter.

(continued)

Top with the remaining ¼ of the nut mixture. Add four more layers of phyllo dough which have been cut down to 13" x 9", brushing each one with melted butter. If any phyllo is still overlapping the sides, fold it back over the top and seal with butter. With a sharp serrated knife, cut partially to the first nut layer 4 lines the length of the pan. Then cut into squares or triangles. Bake until golden, one hour. Meanwhile, cook together in a heavy saucepan, 1½ cups sugar and 1 cup water until the sugar is dissolved. Add grated zest of ½ lemon, 1 cup honey, 1 teaspoon cinnamon, 4 tablespoons lemon juice and 2 tablespoons rum or brandy. Cook for 5 minutes, stirring and remove from heat. Set aside. When you remove the baklava from the oven, cut through the lines you made completely and while the baklava is still hot, stir the cooled honey syrup and pour over the baklava. Makes about 50 pieces.

BLACK AND WHITE COOKIES

½ tsp. baking soda
½ c. hot water
¼ tsp. salt
1 tsp. baking powder
2½ c. flour

⅔ c. buttermilk
1 tsp. vanilla
½ c. Crisco shortening
1 c. sugar
2 eggs

Heat oven to 375°. Grease 2 aluminum baking sheets. Mix the baking soda and hot water together. Set aside to cool. Mix together the flour, baking powder and salt. Set aside. In the bowl of an electric mixer, cream the shortening, sugar and vanilla. Add the eggs and beat until fluffy. Mix in the baking soda and water mixture. On low speed, mix in flour mixture and the buttermilk alternately, beginning and ending with flour. Blend well. Drop batter with a ¼ cup measuring cup 2 inches apart on prepared cookie sheets. Bake for 12-15 minutes, until golden. Transfer to a cake rack to cool. Make icing.

Icing:

Vanilla Icing:

2 c. confectioners' sugar
3 T. milk

1 tsp. vanilla
3 T. butter, softened

Chocolate Icing:

½ recipe for vanilla icing
2 T. cocoa powder

1 T. milk

Beat together the confectioners' sugar, milk, vanilla and butter until smooth. Put ½ the vanilla icing in another bowl and add 2 tablespoons

(continued)

cocoa powder and 1 tablespoon milk. Mix together. When the cookies are cool, turn them over so that the bottoms are facing up. Spread white icing on half of each flat surface and then spread the other half with chocolate icing. Let sit at room temperature for 30 minutes.

BROWNIES

2 1-oz. squares unsweetened chocolate, melted
½ c. butter, softened
1 c. sugar
¼ tsp. salt

2 eggs
1½ tsp. vanilla
½ c. flour
¾ c. coarsely broken walnuts

Heat oven to 325°. Grease and flour an 8" x 8" baking pan. Melt the chocolate. Set aside. In an electric mixer, beat together the softened butter and sugar until creamy. Add eggs and beat until fluffy. Put the speed on low and blend in the melted chocolate, salt and vanilla. Stir in the flour. Mix thoroughly, scraping down the sides and bottom of the mixing bowl with a rubber spatula. Add the walnuts and blend in. Pour into the prepared pan and bake for 35 minutes. Set the pan on a rack to cool. Cut the brownies into squares.

CARAMEL BARS

1 lb. vanilla caramels, unwrapped
¼ c. water
½ c. peanut butter
4 c. Cheerios

1 c. salted peanuts, without skins
1 c. semi-sweet chocolate chips
¼ c. peanut butter
2 T. butter

Butter a 13" x 9" baking pan or glass baking dish. Combine caramels and water and melt in top of a double boiler, with boiling water in the bottom pan. When smooth, stir in ½ cup peanut butter and stir until blended. Put the Cheerios in a large bowl. Pour the mixture over the Cheerios and mix well. Add the peanuts and mix until blended. Press into the prepared pan. Place the semi-sweet chocolate chips, ¼ cup peanut butter and 2 tablespoons butter in the top of a double boiler with boiling water in the bottom pan. Melt and blend together. Spread over the cereal mixture. Let stand until firm.

CUSCINETTI ABRUZZESE

Vegetable Oil for frying

Dough:

2 eggs	¼ tsp. salt
6 T. sugar	2 c. flour
1 tsp. vanilla	2 T. olive oil

Filling:

1 can chick peas, rinsed and drained	2 tsp. orange extract
	¼ c. honey
6-oz. chocolate bar, grated	½ tsp. cinnamon

Grate the chocolate in a food processor into granules. Put into a mixing bowl. Purée the chick peas in a food processor. Add to the chocolate. Add the orange extract, honey and cinnamon. Mix well. For the dough, beat the eggs with the sugar, vanilla, salt and oil. Stir in the flour until dough holds its shape. Divide the dough into 24 balls. Roll out each ball of dough into a 5½" circle. Divide the filling into 24 balls, rounding out in your hands. Put rounded balls of mixture on the dough rounds. Moisten the edges of the circles of dough. Fold one half over the other and press to seal. Then press each one around the edges with a fork to seal. Heat oil to 2" deep to 375° in an electric frying pan or a deep fryer. Fry, a few at a time, until golden, turning to cook each side. Makes 24.

CHERRY COOKIES

½ c. shortening	1 tsp. almond flavor
1 c. sugar	1 tsp. vanilla
2 tsp. baking powder	2½ c. flour
½ tsp. salt	granulated sugar for sprinkling
2 large eggs	maraschino cherries, sliced in half horizontally
juice from 6-oz. jar of maraschino cherries	

Heat oven to 350°. Grease two aluminum cookie sheets. In electric mixer, cream together the shortening and sugar. Add the eggs and beat together. Add the almond flavoring, vanilla and juice from jar of cherries. Stir in the baking powder and salt. Stir in the flour, one half cup at a time. Drop on prepared cookie sheets 1" apart. Sprinkle with sugar with a small spoon, flattening the cookies a little. Slice the cherries in half

(continued)

lengthwise and place one half of a cherry on each cookie. Bake 10-12 minutes until they are beginning to brown.

CHERRY WINKS

2¼ c. flour
1 tsp. baking powder
½ tsp. baking soda
½ tsp. salt
¾ c. Crisco shortening
1 c. sugar
2 eggs

2 T. milk
1 tsp. vanilla
1 c. chopped pecans
1 c. chopped dates
⅓ c. maraschino cherries
crushed Cornflakes for rolling in
maraschino cherries for topping

Heat oven to 350°. Mix together the flour, baking powder, baking soda and salt. Cream together in electric mixer the shortening and sugar. Add the eggs and beat until fluffy. Add 2 tablespoons milk and the vanilla and mix. On low speed, add the dry ingredients. Stir in the pecans, dates and cherries. Form into balls about the size of a walnut. Sprinkle the crushed Cornflakes on wax paper. Roll the balls into the Cornflakes and place on ungreased aluminum cookie sheets 1" apart. Press down with ¼ of a cherry in the middle. Bake for 10-12 minutes until golden.

CHOCOLATE BUTTERSCOTCH BARS

¼ lb. butter
1 c. graham cracker crumbs
  (about 6 whole graham crackers)
1 c. semi-sweet chocolate chips

1 c. butterscotch chips
1 c. flaked coconut
1 c. broken pecans
1 15-oz. can condensed milk

Heat oven to 350°. Melt butter in 9" x 13" baking pan. Sprinkle the graham cracker crumbs over the butter. Sprinkle evenly over the crumbs: 1 cup chocolate chips, then 1 cup butterscotch chips, then 1 cup coconut, then 1 cup broken pecans. Drizzle over 1 can condensed milk. Bake for 30 minutes. Cool and cut into squares.

CHOCOLATE CHIP HEATH BAR COOKIES LEE ANNE

2¼ c. flour
1 tsp. baking soda
1 tsp. salt
½ c. butter, softened
½ c. Crisco shortening
1½ c. granulated sugar
1 tsp. vanilla
2 large eggs
2 c. Hershey's semi-sweet chocolate chips
1 c. chopped walnuts or pecans
1 8-oz. pkg. Heath Bar chips

Heat oven to 350°. Combine flour, baking soda and salt in a bowl. In an electric mixer, beat together the butter, shortening, granulated sugar and vanilla until creamy. Add eggs, one at a time, beating well after each addition. On low speed, gradually beat in flour mixture. Stir in chocolate chips, nuts and Heath Bar chips. Drop by rounded tablespoonfuls onto ungreased aluminum baking sheets. Bake for 11 minutes or until golden. Let stand for 2 minutes. Remove to platter to cool completely.

CHOCOLATE COOKIES

½ c. oil
½ c. sugar
1 tsp. vanilla
¼ tsp. salt
2 eggs
½ c. cocoa
½ c. milk
2 tsp. baking powder
½ c. semi-sweet chocolate chips
½ c. chopped walnuts
2½ c. flour
4 c. confectioners' sugar
approximately ½ c. milk

Heat oven to 350°. Mix together the oil, sugar, vanilla, salt, ½ cup milk and eggs beat on medium speed of electric mixer. Put speed on low and stir in cocoa and baking powder. Stir in flour, a cup at a time, and beat on medium speed for 1 minute. Lower speed and stir in chocolate chips and nuts. Roll dough into balls the size of a walnut. Put on ungreased aluminum baking sheets. Bake for 10 minutes. When completely cool, dip in a mixture of powdered sugar mixed with ½ cup milk, thick enough to glaze cookies. Set on wax paper to dry. Let dry thoroughly before packing, preferably overnight.

CHOCOLATE COOKIES WITH WHITE CHOCOLATE CHIPS

2¼ c. all-purpose flour
⅔ c. cocoa
1 tsp. baking soda
¼ tsp. salt
½ c. butter
½ c. Crisco shortening

¾ c. granulated sugar
⅔ c. packed brown sugar
1 tsp. vanilla
2 eggs
2 c. white chocolate chips (12-oz. pkg.)

Heat oven to 350°. Combine flour, cocoa, baking soda and salt in small bowl. With electric mixer, in large bowl, beat together butter, shortening, granulated sugar, brown sugar and vanilla until creamy. Beat in eggs. On low speed, gradually beat in flour mixture. Stir in white chocolate chips. Drop by heaping teaspoonfuls onto ungreased aluminum baking sheets. Bake for 9 to 11 minutes. Let stand for 2 minutes. Remove to wire racks to cool completely. Makes about 5 dozen.

CHOCOLATE CRINKLES

½ c. Crisco shortening
1⅔ c. sugar
2 tsp. vanilla
2 eggs
2 1-oz. squares unsweetened chocolate, melted

2 c. all-purpose flour
2 tsp. baking powder
½ tsp. salt
⅓ c. milk
½ c. chopped walnuts
sifted confectioners' sugar

Heat oven to 350°. Melt chocolate in microwave or in top of double boiler over boiling water. Grease aluminum cookie sheets. Cream shortening, sugar and vanilla. Beat in eggs, one at a time, then stir in melted chocolate. Sift together flour, baking powder and salt. Blend in dry ingredients with milk. Add nuts. Chill dough in refrigerator for 45 minutes. Form into 1" balls. Roll in confectioners' sugar. Place on prepared cookie sheet 2" apart. Bake about 15 minutes. Cool for 5 minutes and remove from pan onto platter.

CHOCOLATE FILLED COOKIES

Filling:

1 15-oz. can condensed milk
1 12-oz. pkg. semi-sweet chocolate chips
1 c. chopped nuts

Dough:

½ c. sugar
4 eggs
¼ c. oil
2 tsp. vanilla
4 tsp. baking powder
4 c. flour

Frosting:

2 c. confectioners' sugar
3 T. milk
1 tsp. vanilla
3 T. butter, softened
Multi-colored nonpareils for sprinkling

Heat oven to 350°. In a saucepan, over a low flame, melt the chocolate chips with the milk. Stir until thick. Add the nuts and let cool. In an electric mixer, mix together the sugar, eggs, oil and vanilla until fluffy. Add the baking powder and mix. On low speed mix in the flour, one cup at a time, until a soft dough is formed. On a lightly floured surface, shape the dough into 4 balls. Roll each one into a 14" x 4" rectangle. Spoon one-fourth of the filling lengthwise down the center of each rectangle in a 1" in diameter strip. From the long side, lift one side of the dough over to cover the filling and lift the other side up and over. Seal edges. Transfer to an ungreased cookie sheet, seam side down. Repeat with the remaining dough and filling. Bake for 15 minutes, until golden. Cool and frost. To make frosting, on low speed of electric mixer, stir together the confectioners' sugar, milk, vanilla and butter. On high speed, beat for 4 minutes. Frost the cookies and sprinkle with multi-colored nonpareils. Slice into 2" pieces.

CHOCOLATE KISS COOKIES

1 c. butter, softened
½ c. sugar
1 tsp. vanilla
1¾ c. flour
1 c. pecans, chopped
1 9-oz. pkg. chocolate candy kisses, unwrapped
confectioners' sugar for rolling

Heat oven to 350°. Cream butter and sugar together with vanilla. Add flour gradually until well blended. Stir in pecans. Chill dough for an hour. Mold about 1 tablespoon of cookie dough around each chocolate

(continued)

kiss, covering candy completely. Bake on aluminum cookie sheet until they just turn golden around the edges, about 10 minutes. Let cool slightly before removing from cookie sheet, about 5 minutes. Pour 1 cup confectioners' sugar in a shallow dish. When completely cool, roll in confectioners' sugar. Makes about 3 dozen.

COCOA OATMEAL NUGGETS

8 T. butter
2 c. sugar
¼ c. cocoa
½ c. milk
pinch salt

3 c. oatmeal
½ c. flaked coconut
½ c. chopped nuts
2 heaping T. peanut butter
1 tsp. vanilla

In a saucepan, melt the butter. Remove from heat. Stir in 2 cups sugar, ¼ cup cocoa, ½ cup milk and a pinch of salt. Return to heat. Bring to a full boil. Stir and cook 2½ minutes. Remove from heat. Add ½ cup flaked coconut, ½ cup chopped nuts, two heaping tablespoons peanut butter and 1 teaspoon vanilla and mix together. Stir in 3 cups oatmeal. Drop by heaping teaspoons onto wax paper. Let stand until firm.

COCONUT BARS

½ c. shortening
½ c. brown sugar
½ tsp. salt
1 c. all-purpose flour
2 eggs
1 tsp. vanilla
1 c. brown sugar

2 T. all-purpose flour
1 tsp. baking powder
½ tsp. salt
1¼ c. flaked coconut
1 c. chopped walnuts
Confectioners' Sugar Frosting, if desired

Heat oven to 350°. Cream together ½ cup shortening, ½ cup brown sugar and ½ teaspoon salt. Stir in 1 cup flour. Pat dough into ungreased 13" x 9" x 2" pan. Bake for 15 minutes. Meanwhile, beat eggs slightly and add vanilla. Gradually add 1 cup brown sugar, beating just until fluffy. Add 2 tablespoons flour, baking powder and ½ tsp. salt. Stir in coconut and walnuts. Spread over baked layer. Bake 20 to 25 minutes longer or until round toothpick comes out clean. Cool. If desired, frost with a light coating of confectioners' icing. Cut in diamonds or squares. Makes 2 dozen.

(continued)

Confectioners' Sugar Frosting:

1 c. confectioners' sugar
2 T. milk
½ tsp. vanilla
1 T. butter, softened

Stir together the sugar, milk, vanilla and butter in a bowl with an electric mixer. When mixed together, put the speed on high and beat until fluffy.

COCONUT TOPPED BROWNIES

1 4-oz. pkg. sweet cooking chocolate
⅓ c. butter
⅔ c. all-purpose flour
½ tsp. baking powder
¼ tsp. salt
2 eggs
½ c. sugar
1 tsp. vanilla
⅔ c. chopped nuts
½ c. mini semi-sweet chocolate chips
2 T. cream
1⅓ c. coconut
¼ c. brown sugar

Heat oven to 350°. Melt chocolate and butter over low heat in a saucepan, stirring. Set aside. Cool. Sift together flour, baking powder and salt. Beat eggs with an electric mixer. Gradually beat in sugar and vanilla. Add chocolate mixture and stir. With low speed, add flour mixture. Stir in nuts and mini semi-sweet chocolate chips. Spread in greased and floured 9" square pan. Mix together the cream, coconut and brown sugar. Spread over batter. Bake for 25 to 30 minutes.

CRUNCHY PEANUT BUTTER BALLS

1 c. crunchy peanut butter
⅔ c. sifted powdered sugar
⅔ c. powdered skim milk
4 T. honey
2 tsp. vanilla
pinch salt
½ c. chopped peanuts for rolling in

Mix together the peanut butter, powdered sugar, powdered milk, honey, vanilla and salt. Shape into balls. Put chopped peanuts on wax paper. Roll balls in peanuts. Chill.

FATTIGMAND COOKIES

6 egg yolks
1 T. melted butter
⅛ tsp. salt
6 T. cream
4 T. sugar

½ tsp. ground cardamom
2 c. flour
vegetable oil for frying
confectioners' sugar for
 sprinkling

    Beat egg yolks until lemon colored. Add sugar and mix well. Add melted butter, salt, cardamom and cream. Mix. Gradually mix in flour on a low speed of mixer. On a floured surface, roll out thin. Cut into diamond shapes. Heat the oil 3" deep in a saucepan or deep fryer to 375°. Fry for 2-3 minutes, turning, until light brown. When cool, dust with confectioners' sugar.

FIG COOKIES

½ c. butter
¼ c. granulated sugar
¼ c. brown sugar
¼ tsp. baking soda
1 egg
1 tsp. vanilla
1¾ c. all-purpose flour
1 c. dried figs, stems removed,
 finely chopped
⅔ c. raisins, finely chopped

⅓ c. diced mixed candied fruit
 and peels, finely chopped
½ c. orange juice
2 T. granulated sugar
1 tsp. grated lemon zest
¼ tsp. ground cinnamon
½ c. chopped almonds
Confectioners' sugar glaze
Multi-colored nonpareils for
 sprinkling

    Heat oven to 350°. Beat butter with an electric mixer in a medium mixing bowl. Add the ¼ cup granulated sugar, brown sugar and baking soda. Beat until fluffy. Beat in egg and vanilla until combined. Beat in enough of the flour to form a dough you can roll out. Set aside. Combine figs, raisins, candied fruit and peels, orange juice, the 2 tablespoons granulated sugar, lemon zest and cinnamon in a small saucepan. Bring to just boiling. Reduce heat. Cover and simmer for 5 to 8 minutes or until fruit is softened and mixture is thick, stirring occasionally. Stir in almonds. Cool to room temperature. Divide dough in half. Roll one portion out on a floured surface into a 10" x 8" rectangle. Cut from the 8" side into two strips, 4" x 10". Spoon one-fourth of the filling lengthwise down center of each piece of dough in a 1" wide strip. Lift one side of dough up to cover filling. Lift opposite side of dough up and over the first side. Seal edges, forming a long rope. Transfer to an ungreased cookie sheet, seam side down. Repeat with remaining dough and filling. Bake for 15 minutes, until lightly browned. Frost with Confectioners'

(continued)

Sugar Glaze when cool. Sprinkle with multi-colored nonpareils. Cut into 1½" pieces at a diagonal.

Confectioners' Sugar Glaze:

2 c. confectioners' sugar
3 T. milk
1 tsp. vanilla
3 T. butter, softened

Stir together the sugar, milk, vanilla and butter in a bowl with an electric mixer. When mixed together, put the speed on high and beat until fluffy.

FRUIT BARS

1 c. Crisco shortening
1 c. sugar
1 tsp. salt
1 tsp. cinnamon
1 tsp. baking soda
½ tsp. ground ginger
3 eggs
1 c. molasses
4 c. flour
1 c. raisins
1 c. pecans

Heat oven to 350°. Grease and flour a 15½" x 10½" x 1" jelly roll pan. Beat together the shortening and sugar until creamy. Add the eggs and beat until fluffy. Add the salt, cinnamon, baking soda, ginger and mix in. Add the molasses and mix. On low speed, gradually add the flour. Stir in the raisins and pecans. Spread onto prepared pan. Bake for 18 minutes. While warm, ice with a thin coating of Confectioners' Sugar Frosting. Let cool and cut into bars.

Confectioners' Sugar Frosting:

2 c. confectioners' sugar
3 T. milk
1 tsp. vanilla
3 T. butter, softened

Stir together the sugar, milk, vanilla and butter in a bowl with an electric mixer. When mixed together, put the speed on high and beat until fluffy.

FUDGE NUT BARS

1 12-oz. pkg. semi-sweet chocolate chips
1 can condensed milk
2 T. butter
½ tsp. salt
1 c. chopped walnuts
2 tsp. vanilla
1 c. butter, softened
2 c. brown sugar
2 beaten eggs
2 tsp. vanilla
2½ c. all-purpose flour
1 tsp. salt
1 tsp. baking soda
3 c. oatmeal
½ c. chopped nuts

Heat oven to 350°. Melt together over low heat the chocolate chips, condensed milk, butter and salt, stirring constantly. When melted, add 1 cup chopped nuts and 2 teaspoons vanilla. Set aside. Cream 1 cup butter and 2 cups brown sugar. Add 2 beaten eggs and 2 teaspoons vanilla. Blend well. Stir in 2½ cups all-purpose flour and 1 teaspoon salt, 1 teaspoon baking soda and 3 cups oatmeal. Press ⅔ of this mixture in a 10½" x 15½" x 1" jelly roll pan. Spread with the chocolate filling. Add ½ cup chopped nuts to the remaining oatmeal mixture and sprinkle over filling. Press down slightly, but not too much. Bake for 25-30 minutes. Do not overbake. Cool. Cut into bars.

GINGER COOKIE PEOPLE

1 c. shortening
1½ c. sugar
2 eggs
4 T. molasses
3 c. all-purpose flour
2 tsp. baking soda
2 tsp. cinnamon
1 tsp. ginger
½ tsp. cloves
½ tsp. salt
Icing for decorating
Raisins for decorating

Heat oven to 350°. Cream shortening and sugar. Add eggs. Beat until fluffy. Add molasses. Mix well. Sift together dry ingredients. Stir into creamed mixture. Chill dough for 1 hour. Roll out dough on floured surface ¼" thick. Cut with a ginger boy/girl cookie cutter. Place 1" apart on ungreased cookie sheets. Use scraps to make more cookies. Bake for 8 to 10 minutes. Decorate with icing and raisins.

Icing:

2 c. confectioners' sugar
3 T. milk
1 tsp. vanilla
3 T. butter, softened

(continued)

Stir together the sugar, milk, vanilla and butter in a bowl with an electric mixer. When mixed together, put the speed on high and beat until fluffy.

HERMITS

½ c. shortening
½ c. brown sugar
¼ tsp. ground ginger
¼ tsp. ground cloves
½ tsp. baking soda
½ tsp. ground cinnamon
½ tsp. ground nutmeg
2 eggs

¼ c. molasses
2 T. milk
1 tsp. vanilla
2 c. all-purpose flour
1 c. chopped dates
½ c. chopped walnuts
1½ c. sifted confectioners' sugar
2 T. milk

Heat oven to 350°. Grease and flour a 15½" x 10½" x 1" jelly roll pan. In a large bowl, beat together shortening, sugar, ginger, cloves, baking soda, cinnamon and nutmeg. On low speed, beat in eggs, molasses, the 2 tablespoons milk and vanilla. Add the flour, a cup at a time, and mix in. Mix in the dates and nuts. Spread onto prepared pan. Bake for 15-20 minutes, or until a round toothpick inserted in center comes out clean. Cool. Mix together the confectioners' sugar and milk. Spread over top. Cut into 24 bars.

HOLIDAY MINCE SQUARES

2 c. oatmeal
2 c. flour
1¾ c. brown sugar
1½ tsp. salt
1 tsp. cinnamon

½ c. oil
½ c. milk
½ tsp. baking soda
1 28-oz. jar mincemeat
½ c. chopped nuts

Heat oven to 350°. Grease a 13" x 9" x 2" baking pan. Combine in a large bowl 2 cups oatmeal, 2 cups flour, 1¾ cup brown sugar, 1½ teaspoons salt and 1 teaspoon cinnamon. Cut in with a fork ½ cup oil, ½ c. milk and ½ tsp. baking soda until mixture is crumbly. Put ⅔ of crumb mixture into prepared pan. Spoon evenly over the top one 28-oz. jar of mincemeat. Mix ½ cup chopped nuts into remaining third of crumb mixture. Sprinkle over and gently press into mincemeat. Bake for 60 minutes. Cool. Cut into 1½" squares.

ITALIAN ROSETTES

Dough:

¼ c. vegetable oil
4 eggs
5 T. sugar

4 tsp. baking powder
2 tsp. vanilla
4 c. flour

Filling:

1 c. melted butter
5 c. finely chopped walnuts

1 T. cinnamon
½ c. sugar

Heat oven to 350°. To make the dough, mix together the vegetable oil, eggs, sugar, baking powder and vanilla with electric mixer. On low speed, add flour, 1 cup at a time. Divide the ball of dough in half. On floured surface roll out a ball of dough into 12" x 6" rectangle. Mix together the walnuts, cinnamon and sugar. Lightly brush the dough with melted butter. Sprinkle one-half of the mixture on the dough. Roll up the rectangle from the 12" side. Cut the roll into 1½" lengths. Pinch the sides of each piece, forming into a rosette, and place on ungreased cookie sheet, 1" apart. Repeat with second ball of dough. Bake for 15-20 minutes, until they turn golden brown.

LACKERLI

2 c. milk
1 c. butter
1 c. sugar
⅔ c. molasses
4 c. all-purpose flour
1 tsp. salt
2 tsp. cinnamon
½ tsp. ginger

½ tsp. cloves
½ tsp. nutmeg
1½ tsp. baking soda
2 T. cocoa
1 c. chopped nuts
1 c. raisins
Confectioners' Sugar Icing

Heat oven to 350°. Grease and flour two 15½" x 10½" x 1" jelly roll pans. Scald the milk by heating until tiny bubbles appear. Add the butter, sugar, and molasses to the milk. Turn into a large bowl to cool. In another bowl, mix together flour, salt, cinnamon, ginger, cloves, nutmeg, baking soda and cocoa. Gradually add to the milk-molasses mixture, beating well after each addition. Stir in the nuts and raisins. Divide the batter between the two prepared pans. Spread to the edges of the pans. Batter should be about ½" thick. Bake for 20 minutes. Cool and frost with confectioners' sugar icing. Cut diagonally into diamonds. Makes about 5 dozen cookies.

(continued)

Confectioners' Sugar Icing:

2 c. confectioners' sugar
3 T. milk

1 tsp. vanilla
3 T. butter, softened

Stir together the sugar, milk, vanilla and butter in a bowl with an electric mixer. When mixed together, put the speed on high and beat until fluffy.

LEBKUCHEN

3 c. flour
1 tsp. baking soda
½ tsp. salt
1 tsp. allspice
1 tsp. nutmeg
1 tsp. cinnamon
1 tsp. cloves
¼ c. finely chopped citron

½ c. finely chopped walnuts
¾ c. honey
¼ c. molasses
¾ c. light brown sugar
1 egg
1 T. lemon juice
2 tsp. grated lemon zest

Glaze:

2 c. sifted confectioners' sugar   3 T. water

Sift flour with baking soda, salt, allspice, nutmeg, cinnamon and cloves. Warm honey and molasses in small saucepan. Remove from heat. In a large bowl, with electric mixer, beat together brown sugar and egg until smooth and fluffy. Add lemon juice and honey-molasses mixture. Beat well. Beat in lemon zest and 1 cup of the flour mixture until smooth. Beat in another cup of the flour mixture. Stir in the citron and nuts. Stir in the rest of the flour mixture. Refrigerate dough, covered, overnight. Preheat oven to 375°. Lightly grease 2 aluminum cookie sheets. On lightly floured surface, roll out dough, ½ at a time, to ¼" thick. Using floured 2" round cookie cutters, cut out cookies. Place 2" apart on prepared cookie sheets. Bake 12 minutes. When cookies are baked, cool slightly. Make glaze by combining confectioners' sugar with the water, stirring until smooth. Brush glaze on warm cookies. Makes 3 dozen. Store, tightly covered, in a cool, dry place two weeks before using. (To keep moist, keep a slice of bread in container, changing bread every few days, to prevent molding.)

LEMON BARS

12 T. butter, softened
2 c. flour
½ c. light brown sugar
½ t. salt
4 eggs

1½ c. granulated sugar
¾ c. fresh lemon juice
⅓ c. all-purpose flour
½ tsp. baking powder
confectioners' sugar

Heat oven to 350°. Put the 2 cups flour and salt into a bowl. Cut the butter into the flour with a fork until crumbly. Mix the light brown sugar in until well blended. Press the dough onto the bottom and ½" up the sides of a lightly greased 13" x 9" x 2" pan. Bake for 20 minutes. Remove from the oven and cool. Beat the eggs and granulated sugar with an electric mixer. Stir in the lemon juice, flour and baking powder. Pour lemon mixture over the baked crust. Put into the oven and bake until set, about 20 minutes. Cool to room temperature. Sift confectioners' sugar over before serving. Cut into bars.

LEMON COOKIES

4 T. butter, softened
4 T. shortening
¾ c. sugar
1 egg
½ tsp. lemon extract
2 tsp. grated lemon zest
1 T. milk

1¼ c. flour
¼ tsp. salt
¼ tsp. baking soda
¼ tsp. baking powder
confectioners' sugar for sifting on top

Heat oven to 350°. With an electric mixer, cream the butter and shortening together. Gradually add the sugar, beating until light. Add the egg, lemon extract, lemon zest and milk and beat thoroughly. Mix together the flour, salt, baking soda and baking powder. On low speed of mixer, stir in the flour mixture. Drop by rounded teaspoonfuls on lightly greased aluminum cookie sheets, 2" apart. Bake for 10 minutes until lightly browned. Let sit on the cookie sheets for 5 minutes. Remove to a platter with a metal spatula. Let cool and sift confectioners' sugar over the tops.

MACADAMIA NUT SQUARES

1 c. flour
½ c. butter, softened
2 eggs, slightly beaten
½ c. flaked coconut
2 T. flour
1½ c. brown sugar, firmly packed
¼ tsp. baking powder
½ tsp. salt

1 tsp. vanilla
1 c. chopped macadamia nuts
2 T. butter, softened
1½ c. confectioners' sugar
3 T. orange juice
1 tsp. lemon juice
½ c. ground macadamia nuts

Heat oven to 350°. Grease a 9" square baking pan. Mix the 1 cup flour and ½ cup butter to fine crumbs. Pat into the bottom of prepared pan. Bake 15 minutes. Remove from oven. Mix together the eggs, coconut, 2 tablespoons flour, brown sugar, baking powder, salt, vanilla and chopped nuts. Cover the crust with mixture and bake for 20 minutes. Remove from oven and cool. Mix together the 2 tablespoons butter, confectioners' sugar, orange juice and lemon juice and spread over mixture. Sprinkle ground nuts over top. Cut into small squares.

MAGIC PEANUT BUTTER MIDDLES

Dough:

1½ c. flour
½ c. cocoa
½ tsp. baking soda
½ c. granulated sugar
½ c. brown sugar

½ c. butter
¼ c. peanut butter
1 tsp. vanilla
1 egg

Filling:

¾ c. peanut butter
¾ c. confectioners' sugar

Heat oven to 375°. In small bowl, combine flour, baking soda and cocoa. In large bowl, beat granulated sugar, brown sugar, butter and ¼ cup peanut butter until light and fluffy. Add vanilla and egg. Beat well. Stir in flour mixture until blended. set aside. In small bowl, combine ¾ cup peanut butter and ¾ cup confectioners' sugar. Roll into 30 1" balls. Shape 1 tablespoon dough around each peanut butter ball, covering completely. Place 2" apart on ungreased cookie sheet. Flatten with bottom of a glass dipped in granulated sugar. Bake 7-9 minutes or until set and slightly cracked. Cool. Makes 30.

MERINGUES GLACÉS

2 egg whites
½ c. sugar
4 T. unsweetened, sifted cocoa
¼ tsp. cream of tartar

1 tsp. vanilla
Vanilla Ice Cream
Regal Chocolate Sauce

Heat oven to 300°. Prepare Regal Chocolate Sauce and set aside to cool. Grease an aluminum cookie sheet. Make chocolate meringues: In small bowl, with electric mixer at high speed, beat egg whites with cream of tartar just until soft peaks form when beater is slowly raised. Add sugar, 1 tablespoon at a time, beating well after each addition. Continue beating until stiff peaks form when beater is slowly raised. Fold in cocoa and vanilla with a spatula. Drop by heaping tablespoonfuls, 1" apart, onto prepared cookie sheet, making 12 mounds. Bake 15 minutes. Turn off oven heat. Leave meringues in oven 1½ to 2 hours, or until completely dry and crisp. To serve: For each serving, place a ball of ice cream in a dessert dish. Press a meringue, rounded side out, against one side, another against opposite side. Pass chocolate sauce (either Regal Chocolate Sauce or purchased). Makes 6 servings.

Regal Chocolate Sauce:

½ c. light corn syrup
1 c. sugar
1 c. water
3 1-oz. squares unsweetened chocolate, broken up, or grated in food processor

1 tsp. vanilla
½ c. evaporated milk

Combine corn syrup, sugar and water. Cook to soft ball stage (236°). Remove from heat and add grated chocolate. Stir until melted. Add vanilla. Slowly add evaporated milk. Mix well. Cool. Makes 1¾ cup sauce.

MOLASSES COOKIES

½ c. Crisco shortening
½ c. firmly packed brown sugar
1 egg, beaten
½ c. molasses
1 T. vinegar
½ c. hot water
2½ c. sifted all-purpose flour

1 tsp. baking powder
¼ tsp. baking soda
½ tsp. salt
½ tsp. ginger
½ tsp. cloves
½ tsp. cinnamon
½ c. raisins

(continued)

Heat oven to 350°. Grease two aluminum cookie sheets. Cream shortening and brown sugar together with electric mixer. Beat in egg until light and fluffy. Combine molasses, vinegar and the hot water. Sift flour and combine with baking powder, baking soda, salt, ginger, cloves and cinnamon. Add alternately with the liquids to the creamed mixture. Beat until blended after each addition. Stir in raisins. Drop by teaspoonfuls onto prepared cookie sheets. Bake 15 minutes. Makes 7 dozen.

MOUNDS BARS

½ c. butter, softened
1½ c. sugar
3 T. cocoa
3 eggs
1 c. flour

1 c. chopped walnuts
½ tsp. salt
1 tsp. vanilla
1 15-oz. can condensed milk
2¼ c. flaked coconut

Heat oven to 350°. Grease a 13" x 9" baking pan. Mix together the butter, sugar, cocoa, eggs, flour, salt, vanilla and walnuts. Pour into prepared pan. Bake 20-25 minutes. Mix condensed milk and coconut. Spread evenly over bars. Return to oven and bake for 15-20 minutes until set. Cool and frost.

Frosting:

1 c. granulated sugar
¼ c. shortening

¼ c. milk
½ c. chocolate chips

In a saucepan, bring the milk, sugar and shortening to a boil and stir until the sugar is dissolved. Remove from heat and stir in the chocolate chips.

NORWEGIAN KAKE

1 c. butter, softened
1 c. sugar
2 tsp. baking powder
¼ tsp. salt
2 eggs
1 tsp. almond extract

2¾ c. all-purpose flour
1 slightly beaten egg white
1 T. water
1 T. sugar
⅓ c. finely chopped almonds

Heat oven to 350°. In a large bowl with electric mixer, beat butter and sugar until creamed. Add the baking powder and salt. Mix. Beat in eggs and almond extract until combined. On low speed, beat in flour.

(continued)

Divide dough into thirds. On lightly floured surface, roll each portion into a 7" long roll. Place rolls 3 inches apart on aluminum cookie sheet. Flatten each slightly to about 7" long and 2" wide. Combine egg white and 1 tablespoon water. Brush on tops of rolls. Mix together the sugar and almonds and sprinkle on tops of rolls. Press lightly into dough. Bake for 30 minutes. Cut diagonally into ½" thick slices. Place slices, cut side down, on cookie sheets. Lower oven to 325°. Bake 5 minutes on one side. Turn over on other side and bake 5 minutes longer. Remove and cool on wire racks. Makes about 30.

NORWEGIAN ROSETTES

2 eggs
1 T. sugar
1 tsp. vanilla
¼ tsp. salt
1 c. milk

1 c. flour
oil for frying
confectioners' sugar for sprinkling

In a large bowl, beat eggs slightly. Add sugar, vanilla, salt and milk. Add ½ cup flour and stir. Add ½ cup more of the flour and mix until smooth. Set deep fat fryer to 375°. Add 5" of oil and heat. Or heat 5" of oil in a saucepan and heat to 375°, using a candy thermometer. Heat a rosette iron in hot oil for 30 seconds, briefly drain on paper towels, then dip iron into batter three-fourths of the way up, being sure not to get batter over top of iron. Fry until light brown (it doesn't take very long), remove from oil and tip slightly to drain. Push rosette off iron with fork and drain upside down on paper towels. Repeat with remaining batter, reheating iron about 10 seconds each time. Sift confectioners' sugar over rosettes.

NUTMEG COOKIES

½ c. Crisco shortening
½ c. brown sugar
½ c. granulated sugar
½ tsp. salt
1 tsp. vanilla
1 tsp. baking powder

2 eggs
1 c. flour
½ tsp. nutmeg
1 c. raisins
1 c. chopped walnuts

Heat oven to 350°. Grease aluminum baking sheets. Beat shortening, brown sugar and granulated sugar in bowl with electric mixer. Add eggs and vanilla. Beat. Add salt, baking powder and nutmeg. Mix together.

(continued)

On low speed mix in flour. Mix in raisins and nuts. Drop by tablespoonfuls on baking sheet. Bake for 12 minutes.

OATMEAL CARAMEL BARS

32 vanilla caramels, unwrapped
5 tsp. milk
1 c. flour
¾ c. brown sugar
1 c. oatmeal

¼ tsp. salt
½ tsp. baking soda
¾ c. butter, softened
1 c. chocolate chips
½ c. chopped walnuts

Heat oven to 350°. Melt in the top of a double boiler, with boiling water underneath, the caramels and milk. In a bowl, mix together the flour, brown sugar, oatmeal, salt, butter and baking soda until crumbly and well mixed. Put ½ of crumb mixture in 7" x 11" baking pan. Bake 5 minutes. Sprinkle evenly over top the chocolate chips and walnuts. Pour caramel mixture evenly over. Sprinkle with remaining crumb mixture. Press down slightly. Bake 15-20 minutes, until golden brown. Remove from oven and cool. Cut into squares.

OATMEAL CHOCOLATE CHIP COOKIES

1 c. Crisco shortening
¾ c. brown sugar
¾ c. granulated sugar
1 egg
¼ c. ice water
1 tsp. vanilla
¾ c. flour
1 tsp. salt

1 tsp. baking soda
⅛ tsp. mace
½ tsp. cinnamon
½ tsp. allspice
3 c. oatmeal
1 c. chopped walnuts
¾ c. golden raisins
1 c. chocolate chips

Heat oven to 350°. Beat shortening, brown sugar and granulated sugar with electric mixer. Add egg and slowly add ¼ cup ice water. Add vanilla, salt, baking soda, mace, cinnamon and allspice. Mix together. Add flour and mix. Add oatmeal and mix. Then add raisins and mix, add walnuts and mix and add chocolate chips and mix. Drop by tablespoonfuls on aluminum baking sheet (12 cookies per sheet). Bake for 13 minutes. Remove from oven. Cool. Remove from baking sheet with a metal spatula. Makes 4 dozen cookies.

PEANUT BLOSSOM COOKIES

1¾ c. flour
1 tsp. baking soda
½ tsp. salt
½ c. Crisco shortening
½ c. peanut butter
½ c. granulated sugar
½ c. firmly packed brown sugar

1 egg
2 T. milk
1 tsp. vanilla
1 9-oz. pkg. solid milk chocolate
  candy kisses, unwrapped
granulated sugar for rolling in

Heat oven to 375°. Sift together the flour, baking soda and salt. With electric mixer, cream together the shortening and peanut butter. Gradually add the granulated sugar and then the brown sugar, creaming well. Add the egg, milk and vanilla. Mix together. On low speed of mixer, blend in the dry ingredients gradually and mix well. Shape by rounded teaspoonfuls into balls. Put ¼ cup granulated sugar in a small dish. Roll the balls in the sugar. Place on ungreased aluminum cookie sheets. Bake for 8 minutes. Remove from oven and place a solid milk chocolate candy kiss on top of each cookie, pressing down so that cookie cracks around the edge. Return to the oven. Bake 2 to 4 minutes longer.

PINE NUT COOKIES

½ c. granulated sugar
½ c. confectioners' sugar
¼ c. all-purpose flour
⅛ tsp. salt
1 8-oz. can almond paste

2 egg whites, slightly beaten
3 oz. pine nuts
confectioners' sugar for
  sprinkling

Heat oven to 300°. Lightly grease 2 aluminum cookie sheets. Sift granulated sugar, confectioners' sugar, flour and salt together. In medium bowl, break up almond paste with fork. Add egg whites and beat until well blended and fairly smooth. Stir in flour mixture until well blended. Drop mixture by slightly rounded teaspoonfuls, 2" apart, on prepared cookie sheets. Lightly press into rounds, 1½" in diameter. Press some pine nuts into each. Bake 20 to 25 minutes, or until golden. Remove to wire rack. Cool. Sprinkle with confectioners' sugar. Makes about 2½ dozen.

RAISIN SUGAR COOKIES

1½ c. sugar
¾ c. Crisco shortening
2 tsp. vanilla
2 eggs, beaten
½ c. buttermilk
½ tsp. baking soda
2 tsp. baking powder

4 c. all-purpose flour
½ tsp. nutmeg
½ tsp. cinnamon
½ tsp. salt
1 c. raisins
granulated sugar for dipping

Heat oven to 375°. Grease aluminum cookie sheets. With electric mixer, in a large bowl, cream together sugar, shortening and vanilla. Add eggs and beat until fluffy. Sift together the flour, baking soda, baking powder, nutmeg, cinnamon and salt. On low speed, add dry ingredients alternately with buttermilk. Add raisins. Refrigerate dough until it is easy to handle. Pour ½ cup of granulated sugar in a small dish. Roll balls of dough, about 1" in diameter, between palms of hands. Dip tops of balls in sugar and place on prepared cookie sheets. Press them down a little. Bake for 10 to 15 minutes, depending upon the thickness of the cookie, until they get golden brown around edges. Let cookies stand a few minutes on cookie sheets, then remove them with a spatula and transfer to racks to cool. Makes about 4 dozen.

REFRIGERATOR CHOCOLATE BARS

First Layer:

½ c. butter
¼ c. granulated sugar
¼ c. cocoa
¼ c. milk
1 egg, slightly beaten
1 tsp. vanilla

1⅔ c. graham cracker crumbs
  (about 10 whole graham
  crackers)
1¼ c. flaked coconut
¾ c. finely chopped walnuts

Second Layer

6 T. butter, softened
1½ c. confectioners' sugar

1 T. milk
1 tsp. vanilla

Third Layer:

1 c. semi-sweet chocolate chips
2 T. butter
1½ T. milk

3 T. chopped walnuts for
  sprinkling

(continued)

Butter a 9" square pan. Melt butter in a saucepan and stir in sugar and cocoa until smooth. Add milk. Heat to boiling. Blend a small amount of hot mixture to egg and return to saucepan. Stir until slightly thickened. Add vanilla. Stir in graham cracker crumbs, coconut and nuts. Press into the bottom of prepared pan. Cream butter and stir in confectioners' sugar and beat with milk and vanilla until fluffy. Spread over crumb mixture and chill for 15 minutes. Heat chocolate chips, butter and milk, stirring until smooth. Spread over chilled layers and sprinkle with chopped nuts. Chill. When firm, cut into 1½" x 1" pieces. Makes 30 pieces.

SANDIES

1 c. butter
⅓ c. confectioners' sugar
2 tsp. vanilla
2 tsp. water

2 c. all-purpose flour
1 c. chopped pecans
confectioners' sugar for rolling in

Heat oven to 325°. Cream butter and confectioners' sugar. Add vanilla and water. Mix together. Add flour and mix well. Stir in chopped pecans. Shape into small balls. Bake on ungreased aluminum cookie sheets for 20 minutes. Remove to rack to cool. Roll in confectioners' sugar. Makes 3 dozen.

TARALLI ABRUZZESE

2½ c. flour
4 eggs
2 T. sugar

2 T. olive oil
2 tsp. anise seed

Heat oven to 350°. Bring a large pot of water to a boil. Mix together the eggs, sugar and olive oil. Add flour slowly, mixing, until a dough is formed, not too soft or not hard. Divide dough into 16 balls. Roll between your palms into 6" long ropes. Shape each rope into a ring, pressing ends together. Smooth out. Drop the taralli into boiling water. Do not crowd. Cook in 2 batches. Do not touch or stir until they have risen to the surface. Boil for 1 minute longer. Remove from boiling water with a slotted spoon and lay on a damp towel. When cold, bake on aluminum cookie sheets for 30 minutes, or until golden.

WHISKEY BALLS

2 lbs. vanilla wafers
1½ c. crushed pecans
1 c. confectioners' sugar
½ c. white corn syrup
¾ c. bourbon whiskey
confectioners' sugar for rolling in

Roll and crush wafers until fine. Mix with sugar and syrup, then add whiskey and pecans. Roll into balls and roll in sifted confectioners' sugar. Makes about 4 dozen.

WHOOPIES

1 tsp. baking soda
½ c. hot water
⅔ c. buttermilk
½ c. Crisco shortening
1 c. sugar
1 tsp. vanilla
2 eggs
⅔ c. cocoa
¼ tsp. salt
1 tsp. baking powder
2 c. flour
Seven-Minute Frosting

Heat oven to 375°. Grease 2 aluminum baking sheets. Mix the baking soda and hot water together. Set aside to cool. Mix together the cocoa, salt, baking powder and flour. Set aside. In the bowl of an electric mixer, cream the shortening, sugar and vanilla. Add the eggs and beat until fluffy. Mix in the baking soda and water mixture. On low speed, mix in the flour mixture and the buttermilk alternately. Blend well. Place by heaping tablespoonfuls 2" apart on baking sheets. Bake for 10 minutes (when the top of cookie is gently touched, it should spring back). Remove from oven when done, and place on a wire rack until cool. Spread 2 tablespoons of frosting on the bottom of half of the cookies. Top with the other half of the cookies, placing the bottom half on the frosting.

Seven Minute Frosting:

1½ c. sugar
¼ tsp. cream of tartar
⅛ tsp. salt
2 egg whites
¼ c. water
2 tsp. vanilla

Mix sugar, cream of tartar, salt, egg whites and ¼ cup water in the top of a double boiler with boiling water in the bottom pan. Beat with a hand-held electric mixer until the frosting stands in peaks, about 5-7 minutes, no more. Remove from heat. Beat in the vanilla.

ZINFANDEL COOKIES

¼ c. zinfandel wine
3 T. vegetable oil
½ c. sugar
2 tsp. baking powder
1 tsp. anise seed

1½ c. flour
1 egg yolk, beaten, and mixed with 2 tsp. water, for brushing
granulated sugar for sprinkling

Heat oven to 350°. Lightly grease aluminum cookie sheets. Mix together the wine, oil and sugar. Add the baking powder and anise seed and mix together. Add the flour, a half cup at a time, until a soft dough is formed. Divide dough into 32 pieces. Roll each piece into a ball and then into into a 4" rope. Shape each rope into a wreath, overlapping ends. Brush egg mixture over cookies and sprinkle with sugar. Place on prepared cookie sheets and bake 10-12 minutes. Makes 32 cookies.

Recipe Favorites

Pies
Pastry
Desserts

My Sister Dawn

Helpful Hints

- Keep eggs at room temperature for greater volume when whipping egg whites to make meringue.

- Pie dough can be frozen. Roll dough out between sheets of plastic wrap, stack in a pizza box, and keep the box in the freezer. Defrost in the fridge and use as needed. Use within 2 months.

- Place your pie plate on a cake stand when ready to flute the edges of the pie. The cake stand will make it easier to turn the pie plate, and you won't have to stoop over.

- When making decorative pie edges, use a spoon for a scalloped edge. Use a fork to make crosshatched and herringbone patterns.

- When cutting butter into flour for pastry dough, the process is easier if you cut the butter into small pieces before adding it to the flour.

- Pumpkin and other custard-style pies are done when they jiggle slightly in the middle. Fruit pies are done when the pastry is golden, juices bubble, and fruit is tender.

- Keep the cake plate clean while frosting by sliding 6-inch strips of waxed paper under each side of the cake. Once the cake is frosted and the frosting is set, pull the strips away, leaving a clean plate.

- Create a quick decorating tube to ice your cake with chocolate. Put chocolate in a heat-safe, zipper-lock plastic bag. Immerse it in simmering water until the chocolate is melted. Snip off the tip of one corner, and squeeze the chocolate out of the bag.

- Achieve professionally decorated cakes with a silky, molten look by blow-drying the frosting with a hair dryer until the frosting melts slightly.

- To ensure that you have equal amounts of batter in each pan when making a layered cake, use a kitchen scale to measure the weight.

- Help prevent cracking in your cheesecake during baking by placing a shallow pan of hot water on the bottom oven rack. Do not open the oven door during baking.

- A cheesecake needs several hours to chill and set.

- For a perfectly cut cheesecake, first dip the knife into water, and clean it after each cut. Or hold a length of dental floss taut between your hands and pull the floss down through the cheesecake, making a clean cut across the diameter of the cake.

Pies/Pastry/Desserts

PIE CRUST

For 8" or 9" single pie shell:

1 ⅓ c. flour   ½ c. Crisco shortening
½ tsp. salt   ¼ c. cold water

For 8" or 9" Two-Crust Pie:

2 c. flour   ¾ c. Crisco shortening
1 tsp. salt   ⅓ c. cold water

Combine flour and salt in a bowl. Cut in shortening with a pastry blender or a fork until mixture resembles coarse meal or very tiny peas. (Texture will not be uniform, but will contain varying sizes of bits and pieces.) Sprinkle water over, a tablespoon at a time, mixing with a fork, until mixture holds together when pressed gently into a ball. For double crust, divide dough in half. For bottom crust, sprinkle flour on surface and on top of ball of dough. Roll out dough 2" larger than the pie pan. For ease of handling, carefully fold crust in half and place fold in center of pie pan, then unfold in pan and fit crust in pan. Trim edge even with outside edge of plate. Add filling and roll other half of dough and place over filling. Trim edge about ½" beyond edge of plate. Fold under edge of bottom crust and flute to seal. Prick steam vents in top crust with a fork. Bake at temperature required for pie recipe. For single pastry shell, roll out dough 2" larger than the pie pan. For ease of handling, carefully fold crust in half and place fold in center of pie pan, then unfold in pan and fit crust in pan. Trim ½" beyond edge of plate. Fold edge under and flute. Prick bottom and sides with a fork in several places. Bake at 400° for 12 to 15 minutes or until lightly browned.

APPLE PIE

2½ lb. apples (5 to 6 med. to large) (Rome Beauty are an excellent choice)
1 c. sugar
3 T. flour
1 tsp. cinnamon
¼ tsp. nutmeg
¼ tsp. allspice
⅛ tsp. cloves
⅛ tsp. salt
2 T. butter
Pie Crust recipe for two-crust pie in this book
1 beaten egg white
1 T. milk
2 tsp. sugar

(continued)

Prepare pie crust for two-crust pie in this book. Heat oven to 375°. Pare and core apples and slice thinly. Put in a large bowl. Combine sugar, flour, cinnamon, nutmeg, allspice, cloves and salt. Mix with apples. Line 9" pie plate with pastry. Brush some egg white on bottom crust. Fill with apple mixture. Dot with butter. Put on top crust following directions for double crust pie, according to Pie Crust directions. Brush with 1 tablespoon milk and sprinkle with 2 teaspoons sugar. Prick steam vents on top with a fork. Bake for 50 minutes, or until crust is golden.

BANANA COCONUT CREAM PIE

¾ c. sugar
3 T. cornstarch
¼ tsp. salt
2 c. milk
3 egg yolks
2 T. butter

1 tsp. vanilla
2 bananas
¾ c. flaked coconut
Pie Crust recipe for 9" single baked pie shell in this book
1 recipe Meringue

Prepare baked pie shell using Pie Crust recipe for 9" Pie Crust recipe in this book. Set aside to cool. In saucepan, combine sugar, cornstarch and salt. Gradually stir in milk. Cook and stir over medium heat until mixture boils. Cook 2 minutes longer. Remove from heat. Stir small amount of hot mixture into slightly beaten egg yolks. Return to hot mixture and cook, stirring, 2 minutes longer. Remove from heat. Add butter and vanilla. Cool to room temperature. When cooled, slice bananas into cooled pie shell. Sprinkle ¾ cup coconut over bananas. Pour cooled custard mixture over the coconut. Prepare meringue.

Meringue:

3 egg whites
¼ tsp. cream of tartar

6 T. sugar
¼ c. flaked coconut

Beat egg whites and cream of tartar with electric mixer to soft peaks. Gradually add the sugar, beating to stiff peaks. Pour over top of pie, spreading to edges to completely cover filling. Sprinkle top with ¼ cup flaked coconut. Bake in hot oven (400°) about 8 minutes, or until meringue is golden.

BLUEBERRY PIE

4 c. fresh or frozen blueberries
1 c. sugar
1 T. fresh lemon juice
⅛ tsp. salt
3 T. flour
½ tsp. cinnamon, if desired

1 T. butter
Pie Crust recipe for two-crust pie in this book
1 egg white, beaten
1 T. milk
2 teaspoons sugar

Heat oven to 400°. Prepare pie crust for a 2-crust pie using Pie Crust recipe in this book. Line a 9" pie plate with pastry. Brush some egg white over bottom of pie shell. Combine 4 cups blueberries with the sugar, flour, lemon juice, salt and cinnamon, if desired. Fill pie shell. Dot with butter. Put on top crust following directions for double crust pie, according to Pie Crust directions. Brush with 1 tablespoon milk. Sprinkle with 2 teaspoons sugar. Prick steam vents on top with a fork. Bake for 10 minutes, then lower heat to 350° and bake for 30-40 minutes or until the top is golden brown.

CHERRY-BANANA PIE

2 medium bananas
1 No. 2 can cherry pie filling
1 c. whipping cream, whipped stiff

Pie Crust recipe for 9" single baked pie shell in this book

Prepare baked pie shell using Pie Crust recipe for 9" single pie shell and cool. Place layers of sliced bananas in pie shell. Pour cherry pie filling over bananas. Spoon wreath of whipped cream on pie. Chill.

CHOCOLATE PIE

2½ c. milk
3 squares unsweetened chocolate
1 c. sugar
4 T. flour
1 tsp. salt
4 egg yolks

2 T. butter
1 tsp. vanilla
1 c. heavy cream
Pie Crust recipe for 9" single baked pie shell in this book

Prepare baked pie shell using Pie Crust recipe for 9" single pie shell. Set aside to cool. Scald milk by cooking in top of double boiler, with boiling water in pan below, until tiny bubbles appear. Add chocolate, stirring to melt. Remove from heat. Set aside. Beat egg yolks until fluffy

(continued)

and pale yellow. Mix sugar, flour and salt and gradually add to egg yolks. Mix well. Pour small amount of scalded milk mixture over egg-sugar mixture and beat well. Gradually add rest of milk mixture. Return to double boiler top and cook over medium heat until custard is quite thick. Remove from stove and add butter and vanilla. Cool and chill in refrigerator for several hours. When ready to serve, put filling in baked pie shell. Whip cream and spread over top.

LEMON PIE

4 egg yolks
½ c. sugar
⅓ c. fresh lemon juice
3 T. orange juice
½ tsp. salt
1 envelope plain gelatin
¼ c. cold water

½ tsp. grated lemon zest
½ tsp. grated orange zest
¼ c. sugar
4 stiffly beaten egg whites
Pie Crust recipe for 9" single baked pie shell in this book
1 c. heavy cream

Prepare baked pie shell using Pie Crust recipe for 9" single pie shell in this book. Beat egg yolks until pale with ½ cup sugar. Add lemon juice, orange juice and salt and mix. Mix gelatin with ¼ cup cold water to dissolve gelatin and set aside. Cook egg yolk mixture on top of double boiler, with hot water in lower pan, until thick, stirring constantly. Stir gelatin mixture and add to egg yolk mixture. Add lemon zest and orange zest. Stir. Put into a large bowl and cool until partially set. With electric mixer, beat egg whites, gradually adding ¼ cup sugar, until whites are stiff. Fold into cooled egg mixture and blend. Pour into pie shell and chill in refrigerator until firm. Whip cream and spread over top.

LIME CHIFFON PIE

1 envelope plain gelatin
⅛ c. cold water
4 eggs, separated
½ c. fresh lime juice
1 c. sugar
¼ tsp. salt

1 tsp. grated lime zest
½ c. heavy cream, whipped
½ c. grated coconut
Pie Crust recipe for 9" single baked pie shell in this book

Prepare baked pie shell using Pie Crust recipe for 9" single pie shell in this book and set aside to cool. Lower oven to 350°. Spread coconut in shallow pan and toast coconut for 8 minutes, stirring frequently, until golden brown. Watch carefully so it doesn't burn. Soften gelatin in cold

(continued)

water. With electric mixer, beat egg yolks until pale with ½ cup sugar and add lime juice and salt. Put mixture in top of double boiler, with hot water in bottom pan. Cook, stirring constantly, until mixture thickens slightly. Remove from heat. Stir gelatin and add, stirring. Add lime zest. Cool to room temperature. Beat egg whites until stiff peaks form. Gradually beat in remaining ½ cup sugar. Fold gelatin mixture into egg whites. Beat cream. Fold in whipped cream. Turn into baked pie shell. Sprinkle with toasted coconut. Chill in refrigerator.

PEACH PIE

2½ lb. peaches, peeled, pitted and sliced ¼" thick
¾ c. sugar
¼ tsp. nutmeg
⅛ tsp. salt
3 T. flour
2 T. butter
Pie Crust recipe for two-crust pie in this book
1 egg white, beaten
1 T. milk
2 teaspoons sugar

Prepare pie crust for two-crust pie using Pie Crust recipe in this book. Heat oven to 375°. To peel peaches easily, drop them in boiling water for 1 minute, then slip off the skins. Pit the peaches, then slice them ¼" thick. Put the peaches in a large bowl. Combine the sugar, flour, nutmeg and salt. Lightly stir into the peaches. Line a 9" pie plate with bottom crust. Brush the crust with some egg white. Put filling in and dot with the butter. Cover with top crust according to directions in Pie Crust recipe. Brush on 1 tablespoon milk. Sprinkle with 2 teaspoons sugar. Prick steam vents on top with a fork. Bake 50 minutes, or until crust turns golden brown.

PECAN PIE

3 eggs
¼ tsp. salt
1 lb. light brown sugar
¾ c. water
¼ c. soft butter
1 tsp. vanilla
1½ c. pecan halves
Pie Crust recipe for 9" single pie crust in this book, unbaked
1 beaten egg white
Optional topping: Whipped Cream

Heat oven to 350°. Prepare pie crust for single crust pie. Line 9" pie pan with crust. Beat eggs in medium mixing bowl until frothy. Set aside. Combine sugar and salt with water in 2-quart saucepan. Place over moderate heat, stirring until sugar dissolves. Bring to a full boil and

(continued)

cook for 3 minutes. Gradually stir hot syrup into eggs. Blend butter and vanilla into mixture. Add 1½ cup pecans. Brush bottom of crust with some egg white. Turn mixture into pastry-lined pie pan. Bake for 50 minutes. Remove to cooling rack. Top with whipped cream if you like. (You can add ¼ c. bourbon and/or ½ c. chocolate chips to filling.)

PINEAPPLE PIE

1 fresh pineapple, trimmed, peeled and cored
2 eggs
1½ c. sugar
2 T. flour
⅛ tsp. salt
1 T. grated lemon zest

1 T. lemon juice
Pie Crust recipe for two-crust pie in this book
1 beaten egg white
1 T. milk
2 tsp. sugar

Heat oven to 350°. Make pie crust for two-crust pie. Roll out half of the pastry and put into 9" pie pan according to Pie Crust recipe and trim edge ½" beyond edge of plate. Beat eggs with sugar, flour, salt, grated lemon zest and lemon juice until blended. Cut pineapple into small chunks. Fold into egg mixture. Brush some egg white on bottom of shell. Spread filling in the pie shell. Roll out top half and place over filling. Fold under edge of bottom crust and flute to seal. Brush crust with milk and sprinkle with sugar. Prick the top crust with a fork to allow steam to escape. Bake for 40-50 minutes until crust is golden.

PUMPKIN PIE

2 eggs, slightly beaten
1 16-oz. can Libby's Solid Pack pumpkin
¾ c. sugar
½ tsp. salt
1 tsp. cinnamon
½ tsp. ginger
½ tsp. allspice

½ tsp. nutmeg
¼ tsp. cloves
1⅔ c. (13 oz.) evaporated milk or light cream
Pie Crust recipe for 9" single pie shell in this book, unbaked
1 beaten egg white
Optional topping: Whipped Cream

Heat oven to 400°. Make pie crust, but do not bake. Whisk together in a large bowl the eggs, pumpkin, sugar, salt, cinnamon, ginger, allspice, nutmeg, cloves and the evaporated milk. Brush bottom of crust with some egg white. Pour filling into pie shell. Bake for 15 minutes. Reduce temperature to 350° and continue baking for 45 minutes or until knife

(continued)

inserted in center of pie filling comes out clean. Cool. Top with whipped cream, if desired.

RICE TORTE

Crust:

2 c. all-purpose flour
1/8 tsp. salt
1 T. baking powder
1/2 c. sugar
2/3 c. butter, softened
3 eggs
2 T. anisette

1 egg yolk beaten with 2 teaspoons water to brush on top
1 egg white, beaten, to brush on bottom crust
confectioners' sugar for sprinkling

Filling:

3 c. cooked rice
3 eggs
1 T. flour
1/2 c. sugar
1 tsp. vanilla
1/2 tsp. nutmeg

1/2 tsp. cinnamon
1 c. raisins
1/4 c. chopped candied citron
1/2 c. pine nuts
1/2 c. grated milk chocolate

Heat oven to 350°. To make the rice, bring 1 3/4 cups water to a boil. Add 1/2 tsp. salt and pour in 1 cup rice. Return to boil, lower heat and simmer until water evaporates, about 20 minutes. Meanwhile, make the pie crust by mixing the flour, salt, baking powder and sugar together in a large mixing bowl. Cut in the butter with a pastry cutter or a fork until mixture is crumbly. Beat the eggs, mixing in the anisette. Mix lightly into the crumbly mixture just until pastry holds together. Shape the dough into a ball. Put three-fourths of the dough on a floured surface, sprinkle some flour on top and roll the dough 2" larger than a 9" pie pan. Carefully fold the dough in half and place fold in center of the pie pan, then unfold in pan and fit dough in pan. Trim edge about 1/2" beyond edge of pan. Flute the edges. Brush some egg white on bottom of crust. To make the filling, whisk together the eggs with the flour, sugar, vanilla, nutmeg and cinnamon until well blended. Stir in the cooked rice, raisins, citron, pine nuts and grated chocolate. Pour into pie crust. Roll out the remaining dough into a 10" x 8" rectangle. Cut the dough lengthwise into 3/4" strips with a pastry wheel or a knife. Weave strips over filling to make a lattice design. Trim overhang so it is flush with the inside edge. Beat the egg yolk with 2 teaspoons water, and brush the top crust and along the top of the edges of the crust.

(continued)

Bake for 50 minutes, until the pastry is golden. Cool on wire rack. After it is cooled, sift confectioners' sugar over top.

RICOTTA PIE

Crust:

2 c. all-purpose flour	3 eggs
1/8 tsp. salt	grated zest of 1 lemon
1 T. baking powder	1 tsp. vanilla
1/2 c. sugar	confectioners' sugar for sprinkling
2/3 c. butter, softened	

Filling:

1 1/2 lb. ricotta cheese	3 T. chopped candied citron
4 eggs	3 T. chopped candied orange peel
2 T. flour	(use recipe in this book)
1 c. sugar	1 egg yolk beaten with two teaspoons water, to brush over top
2 tsp. vanilla	
1/4 tsp. cinnamon	
1/4 c. mini semi-sweet chocolate chips	1 egg white, beaten to brush on bottom crust

Heat oven to 350°. To make crust, mix the flour, salt, baking powder and sugar together in a large mixing bowl. Cut in the butter with a pastry cutter or a fork until mixture is crumbly. Beat the eggs, mixing in the lemon zest and vanilla. Mix lightly into the crumbly mixture just until pastry holds together. Shape the dough into a ball. Put three-fourths of the dough on a floured surface, sprinkle some flour on top and roll the dough 2" larger than a 10" pie pan. Carefully fold the dough in half and place fold in center of the pie pan, then unfold in pan and fit dough in pan. Trim edge about 1/2" beyond edge of pan. Flute the edges. Brush some beaten egg white on the bottom. To make the filling, with electric mixer, beat the eggs until they are light. Add the flour, sugar, vanilla and cinnamon and beat. Stir in the ricotta, then the chocolate chips, candied citron and candied orange peel. Blend well. Pour into the pie crust. Roll out the remaining dough into a 10" x 8" rectangle. Cut the dough lengthwise into 3/4" strips with a pastry wheel or a knife. Weave strips over filling to make a lattice design. Trim overhang so it is flush with the inside edge. Beat the egg yolk with two teaspoons water, and brush the top crust and along the top of the edges of the crust. Bake for 50-60 minutes, until the pastry is golden. Cool on wire rack. After it is cooled, sift confectioners' sugar over top.

STRAWBERRY RHUBARB PIE

1¼ c. sugar
¼ c. flour
1 c. fresh strawberries
2 c. diced rhubarb
2 T. butter

Pie Crust recipe for two-crust pie in this book
1 beaten egg white
1 T. milk
2 tsp. sugar

Heat oven to 400°. Prepare pie crust using recipe in this book for two-crust pie. Slice the strawberries. Put them in a bowl with the diced rhubarb. Sift sugar and flour together and combine ¾ of it with the fruits. Line pie pan with pastry. Brush some beaten egg white on bottom. Sprinkle remaining dry mixture over bottom and add the filling. Dot with butter and arrange top over filling following directions in Pie Crust recipe. Brush top with 1 tablespoon milk. Sprinkle with 2 teaspoons sugar. Prick steam vents on top with a fork. Bake for 10 minutes. Lower heat to 350° and bake 30 minutes longer, or until top is golden brown.

SUPER STRAWBERRY PIE

Crumb Crust:

1½ c. finely crushed graham crackers (about 9 whole graham crackers)
5 T. melted butter
2 T. sugar
¼ tsp. cinnamon

Filling:

2 pt. hulled fresh strawberries
¼ c. cornstarch
1 c. granulated sugar
2 T. lemon juice
1 c. heavy cream

Heat oven to 350°. Crush the graham crackers by rolling 2 crackers at a time between 2 sheets of wax paper. Mix together the cracker crumbs, sugar and cinnamon. Mix in the melted butter with a fork. Press into the bottom and up the sides of a 9" pie pan. Bake until lightly browned, 10-15 minutes. Set aside to cool. In saucepan, with fork or potato masher, crush 1 pint strawberries. Stir in ¼ cup cornstarch, 1 cup sugar and 2 tablespoons lemon juice. Cook over moderate heat, stirring, until clear and thickened. Cool. Slice the other pint of strawberries in half. Fold into the cooled mixture. Pour into crust. Refrigerate until well chilled. When ready to serve, whip the cream and spread over top.

SWEET POTATO PIE

1½ lb. sweet potatoes
¾ c. sugar
¼ c. firmly packed light brown sugar
2 T. all-purpose flour
2 large eggs
1 c. evaporated milk
½ tsp. salt
1 tsp. nutmeg
½ tsp. allspice
½ tsp. cinnamon
½ tsp. ginger
1 tsp. vanilla
Pie Crust recipe for 9" single pie shell in this book, unbaked
1 beaten egg white

Cover the potatoes with water and bring to a boil. Boil 45 minutes or until tender. Drain and cool. Heat oven to 400°. While the potatoes are cooking, make the pie crust for single-crust pie. Peel the potatoes and mash them with an electric mixer until smooth. Add the eggs, granulated sugar, brown sugar, flour, evaporated milk, salt, nutmeg, allspice, cinnamon, ginger and vanilla. Brush some egg white on bottom of crust. Pour filling into pie crust. Bake for 10 minutes, lower the temperature to 350° and bake for 45 to 50 minutes longer, until knife inserted into center comes out clean.

APPLE DUMPLINGS

1½ c. packed light brown sugar
2 c. water
½ tsp. cinnamon
½ tsp. nutmeg
¼ c. butter
6 small Rome beauty apples, peeled and cored
½ c. brown sugar
½ tsp. cinnamon
¼ tsp. salt
3 T. butter, softened
Pie Crust recipe for two-crust pie in this book

Heat oven to 375°. Bring 1½ cups sugar, 2 cups water, ½ teaspoon cinnamon and ½ teaspoon nutmeg to a boil in a saucepan. Reduce heat. Simmer 5 minutes. Remove from heat. Stir in ¼ cup butter. Set aside. Prepare pie crust dough. Shape into a ball. Turn dough out onto a floured surface and sprinkle flour on top of the dough. Roll out into an 18" x 12" rectangle. Cut into six 6" squares. Place one apple in center of each square. Combine ½ cup brown sugar, ½ teaspoon cinnamon and salt. Sprinkle some over each apple. Put ½ tablespoon butter on top of each apple. Moisten dough edges with water. Pull corners over apples, pinching to seal. Prick the top of each pastry several times and place dumplings in a lightly greased 13" x 9" baking dish. Bake for 15 minutes. Pour syrup over and reduce heat to 350°.

(continued)

Bake 30 to 35 minutes more, basting with juices in the pan every 10 minutes. When the apples are golden brown, they are done.

BAKED ALASKA

2 eggs, separated
¼ c. hot water
1 tsp. vanilla
¾ c. sugar
⅛ tsp. salt
1 c. cake flour

1¼ tsp. baking powder
3 T. brandy or rum
½ gal. vanilla ice cream
1 recipe meringue
confectioners' sugar, for topping

Heat oven to 325°. Line the bottom of a 9" round cake pan with wax paper. Mix together the flour and baking powder and set aside. Beat the egg yolks, ¼ cup hot water and vanilla together until very thick and pale. Slow beat in ½ cup of the sugar. Set aside. Beat the egg whites until foamy, add the salt and continue beating until they hold soft peaks. Gradually beat in the remaining ¼ cup of sugar and beat until stiff but not dry. Stir a fourth of the whites into the yolk mixture. Spoon the remaining whites onto the yolk mixture and sprinkle the flour and baking powder over them. Gently fold the flour mixture into the batter until blended. Spoon into the pan and bake 25-30 minutes. Invert the pan on a rack. Remove the wax paper. Let the cake cool completely. While the cake is baking, soften the ice cream a bit, and put the ice cream in a 7" in diameter bowl. Put the bowl of ice cream in the freezer. When the cake is cool, put it on a piece of cardboard, larger in diameter than the cake, which has been wrapped with aluminum foil. Sprinkle the cake with brandy or rum. Invert the bowl of ice cream onto the cake. The cake will be 1" larger all around than the dome of ice cream. At this point, you can put the cake in the freezer until ready to serve. When ready to serve, heat the oven to 400°. Make the meringue. Remove the cake from the freezer and place it on an ovenproof platter (not metal). Quickly frost it with the meringue, making sure there are no gaps or thin spots and it is well covered. Swirl the topping on the cake with the back of a spoon so it looks decorative. Sift confectioners' sugar over and put it in the oven until it turns golden, about 5-8 minutes. Remove from oven and serve at once.

Meringue:

4 egg whites
⅛ tsp. cream of tartar

½ c. sugar

(continued)

Put the egg whites and cream of tartar in a bowl and beat until foamy. Slowly add the sugar and continue to beat until stiff but not dry.

BANANA SPLIT

For Each Banana Split:

1 banana, peeled and halved lengthwise	chopped nuts
3 scoops ice cream (your favorite)	whipped cream
hot fudge sauce	grated coconut
caramel sauce	maraschino cherries with stems on
frozen strawberries in sugar syrup, thawed	

Hot Fudge Sauce:

1 6-oz. pkg. semi-sweet chocolate pieces	½ c. evaporated milk

Caramel Sauce:

28 vanilla caramels, unwrapped	½ c. hot water

To make a quick fudge sauce, heat 1 6-oz. package semi-sweet chocolate pieces and ½ cup evaporated milk in a saucepan over medium heat, stirring constantly until blended. Keep warm. For Caramel sauce, combine 28 vanilla caramels with ½ cup hot water in top of double boiler with hot water in pan underneath over low heat. Stir occasionally until caramels melt. Keep warm. To assemble splits, place 1 halved banana in a long dish. Place three scoops of ice cream in between. Pour hot fudge sauce over, then caramel sauce. Top with some thawed strawberries, chopped nuts, whipped cream, coconut and a maraschino cherry.

BERRY COBBLER

1 pt. fresh raspberries, or 1 16-oz. bag frozen, thawed
1 pt. fresh blueberries or sliced strawberries, or 1 16-oz. bag frozen, thawed
⅓ c. sugar
2 T. cornstarch (3 T. if you use frozen berries)

1 c. all-purpose flour
1 T. sugar
1½ tsp. baking powder
¼ tsp. salt
¼ tsp. ground nutmeg
½ c. milk
⅓ c. butter, melted

Heat oven to 375°. If you use frozen, thawed berries, use the juice and increase cornstarch to 3 tablespoons. Combine berries, ⅓ cup sugar and cornstarch in medium bowl. Toss lightly with a rubber spatula. Spoon into a 1½-quart or 8"-square baking dish. Combine flour, 1 tablespoon sugar, baking powder, salt and nutmeg in a medium bowl. Add milk and melted butter. Mix just until dry ingredients are moistened. Drop batter by six heaping tablespoonfuls for even distribution over berries. Bake 25 minutes or until topping is golden brown and fruit is bubbly. Cool on wire rack. Serve warm or at room temperature.

BISQUE TORTONI

3 egg whites
⅛ tsp. salt
¼ c. water
¾ c. sugar
¼ c. slivered almonds

¼ tsp. almond extract
1½ tsp. almond extract
1 tsp. vanilla extract
1½ c. heavy cream
12 candied cherries

Put egg whites in large bowl and let warm to room temperature. Heat oven to 350°. Place almonds in shallow pan, and bake just until toasted - about 5 minutes. Finely grind almonds in blender. Turn into a small bowl. Blend in 1½ teaspoons almond extract. Set aside. Combine ¼ cup water with the sugar in a 1-quart saucepan. Cook over low heat, stirring, until sugar is dissolved. Bring to boiling over medium heat. Boil, uncovered, without stirring, and bring to 236° on candy thermometer. Meanwhile, while syrup is boiling, at high speed, beat egg whites with salt just until stiff peaks form when beater is slowly raised. Pour hot syrup in thin stream over egg whites, beating constantly until mixture forms very stiff peaks when beater is raised. In medium bowl, beat cream with ¼ teaspoon almond extract and the vanilla until stiff. With a rubber spatula, fold whipped cream into egg white mixture until thoroughly blended. Spoon into 12 paper cups set into 2½" muffin pan cups. Sprinkle with almond mixture. Top with a cherry. Cover with foil.

(continued)

Put into freezer until firm -- several hours or overnight. Serve right from freezer.

BREAD PUDDING

6 c. cubed white bread
4 c. half and half
5 eggs, beaten
1 c. sugar
1 T. butter, melted

¼ tsp. salt
¼ tsp. nutmeg
½ tsp. cinnamon
2 t. vanilla
¾ c. raisins

Heat oven to 350°. Put the cubed bread in a large bowl and pour the half and half over. Soak for 5 minutes. In another bowl, beat the eggs, slowing adding the sugar, until frothy. Stir in the butter, salt, nutmeg, cinnamon, vanilla and raisins. Pour slowly over the bread. Mix together. Pour into a 2½-quart buttered baking dish. Put the dish in a pan of hot water, 1" deep. Bake for 1 hour. Serve with the following sauce if you like.

Caramel Sauce:

½ c. granulated sugar
½ c. brown sugar
½ c. butter

½ c. whipping cream
1 tsp. vanilla

Mix together the granulated sugar, brown sugar, butter and cream in a 1-quart saucepan. Heat until mixture is thick and comes to a boil. Remove from heat and add vanilla. Serve warm over bread pudding.

CANNOLI

Dough for Shells:

2 T. shortening
¼ tsp. cinnamon
1 tsp. vanilla
½ c. Marsala wine
¼ tsp. salt

1 tsp. sugar
1½ c. flour
1 egg yolk for sealing
Vegetable oil for frying

Filling:

2 lb. ricotta cheese
1½ c. confectioners' sugar
½ c. mini semi-sweet chocolate pieces
½ c. chopped citron

2 tsp. vanilla
¾ c. chopped pistachio nuts for dipping in
confectioners' sugar for dusting

To make cannoli shells, you will need either metal tubes or wooden dowels, 5" long and 1" in diameter. In a large bowl, combine the flour, cinnamon, sugar and salt and cut in the shortening with a pastry cutter or a fork until the mixture resembles coarse crumbs. Add the vanilla and wine and blend well. The dough will be rather firm. Knead the dough for 5 minutes into a ball. Set aside. In a mixing bowl, beat together the ricotta, confectioners' sugar and vanilla until smooth and creamy. Stir in the chocolate pieces and citron and blend well. Put the filling into the refrigerator to chill. Make the shells by dividing the dough into 30 pieces, shaping each piece into a ball and rolling each one out on a lightly floured surface into a 4½" circle. Heat the oil to 3" deep in a saucepan or deep fryer to 375°. Fold the circles of dough over the tubes or dowels, moistening with a bit of egg yolk to seal. Drop two dough-covered forms at a time into the hot oil for one minute, turning to get them golden brown on all sides. With tongs, remove from oil, tipping slightly to drain off the oil and place on paper towels to drain. When they are cool enough to handle, carefully remove forms. Set aside to cool. Have two more ready to cook, but be sure the oil has reheated to 375° before dropping them in. Continue cooking all the circles of dough. Don't fill until just before serving or they will get soggy. You may make the shells a day in advance and store on a tray in a dry place, covered with a tea towel. When you are ready to fill, you can fill with a pastry bag or a small spoon. Chop the pistachio nuts into small pieces and dip the ends of the cannoli into the nuts. Sift confectioners' sugar over the cannoli.

CHOCOLATE FONDUE

3 7-oz. bars Hershey plain chocolate
½ c. heavy cream
2 T. cherry brandy

cubes of angel food cake
pineapple chunks, fresh or canned, drained
bananas, sliced ½" thick

Melt the chocolate and cream together in the top of a double boiler with hot water underneath. Stir in the flavoring. Pour the chocolate mixture into your cheese fondue pot and light a candle underneath the pot to keep the chocolate warm. Place a variety of the cubes of cake and fruit on a platter next to the fondue pot. Set out some fondue forks and small plates and let guests spear the fruit or cake with the forks and dip into the chocolate. Stir the chocolate occasionally.

CHOCOLATE PUDDING

3 T. cornstarch
4 T. sugar
⅛ tsp. salt
2 c. milk

1 tsp. vanilla
2 oz. semi-sweet chocolate
4 maraschino cherries

Mix the cornstarch, sugar and salt with ¼ cup of the milk in a saucepan. In another saucepan, heat the remaining milk with the semi-sweet chocolate, stirring, until chocolate is melted. Slowly add it to the cornstarch mixture, stirring constantly. Cook until thickened, stirring constantly over moderately low heat or in a double boiler over simmering water. Continue to cook for about 15 minutes until smooth and creamy. Let cool, then add the vanilla. Spoon into four serving dishes, cover and chill. To serve, place a maraschino cherry on top.

CREAM PUFFS

Cream Puffs:

1 c. cold water
½ c. butter
¼ tsp. salt

1 c. all-purpose flour
4 eggs

Chocolate Frosting For Cream Puffs and Éclairs:

3 oz. semi-sweet chocolate

2 T. butter

(continued)

Heat oven to 375°. Combine 1 cup water, salt and the butter in a saucepan and bring to a boil. Remove from the heat and add the flour all at once, stirring vigorously with a wooden spoon. Return to moderate heat and stir constantly until the dough leaves the sides of the pan and forms a ball. Remove from the heat and let cool for about 5 minutes. Add the eggs, one at a time, beating hard until the dough is smooth. Place large, rounded tablespoons of dough on an ungreased cookie sheets, 2" apart. Bake for 30 minutes or until the puffs are golden. Carefully slice the tops off the puffs. Set aside. Scoop out the centers. Discard. Cool on a rack. Fill with Cream Filling. Replace the tops and cover them with Chocolate Frosting For Cream Puffs and Éclairs. For the frosting, melt the chocolate and the butter in a small pan over moderate heat, stirring constantly until smooth. Spoon over filled cream puffs or éclairs and let drip down the sides.

Basic Cream Filling:

1 c. milk	⅛ tsp. salt
½ c. sugar	2 egg yolks, slightly beaten
3 T. flour	2 tsp. vanilla

Heat the milk in a heavy-bottomed saucepan until very hot but not boiling. Mix the sugar, flour and salt together in a bowl and stir in the hot milk, and beat with a whisk until well blended. Pour back into the pan, scraping the bowl with a spatula and continue to stir vigorously over low heat for 4-5 minutes, until very thick and smooth. Add the egg yolks and cook for a few more minutes, stirring. Cool, stirring from time to time, then add the vanilla.

CRÈME BRÛLÉE

2½ c. heavy cream	1 tsp. cornstarch
6 eggs	1 tsp. vanilla
6 T. granulated sugar	½ c. brown sugar
¼ tsp. salt	

In top of double boiler heat cream over hot, not boiling, water just until light skin forms on top. Remove from heat and set aside. Beat eggs until thick. Mix granulated sugar and salt with cornstarch and add to eggs gradually, beating. Add slightly cooled cream slowly, stirring. Return mixture to double boiler top and cook over simmering water. Stir until mixture will coat the spoon. Remove from heat. Stir in vanilla. Strain through a sieve into a 1-quart shallow baking dish or 6 individual heat-proof ramekins. Stir gently twice during first 10 minutes of cooling to prevent skin from forming. When lukewarm, put in the refrigerator to

(continued)

chill for 6-8 hours for the 1-quart baking dish and 3-4 hours for the individual ramekins. Just before serving, sprinkle top with lump-free brown sugar. Set dish in shallow pan of ice cubes and cold water. Broil 8" from broiler 5 minutes or until bubbly crust forms. Serve immediately.

ÉCLAIRS

Prepare one recipe for Cream Puffs
Prepare Basic Cream Filling under recipe for Cream Puffs
Prepare Chocolate Frosting For Cream Puffs and Éclairs in recipe for Cream Puffs

Put the dough in a pastry bag and pipe onto an ungreased cookie sheet in strips about 4½" long and 1" wide. Bake for 30 minutes or until the éclairs are golden. Carefully split the éclairs lengthwise and cool them on a rack. Scoop out the insides and discard. Fill with Basic Cream Filling or with whipped cream. Replace the top halves and frost with Chocolate Frosting For Cream Puffs and Éclairs.

FLAN (CARAMEL CUSTARD)

1½ c. sugar
1 qt. milk
6 eggs
⅛ tsp. salt
1 tsp. vanilla

Heat oven to 325°. Place 1 cup sugar in a heavy skillet. Cook over low heat, without stirring, until the sugar forms a light-brown syrup. Then stir to blend. Use the syrup to coat a 1½-quart casserole by holding the casserole with a pot holder, and slowing pouring in the hot syrup, turning the casserole to coat the bottom and side. To make the custard, heat the milk just until bubbles form around the edge of the saucepan. Turn off heat. In a large bowl, with electric beater, beat eggs slightly. Add remaining ½ cup sugar, the salt and the vanilla to the eggs and mix. Gradually pour in the hot milk, stirring constantly. Pour into the syrup-coated casserole. Set the casserole in a shallow pan of hot water, 1" deep. Bake 1 hour and 35 minutes, or until silver knife inserted in center comes out clean. Let custard cool, then cover with plastic wrap and refrigerate overnight. To serve, run small spatula around edge of casserole to loosen. Invert on shallow serving dish. The dish must be large enough in diameter to catch the syrup. Shake gently to release. If you have difficulty releasing the mold, dip the bottom and sides for a

(continued)

few seconds in hot water and then loosen with the spatula. The caramel acts as a sauce. Serves 8.

ICE CREAM NUT BALLS

½ gallon vanilla ice cream
3 c. broken walnuts

Chocolate Sauce:

½ c. sugar
¼ c. cocoa
¼ tsp. salt
½ c. water
1 c. heavy cream
1 c. light corn syrup
2 oz. unsweetened chocolate, grated
2 oz. semi-sweet chocolate, grated
4 T. butter, softened
1 T. vanilla

Whirl unsweetened chocolate in food processor into granules. Put in a cup and set aside. Then whirl the semi-sweet chocolate in food processor into granules. Put in a cup and set aside. In a large saucepan over medium heat, mix together ½ cup sugar, ¼ cup cocoa, ¼ teaspoon salt and ½ c. water. Stir until sugar is dissolved and simmer for 2 minutes. Remove from heat and whisk in 1 cup heavy cream, 1 cup light corn syrup and 2 ounces unsweetened chocolate. Return to medium heat and boil, while stirring, until bubbles become small and the syrup reaches 225° on a candy thermometer. Remove from heat and add 2 ounces semi-sweet chocolate, 4 tablespoons butter and 1 tablespoon vanilla. Whisk until smooth. Cover. Sprinkle 3 cups of broken walnuts on a large sheet of wax paper. Soften ice cream a bit so that you can shape it into 6 balls of equal size. Roll the balls in the walnuts and put on a tray and return to freezer. When you are ready to serve, place the balls in serving bowls. Sauce should be reheated slightly so it is warm when poured over ice cream balls. Leftover sauce may be refrigerated for up to 2 weeks. Reheat in a saucepan, stirring, over low heat.

ICE CREAM SANDWICHES

2½ c. Rice Krispies
½ c. butter, melted
1 c. flaked coconut
½ c. finely chopped walnuts
1 c. firmly packed light brown sugar
1 quart vanilla ice cream

(continued)

Combine rice cereal, butter, coconut, chopped nuts and brown sugar in a bowl. Toss until thoroughly blended. Spread half of mixture in bottom of 9" square pan. Soften ice cream slightly and spread evenly over the mixture. Spread remaining cereal mixture over the ice cream and press lightly. Freeze until firm and cut into 9 squares.

ITALIAN CREAM WITH FRUIT COCKTAIL

4 c. milk
8 egg yolks
2 c. sugar
$2/3$ c. flour
$1/2$ tsp. salt

3 tsp. vanilla
$1/4$ c. whiskey (optional)
48 ladyfingers
2 29-oz. cans fruit cocktail, well drained

Heat the milk in a large heavy-bottomed saucepan until very hot but not boiling, Mix the sugar, flour and salt together in a bowl and stir in 1 cup of the hot milk, beating with a whisk until well blended. Pour back into the saucepan, scraping the bowl with a spatula, and continue to whisk vigorously over low heat for 8-10 minutes, until very thick and smooth. Stir in the egg yolks and cook for a few more minutes. Cool, stirring from time to time, then add the vanilla. In a 13" x 9" x 2" glass baking dish, lay 24 ladyfingers on the bottom of the dish. Sprinkle the whiskey over the ladyfingers. Pour $1/2$ of the custard over. Then spoon the drained fruit cocktail over the custard. Lay 24 ladyfingers on top of the fruit cocktail. Spread the other half of the custard over the ladyfingers. Cover with plastic wrap and refrigerate. Serve cold.

ITALIAN TRIFLE

24 ladyfingers
4 oz. rum
4 oz. creme de cacao
1 12-oz. jar raspberry preserves
1 c. heavy cream
3 T. confectioners' sugar
$1/4$ c. slivered almonds

8 egg yolks
$1/2$ c. sugar
$1/4$ tsp. salt
4 c. milk
6 T. flour
1 tsp. vanilla

Heat the milk in a large heavy-bottomed saucepan until very hot but not boiling. Mix the sugar, flour and salt together in a bowl and stir in 1 cup of the hot milk, beating with a whisk until well blended. Pour back into the saucepan, scraping the bowl with a spatula, and continue to whisk vigorously over low heat for 8-10 minutes, until very thick and

(continued)

smooth. Stir in the egg yolks and cook for a few more minutes. Cool, stirring from time to time, then add the vanilla. Sprinkle half the ladyfingers with rum and the other half with creme de cacao. Place a layer of rum ladyfingers in a 2-quart soufflé dish or glass bowl. Spread with some preserves. Spread with a layer of the custard. Add a layer of creme de cacao ladyfingers and spread with some preserves. Spread with a layer of the custard. Repeat until dish is filled, reserving a few ladyfingers for the around the sides. Finish with the custard layer on top. Whip the cream with the confectioners' sugar until stiff. Spread over the top of the custard. Garnish with slivered almonds. Refrigerate for at least an hour before serving.

MACEDONIA OF FRUIT

1 pineapple
3 oranges
1 small melon
2 apples
½ c. purple or green seedless grapes
¼ c. brandy or any orange liqueur
½ c. sliced almonds
¼ c. shredded coconut

Wash, dry and peel pineapple, oranges, melon and apples, then dice large. Wash and dry grapes. Put the fruit in a glass or ceramic bowl. Pour brandy or orange liqueur over. Marinate for 2 hours. Fold in almonds and coconut. Serve in chilled fruit bowls. Serves 6.

MOUSSE AU CHOCOLAT

5 egg whites
¼ tsp. cream of tartar
1 c. sugar
5 egg yolks
⅛ tsp. salt
2 tsp. vanilla
4 squares unsweetened chocolate, melted and cooled
1⅔ c. heavy cream
½ c. heavy cream for whipping for top
2 T. semi-sweet chocolate curls

Melt chocolate in microwave or in top pan of double boiler with boiling water in the bottom pan. In large bowl, with electric mixer at high speed, beat egg whites with cream of tartar until soft peaks form when beater is slowly raised. Gradually add ¾ cup sugar, 2 tablespoons at a time, beating well after each addition. Continue to beat until stiff peaks form. In small bowl, with same beater, beat egg yolks with salt until thick and lemon-colored. Gradually add remaining sugar, beating well. Gradually

(continued)

beat in vanilla, melted chocolate and ⅓ cup cream until mixture is smooth and thickened. Whip remaining cream until stiff. Fold whipped cream with chocolate mixture into egg whites. Gently turn into a 2-quart serving dish, spreading evenly. Refrigerate 24 hours. To serve: Decorate top of mousse with additional whipped cream and semi-sweet chocolate curls. Makes 8 servings.

PASTICCIOTTI

1 recipe Chocolate Pudding in this book

Dough:

½ c. packed brown sugar
2 eggs
2 T. vegetable oil
1 tsp. vanilla

2 tsp. baking powder
2 c. flour
1 egg yolk mixed with 2 teaspoons water

Heat oven to 350°. Make Chocolate Pudding using recipe in this book. Let pudding cool. Meanwhile, make dough. Beat together with an electric beater the brown sugar, eggs, oil and vanilla in a large bowl. Add the baking powder and stir. Add the flour, one cup at a time, and stir. Form the dough into a ball. Roll out into a large circle ⅛" thick. Using round cookie cutters or tops of bowls or jars, cut out eight 4½" circles and eight 3" circles. You may have to re-roll the scraps to make some of the circles. Fit the 4½" circles into 2" in diameter cupcake tins, leaving a ⅜" overhang. Fill with 2 rounded tablespoonfuls of the cooled pudding, ⅔ full. (Do not overfill. There will be a small amount of leftover filling.) Moisten the underside edges of the 3" circles with a little water and fit them over the top. Press the edges together to seal well so the pudding won't escape. Brush some egg yolk mixed with water on the tops, blotting any excess with a paper towel. Bake for 15 minutes, then lower the heat to 325° and bake 15 minutes longer. Remove from oven and cool. Refrigerate until chilled and serve.

RASPBERRIES SABAYON

Sabayon Sauce:

4 egg yolks	2 pt. red raspberries, washed and drained until dry;
2 T. sugar	or 3 pkg. 10-oz. size, frozen raspberries, thawed and drained
¼ c. Grand Marnier	
⅓ c. heavy cream, whipped	

Whip cream and set aside. Make Sabayon Sauce: In double boiler top (before putting on heat), with electric mixer at medium speed, beat egg yolks until thick. Gradually beat in sugar. Beat until mixture is light and soft peaks form when beater is slowly raised. Place double boiler top over bottom pan with simmering water (water in bottom should not touch base of top). Slowly beat in Grand Marnier. Continue beating until mixture is fluffy and mounds, about 5 minutes. Remove double boiler top from hot water and set in ice water. Beat the custard mixture until cool. Gently fold in whipped cream. Refrigerate sauce, covered with plastic wrap, until you are ready to serve. To serve: place berries in serving bowl or dessert dishes. Stir sauce and pour over fruit. Serves 6.

RICE PUDDING

1 c. cooked rice	3 eggs, beaten
½ c. sugar	1 tsp. vanilla
3 c. milk	⅔ c. raisins
3 T. butter, melted	½ tsp. cinnamon
⅛ tsp. salt	¼ tsp. nutmeg

Cook rice by adding ½ cup rice to 1 cup boiling water. Cover and cook over moderate heat for 15-20 minutes, or until all water is absorbed. Heat oven to 350°. Mix together the sugar and eggs and beat with an electric mixer until frothy. Stir in the milk, butter, salt, vanilla, cinnamon, nutmeg, rice and raisins. Pour into a 1½-quart casserole. Place casserole in shallow pan and pour hot water 1" deep into pan. Bake, stirring once, until pudding is creamy and most liquid is absorbed, about 1½ to 2 hours. Remove casserole from oven. Serve warm.

RICE PUDDING WITH CARDINAL SAUCE

2 c. cooked rice (chilled)
1½ c. miniature marshmallows
2 c. fresh or canned pineapple chunks, drained

1 c. heavy cream
¼ c. confectioners' sugar
¼ tsp. almond extract
1 tsp. vanilla extract

Cardinal Sauce:

1 10-oz. pkg. frozen raspberries, thawed and drained, reserving juice
enough water to add to reserved juice to make 1 c.

1 T. cornstarch
¼ c. current jelly

Cook the rice according to package directions to make 2 cups cooked. Mix the chilled rice, marshmallows and pineapple in a bowl. Refrigerate 2 hours. Make Sauce: In small saucepan, combine the juice which has been drained from the raspberries, adding enough water to make 1 cup, with the cornstarch. Boil for 1 minute. Add thawed raspberries and current jelly. Stir well until a bit thickened. Remove from heat and refrigerate 1 hour. Just before serving, whip the cream with the confectioners' sugar. Add the whipped cream, the almond extract and vanilla extract to the rice mixture. Fold together with a rubber spatula and blend lightly. Serve in dessert dishes. Pour raspberry sauce over pudding.

SOPAPILLAS

2 c. flour
1 T. baking powder
½ tsp. salt
2 T. shortening

⅔ c. lukewarm water
Oil for frying
honey

Sift together flour, baking powder and salt. Cut in shortening until mixture is crumbly. Add enough water to make a soft dough. Roll out dough on a floured surface until it is ¼" thick. Cut into 3" squares. Put 4" of vegetable oil into a saucepan or a deep-fat fryer. Heat to 375°. Fry the squares, a few at a time, until golden brown. Drain on paper towels. Be sure the oil has reheated to 375° before adding each batch. Serve with warm honey.

SOUFFLÉ WITH STRAWBERRY SAUCE

6 T. butter, softened
2 T. sugar
¾ c. sugar
1 c. milk
2 tsp. vanilla
¼ c. sifted all-purpose flour

⅓ c. cold milk
4 egg yolks
5 egg whites
⅛ tsp. salt
2 T. superfine sugar

Heat oven to 375°. Generously coat the soufflé dish with 1 tablespoon of the butter. Sprinkle in the 2 tablespoons sugar and tilt the dish in all directions so that interior is fully encrusted with sugar. Shake off excess. Place the 1 cup milk in a saucepan. Bring to a simmer. Remove from the stove, stir in ⅓ cup of the sugar, cover the pan, and let steep for 15 minutes. Mix the flour with the cold milk, stirring until the mixture is a smooth paste. Beating with a wire whisk, add this to the milk/sugar mixture. Place the pan over a moderate heat, and beating constantly with the wire whisk, bring to a boil. Let it cook for 5 minutes, beating with the whisk to prevent lumps and avoid scorching. Remove from heat. Let cool for 5 minutes. Beat in egg yolks, 1 at a time, beating well after each addition. Beat in the rest of the butter until it has melted into the mixture. Add the vanilla and mix in. Beat the egg whites with an electric mixer with the salt until foamy. Gradually add the remaining sugar and beat until the whites form soft peaks. Stir ⅓ into the egg mixture, mixing until well blended. Fold the rest in with a rubber spatula. Pour into the prepared soufflé dish and run the point of a sharp knife around the top, about 1" in from the side. This makes the top of the soufflé rise like a "hat." Place the dish in the oven and lower the heat to 350°. Bake for 30 minutes, then open the oven and slide out the rack and quickly sprinkle the top of the soufflé with a little superfine sugar. Push the rack back in, and slide the soufflé to the back of the oven. Raise the heat to 400°, and bake for another 2 or 3 minutes, or until the top is slightly glazed. Serve at once with Strawberry Sauce.

Strawberry Sauce:

4 c. strawberries, hulled
1½ c. sugar

¾ c. water
2 slices lemon

Cut the berries into small pieces. Cook the sugar and water in a small saucepan over high heat until it reaches 238° on the candy thermometer. Add the berries and the lemon slices, and cook until the berries are mushy, mashing them with a potato masher. Remove from the stove and discard the lemon slices. Makes 2½ cups. If frozen strawberries are used, defrost them, drain off their liquid, reduce sugar to ½ cup, cook syrup with berry liquid, and proceed as above.

SPUMONI

3 pt. chocolate ice cream, slightly soft
1 pt. pistachio ice cream, slightly soft
2 pt. vanilla ice cream, slightly soft
½ c. candied mixed fruits
2 tsp. rum flavoring
1½ c. heavy cream, whipped

Place a 2½-quart melon mold in freezer to chill. In large bowl, with mixer, beat the chocolate ice cream until smooth, but not melted. With spoon, quickly press evenly inside the chilled melon mold to make a 1" thick layer. Freeze until it is firm. In a medium bowl, beat the pistachio ice cream until smooth. Then press evenly over the chocolate-ice-cream layer. Freeze until firm. In large bowl, combine the vanilla ice cream, candied fruits and rum flavoring. Stir until blended, but not melted. Press into the center of the mold. Freeze until firm. To unmold: Let spumoni stand at room temperature 5 minutes. Invert over serving plate. Hold hot, damp dishcloth over mold and shake to release. Return to freezer until the surface is firm. Whip the cream until stiff. Spread three-fourths of whipped cream over mold. Place remaining whipped cream in pastry bag with decorating tip, and pipe on mold decoratively. Return to freezer until serving time. Makes 16 to 20 servings.

STRAWBERRIES WITH LEMON

1 pt. fresh strawberries (use wild ones if you can get them)
1 T. granulated sugar
juice of ½ lemon

Wash, hull and dry berries. Slice and put into a bowl. Sprinkle with sugar and lemon and serve.

STRAWBERRIES ROMANOFF

4 c. strawberries, washed, hulled and patted dry
½ c. sugar
½ c. orange juice
⅓ c. Cointreau liqueur
1 c. heavy cream
1 tsp. vanilla
3 T. confectioners' sugar

Place the berries in a crystal bowl. Mix the sugar with the orange juice, stirring until sugar has dissolved. Add the liqueur to the sugar mixture and pour over the berries, tossing lightly with a rubber spatula. Cover the bowl and chill in the refrigerator 2 hours. When ready to

(continued)

serve, whip the cream until stiff, adding the vanilla and confectioners' sugar. Spoon over berries. Place the bowl with the berries in a larger bowl filled with crushed ice and serve.

SUGAR-GLAZED STRAWBERRIES

2 c. sugar
⅔ c. water

1 pt. fresh strawberries, washed and dried (not hulled)

Lightly oil a cookie sheet. Heat sugar and water in saucepan, stirring occasionally, until it reaches 270° on the candy thermometer. Place saucepan in hot water to keep warm. Holding berries by the stems, dip into the syrup. Cover the berry, but not the stem. Place on the oiled cookie sheet to harden.

SUNSHINE SHERBET

¾ c. milk
2 eggs, slightly beaten
½ c. sugar
1 6-oz. can frozen orange juice concentrate, thawed

⅛ tsp. salt
1 c. heavy cream, whipped

Combine milk, eggs and ¼ cup sugar in top of double boiler over hot water. Cook, stirring, until mixture coats spoon. Cool. Mix in remaining sugar, orange juice concentrate and salt. Pour into refrigerator tray and freeze until ice crystals form around edges. Whip the cream. Remove mixture from freezer and fold in the whipped cream. Return to freezer again until firm - 3 hours or overnight. Makes 1 quart.

TIRAMISU

36 ladyfingers
5 egg yolks
⅓ c. sugar
⅓ c. sweet Marsala wine
1 T. water
½ c. heavy cream
2 tsp. vanilla
14 oz. mascarpone cheese, softened

1½ c. cooled expresso or cooled extra-strong coffee
4 T. rum or brandy
3 T. sugar
6 oz. semi-sweet chocolate, grated
1 T. cocoa

(continued)

Heat oven to 350°. Arrange the ladyfingers on a baking sheet. Bake until golden brown and crisp, 8-10 minutes. Let cool. In the top of a double boiler, not over the heat, beat on high speed of electric mixer until thick and pale yellow, the egg yolks and $1/3$ cup sugar. Whisk in $1/3$ cup sweet Marsala and 1 tablespoon water. Set the double boiler top over the bottom pan with hot water in it. Cook until mixture gets hot, whisking, about 5-8 minutes. Remove the bowl from the heat and let cool for about 15 minutes, stirring from time to time. In another bowl, beat $1/2$ cup heavy cream with 2 teaspoons vanilla. Place the mascarpone cheese in a large bowl. Fold in the whipped cream and the cooled egg yolk mixture. Put the coffee, 3 tablespoons sugar and rum or brandy in a small shallow dish. Dip half of the lady fingers in the espresso mixture and arrange in a 9" x 13" x 2" glass baking dish, leaving a little space in between each one. Spread half of the mascarpone filling over the ladyfingers. Sprinkle with half of the grated chocolate. Dip the remaining ladyfingers into the remaining expresso mixture and arrange on top. Spread the remaining filling over and between the ladyfingers and sprinkle with the remaining chocolate. Sift the cocoa over the top. Cover with plastic wrap and refrigerate for at 2 hours before serving. You can refrigerate overnight before serving. Serves 12.

VANILLA PUDDING

3 T. cornstarch
4 T. sugar
$1/8$ tsp. salt

2 c. milk
1 tsp. vanilla
4 maraschino cherries

Mix the cornstarch, sugar and salt with $1/4$ cup of the milk in a saucepan. In another saucepan, heat the remaining milk, then slowly add it to the cornstarch mixture, stirring constantly. Cook until thickened, stirring constantly, over moderately low heat or in a double boiler over simmering water. Continue to cook for about 15 minutes until smooth and creamy. Put into 4 serving dishes, cover and chill in the refrigerator. When ready to serve, place a maraschino cherry on top.

Beverages

My Brother Natalino hunted down his first deer with a bow and arrow.

Helpful Hints

- To add flavor to tea, dissolve old-fashioned lemon drops or hard mint candies in tea. They melt quickly and keep the tea brisk.

- Make your own spiced tea or cider. Place orange peels, whole cloves, and cinnamon sticks in a 6-inch square piece of cheesecloth. Gather the corners and tie with a string. Steep in hot cider or tea for 10 minutes or longer if you want a stronger flavor.

- Always chill juices or sodas before adding them to beverage recipes.

- Calorie-free club soda adds sparkle to iced fruit juices and reduces calories per portion.

- To cool your punch, float an ice ring made from the punch rather than using ice cubes. It appears more decorative and also inhibits melting and diluting.

- Place fresh or dried mint in the bottom of a cup of hot chocolate for a cool and refreshing taste.

- When making fresh orange juice or lemonade, one lemon yields about ¼ cup juice, and one orange yields about ⅓ cup juice.

- Never boil coffee; it brings out acids and causes a bitter taste. Store ground coffee in the refrigerator or freezer to keep it fresh.

- Always use cold water for electric drip coffee makers. Use 1–2 tablespoons ground coffee for each cup of water.

- How many appetizers should you prepare? Allow 4–6 appetizers per guest if a meal quickly follows. If a late meal is planned, allow 6–8 appetizers per guest. If no meal follows, allow 8–10 pieces per guest.

- If serving appetizers buffet-style or seating is limited, consider no-mess finger foods that don't require utensils to eat.

- Think "outside the bowl." Choose brightly-colored bowls to set off dips. Or get creative with hollowed-out loaves of bread, bell peppers, heads of cabbage, or winter squash.

- Cheeses should be served at room temperature, approximately 70°.

- To keep appetizers hot, make sure you have enough oven space and warming plates to maintain their temperature.

- To keep appetizers cold, set bowls on top of ice or rotate bowls of dips from the fridge every hour or as needed.

Copyright © Morris Press Cookbooks

Beverages

BANANA DAIQUIRI

1 c. crushed ice
¼ c. light rum
¼ c. banana liquor

2 T. lime juice
1 ripe banana, cut up
fresh mint

Put the ice, light rum, banana liquor and lime juice in the blender. Cover and blend for 10 seconds. Add banana. Blend 45 seconds or until mixture has consistency of snow. Pick out any remaining large particles and serve in chilled saucer champagne glasses. Garnish with mint.

BLACK COW

2 T. heavy cream
root beer

2 scoops vanilla ice cream

Put the heavy cream in a 10-oz. glass. Fill nearly to the top with cold root beer. Add 2 small scoops vanilla ice cream.

BLOODY MARY

ice cubes
1 shot (1½ oz.) vodka
1 c. tomato juice
⅛ tsp. salt
Worcestershire sauce

Tabasco sauce
freshly ground black pepper
lime wedge or small celery rib
with leaves attached, for
garnish

Fill a tall glass one-half full with ice. Pour in the vodka, tomato juice juice, salt, a couple of dashes Worcestershire and a couple of dashes Tabasco sauce to taste. Stir. Sprinkle top with fresh pepper and garnish with lime wedge or celery rib. Serves 1.

BRANDY ALEXANDER

2 c. vanilla ice cream
3 T. brandy

3 T. white creme de cacao
1 T. white chocolate shavings

(continued)

Combine the ice cream, brandy and white creme de cacao in the blender. Process until smooth. Spoon into saucer champagne glasses. Garnish, if desired, with white chocolate shavings. Two servings.

BROADWAY

2 T. heavy cream
2 T. chocolate syrup
club soda
2 small scoops coffee ice cream

Put the cream and chocolate syrup into a 10-ounce glass. Stir. Fill glass near to top with club soda. Add 2 small scoops coffee ice cream.

CAFÉ BRÛLOT

2 3" cinnamon sticks
1 small orange washed and dried and studded with 12 whole cloves
2 slices of an orange (sliced thinly)
1 ribbon of lemon peel
8 cubes sugar
1 c. brandy
3 c. hot strong coffee

Heat (do not boil) the brandy. Put the cinnamon sticks, orange, orange slices, lemon peel, sugar and heated brandy in a silver chafing dish with a flame underneath. Put the chafing dish on a tray and bring to the dining table. Lift out a ladleful of the brandy mixture and ignite. Ladle the brandy over the sugar a few times until it is melted. Slowly pour in the hot coffee. When the flames dies, ladle the mixture into demitasse cups and serve.

CHAMPAGNE PUNCH

1 qt. champagne
1 qt. ginger ale
1 qt. soda water
1 qt. Rhine wine
4 jiggers orange juice
4 jiggers lemon juice
4 jiggers light rum
4 jiggers curaçao
1 dash bitters
1 block of ice

Freeze 1 quart of water in a rounded metal bowl to make a block of ice for the punch. Mix together the wine, orange juice, lemon juice, rum,

(continued)

curaçao and a dash of bitters in the punch bowl. Stir. Put in the block of ice. Pour over the champagne, ginger ale and soda water. Stir again. Serves 20.

CHILDREN'S MARTINI LEE ANNE & AMY JO

1 jigger grape juice
2 jiggers orange juice
2 jiggers lemonade
1 Maraschino cherry
1 slice of orange
2 ice cubes
4 jiggers 7-Up

Mix all ingredients together in a glass and stir.

CREAMY STRAWBERRY DAIQUIRIS

1 c. crushed ice
1 c. sliced fresh strawberries
½ c. light rum
⅓ c. frozen pink lemonade concentrate, thawed
1 pt. vanilla ice cream

Combine half the ingredients in a blender and process until mixture is smooth. Turn out into a cold bowl. Process the other half of the ingredients in the blender and process until mixture is smooth. Turn out into the bowl, mix together and spoon into chilled champagne glasses. Makes 1 quart.

EGGNOG

2 c. sugar
12 egg yolks, well beaten
1 pt. brandy
1 pt. dark rum
1 qt. milk
1 qt. cream
freshly grated nutmeg

Beat egg yolks until pale yellow, gradually stirring in sugar, until sugar is dissolved. Stir in brandy and rum gradually. Chill several hours. When ready to serve, fold in milk and cream. Pour into punch bowl and ladle into punch glasses. Sprinkle with freshly grated nutmeg. Stir eggnog before refilling glasses. Makes 50-60 servings.

FROSTY DRINK

1 10-oz. pkg. frozen strawberries, partially thawed
1 6-oz. can frozen orange juice, thawed
3 orange juice cans cold water
1 pt. vanilla ice cream

Put half of the ingredients in a blender and process only until blended. Pour into a cold bowl. Put the other half of the ingredients in the blender and process until blended. Pour into the bowl and stir. Pour into glasses. Serves 12.

FRUIT PUNCH

block of ice
1 c. sugar
1 c. water
1 qt. orange juice
1 c. lemon juice
1 pt. pineapple juice
1 pt. grapefruit juice
1 c. rum
1 c. brandy
1 qt. club soda
orange slices
lime slices

To make a block of ice, put cold water in a 1-quart rounded bowl and freeze. In a saucepan, stir the sugar and water together over medium heat until the sugar is dissolved. Cool. In a large pan, mix together the orange juice, lemon juice, pineapple juice and grapefruit juice. Stir in the cooled sugar water. Put into refrigerator to chill. When ready to serve, put the block of ice in the punch bowl, pour in the fruit juices and add the rum and brandy. Stir, and then add the club soda. Slice an orange and a lime and float slices on top.

FRUIT SLUSH

4 c. sugar
6 c. water
1 46-oz. can pineapple juice
2 12-oz. cans frozen orange juice, thawed
1 12-oz. can frozen lemonade, thawed
1 10-oz. pkg. frozen strawberries, thawed

Bring sugar and water to a boil in a large pan. Stir until sugar is dissolved. Cool. Purée the strawberries in the blender. Put into a large bowl. Add the pineapple juice, orange juice, lemonade and cooled sugar

(continued)

water to the strawberries. Stir and freeze in plastic containers. When ready to use, put 2 scoops into a glass and fill with ginger ale or 7-Up.

GRASSHOPPERS

1 pt. vanilla ice cream
¼ c. white creme de cacao
¼ c. green creme de menthe

In a blender container, combine ice cream, creme de cacao and creme de menthe. Cover and blend until smooth. Makes 4 servings.

HOT BUTTERED RUM

1 lb. butter, melted
1 16-oz. box dark brown sugar
1 16-oz. box confectioners' sugar
2 T. cinnamon
1 tsp. nutmeg
1 qt. softened vanilla ice cream

Mix together the brown sugar, confectioners' sugar, cinnamon and nutmeg. Then add the ice cream and mix. Then add the melted butter and mix all together. Put into a plastic container and put into the freezer. To mix one drink, put 2 tablespoons of the mixture into a cup with 1 jigger rum. Fill with hot water.

ICED CAPPUCCINO

1 c. granulated sugar
½ c. cocoa
½ c. instant coffee granules
1 c. hot water
6 c. cold milk
1 T. vanilla
¼ c. amaretto or ¼ tsp. almond extract (optional)
1 pt. vanilla ice cream
⅛ tsp. cinnamon

Whisk together the sugar, cocoa, coffee granules and hot water in a saucepan until smooth and the sugar is dissolved. Bring to a boil over medium heat, for two minutes. Remove from heat. Cool in refrigerator. Stir in 6 cups cold milk, cinnamon, the vanilla and the amaretto or almond extract, if desired. Put ¼ cup ice cream in a cup or glass and fill with the mixture.

IRISH COFFEE

½ c. sugar
3 c. Irish whiskey
12 c. strong, hot coffee
1 c. whipped cream

For each serving, place 1½ teaspoons sugar in serving glass or cup. Pour in 1½ ounces whiskey. Pour hot coffee into glass or cup, until almost full. Spoon 1 tablespoon whipped cream on top. Serves 16.

KAHLÚA COLADA

4 oz. Coco López real cream of coconut
4 oz. pineapple juice
4 oz. Kahlúa
2½-3 c. vanilla ice cream

Put all ingredients into a blender for a few seconds to blend.

LEMONADE

1⅓ c. sugar
1 c. water
2 c. lemon juice (about 12 lemons)
Ice cubes
cold water
lemon wedges

Combine the sugar and 1 cup water in a small saucepan. Stir over low heat until sugar is dissolved. Cover, bring to boiling, and boil 5 minutes. Remove from heat and set aside to cool. Squeeze enough lemons to make 2 cups liquid. Refrigerate. When syrup is cooled, blend with the lemon juice. Cover and store in refrigerator until ready to use. To serve, put some ice cubes in tall glasses and add ½ cup of the lemon syrup to each glass. Fill glasses with cold water. Stir until blended. garnish with lemon wedges. 8 servings.

LIMONCELLO

2 lbs. fresh lemons
1 qt. grain alcohol
6 c. water
2½ c. sugar

Peel the lemons with a potato peeler, taking care to remove only the zest, or the yellow part. Do not remove any of the pith, or the white part. Put the lemon zest into a half-gallon jar with a tight-fitting lid. Pour

(continued)

on the alcohol. Let stand for 2-4 days, in a cool, darkened area. Shake the jar several times a day. When you see the lemons are getting pale, the oil has been extracted and you can strain the liquid and discard the zest. In a saucepan over low heat, mix together the water and sugar and stir until the sugar is dissolved and the syrup is clear. Let cool to room temperature and mix with the alcohol. Strain through a double thickness of cheesecloth into a clean bowl. Using a funnel, transfer the liquid into a clean, attractive bottle. Close the top with a cork or lid and store in the refrigerator. Serve well chilled as an after-dinner drink. Makes 2 quarts. (If grain alcohol is hard to find, substitute vodka.)

MARGARITA

½ oz. triple sec
1½ oz. tequila

½ oz. lime juice
shaved ice

Put the triple sec, tequila and lime juice in a shaker with shaved ice. Shake hard and pour into an on-the-rocks glass with salted rim (sprinkle coarse salt on wax paper, moisten rim of glass and dip in salt).

MILK SHAKES

Chocolate Milk Shake:

¾ c. milk
¼ c. chocolate syrup

3 scoops chocolate ice cream

Vanilla Milk Shake:

¾ c. milk
2 tsp. vanilla

3 scoops vanilla ice cream

Strawberry Milk Shake:

⅓ c. milk
½ c. sliced strawberries

3 scoops strawberry ice cream

For each shake, put ingredients for that flavor into blender. Cover and blend on high speed 2 seconds, then on low speed 5 seconds longer.

MIMOSA

juice of ½ orange
chilled champagne
ice

For each Mimosa, put 1 cube of ice into a champagne glass. Add juice of ½ orange. Fill with chilled champagne.

RAMOS FIZZ

2 jiggers gin
1 jigger lime juice
1 jigger lemon juice
2 egg whites
2 jiggers soda water
2 tsp. sugar syrup
1 pony heavy cream
2 dashes orange flower water
4 ice cubes

Mix together in blender all ingredients for 20-30 seconds. Strain and serve in 8-ounce glasses.

SANGRIA

½ c. water
½ c. sugar
juice of 1 lemon
juice of 1 orange
1 750-milliliter bottle dry, red wine
¼ c. brandy
2 c. chilled club soda
block of ice
orange and lemon slices

To make block of ice, put 1 quart of water in a rounded bowl and freeze. Bring sugar and water to a boil and stir until sugar is dissolved. Remove from heat and cool. When ready to serve, put block of ice in punch bowl. In a large pan, stir together the sugar water, lemon and orange juices, wine and brandy. Pour into punch bowl. Pour in chilled club soda. Slice an orange and a lemon and float some slices on top.

SPICED WINE

zest of 4 lemons
zest of 4 oranges
2 3" cinnamon sticks
10 whole cloves
2 c. sugar
2 c. water
juice of 1 lemon
12 c. burgundy wine

(continued)

Mix the lemon zest, orange zest, cinnamon sticks, cloves, sugar and water in a large pan. Bring to a boil and stir until the sugar is dissolved. Lower heat, cover and simmer for 20 minutes. Squeeze the juice of 1 lemon into the mix and pour in 12 cups of burgundy wine. Heat slowly over low heat. Do not boil. Ladle into mugs or punch cups from pan. Keep warm over very low heat.

WASSAIL BOWL

½ c. sugar
½ c. water
12 whole cloves
2 3" sticks cinnamon

1½ qt. fresh orange juice
2 c. fresh ruby red grapefruit juice
1 qt. sweet cider
1 orange, sliced

Combine sugar, water, cloves and cinnamon in saucepan over medium heat. Stir until sugar is dissolved. Cover and simmer 10 minutes over low heat. Strain. Add orange, grapefruit juices and cider. Reheat and serve hot in metal punch bowl. (Hot liquid will crack a glass bowl.) Slice orange and float slices on top.

Recipe Favorites

Sample Menus
Entertaining

My Brother David

Helpful Hints

- Unbaked cookie dough can be covered and refrigerated for up to 24 hours or frozen in an airtight container for up to 9 months.

- Bake one cookie sheet at a time using the middle oven rack.

- Decorate cookies with chocolate by placing cookies on a rack over waxed paper. Dip the tines of a fork into melted chocolate, and wave the fork gently back and forth to make wavy line decorations.

- Some cookies need indentations on top to fill with jam or chocolate. Use the rounded end of a honey dipper.

- Dip cookie cutters in flour or powdered sugar and shake off excess before cutting. For chocolate dough, dip cutters in baking cocoa.

- Tin coffee cans make excellent freezer containers for cookies.

- If you only have one cookie sheet on hand, line it with parchment paper. While one batch is baking, load a second sheet of parchment paper to have another batch ready to bake. Cleaning is also easier.

- When a recipe calls for packed brown sugar, fill the correct size measuring cup with sugar, and then use one cup size smaller to pack the brown sugar into its cup.

- Cut-up dried fruit often sticks to the blade of your knife. To prevent this problem, coat the blade of your knife with a thin film of vegetable spray before cutting.

- Instead of folding nuts into brownie batter, sprinkle on top of batter before baking. This keeps nuts crunchy instead of soggy.

- Only use glass or shiny metal pans. Dark or nonstick pans will cause brownies to become soggy and low in volume.

- When making bars, line pan with aluminum foil and prepare as directed. The bars can be lifted out, and cleanup is easy.

- Cutting bars is easier if you score the bars right as the pan leaves the oven. When the bars cool, cut along the scored lines.

- Use a double boiler for melting chocolate to prevent it from scorching. A slow cooker on the lowest setting also works well for melting chocolate, especially when coating a large amount of candy.

- Parchment paper provides an excellent nonstick surface for candy. Waxed paper should not be used for high-temperature candy.

Copyright © Morris Press Cookbooks

Brunch:	Luncheon:
Mimosas	Orvieto Wine
Baked Chiles Rellenos With Cheese	Norwegian Creamed Herring
	Quiche Lorraine
Creamed Chicken/Potato Nests	Artichokes Pizzaiola
Fruit Salad	Lime Chiffon Pie
Cinnamon Buns	
Children's Lunch or Dinner	
Celery and Carrots Toscano	Fruit Kabobs With Dip
Grilled Beefburgers	Macaroni and Cheese Laurina
Onion Strings	Zucchini Sauté
Milk Shakes	Frosty Drink
Sugar-Glazed Strawberries	Chocolate Pudding
Dinners	
Guacamole Dip/Tortilla Chips	Corn Chowder
Sangria	Chianti Wine
Southwestern Chili Casserole	Beef Braciola
Mixed Greens, Pear & Pecan Salad	Green Beans and Potatoes
	Ice Cream Nut Balls
Macedonia of Fruit	
Lorenzo Alla Filippini	Spanakopita
Chardonnay Wine	Sangiovese de Romagna Wine
Osso Buco	Grilled Lamb Chops
Risotto Milanese	Risi e Bisi
Roasted Red Peppers	Greek Salad
Bisque Tortoni	Orange Torte
Coconut Shrimp	Antipasto
Orvieto Wine	Pinot Grigio Wine
Baked Stuffed Sea Bass	Agnolotti
Roasted Potatoes	Lemon Raspberry Cake
Asparagus	
Chocolate Pie	
Artichoke/Crab Dip	Pot Stickers
Montepulciano d'Abruzzo Wine	Riesling Wine
Mongolian Barbecue	Paella
Fruit Salad	Spinach Salad
Baked Alaska	Flan

Fruit Cocktail Salad Trebbiano d'Abruzzo Wine Stuffed Pork Chops Potato Casserole Green Beans Stir Fry Crème Brûlée	Kiwi Tomato Salad Chenin Blanc Wine Chicken With Creamy Swiss Cheese Sauce Couscous Celery Amandine Banana Coconut Cream Pie
Butternut Squash Soup Riesling Wine Roast Duck Creamed Spinach Smashed Red Potatoes Peach Pie	Won Ton Soup Sake Wine Kung Pao Shrimp With Cashews Broccoli Lemon Bars
Hummus with Tahini Lee Anne Chenin Blanc Wine Chicken in Creamed Coconut Sauce/Basmati Rice Asparagus Berry Cobbler ――――――――― Fruit Kabobs With Dip Merlot Wine Hungarian Goulash/Spätzle Beets Chocolate Cake	Cocktail Party I Cheese Ball With Crackers Chicken Drumsticks Cocktail Frankfurters Raw Vegetables With Dip Liverwurst Pâté With Crackers Meatballs With Sour Cream Sauce Quiche Shrimp Spanakopita Rumaki Pulled Pork/Rolls

Cocktail Party II
Beef Bourguignon
Brie en Croute With Crackers
Caponata With Pita Chips
Stuffed Mushrooms
Coconut Curried Chicken Balls
Crisp Shrimp With Sweet and
  Sour Sauce
Guacamole Dip/Tortilla Chips
Layered Bean Dip/Corn Chips
Stuffed Celery
Ham With Mustard and Sweet
  and Sour Sauce/Rolls
	Cocktail Party III
	Sweet/Sour Spareribs
	Artichoke/Crab Dip/Bread
	Cheddar/Olive Balls
	Chinese Egg Rolls
	Coconut Shrimp
	Salmon Ball/Crackers
	Japanese Chicken
	Ham and Cheese Log/Crackers
	Pigs in Blanket
	Roast Beef With Horseradish
	  Sauce/Rolls

INDEX OF RECIPES

Appetizers/Soups/Salads/Sandwiches

ALMOND CHICKEN SALAD SANDWICH	57
ANTIPASTO	1
ARTICHOKE CRAB DIP	1
ASPARAGUS SOUP	29
BAKED POTATO SOUP	30
BAKED TOMATO CHEESE SANDWICHES	58
BARLEY SALAD	40
BEEF BARLEY SOUP	30
BEEF BOURGUIGNON	2
BEEF FAJITAS	58
BLACK BEAN SOUP	31
BLUE CHEESE DRESSING	56
BRIE EN CROUTE	2
BROCCOLI SOUP	31
BUTTERNUT SQUASH SOUP	32
BUTTERY BOURSIN CHEESE SPREAD	3
CALIFORNIA SHRIMP BOAT	40
CANAPÉS DE NAPOLI	3
CAPONATA	3
CAPRESE SALAD	40
CELERY AND CARROTS TOSCANO (PINZIMONIO)	4
CEVICHE	32
CHEDDAR/OLIVE BALLS	4
CHEESE BALL	4
CHEESE DIP	5
CHEESE FONDUE	5
CHEESY CHILI DIP	5
CHICK PEAS WITH DITALINI SOUP	33
CHICKEN AND BACON SANDWICH	59
CHICKEN DRUMSTICKS	6
CHICKEN SALAD	41
CHICKEN SOUP	33
CHICKEN SOUP WITH MATZO BALLS	34
CHILES RELLENOS SQUARES	6
CHINESE CHICKEN SALAD	41
CHINESE EGG ROLLS	6
CHINESE VEGETABLE SALAD	42
COBB SALAD	43
COCKTAIL FRANKFURTERS	7
COCONUT CURRIED CHICKEN BALLS	7
COCONUT SHRIMP	8
COLESLAW	43
CORN CHOWDER	34
COUSCOUS SALAD	44
CRAB SPREAD	8
CRANBERRY ORANGE RELISH	44
CRISP SHRIMP WITH SWEET/SOUR SAUCE	9
CURRIED CHICKEN SANDWICHES	59
DANDELION SALAD	44
DEVILED EGGS	9
DIP FOR RAW VEGETABLES	10
DOLMADES (STUFFED GRAPE LEAVES)	10
DUTCH SPLIT PEA SOUP	35
EGG AND OLIVE SANDWICHES	59
EMPANADAS	11
ESCARGOTS (SNAILS IN GARLIC BUTTER)	11
ESCAROLE SOUP	35
FRIED DOUGH WITH ANCHOVIES	12
FRIED DOUGH WITH MOZZARELLA CHEESE	12
FROZEN GREEN SALAD	45
FRUIT COCKTAIL SALAD	45
FRUIT KABOBS WITH DIP	13
FRUIT SALAD	45
GREEK SALAD	46
GUACAMOLE DIP	13
HAM AND CHEESE APPETIZERS	13
HAM AND CHEESE LOGS	14
HAM SALAD	46
HERB DRESSING	57
HOT CRAB FONDUE	14
HUMMUS WITH TAHINI (HOMOS BI TIHINEH) LEE ANNE	14
INDIAN CURRY BALLS	15
ITALIAN HERO SANDWICH	60
ITALIAN SEAFOOD SALAD	47
JAPANESE CHICKEN	15
KIWI TOMATO SALAD	47
LAYERED BEAN DIP	15
LIVERWURST AND TOMATO SANDWICH	60
LIVERWURST PÂTÉ	16
LOBSTER BISQUE	36
LORENZO ALLA FILIPPINI	16
MACARONI SALAD	48
MARINATED MUSHROOMS	16
MARINATED SHRIMP	17
MARINATED VEGETABLE SALAD	48
MARYLAND CRAB CHOWDER	36
MEATBALL AND PROVOLONE SANDWICH	60
MEATBALLS WITH SOUR CREAM SAUCE	17

MINESTRONE	37
MIXED GREENS, PEAR AND PECAN SALAD	49
MOZZARELLA PUFFS	18
ORGANIC SANDWICH	61
OYSTER CRACKER SNACKS	18
PASTA CON FAGIOLI (PASTA AND BEANS)	37
PASTA SALAD	49
PASTA SALAD WITH CHICKEN	50
PIGS IN BLANKET	18
PINEAPPLE BOATS	50
PINEAPPLE CRANBERRY SALAD	51
PITA POCKETS THAI	61
POT STICKERS	19
POTATO SALAD	51
POTATO SALAD ROLL	52
QUICHE SQUARES	20
QUICHES WITH SHRIMP	19
RED PEPPER DIP	20
RED PEPPER SALAD	52
RIBOLLITA	38
RICE SALAD	52
ROAST BEEF CLUB SANDWICH	61
RUMAKI	21
SALMON BALL	21
SALSA WITH CHIPS AMY JO	22
SAUSAGE AND PEPPERS SANDWICH	62
SAUSAGE BALLS	22
SCALLOPS WITH REMOULADE DIP	22
SESAME DRESSING	56
SHRIMP DIP	23
SHRIMP MOUSSE	23
SHRIMP SPREAD	23
SOUTHWESTERN CHICKEN SOUP	38
SPANAKOPITA APPETIZERS	24
SPINACH DIP WITH FRESH VEGETABLES	24
SPINACH SALAD	53
SPRING ROLLS	25
STRACCIATELLA	39
STRAWBERRY CREAM SQUARES	53
STUFFED CELERY	26
STUFFED MUSHROOMS	26
STUFFED ZUCCHINI BLOSSOMS	26
SWEET/SOUR SPARERIBS	27
TACO SALAD	54
TEQUILA DIP	27
TOMATO BISQUE	39
TOMATO SALAD	55
TOMATO SANDWICH	62
TORTELLINI SALAD	55
TUNA AND BEAN SALAD	55
TUNA MELT WITH TOMATO	63
VEGETARIAN SANDWICH	63
VIETNAMESE EGG ROLLS	28
VINAIGRETTE DRESSING	57
WALDORF SALAD	56
WONTON FILLED WITH PORK	28
WONTON SOUP	39
ZUCCHINI SQUARES	29

Pasta/Rice/Casseroles/Main Dishes/Eggs/Sauces/ Marinades/Stuffings/ Vegetables

AGNOLOTTI	65
ANGEL HAIR PASTA WITH OLIVE OIL & HERBS	66
ARTICHOKES PIZZAIOLA	113
ARTICHOKES WITH STUFFING	113
ASPARAGUS	114
BAKED ACORN SQUASH	114
BAKED BEANS	115
BAKED CHICKEN AND RICE	86
BAKED CHILIES RELLENOS WITH CHEESE	101
BAKED STUFFED AVOCADOS	87
BAKED VEGETABLES	115
BAKED ZITI	66
BARLEY CASSEROLE	87
BEANS ALLA TOSCANO	116
BEANS AND RICE	67
BÉCHAMEL SAUCE	104
BEEF AND EGGS	101
BEETS	116
BLACK-EYED PEAS	116
BROCCOLI	117
BURRITOS CON QUESO	88
BUTTERNUT SQUASH	117
CABBAGE WITH CANNELLINI BEANS	117
CANDIED SWEET POTATOES	118
CANNELLONI	67
CARIB BREAKFAST CASSEROLE	102
CARROTS WITH BRANDY	118
CAULIFLOWER WITH BÉCHAMEL	118
CELERY AMANDINE	119
CHICK PEAS	119
CHICKEN CHIP BAKE	88
CHICKEN CURRY	88
CHICKEN POT PIE	89
CHILI CON CARNE	90
CHIMICHURRI SAUCE	104
CHINESE GREEN BEANS	119
CHINESE SAUCE	105
CHOUCROUTE GARNIE	91

CORN SOUFFLÉ	120
COUSCOUS	68
CREAMED SPINACH	120
CROQUE MONSIEUR	102
CURRIED RICE	69
DUMPLINGS	69
EGGPLANT PARMIGIANA	121
ENCHILADA CASSEROLE	91
FETTUCCINE PRIMAVERA	71
FETTUCCINE WITH CREAM	69
FETTUCCINE WITH FOUR CHEESES	70
FETTUCCINE WITH LAMB SAUCE	70
FETTUCCINE WITH PORCINI MUSHROOMS	71
FRIED RICE	72
FRITTATA	102
GNOCCHI	72
GREEN BEANS AND POTATOES	121
GREENS, BEANS AND SAUSAGE	92
HOLLANDAISE SAUCE	105
HORSERADISH SAUCE	105
HOT MUSTARD SAUCE	105
HUNGARIAN GOULASH WITH SPÄTZLE	92
KALE	121
LASAGNA	73
LENTILS	122
LINGUINE WITH CLAM SAUCE	73
LINGUINE WITH PROSCIUTTO AND MUSHROOMS	74
LINGUINE WITH SHRIMP AND SCALLOPS	74
LINGUINE WITH ZUCCHINI	75
MACARONI AND CHEESE LAURINA	94
MACARONI AND CHEESE WITH ZUCCHINI	94
MACARONI WITH ARTICHOKES AND MOZZARELLA CHEESE	93
MARINADE	106
MARINARA SAUCE	106
MARINATED VEGETABLES	122
MEXICAN CHEESE PUFF	95
ONION STRINGS	123
PAELLA	95
PASTA DOUGH	75
PASTA WITH PEAS	76
PASTA WITH SEAFOOD SAUCE	77
PENNE PASTA WITH MARINARA SAUCE	77
PENNE PASTA WITH MEAT SAUCE	78
PESTO ALLA GENOVESE	106
PICO DE GALLO SAUCE	107
PIEROGI	96
PLUM SAUCE	107
POLENTA BROILED	78
POLENTA FRIED	79
POLENTA MARINARA	79
POLENTA WITH BUTTER AND CHEESE	79
POLENTA WITH VEGETABLES	80
POTATO CASSEROLE	123
POTATO CHIPS	123
POTATO NESTS	124
POTATOES AND EGGS	103
POTATOES AND EGGS WITH PEPPERS	103
POTATOES AU GRATIN	124
QUICHE LORRAINE	100
QUICHE WITH SPINACH AND MUSHROOMS	100
RAVIOLI WITH MEAT	80
RAVIOLI WITH SALMON	81
RED CABBAGE AU CARAMEL	125
RED CLAM SAUCE	108
RED WINE SAUCE	109
REFRIED BEANS	125
RICE CASSEROLE	97
RIGATONI WITH SAUSAGE AND PEPPERS	82
RISI E BISI (RICE AND PEAS)	82
RISOTTO ALLA MILANESE	83
ROASTED POTATOES	126
ROASTED RED PEPPERS	126
SAUSAGE STUFFING	110
SCALLOPED HAM AND EGGS	104
SCALLOPED POTATOES	127
SEAFOOD COCKTAIL SAUCE	109
SHEPHERD'S PIE	97
SICHUAN NOODLE TOSS	83
SMASHED RED POTATOES	127
SOUTHWESTERN CHILI CASSEROLE	98
SPAGHETTI CARBONARA	84
SPAGHETTINI WITH SMOKED SALMON	84
SPANISH RICE	84
SPINACH SAUTÉ	127
STUFFED BAKED ONIONS	128
STUFFED BAKED POTATOES	128
STUFFED CABBAGE ROLLS	98
STUFFED RED PEPPERS	99
STUFFING	110
STUFFING WITH OYSTERS	111
SWEET AND SOUR SAUCE	111
TARTAR SAUCE	111
TOMATO SAUCE	112
TOMATO SAUCE WITH BEEF	112
TOMATO SAUCE WITH LAMB	112
TOMATO SAUCE WITH PORK	113
TOMATOES, OVEN DRIED	128
TORTELLINI ALLA BOLOGNESE	85
TUNA NOODLE CASSEROLE	99

VEGETABLE STIR FRY	129
VEGETARIAN LASAGNA	86
YELLOW SQUASH	129
ZUCCHINI SAUTÉ	129

Meats And Poultry

BARBECUED SPARERIBS	155
BEEF BRACIOLA	131
BEEF BURGUNDY	131
BEEF GRILL	132
BEEF TACOS	132
BEEF TERIYAKI	133
BEEF WITH CREAM	133
BROILED MARINATED LAMB CHOPS	152
CARBONADE OF BEEF FLAMANDE	134
CHICKEN AMANDINE	161
CHICKEN AND SAUSAGE	166
CHICKEN AND WALNUTS	169
CHICKEN BAKED WITH PARMESAN CHEESE	161
CHICKEN CACCIATORE WITH POLENTA	162
CHICKEN CREOLE	164
CHICKEN CROQUETTES	164
CHICKEN FRIED	165
CHICKEN IN CREAMED COCONUT SAUCE	162
CHICKEN KIEV	165
CHICKEN QUESADILLA	166
CHICKEN SCALLOPS	167
CHICKEN TANDOORI	167
CHICKEN TENDERS WITH HONEY MUSTARD	168
CHICKEN WITH CREAMY SWISS CHEESE SAUCE	163
CHICKEN WITH TOMATO/SOUR CREAM SAUCE	168
CORNED BEEF AND CABBAGE	134
CURRIED LOIN OF PORK	155
GIAMBOTTE (ITALIAN SAUSAGE AND PEPPERS)	156
GRILLED BEEFBURGERS	135
HONEY-BASTED CHICKEN BREASTS	169
KUNG PAO BEEF	135
KUNG PAO CHICKEN	170
KUNG PAO PORK	156
LAMB CURRY	152
LAMB SHISH KABOBS (SOUVLAKIA)	153
LIVER AND ONIONS	136
MEAT LOAF	137
MEATBALLS	136
MONGOLIAN BARBEQUE	137
MOO SHU PORK	157
OSSO BUCO ALLA MILANESE	145
PARTY CHICKEN BREASTS	171
PEPPER STEAK	138
PORK SATAY	158
POT ROAST	139
PULLED PORK	158
ROAST BEEF	139
ROAST CHICKEN	171
ROAST DUCK	172
ROAST LEG OF LAMB	154
ROAST PORK ALLA TOSCANA	159
ROAST RACK OF LAMB	154
ROAST VEAL	146
ROASTED FRESH HAM	159
SALTIMBOCCA	147
SAUERBRATEN	140
SAUSAGE	160
SAVORY SPANAKOPITAS	140
SESAME BEEF	141
SESAME CHICKEN	171
SHORT RIBS ROGER	142
STEAK AUDREE	142
STEAK DIANE	143
STEAK WITH OYSTERS	144
STUFFED CHICKEN BREASTS	172
STUFFED FLANK STEAK	144
STUFFED PORK CHOPS	160
STUFFED VEAL	147
SUKIYAKI	145
VEAL BIRDS	148
VEAL CHOPS	148
VEAL CORDON BLEU	149
VEAL MARSALA	149
VEAL PARMIGIANA	150
VEAL PICCATA	150
VEAL STEW	151
VITELLO TONNATO	151

Fish/Seafood

BAKED SNAPPER	175
BAKED STUFFED SEA BASS	175
BROILED SALMON	176
COD	176
CRAB CAKES	177
DOVER SOLE IN LEMON BUTTER	177
FRIED CALAMARI WITH SAUCE	178
FRIED SMELT	178
FRITTO MISTO	179
HALIBUT FLORENTINE	180
JAMBALAYA	181
KUNG PAO SHRIMP WITH CASHEWS	181
LOBSTER IN THE MOON	182
LOBSTER THERMIDOR	183
LUTEFISK	183

NORWEGIAN CREAMED HERRING	183
OYSTER FRITTERS	184
SALMON PIE	184
SALMON, POACHED	185
SAUTÉED SHRIMP	185
SHRIMP CREOLE	186
SHRIMP CURRY	186
SHRIMP ÉTOUFFÉE	187
STIR-FRY SHRIMP AND VEGETABLES	187
STUFFED BAKED CALAMARI	188
STUFFED FLOUNDER	188
STUFFED SHRIMP WITH CRAB	189
TROUT AMANDINE	189

Bread/Rolls/Pancakes/ Muffins/Cakes/Frostings/ Candy/Cookies/Bars

ALMOND BISCOTTI	239
ALMOND CARAMEL CANDY	231
ALMOND CRUNCH	231
ANGEL CUSTARD CAKE	213
ANISE COOKIES	240
APPLE BRAN MUFFINS	191
APPLE CAKE	213
APPLE FRITTERS	191
AVOCADO BREAD	192
BAGUETTES	192
BAKED CARAMEL CORN	232
BAKLAVA	240
BANANA BREAD	193
BANANA PINEAPPLE CAKE WITH PECANS	214
BANANA POUND CAKE	214
BLACK AND WHITE COOKIES	241
BLUEBERRY CITRUS CAKE	215
BLUEBERRY STREUSEL MUFFINS	193
BREAD DOUGH	194
BREAD STICKS WITH SESAME SEEDS	194
BROWNIES	242
BUCCELLATO (ITALIAN EASTER BREAD)	195
BUTTERMILK BISCUITS	195
CANDIED APPLES	232
CANDIED CITRUS PEEL	233
CANNOLI CAKE	216
CARAMEL APPLES	233
CARAMEL BARS	242
CARAMEL CRUSHES	233
CARAMEL PECAN LOGS	234
CARROT CAKE	217
CASSATA ALLA SICILIANA	218
CHEESE BREAD	196
CHEESECAKE	219

CHERRY COOKIES	243
CHERRY WINKS	244
CHOCOLATE ALMOND BARK	235
CHOCOLATE BUTTERSCOTCH BARS	244
CHOCOLATE CAKE	221
CHOCOLATE CHEESECAKE	220
CHOCOLATE CHIP HEATH BAR COOKIES LEE ANNE	245
CHOCOLATE COOKIES	245
CHOCOLATE COOKIES WITH WHITE CHOCOLATE CHIPS	246
CHOCOLATE CRINKLES	246
CHOCOLATE FILLED COOKIES	247
CHOCOLATE KISS COOKIES	247
CHOCOLATE NUT CARAMELS	235
CHOCOLATE ROLL	222
CHOCOLATE TRUFFLES	236
CINNAMON BUNS	196
COCOA OATMEAL NUGGETS	248
COCONUT BARS	248
COCONUT TOPPED BROWNIES	249
CRANBERRY FRUIT NUT BREAD	197
CRÊPE BATTER	197
CRUNCHY PEANUT BUTTER BALLS	249
CUPCAKES WITH FILLING	223
CUSCINETTI ABRUZZESE	243
DATE LOAF	198
DILLY CASSEROLE BREAD	198
DINNER ROLLS	199
DOUGHNUTS, BAKED	200
DOUGHNUTS FILLED WITH JELLY	201
FATTIGMAND COOKIES	250
FIG COOKIES	250
FRIED BREAD	201
FRUIT BARS	251
FRUIT CAKE	224
FUDGE NUT BARS	252
GERMAN STOLLEN	202
GERMAN SWEET CHOCOLATE CAKE	225
GINGER COOKIE PEOPLE	252
GORP	236
HEATH BAR CAKE	226
HERMITS	253
HOLIDAY MINCE SQUARES	253
ITALIAN ROSETTES	254
JULE KAGE	202
LACKERLI	254
LEBKUCHEN	255
LEFSE	203
LEMON BARS	256
LEMON COOKIES	256
LEMON RASPBERRY CAKE	226
MACADAMIA NUT SQUARES	257

MAGIC PEANUT BUTTER MIDDLES	257
MARSHMALLOW CREAM FUDGE	236
MERINGUES GLACÉS	258
MINTS	237
MOLASSES COOKIES	258
MOUNDS BARS	259
NORWEGIAN CHRISTMAS BREAD	203
NORWEGIAN KAKE	259
NORWEGIAN ROSETTES	260
NUTMEG COOKIES	260
OATMEAL CARAMEL BARS	261
OATMEAL CHOCOLATE CHIP COOKIES	261
OLIVE BREAD	204
ORANGE TORTE	227
PANCAKES - LAURINA'S	204
PANETTONE (ITALIAN CHRISTMAS BREAD)	227
PEANUT BLOSSOM COOKIES	262
PEANUT BRITTLE	237
PEANUT BUTTER CHEWIES	238
PINE NUT COOKIES	262
PIZZA VEGETARIAN	206
PIZZA WITH ANCHOVIES	205
PIZZA WITH MEAT	206
PIZZA WITH TOMATO AND CHEESE	205
POUND CAKE	228
PRETZELS - AMY JO	207
PUMPKIN BREAD	208
RAISIN NUT BREAD	208
RAISIN SUGAR COOKIES	263
REFRIGERATOR CHOCOLATE BARS	263
SANDIES	264
SAUSAGE BREAD	209
SOUR CREAM PEAR COFFEE CAKE	229
SOURDOUGH BREAD	210
SOURDOUGH ENGLISH MUFFINS	210
SOURDOUGH STARTER	209
STRAWBERRY CAKE	229
STUFFED CALZONE	211
TARALLI ABRUZZESE	264
TORRONE (NOUGAT CANDY)	238
TURTLES	239
WHEAT BREAD	212
WHISKEY BALLS	265
WHITE CAKE/WEDDING CAKE	230
WHOOPIES	265
ZINFANDEL COOKIES	266
ZUCCHINI BREAD	212

Pies/Pastry/Desserts

APPLE DUMPLINGS	276
APPLE PIE	267
BAKED ALASKA	277
BANANA COCONUT CREAM PIE	268
BANANA SPLIT	278
BERRY COBBLER	279
BISQUE TORTONI	279
BLUEBERRY PIE	269
BREAD PUDDING	280
CANNOLI	281
CHERRY-BANANA PIE	269
CHOCOLATE FONDUE	282
CHOCOLATE PIE	269
CHOCOLATE PUDDING	282
CREAM PUFFS	282
CRÈME BRÛLÉE	283
ÉCLAIRS	284
FLAN (CARAMEL CUSTARD)	284
ICE CREAM NUT BALLS	285
ICE CREAM SANDWICHES	285
ITALIAN CREAM WITH FRUIT COCKTAIL	286
ITALIAN TRIFLE	286
LEMON PIE	270
LIME CHIFFON PIE	270
MACEDONIA OF FRUIT	287
MOUSSE AU CHOCOLAT	287
PASTICCIOTTI	288
PEACH PIE	271
PECAN PIE	271
PIE CRUST	267
PINEAPPLE PIE	272
PUMPKIN PIE	272
RASPBERRIES SABAYON	289
RICE PUDDING	289
RICE PUDDING WITH CARDINAL SAUCE	290
RICE TORTE	273
RICOTTA PIE	274
SOPAPILLAS	290
SOUFFLÉ WITH STRAWBERRY SAUCE	291
SPUMONI	292
STRAWBERRIES ROMANOFF	292
STRAWBERRIES WITH LEMON	292
STRAWBERRY RHUBARB PIE	275
SUGAR-GLAZED STRAWBERRIES	293
SUNSHINE SHERBET	293
SUPER STRAWBERRY PIE	275
SWEET POTATO PIE	276
TIRAMISU	293
VANILLA PUDDING	294

Beverages

BANANA DAIQUIRI	295
BLACK COW	295
BLOODY MARY	295
BRANDY ALEXANDER	295
BROADWAY	296
CAFÉ BRÛLOT	296
CHAMPAGNE PUNCH	296
CHILDREN'S MARTINI LEE ANNE & AMY JO	297
CREAMY STRAWBERRY DAIQUIRIS	297
EGGNOG	297
FROSTY DRINK	298
FRUIT PUNCH	298
FRUIT SLUSH	298
GRASSHOPPERS	299
HOT BUTTERED RUM	299
ICED CAPPUCCINO	299
IRISH COFFEE	300
KAHLÚA COLADA	300
LEMONADE	300
LIMONCELLO	300
MARGARITA	301
MILK SHAKES	301
MIMOSA	302
RAMOS FIZZ	302
SANGRIA	302
SPICED WINE	302
WASSAIL BOWL	303

PANTRY BASICS

A WELL-STOCKED PANTRY provides all the makings for a good meal. With the right ingredients, you can quickly create a variety of satisfying, delicious meals for family or guests. Keeping these items in stock also means avoiding extra trips to the grocery store, saving you time and money. Although everyone's pantry is different, there are basic items you should always have. Add other items according to your family's needs. For example, while some families consider chips, cereals and snacks as must-haves, others can't be without feta cheese and imported olives. Use these basic pantry suggestions as a handy reference list when creating your grocery list. Don't forget refrigerated items like milk, eggs, cheese and butter.

STAPLES

- Baker's chocolate
- Baking powder
- Baking soda
- Barbeque sauce
- Bread crumbs (plain or seasoned)
- Chocolate chips
- Cocoa powder
- Cornmeal
- Cornstarch
- Crackers
- Flour
- Honey
- Ketchup
- Lemon juice
- Mayonnaise or salad dressing
- Non-stick cooking spray
- Nuts (almonds, pecans, walnuts)
- Oatmeal
- Oil (olive, vegetable)
- Pancake baking mix
- Pancake syrup
- Peanut butter
- Shortening
- Sugar (granulated, brown, powdered)
- Vinegar

PACKAGED/CANNED FOODS

- Beans (canned, dry)
- Broth (beef, chicken)
- Cake mixes with frosting
- Canned diced tomatoes
- Canned fruit
- Canned mushrooms
- Canned soup
- Canned tomato paste & sauce
- Canned tuna & chicken
- Cereal
- Dried soup mix
- Gelatin (flavored or plain)
- Gravies
- Jarred Salsa
- Milk (evaporated, sweetened condensed)
- Non-fat dry milk
- Pastas
- Rice (brown, white)
- Spaghetti sauce

SPICES/SEASONINGS

- Basil
- Bay leaves
- Black pepper
- Bouillon cubes (beef, chicken)
- Chives
- Chili powder
- Cinnamon
- Mustard (dried, prepared)
- Garlic powder or salt
- Ginger
- Nutmeg
- Onion powder or salt
- Oregano
- Paprika
- Parsley
- Rosemary
- Sage
- Salt
- Soy sauce
- Tarragon
- Thyme
- Vanilla
- Worcestershire sauce
- Yeast

Copyright © 2006
Morris Press Cookbooks
All Rights Reserved.

HERBS & SPICES

DRIED VS. FRESH. While dried herbs are convenient, they don't generally have the same purity of flavor as fresh herbs. Ensure dried herbs are still fresh by checking if they are green and not faded. Crush a few leaves to see if the aroma is still strong. Always store them in an air-tight container away from light and heat.

BASIL — Sweet, warm flavor with an aromatic odor. Use whole or ground. Good with lamb, fish, roast, stews, beef, vegetables, dressing and omelets.

BAY LEAVES — Pungent flavor. Use whole leaf but remove before serving. Good in vegetable dishes, seafood, stews and pickles.

CARAWAY — Spicy taste and aromatic smell. Use in cakes, breads, soups, cheese and sauerkraut.

CELERY SEED — Strong taste which resembles the vegetable. Can be used sparingly in pickles and chutney, meat and fish dishes, salads, bread, marinades, dressings and dips.

CHIVES — Sweet, mild flavor like that of onion. Excellent in salads, fish, soups and potatoes.

CILANTRO — Use fresh. Excellent in salads, fish, chicken, rice, beans and Mexican dishes.

CINNAMON — Sweet, pungent flavor. Widely used in many sweet baked goods, chocolate dishes, cheesecakes, pickles, chutneys and hot drinks.

CORIANDER — Mild, sweet, orangy flavor and available whole or ground. Common in curry powders and pickling spice and also used in chutney, meat dishes, casseroles, Greek-style dishes, apple pies and baked goods.

CURRY POWDER — Spices are combined to proper proportions to give a distinct flavor to meat, poultry, fish and vegetables.

DILL — Both seeds and leaves are flavorful. Leaves may be used as a garnish or cooked with fish, soup, dressings, potatoes and beans. Leaves or the whole plant may be used to flavor pickles.

FENNEL — Sweet, hot flavor. Both seeds and leaves are used. Use in small quantities in pies and baked goods. Leaves can be boiled with fish.

HERBS & SPICES

GINGER — A pungent root, this aromatic spice is sold fresh, dried or ground. Use in pickles, preserves, cakes, cookies, soups and meat dishes.

MARJORAM — May be used both dried or green. Use to flavor fish, poultry, omelets, lamb, stew, stuffing and tomato juice.

MINT — Aromatic with a cool flavor. Excellent in beverages, fish, lamb, cheese, soup, peas, carrots and fruit desserts.

NUTMEG — Whole or ground. Used in chicken and cream soups, cheese dishes, fish cakes, and with chicken and veal. Excellent in custards, milk puddings, pies and cakes.

OREGANO — Strong, aromatic odor. Use whole or ground in tomato juice, fish, eggs, pizza, omelets, chili, stew, gravy, poultry and vegetables.

PAPRIKA — A bright red pepper, this spice is used in meat, vegetables and soups or as a garnish for potatoes, salads or eggs.

PARSLEY — Best when used fresh, but can be used dried as a garnish or as a seasoning. Try in fish, omelets, soup, meat, stuffing and mixed greens.

ROSEMARY — Very aromatic. Can be used fresh or dried. Season fish, stuffing, beef, lamb, poultry, onions, eggs, bread and potatoes. Great in dressings.

SAFFRON — Aromatic, slightly bitter taste. Only a pinch needed to flavor and color dishes such as bouillabaisse, chicken soup, rice, paella, fish sauces, buns and cakes. Very expensive, so where a touch of color is needed, use turmeric instead, but the flavor will not be the same.

SAGE — Use fresh or dried. The flowers are sometimes used in salads. May be used in tomato juice, fish, omelets, beef, poultry, stuffing, cheese spreads and breads.

TARRAGON — Leaves have a pungent, hot taste. Use to flavor sauces, salads, fish, poultry, tomatoes, eggs, green beans, carrots and dressings.

THYME — Sprinkle leaves on fish or poultry before broiling or baking. Throw a few sprigs directly on coals shortly before meat is finished grilling.

TURMERIC — Aromatic, slightly bitter flavor. Should be used sparingly in curry powder and relishes and to color cakes and rice dishes.

Use 3 times more fresh herbs if substituting fresh for dried.

BAKING BREADS

HINTS FOR BAKING BREADS

- Kneading dough for 30 seconds after mixing improves the texture of baking powder biscuits.

- Instead of shortening, use cooking or salad oil in waffles and hot cakes.

- When bread is baking, a small dish of water in the oven will help keep the crust from hardening.

- Dip a spoon in hot water to measure shortening, butter, etc., and the fat will slip out more easily.

- Small amounts of leftover corn may be added to pancake batter for variety.

- To make bread crumbs, use the fine cutter of a food grinder and tie a large paper bag over the spout in order to prevent flying crumbs.

- When you are doing any sort of baking, you get better results if you remember to preheat your cookie sheet, muffin tins or cake pans.

3 RULES FOR USE OF LEAVENING AGENTS

1. In simple flour mixtures, use 2 teaspoons baking powder to leaven 1 cup flour. Reduce this amount ½ teaspoon for each egg used.

2. To 1 teaspoon soda, use 2 ¼ teaspoons cream of tartar, 2 cups freshly soured milk or 1 cup molasses.

3. To substitute soda and an acid for baking powder, divide the amount of baking powder by 4. Take that as your measure and add acid according to rule 2.

PROPORTIONS OF BAKING POWDER TO FLOUR

biscuits	to 1 cup flour use 1 ¼ tsp. baking powder
cake with oil	to 1 cup flour use 1 tsp. baking powder
muffins	to 1 cup flour use 1 ½ tsp. baking powder
popovers	to 1 cup flour use 1 ¼ tsp. baking powder
waffles	to 1 cup flour use 1 ¼ tsp. baking powder

PROPORTIONS OF LIQUID TO FLOUR

pour batter	to 1 cup liquid use 1 cup flour
drop batter	to 1 cup liquid use 2 to 2 ½ cups flour
soft dough	to 1 cup liquid use 3 to 3 ½ cups flour
stiff dough	to 1 cup liquid use 4 cups flour

TIME & TEMPERATURE CHART

Breads	Minutes	Temperature
biscuits	12 - 15	400° - 450°
cornbread	25 - 30	400° - 425°
gingerbread	40 - 50	350° - 370°
loaf	50 - 60	350° - 400°
nut bread	50 - 75	350°
popovers	30 - 40	425° - 450°
rolls	20 - 30	400° - 450°

BAKING DESSERTS

PERFECT COOKIES

Cookie dough that must be rolled is much easier to handle after it has been refrigerated for 10 to 30 minutes. This keeps the dough from sticking, even though it may be soft. If not done, the soft dough may require more flour and too much flour makes cookies hard and brittle. Place on a floured board only as much dough as can be easily managed. Flour the rolling pin slightly and roll lightly to desired thickness. Cut shapes close together and add trimmings to dough that needs to be rolled. Place pans or sheets in upper third of oven. Watch cookies carefully while baking in order to avoid burned edges. When sprinkling sugar on cookies, try putting it into a salt shaker in order to save time.

PERFECT PIES

- Pie crust will be better and easier to make if all the ingredients are cool.

- The lower crust should be placed in the pan so that it covers the surface smoothly. Air pockets beneath the surface will push the crust out of shape while baking.

- Folding the top crust over the lower crust before crimping will keep juices in the pie.

- When making custard pie, bake at a high temperature for about 10 minutes to prevent a soggy crust. Then finish baking at a low temperature.

- When making cream pie, sprinkle crust with powdered sugar in order to prevent it from becoming soggy.

PERFECT CAKES

- Fill cake pans two-thirds full and spread batter into corners and sides, leaving a slight hollow in the center.

- Cake is done when it shrinks from the sides of the pan or if it springs back when touched lightly with the finger.

- After removing a cake from the oven, place it on a rack for about 5 minutes. Then, the sides should be loosened and the cake turned out on a rack in order to finish cooling.

- Do not frost cakes until thoroughly cool.

- Icing will remain where you put it if you sprinkle cake with powdered sugar first.

TIME & TEMPERATURE CHART

Dessert	Time	Temperature
butter cake, layer	20-40 min.	380° - 400°
butter cake, loaf	40-60 min.	360° - 400°
cake, angel	50-60 min.	300° - 360°
cake, fruit	3-4 hrs.	275° - 325°
cake, sponge	40-60 min.	300° - 350°
cookies, molasses	18-20 min.	350° - 375°
cookies, thin	10-12 min.	380° - 390°
cream puffs	45-60 min.	300° - 350°
meringue	40-60 min.	250° - 300°
pie crust	20-40 min.	400° - 500°

VEGETABLES & FRUITS

COOKING TIME TABLE

Vegetable	Cooking Method	Time
artichokes	boiled	40 min.
	steamed	45-60 min.
asparagus tips	boiled	10-15 min.
beans, lima	boiled	20-40 min.
	steamed	60 min.
beans, string	boiled	15-35 min.
	steamed	60 min.
beets, old	boiled or steamed	1-2 hours.
beets, young with skin	boiled	30 min.
	steamed	60 min.
	baked	70-90 min.
broccoli, flowerets	boiled	5-10 min.
broccoli, stems	boiled	20-30 min.
brussels sprouts	boiled	20-30 min.
cabbage, chopped	boiled	10-20 min.
	steamed	25 min.
carrots, cut across	boiled	8-10 min.
	steamed	40 min.
cauliflower, flowerets	boiled	8-10 min.
cauliflower, stem down	boiled	20-30 min.
corn, green, tender	boiled	5-10 min.
	steamed	15 min.
	baked	20 min.
corn on the cob	boiled	8-10 min.
	steamed	15 min.
eggplant, whole	boiled	30 min.
	steamed	40 min.
	baked	45 min.
parsnips	boiled	25-40 min.
	steamed	60 min.
	baked	60-75 min.
peas, green	boiled or steamed	5-15 min.
potatoes	boiled	20-40 min.
	steamed	60 min.
	baked	45-60 min.
pumpkin or squash	boiled	20-40 min.
	steamed	45 min.
	baked	60 min.
tomatoes	boiled	5-15 min.
turnips	boiled	25-40 min.

DRYING TIME TABLE

Fruit	Sugar or Honey	Cooking Time
apricots	¼ c. for each cup of fruit	about 40 min.
figs	1 T. for each cup of fruit	about 30 min.
peaches	¼ c. for each cup of fruit	about 45 min.
prunes	2 T. for each cup of fruit	about 45 min.

VEGETABLES & FRUITS

BUYING FRESH VEGETABLES

Artichokes: Look for compact, tightly closed heads with green, clean-looking leaves. Avoid those with leaves that are brown or separated.

Asparagus: Stalks should be tender and firm; tips should be close and compact. Choose the stalks with very little white; they are more tender. Use asparagus soon because it toughens quickly.

Beans, Snap: Those with small seeds inside the pods are best. Avoid beans with dry-looking pods.

Broccoli, Brussels Sprouts and Cauliflower: Flower clusters on broccoli and cauliflower should be tight and close together. Brussels sprouts should be firm and compact. Smudgy, dirty spots may indicate pests or disease.

Cabbage and Head Lettuce: Choose heads that are heavy for their size. Avoid cabbage with worm holes and lettuce with discoloration or soft rot.

Cucumbers: Choose long, slender cucumbers for best quality. May be dark or medium green, but yellow ones are undesirable.

Mushrooms: Caps should be closed around the stems. Avoid black or brown gills.

Peas and Lima Beans: Select pods that are well-filled but not bulging. Avoid dried, spotted, yellow or limp pods.

BUYING FRESH FRUITS

Bananas: Skin should be free of bruises and black or brown spots. Purchase them slightly green and allow them to ripen at room temperature.

Berries: Select plump, solid berries with good color. Avoid stained containers which indicate wet or leaky berries. Berries with clinging caps, such as blackberries and raspberries, may be unripe. Strawberries without caps may be overripe.

Melons: In cantaloupes, thick, close netting on the rind indicates best quality. Cantaloupes are ripe when the stem scar is smooth and the space between the netting is yellow or yellow-green. They are best when fully ripe with fruity odor.

Honeydews are ripe when rind has creamy to yellowish color and velvety texture. Immature honeydews are whitish-green.

Ripe watermelons have some yellow color on one side. If melons are white or pale green on one side, they are not ripe.

Oranges, Grapefruit and Lemons: Choose those heavy for their size. Smoother, thinner skins usually indicate more juice. Most skin markings do not affect quality. Oranges with a slight greenish tinge may be just as ripe as fully colored ones. Light or greenish-yellow lemons are more tart than deep yellow ones. Avoid citrus fruits showing withered, sunken or soft areas.

NAPKIN FOLDING

FOR BEST RESULTS, use well-starched linen napkins if possible. For more complicated folds, 24-inch napkins work best. Practice the folds with newspapers. Children will have fun decorating the table once they learn these attractive folds!

SHIELD

Easy fold. Elegant with monogram in corner.

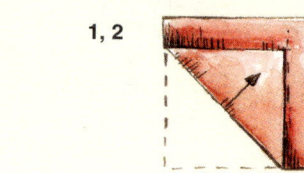

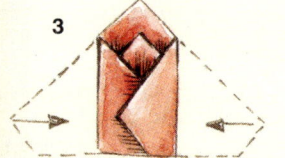

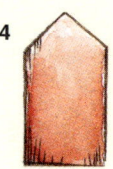

Instructions:
1. Fold into quarter size. If monogrammed, ornate corner should face down.
2. Turn up folded corner three-quarters.
3. Overlap right side and left side points.
4. Turn over; adjust sides so they are even, single point in center.
5. Place point up or down on plate, or left of plate.

ROSETTE

Elegant on plate.

Instructions:
1. Fold left and right edges to center, leaving ½" opening along center.
2. Pleat firmly from top edge to bottom edge. Sharpen edges with hot iron.
3. Pinch center together. If necessary, use small piece of pipe cleaner to secure and top with single flower.
4. Spread out rosette.

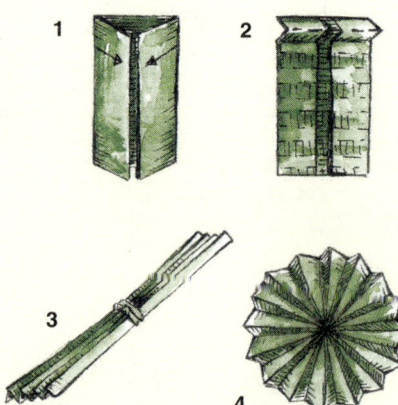

NAPKIN FOLDING

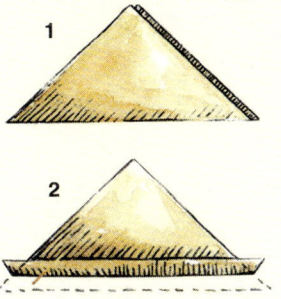

CANDLE

Easy to do; can be decorated.

Instructions:
1. Fold into triangle, point at top.
2. Turn lower edge up 1".
3. Turn over, folded edge down.
4. Roll tightly from left to right.
5. Tuck in corner. Stand upright.

FAN

Pretty in napkin ring or on plate.

Instructions:
1. Fold top and bottom edges to center.
2. Fold top and bottom edges to center a second time.
3. Pleat firmly from the left edge. Sharpen edges with hot iron.
4. Spread out fan. Balance flat folds of each side on table. Well-starched napkins will hold shape.

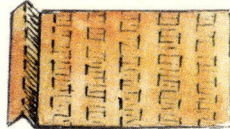

LILY

Effective and pretty on table.

Instructions:
1. Fold napkin into quarters.
2. Fold into triangle, closed corner to open points.
3. Turn two points over to other side. (Two points are on either side of closed point.)
4. Pleat.
5. Place closed end in glass. Pull down two points on each side and shape.

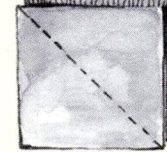

MEASUREMENTS & SUBSTITUTIONS

MEASUREMENTS

a pinch	1/8 teaspoon or less
3 teaspoons	1 tablespoon
4 tablespoons	1/4 cup
8 tablespoons	1/2 cup
12 tablespoons	3/4 cup
16 tablespoons	1 cup
2 cups	1 pint
4 cups	1 quart
4 quarts	1 gallon
8 quarts	1 peck
4 pecks	1 bushel
16 ounces	1 pound
32 ounces	1 quart
1 ounce liquid	2 tablespoons
8 ounces liquid	1 cup

Use standard measuring spoons and cups. All measurements are level.

C° TO F° CONVERSION

120° C	250° F
140° C	275° F
150° C	300° F
160° C	325° F
180° C	350° F
190° C	375° F
200° C	400° F
220° C	425° F
230° C	450° F

Temperature conversions are estimates.

SUBSTITUTIONS

Ingredient	Quantity	Substitute
baking powder	1 teaspoon	1/4 tsp. baking soda plus 1/2 tsp. cream of tartar
chocolate	1 square (1 oz.)	3 or 4 T. cocoa plus 1 T. butter
cornstarch	1 tablespoon	2 T. flour or 2 tsp. quick-cooking tapioca
cracker crumbs	3/4 cup	1 c. bread crumbs
dates	1 lb.	1 1/2 c. dates, pitted and cut
dry mustard	1 teaspoon	1 T. prepared mustard
flour, self-rising	1 cup	1 c. all-purpose flour, 1/2 tsp. salt, and 1 tsp. baking powder
herbs, fresh	1 tablespoon	1 tsp. dried herbs
ketchup or chili sauce	1 cup	1 c. tomato sauce plus 1/2 c. sugar and 2 T. vinegar (for use in cooking)
milk, sour	1 cup	1 T. lemon juice or vinegar plus sweet milk to make 1 c. (let stand 5 minutes)
whole	1 cup	1/2 c. evaporated milk plus 1/2 c. water
min. marshmallows	10	1 lg. marshmallow
onion, fresh	1 small	1 T. instant minced onion, rehydrated
sugar, brown	1/2 cup	2 T. molasses in 1/2 c. granulated sugar
powdered	1 cup	1 c. granulated sugar plus 1 tsp. cornstarch
tomato juice	1 cup	1/2 c. tomato sauce plus 1/2 c. water

When substituting cocoa for chocolate in cakes, the amount of flour must be reduced. Brown and white sugars usually can be interchanged.

EQUIVALENCY CHART

Food	Quantity	Yield
apple	1 medium	1 cup
banana, mashed	1 medium	1/3 cup
bread	1 1/2 slices	1 cup soft crumbs
bread	1 slice	1/4 cup fine, dry crumbs
butter	1 stick or 1/4 pound	1/2 cup
cheese, American, cubed	1 pound	2 2/3 cups
American, grated	1 pound	5 cups
cream cheese	3-ounce package	6 2/3 tablespoons
chocolate, bitter	1 square	1 ounce
cocoa	1 pound	4 cups
coconut	1 1/2 pound package	2 2/3 cups
coffee, ground	1 pound	5 cups
cornmeal	1 pound	3 cups
cornstarch	1 pound	3 cups
crackers, graham	14 squares	1 cup fine crumbs
saltine	28 crackers	1 cup fine crumbs
egg	4-5 whole	1 cup
whites	8-10	1 cup
yolks	10-12	1 cup
evaporated milk	1 cup	3 cups whipped
flour, cake, sifted	1 pound	4 1/2 cups
rye	1 pound	5 cups
white, sifted	1 pound	4 cups
white, unsifted	1 pound	3 3/4 cups
gelatin, flavored	3 1/4 ounces	1/2 cup
unflavored	1/4 ounce	1 tablespoon
lemon	1 medium	3 tablespoon juice
marshmallows	16	1/4 pound
noodles, cooked	8-ounce package	7 cups
uncooked	4 ounces (1 1/2 cups)	2-3 cups cooked
macaroni, cooked	8-ounce package	6 cups
macaroni, uncooked	4 ounces (1 1/4 cups)	2 1/4 cups cooked
spaghetti, uncooked	7 ounces	4 cups cooked
nuts, chopped	1/4 pound	1 cup
almonds	1 pound	3 1/2 cups
walnuts, broken	1 pound	3 cups
walnuts, unshelled	1 pound	1 1/2 to 1 3/4 cups
onion	1 medium	1/2 cup
orange	3-4 medium	1 cup juice
raisins	1 pound	3 1/2 cups
rice, brown	1 cup	4 cups cooked
converted	1 cup	3 1/2 cups cooked
regular	1 cup	3 cups cooked
wild	1 cup	4 cups cooked
sugar, brown	1 pound	2 1/2 cups
powdered	1 pound	3 1/2 cups
white	1 pound	2 cups
vanilla wafers	22	1 cup fine crumbs
zwieback, crumbled	4	1 cups

FOOD QUANTITIES

FOR LARGE SERVINGS

	25 Servings	50 Servings	100 Servings
Beverages:			
coffee	½ pound and 1 ½ gallons water	1 pound and 3 gallons water	2 pounds and 6 gallons water
lemonade	10-15 lemons and 1 ½ gallons water	20-30 lemons and 3 gallons water	40-60 lemons and 6 gallons water
tea	1/12 pound and 1 ½ gallons water	1/6 pound and 3 gallons water	1/3 pound and 6 gallons water
Desserts:			
layered cake	1 12" cake	3 10" cakes	6 10" cakes
sheet cake	1 10" x 12" cake	1 12" x 20" cake	2 12" x 20" cakes
watermelon	37 ½ pounds	75 pounds	150 pounds
whipping cream	¾ pint	1 ½ to 2 pints	3-4 pints
Ice cream:			
brick	3 ¼ quarts	6 ½ quarts	13 quarts
bulk	2 ¼ quarts	4 ½ quarts or 1 ¼ gallons	9 quarts or 2 ½ gallons
Meat, poultry or fish:			
fish	13 pounds	25 pounds	50 pounds
fish, fillets or steak	7 ½ pounds	15 pounds	30 pounds
hamburger	9 pounds	18 pounds	35 pounds
turkey or chicken	13 pounds	25 to 35 pounds	50 to 75 pounds
wieners (beef)	6 ½ pounds	13 pounds	25 pounds
Salads, casseroles:			
baked beans	¾ gallon	1 ¼ gallons	2 ½ gallons
jello salad	¾ gallon	1 ¼ gallons	2 ½ gallons
potato salad	4 ¼ quarts	2 ¼ gallons	4 ½ gallons
scalloped potatoes	4 ½ quarts or 1 12" x 20" pan	9 quarts or 2 ¼ gallons	18 quarts 4 ½ gallons
spaghetti	1 ¼ gallons	2 ½ gallons	5 gallons
Sandwiches:			
bread	50 slices or 3 1-pound loaves	100 slices or 6 1-pound loaves	200 slices or 12 1-pound loaves
butter	½ pound	1 pound	2 pounds
lettuce	1 ½ heads	3 heads	6 heads
mayonnaise	1 cup	2 cups	4 cups
mixed filling			
meat, eggs, fish	1 ½ quarts	3 quarts	6 quarts
jam, jelly	1 quart	2 quarts	4 quarts

QUICK FIXES

PRACTICALLY EVERYONE has experienced that dreadful moment in the kitchen when a recipe failed and dinner guests have arrived. Perhaps a failed timer, distraction or a missing or mismeasured ingredient is to blame. These handy tips can save the day!

Acidic foods – Sometimes a tomato-based sauce will become too acidic. Add baking soda, one teaspoon at a time, to the sauce. Use sugar as a sweeter alternative.

Burnt food on pots and pans – Allow the pan to cool on its own. Remove as much of the food as possible. Fill with hot water and add a capful of liquid fabric softener to the pot; let it stand for a few hours. You'll have an easier time removing the burnt food.

Chocolate seizes – Chocolate can seize (turn coarse and grainy) when it comes into contact with water. Place seized chocolate in a metal bowl over a large saucepan with an inch of simmering water in it. Over medium heat, slowly whisk in warm heavy cream. Use 1/4 cup cream to 4 ounces of chocolate. The chocolate will melt and become smooth.

Forgot to thaw whipped topping – Thaw in microwave for 1 minute on the defrost setting. Stir to blend well. Do not over thaw!

Hands smell like garlic or onion – Rinse hands under cold water while rubbing them with a large stainless steel spoon.

Hard brown sugar – Place in a paper bag and microwave for a few seconds, or place hard chunks in a food processor.

Jello too hard – Heat on a low microwave power setting for a very short time.

Lumpy gravy or sauce – Use a blender, food processor or simply strain.

No tomato juice – Mix 1/2 cup ketchup with 1/2 cup water.

Out of honey – Substitute 1 1/4 cups sugar dissolved in 1 cup water.

Overcooked sweet potatoes or carrots – Softened sweet potatoes and carrots make a wonderful soufflé with the addition of eggs and sugar. Consult your favorite cookbook for a good soufflé recipe. Overcooked sweet potatoes can also be used as pie filling.

Sandwich bread is stale – Toast or microwave bread briefly. Otherwise, turn it into breadcrumbs. Bread exposed to light and heat will hasten its demise, so consider using a bread box.

Soup, sauce, gravy too thin – Add 1 tablespoon of flour to hot soup, sauce or gravy. Whisk well (to avoid lumps) while the mixture is boiling. Repeat if necessary.

Sticky rice – Rinse rice with warm water.

Stew or soup is greasy – Refrigerate and remove grease once it congeals. Another trick is to lay cold lettuce leaves over the hot stew for about 10 seconds and then remove. Repeat as necessary.

Too salty – Add a little sugar and vinegar. For soups or sauces, add a raw peeled potato.

Too sweet – Add a little vinegar or lemon juice.

Undercooked cakes and cookies – Serve over vanilla ice cream. You can also layer pieces of cake or cookies with whipped cream and fresh fruit to form a dessert parfait. Crumbled cookies also make an excellent ice cream or cream pie topping.

COUNTING CALORIES

BEVERAGES

apple juice, 6 oz.	90
coffee (black)	0
cola, 12 oz.	115
cranberry juice, 6 oz.	115
ginger ale, 12 oz.	115
grape juice, (prepared from frozen concentrate), 6 oz.	142
lemonade, (prepared from frozen concentrate), 6 oz.	85
milk, protein fortified, 1 c.	105
skim, 1 c.	90
whole, 1 c.	160
orange juice, 6 oz.	85
pineapple juice, unsweetened, 6 oz.	95
root beer, 12 oz.	150
tonic (quinine water) 12 oz.	132

BREADS

cornbread, 1 sm. square	130
dumplings, 1 med.	70
French toast, 1 slice	135
melba toast, 1 slice	25
muffins, blueberry, 1 muffin	110
bran, 1 muffin	106
corn, 1 muffin	125
English, 1 muffin	280
pancakes, 1 (4-in.)	60
pumpernickel, 1 slice	75
rye, 1 slice	60
waffle, 1	216
white, 1 slice	60-70
whole wheat, 1 slice	55-65

CEREALS

cornflakes, 1 c.	105
cream of wheat, 1 c.	120
oatmeal, 1 c.	148
rice flakes, 1 c.	105
shredded wheat, 1 biscuit	100
sugar krisps, 3/4 c.	110

CRACKERS

graham, 1 cracker	15-30
rye crisp, 1 cracker	35
saltine, 1 cracker	17-20
wheat thins, 1 cracker	9

DAIRY PRODUCTS

butter or margarine, 1 T.	100
cheese, American, 1 oz.	100
camembert, 1 oz.	85
cheddar, 1 oz.	115
cottage cheese, 1 oz.	30
mozzarella, 1 oz.	90
parmesan, 1 oz.	130
ricotta, 1 oz.	50
roquefort, 1 oz.	105
Swiss, 1 oz.	105
cream, light, 1 T.	30
heavy, 1 T.	55
sour, 1 T.	45
hot chocolate, with milk, 1 c.	277
milk chocolate, 1 oz.	145-155
yogurt	
made w/ whole milk, 1 c.	150-165
made w/ skimmed milk, 1 c.	125

EGGS

fried, 1 lg.	100
poached or boiled, 1 lg.	75-80
scrambled or in omelet, 1 lg.	110-130

FISH AND SEAFOOD

bass, 4 oz.	105
salmon, broiled or baked, 3 oz.	155
sardines, canned in oil, 3 oz.	170
trout, fried, 3 1/2 oz.	220
tuna, in oil, 3 oz.	170
in water, 3 oz.	110

COUNTING CALORIES

FRUITS

apple, 1 med.	80-100
applesauce, sweetened, ½ c.	90-115
unsweetened, ½ c.	50
banana, 1 med.	85
blueberries, ½ c.	45
cantaloupe, ½ c.	24
cherries (pitted), raw, ½ c.	40
grapefruit, ½ med.	55
grapes, ½ c.	35-55
honeydew, ½ c.	55
mango, 1 med.	90
orange, 1 med.	65-75
peach, 1 med.	35
pear, 1 med.	60-100
pineapple, fresh, ½ c.	40
canned in syrup, ½ c.	95
plum, 1 med.	30
strawberries, fresh, ½ c.	30
frozen and sweetened, ½ c.	120-140
tangerine, 1 lg.	39
watermelon, ½ c.	42

MEAT AND POULTRY

beef, ground (lean), 3 oz.	185
roast, 3 oz.	185
chicken, broiled, 3 oz.	115
lamb chop (lean), 3 oz.	175-200
steak, sirloin, 3 oz.	175
tenderloin, 3 oz.	174
top round, 3 oz.	162
turkey, dark meat, 3 oz.	175
white meat, 3 oz.	150
veal, cutlet, 3 oz.	156
roast, 3 oz.	76

NUTS

almonds, 2 T.	105
cashews, 2 T.	100
peanuts, 2 T.	105
peanut butter, 1 T.	95
pecans, 2 T.	95
pistachios, 2 T.	92
walnuts, 2 T.	80

PASTA

macaroni or spaghetti, cooked, ¾ c.	115

SALAD DRESSINGS

blue cheese, 1 T.	70
French, 1 T.	65
Italian, 1 T.	80
mayonnaise, 1 T.	100
olive oil, 1 T.	124
Russian, 1 T.	70
salad oil, 1 T.	120

SOUPS

bean, 1 c.	130-180
beef noodle, 1 c.	70
bouillon and consomme, 1 c.	30
chicken noodle, 1 c.	65
chicken with rice, 1 c.	50
minestrone, 1 c.	80-150
split pea, 1 c.	145-170
tomato with milk, 1 c.	170
vegetable, 1 c.	80-100

VEGETABLES

asparagus, 1 c.	35
broccoli, cooked, ½ c.	25
cabbage, cooked, ½ c.	15-20
carrots, cooked, ½ c.	25-30
cauliflower, ½ c.	10-15
corn (kernels), ½ c.	70
green beans, 1 c.	30
lettuce, shredded, ½ c.	5
mushrooms, canned, ½ c.	20
onions, cooked, ½ c.	30
peas, cooked, ½ c.	60
potato, baked, 1 med.	90
chips, 8-10	100
mashed, w/milk & butter, 1 c.	200-300
spinach, 1 c.	40
tomato, raw, 1 med.	25
cooked, ½ c.	30

COOKING TERMS

Au gratin: Topped with crumbs and/or cheese and browned in oven or under broiler.

Au jus: Served in its own juices.

Baste: To moisten foods during cooking with pan drippings or special sauce in order to add flavor and prevent drying.

Bisque: A thick cream soup.

Blanch: To immerse in rapidly boiling water and allow to cook slightly.

Cream: To soften a fat, especially butter, by beating it at room temperature. Butter and sugar are often creamed together, making a smooth, soft paste.

Crimp: To seal the edges of a two-crust pie either by pinching them at intervals with the fingers or by pressing them together with the tines of a fork.

Crudites: An assortment of raw vegetables (i.e. carrots, broccoli, celery, mushrooms) that is served as an hors d'oeuvre, often accompanied by a dip.

Degrease: To remove fat from the surface of stews, soups or stock. Usually cooled in the refrigerator so that fat hardens and is easily removed.

Dredge: To coat lightly with flour, cornmeal, etc.

Entree: The main course.

Fold: To incorporate a delicate substance, such as whipped cream or beaten egg whites, into another substance without releasing air bubbles. A spatula is used to gently bring part of the mixture from the bottom of the bowl to the top. The process is repeated, while slowly rotating the bowl, until the ingredients are thoroughly blended.

Glaze: To cover with a glossy coating, such as a melted and somewhat diluted jelly for fruit desserts.

Julienne: To cut or slice vegetables, fruits or cheeses into match-shaped slivers.

Marinate: To allow food to stand in a liquid in order to tenderize or to add flavor.

Meuniére: Dredged with flour and sautéed in butter.

Mince: To chop food into very small pieces.

Parboil: To boil until partially cooked; to blanch. Usually final cooking in a seasoned sauce follows this procedure.

Pare: To remove the outermost skin of a fruit or vegetable.

Poach: To cook gently in hot liquid kept just below the boiling point.

Purée: To mash foods by hand by rubbing through a sieve or food mill, or by whirling in a blender or food processor until perfectly smooth.

Refresh: To run cold water over food that has been parboiled in order to stop the cooking process quickly.

Sauté: To cook and/or brown food in a small quantity of hot shortening.

Scald: To heat to just below the boiling point, when tiny bubbles appear at the edge of the saucepan.

Simmer: To cook in liquid just below the boiling point. The surface of the liquid should be barely moving, broken from time to time by slowly rising bubbles.

Steep: To let food stand in hot liquid in order to extract or to enhance flavor, like tea in hot water or poached fruit in syrup.

Toss: To combine ingredients with a repeated lifting motion.

Whip: To beat rapidly in order to incorporate air and produce expansion, as in heavy cream or egg whites.